Learning Xcode 8

Learn how to use the power of Xcode to turn your next great app idea into a reality

Jak Tiano

BIRMINGHAM - MUMBAI

Learning Xcode 8

Copyright © 2016 Packt Publishing

First published: November 2016

Production reference: 1111116

Published by Packt Publishing Ltd.
Livery Place
35 Livery Street
Birmingham B3 2PB, UK.

ISBN 978-1-78588-572-3

www.packtpub.com

Credits

Author
Jak Tiano

Reviewer
Vishal Devrajbhai Gabani

Commissioning Editor
Kunal Parikh

Acquisition Editor
Tushar Gupta

Content Development Editor
Deepti Thore

Technical Editor
Rupali R. Shrawane

Copy Editor
Safis Editing

Project Coordinator
Shweta H Birwatkar

Proofreader
Safis Editing

Indexer
Monica Ajmera Mehta

Production Coordinator
Melwyn Dsa

Cover Work
Melwyn Dsa

About the Author

Jak Tiano is an iOS and game developer living in Burlington, VT. In 2015 he graduated with top honors from the game development program at Champlain College, and is now programming educational robotics games at Xemory Software. In his spare time, he always keeping up with the latest iOS technologies.

Jak first learned how to code as a freshman in high school, when the very first iPhone SDK was released. After a year of learning the basics of C++ and Objective-C, he released his first iPhone app in the summer of 2009. Since then, he has programmed over 30 iOS apps and games, releasing a handful along the way. In both 2013 and 2014, he attended Apple's World Wide Developers' Conference in San Francisco on direct scholarship from Apple. He's been programming with Swift exclusively since its release in 2014, and has served as a technical reviewer on *Swift 2 Blueprints, Cecil Costa, Packt Publishing.*

I would like to thank my parents and my friend Chas for giving me the initial nods of encouragement to start writing this book, with a special thanks to my mom for continuing to motivate me throughout. I'd also like to thank Zach and Zach for putting up with me skipping out on plans week after week so that I could write; thanks for still being my friend! I wouldn't have been able to finish the book without the coworking space managed by VCET and the Starbucks on Church Street, which gave me enough space to shake up my writing spots and keep me focused.

Finally, I'd like to thank all of the teachers who have taught, encouraged, and inspired me throughout my education. Without them, I would have neither the technical knowledge nor the language skills needed to write several hundred pages about iOS development.

Also Taylor Swift.

About the Reviewer

Vishal Devrajbhai Gabani is an iOS Developer with more than 6 years of experience in iOS application/framework development. He has 45 developed app under his belt.

Vishal has started his carrier as a Junior iPhone Developer with small company from Ahmedabad, Gujarat (India). He worked with few MNCs during his 5 years stay in Bengaluru, Karnataka (India). He has bachelors degree in Information Technology from Bhavnagar University.

I thank my family for their support. I dedicate this effort to my parents.

www.PacktPub.com

eBooks, discount offers, and more

Did you know that Packt offers eBook versions of every book published, with PDF and ePub files available? You can upgrade to the eBook version at www.PacktPub.com and as a print book customer, you are entitled to a discount on the eBook copy. Get in touch with us at customercare@packtpub.com for more details.

At www.PacktPub.com, you can also read a collection of free technical articles, sign up for a range of free newsletters and receive exclusive discounts and offers on Packt books and eBooks.

https://www2.packtpub.com/books/subscription/packtlib

Do you need instant solutions to your IT questions? PacktLib is Packt's online digital book library. Here, you can search, access, and read Packt's entire library of books.

Why subscribe?

- Fully searchable across every book published by Packt
- Copy and paste, print, and bookmark content
- On demand and accessible via a web browser

Table of Contents

Preface   **xi**

Chapter 1: Starting Your iOS Journey   **1**

A developer's responsibilities   **2**
Pre-production   2
Project setup   3
Development   3
Deployment   3
Working on a team   **4**
Designers   4
Other programmers   5
Project managers   5
Investors   6
The Xcode 8 toolset   **6**
Xcode   6
iOS and watchOS simulator   8
Instruments   9
Application Loader   10
Understanding Model-View-Controller (MVC)   **11**
Model   12
View   14
Controller   15
MVC on the web   16
MVC on iOS   19

Becoming a registered developer   **21**
Which account do you need?   21
Registering a free developer account   22
Registering a paid developer account   22
Summary   **23**

Chapter 2: Welcome to Xcode   **25**
Getting started   **25**
Installing Xcode   26
Adding your developer account   28
Creating a new project   29
Navigating Xcode   **32**
Editor   33
Navigator sidebar   34
Debug area   35
Utilities sidebar   35
Exploring the editor   **36**
Standard editor   36
Assistant editor   40
Version editor   42
Understanding project settings   **42**
Project targets   43
The General tab   44
The Capabilities tab   45
The Info tab   46
Creating and managing files   **47**
Resource types   47
Creating new resources   48
Importing existing files   51
Groups and folders   52
Creating builds   **53**
Build and run   53
Running on a device   54
Applying the basics   **55**
Setting up the workspace   55
Creating the model, view, and controller   57
Testing our work in the simulator   62
Summary   **63**

Chapter 3: Introduction to Swift 3   65

Discovering playgrounds   66
Setting up a playground   66
Resources, pages, and rich comments   73
    Pages   73
    Rich comments   74
Understanding Swift basics   75
Data types, constants, and variables   76
    Data types   76
    Constants   76
    Variables   77
Optionals   78
Collection types   80
    Arrays   80
    Dictionaries   81
Conditional statements   82
    if statement   82
    guard statement   83
    switch statement   83
Loops   84
    for loop   84
    for-in loop   84
    while loop   85
    repeat-while loop   86
Functions   86
Comments and printing   88
Creating classes, structs, and enums   89
Classes   89
Structs   92
Enumerations   94
Using important Swift features   95
Closures   95
Protocols   97
Class extensions   98
Error handling   99
Summary   102

Chapter 4: Using Storyboards, Auto Layout, and Size Classes   103

Storyboards   103
Getting started   104
View controllers and screen flow   106
Understanding segues   111

Auto Layout	**115**
Constraints	117
Resolving issues	123
Size classes	**123**
Devices, orientations, and size classes	124
Size classes in action	125
Summary	**129**
Chapter 5: Taking Advantage of Source Control in Xcode	**131**
Understanding version control	**132**
Introduction to Git	**134**
Setting up Git in Xcode	**135**
Creating a local repository	136
Adding Git to an existing project	137
Using a GitHub hosted repository	141
Using version control in Xcode	**145**
Pull, push, and commit	145
The version editor	147
Creating and merging branches	149
Summary	**151**
Chapter 6: Building Your First iOS App	**153**
Pre-production	**154**
Assembling a feature list	154
Visual design	155
Creating a development plan	157
New snippet	**159**
SnippetData model	160
New snippet button	160
Select snippet type	**163**
Update SnippetData model	164
Create an alert controller	165
Text snippet implementation	**167**
Update SnippetData model	168
Text entry view controller	169
PhotoSnippet implementation	**179**
Update SnippetData model	179
PhotoSnippet data entry	180
Scroll through snippets	**185**
Create prototype cells	186
Populate table view	191

Snippet dates — 196
   Update SnippetData model — 196
   Save data to model — 197
   Update view and controller — 198
Summary — 202
Chapter 7: Integrating Multitouch and Gestures — 203
   Human interface guidelines – gestures — 204
   Standard gestures — 204
   Usage guidelines — 205
   How gestures work — 206
   Adding gestures from the storyboard — 207
   Setting up the storyboard — 207
   Flipping the image — 209
   Adding gestures from code — 211
   Creating a gesture through code — 211
   Changing the scale of our image — 214
   If you're up for a challenge… — 217
   Creating 3D Touch app shortcuts — 217
   Setting up Info.plist — 218
   Handling shortcuts in the app delegate — 220
Summary — 225
Chapter 8: Exploring Common iOS Frameworks — 227
   Frameworks — 227
   What is a framework? — 228
   Linking frameworks in a project — 228
   Understanding UIKit fundamentals — 230
   Application management — 230
     The UIDevice class — 231
   Views — 231
     Drawing — 232
     Hierarchies — 233
     Coordinate systems — 234
   Documents, displays, printing, and more — 235
     Documents — 235
     Displays — 235
     Printing — 236
     And more! — 236
   Using CoreLocation.framework — 236
   Setting up CoreLocation permissions — 236
   Getting the user's location — 240
   Adding location data to Snippets — 243

Using Social.framework   **246**
Setting up the views   246
Posting to Twitter   249
Summary   **252**

Chapter 9: Working with Core Data   **253**
What is Core Data?   **254**
Model revisited   254
Entities, attributes, and relationships   255
   Entities   256
   Attributes   256
   Relationships   256
The data model editor   257
Preparing Snippets for Core Data   **261**
Initializing the Core Data stack   261
   Data model versus object graph   261
   The NSManagedObjectModel   262
   The NSPersistentStoreCoordinator   263
   The NSManagedObjectContext   264
   Final touches   264
Recreating the data model with Core Data   265
Persisting data   **267**
Saving data   268
Fetching data   272
Deleting data   276
Summary   **278**

Chapter 10: Creating a watchOS Companion App   **279**
Designing for the Apple Watch   **279**
Using the watch   280
Intended experience   280
Apple's design principles   281
Components of a watchOS app   **282**
Dock snapshots   283
Notifications   284
Architecture of a watchOS app   **285**
Target bundles   286
   Watch App bundle   286
Interface controller   286
Extension Delegate   287

Snippets for Apple Watch — **288**
Programming the interface controller — 292
Connecting to iOS with Watch Connectivity.framework — 298
Adding a complication — 302
Summary — **306**
Chapter 11: Advanced Input Using Sensors — **307**
Device status with UIDevice — **308**
Accessing orientation state — 308
Checking the proximity sensor — 311
Getting battery status — 313
Introduction to Core Motion — **315**
Accelerometer — 316
CMDeviceMotion — 320
User acceleration — 322
Gravity — 322
Rotation rate — 322
Magnetic field — 322
Charts — 323
Importing the framework — 323
Setting up the storyboard — 324
Filling the chart with data — 325
Pedometer — 328
Altitude — 332
Sensors on Apple Watch — **334**
Setting up an extension — 335
Getting sensor data on Apple Watch — 336
Sending and displaying data on iOS — 337
Summary — **341**
Chapter 12: Sending Notifications — **343**
Introduction to user notifications — **343**
Components of a user notification — 344
Local versus remote notifications — 345
Adding notification support to Snippets — **346**
Getting permission to send notifications — 346
Scheduling a local notification — 347
Advanced notifications — **349**
Categories and actions — 350
Badges — 355
Custom sounds — 356
Receiving notifications while in the app — 358
Summary — **360**

Chapter 13: Writing Unit Tests — 361

Introduction to unit tests — 361
What is a unit? — 362
Why use unit testing in the first place? — 362

Unit tests in action — 363
Setting up the project — 363
Writing tests with XCTest — 365
Running tests — 369

Implementing tests for Snippets — 372
Setting up the Snippets project — 372
Preparing our testing class — 373
Writing a data validation unit test — 375
Checking code coverage — 377

Testing UI in Xcode 8 — 379
How does UI testing work? — 380
Adding the UI testing target — 380
Using the UI recorder — 382

Summary — 384

Chapter 14: Debugging an iOS Application — 385

Basic debugging practices — 385
print() — 386
Breakpoints and the debug area — 386
Variables view — 387
Console — 388
Debug toolbar — 389
The call stack — 393

Advanced debugging tools — 396
Address Sanitizer — 396
Performance gauges — 400
CPU and memory gauge — 401
Disk and network gauge — 402
Energy gauge — 404

Visual debugging — 404

Summary — 408

Chapter 15: Optimizing Your App — 409

Introduction to Instruments — 409
Time Profiler instrument — 410
Anatomy of an Instruments document — 411
Using the Time Profiler — 412
Allocations instrument — 415
Leaks instrument — 418
Slicing — 420

On-demand Resources   426
    Creating tags   427
    Loading resources   428
    Purging resources   429
Summary   **430**

Chapter 16: Distributing an iOS App   **431**

Preparing iTunes Connect   **431**
    Registering a bundle identifier   432
    Creating a new app record in iTunes Connect   435
Uploading to iTunes Connect   **438**
Releasing the app   **442**
    Finalizing store assets   442
    Distributing on TestFlight   446
    Submitting to the App Store   449
Summary   **449**

Index   **451**

Preface

In today's mobile-oriented world, iOS development has become one of the most lucrative skills in the tech industry. Many existing companies can benefit from a well-designed app (just look at Starbucks), and mobile apps have created entirely new businesses by disrupting existing industries (such as Uber) or creating new ones (such as Snapchat).

Over the course of this book, we'll be walking through the basics of iOS development by focusing on the Xcode suite of tools, which is the primary software package used to develop iOS (and watchOS, tvOS, and OSX) applications. Along the way, we'll touch upon many subjects, such as the fundamental concepts behind iOS app architecture, the Swift 3 programming language, creating iOS and watchOS applications from scratch, and much more!

The goal of this book is to give you a wide sampling platter of the many different sides to iOS development. By the end, you will have directly touched many unique aspects of app development and will have built your first app from concept to app store!

Welcome to *Learning Xcode!*

What this book covers

Chapter 1, Starting your iOS Journey, covers the developer's responsibilities, an overview of the Xcode 8 toolset, and an introduction to Model-View-Controller application architecture.

Chapter 2, Welcome to Xcode, looks at the main Xcode application in detail, covering many different areas, modes, and editors.

Chapter 3, Introduction to Swift 3, teaches you the basics of the Swift programming language, from variables and functions to brand new features, such as error handling.

Chapter 4, Using Storyboards, Auto Layout, and Size Classes, covers the visual development side of Xcode, called Interface Builder, in detail.

Chapter 5, Taking Advantage of Source Control in Xcode, gets you up to speed on the concept behind Git version control and how to enable it in Xcode.

Chapter 6, Building your First iOS App, teaches you how to break down an app idea into actionable chunks and then walks you through a full development cycle of app development for an app called Snippets.

Chapter 7, Integrating Multitouch and Gestures, looks at some of the many ways to use advanced touch information in your app through gestures and 3D touch shortcuts.

Chapter 8, Exploring Common iOS Frameworks, covers the concept of code frameworks and then dives into the UIKit, CoreLocation, and Social frameworks.

Chapter 9, Working with CoreData, teaches you the concept behind the CoreData framework and how to use it to save and load user data in an application.

Chapter 10, Creating a watchOS Companion App, looks at how to design and create a companion app for the Apple Watch by using the Snippets app created in Chapter 6.

Chapter 11, Advanced Input Using Sensors, covers the many sensors found in the iPhone using third-party charting frameworks and accessing sensors on Apple Watch.

Chapter 12, Sending Notifications, teaches you how to send the user actionable notifications in addition to displaying application badges and playing alert sounds.

Chapter 13, Writing Unit Tests, introduces the concept of writing code that tests your application code and teaches you how to implement these tests in Xcode.

Chapter 14, Debugging an iOS Application, covers the different ways to search for and eliminate bugs in your application code.

Chapter 15, Optimizing your App, gives you an overview of the tools in Xcode that help speed up the performance of your code and reduce the file size of your app's resources.

Chapter 16, Distributing an iOS App, walks you through the process of taking a finished app from Xcode to the App Store.

What you need for this book

In order to follow along with this book, you'll need a computer running Mac OS X 10.10 or later with Xcode 8 installed (free on the Mac App Store). In Chapter 5, we will also be using GitHub Desktop, which is a free download from the `https://github.com/` website.

To get the most out of the book, you'll also need a recent iOS device (iPhone 6S or newer for the 3D touch segments) and a lightning cable to connect it to your computer. In the final chapter, you will need a paid ($99) Apple Developer Account to follow along with submitting an app to TestFlight and the App Store.

Who this book is for

Learning Xcode is intended for programmers looking to get a jump start into the world of iOS development. Whether you're a young student, who has only spent a few months with Java, or a seasoned developer, who has spent their career developing for a different platform, all that is expected is a basic understanding of a programming language, such as C++, C#, or Java.

Conventions

In this book, you will find a number of text styles that distinguish between different kinds of information. Here are some examples of these styles and an explanation of their meaning.

Code words in text, database table names, folder names, filenames, file extensions, pathnames, dummy URLs, user input, and Twitter handles are shown as follows: "We can include other contexts through the use of the `include` directive".

A block of code is set as follows:

```
struct SnippetData {

    init() {
        print ("new snippet created")
    }

}
```

When we wish to draw your attention to a particular part of a code block, the relevant lines or items are set in bold:

```
func textViewDidEndEditing(textView: UITextView) {
    saveText(text: textView.text)
    dismissViewControllerAnimated(true, completion: nil)
}
```

New terms and **important words** are shown in bold. Words that you see on the screen, for example, in menus or dialog boxes, appear in the text like this: " At the bottom of the window, you should see a drop-down menu for **Command Line Tools**."

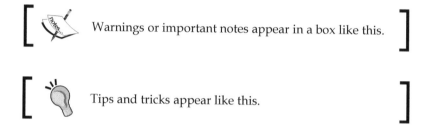

Warnings or important notes appear in a box like this.

Tips and tricks appear like this.

Reader feedback

Feedback from our readers is always welcome. Let us know what you think about this book—what you liked or disliked. Reader feedback is important for us as it helps us develop titles that you will really get the most out of.

To send us general feedback, simply e-mail feedback@packtpub.com, and mention the book's title in the subject of your message.

If there is a topic that you have expertise in and you are interested in either writing or contributing to a book, see our author guide at www.packtpub.com/authors.

Customer support

Now that you are the proud owner of a Packt book, we have a number of things to help you to get the most from your purchase.

Downloading the example code

You can download the example code files for this book from your account at http://www.packtpub.com. If you purchased this book elsewhere, you can visit http://www.packtpub.com/support and register to have the files e-mailed directly to you.

You can download the code files by following these steps:

1. Log in or register to our website using your e-mail address and password.
2. Hover the mouse pointer on the **SUPPORT** tab at the top.
3. Click on **Code Downloads & Errata**.
4. Enter the name of the book in the **Search** box.
5. Select the book for which you're looking to download the code files.
6. Choose from the drop-down menu where you purchased this book from.
7. Click on **Code Download**.

You can also download the code files by clicking on the **Code Files** button on the book's webpage at the Packt Publishing website. This page can be accessed by entering the book's name in the **Search** box. Please note that you need to be logged in to your Packt account.

Once the file is downloaded, please make sure that you unzip or extract the folder using the latest version of:

- WinRAR / 7-Zip for Windows
- Zipeg / iZip / UnRarX for Mac
- 7-Zip / PeaZip for Linux

The code bundle for the book is also hosted on GitHub at `https://github.com/PacktPublishing/Learning-Xcode-8`. We also have other code bundles from our rich catalog of books and videos available at `https://github.com/PacktPublishing/`. Check them out!

Downloading the color images of this book

We also provide you with a PDF file that has color images of the screenshots/diagrams used in this book. The color images will help you better understand the changes in the output. You can download this file from `www.packtpub.com/sites/default/files/downloads/LearningXcode8 _ColorImages.pdf`.

Errata

Although we have taken every care to ensure the accuracy of our content, mistakes do happen. If you find a mistake in one of our books — maybe a mistake in the text or the code — we would be grateful if you could report this to us. By doing so, you can save other readers from frustration and help us improve subsequent versions of this book. If you find any errata, please report them by visiting http://www.packtpub.com/submit-errata, selecting your book, clicking on the **Errata Submission Form** link, and entering the details of your errata. Once your errata are verified, your submission will be accepted and the errata will be uploaded to our website or added to any list of existing errata under the Errata section of that title.

To view the previously submitted errata, go to https://www.packtpub.com/books/content/support and enter the name of the book in the search field. The required information will appear under the **Errata** section.

Piracy

Piracy of copyrighted material on the Internet is an ongoing problem across all media. At Packt, we take the protection of our copyright and licenses very seriously. If you come across any illegal copies of our works in any form on the Internet, please provide us with the location address or website name immediately so that we can pursue a remedy.

Please contact us at copyright@packtpub.com with a link to the suspected pirated material.

We appreciate your help in protecting our authors and our ability to bring you valuable content.

Questions

If you have a problem with any aspect of this book, you can contact us at questions@packtpub.com, and we will do our best to address the problem.

1

Starting Your iOS Journey

When Steve Jobs announced the original iPhone in January of 2007, he referred to it as a combination of three product categories: a widescreen iPod with touch controls, a revolutionary mobile phone, and a breakthrough Internet communications device. When he first announced each of those three feature sets on stage, the iPod and the phone received tremendous applause from the crowd. However, the Internet communications aspect only got a few polite claps. In 2007, the iPhone ran on EDGE (2G) cellular networks. There was no iCloud. The App Store wouldn't exist for over a year; iPhone OS was a closed platform. At the time, there just wasn't anything particularly exciting about an *internet communicator*.

Fast-forward to the present day: our phones are running the 10th version of iOS, and each year iOS developers are getting paid over \$10 B from app sales and in-app-purchases. Since the days of the original iPhone, we've seen the introduction of the iPod Touch, the iPad Air, iPad Mini, and iPad Pro, and in the last year or so the Apple Watch and Apple TV as well. . If it hasn't been made clear yet, the iOS ecosystem's growth has been explosive! While this is nothing but excitement for iOS users, for someone who is about to set off on their journey as an iOS developer, all of these facts just mean that there is much more to learn!

While the *iPod* and the *mobile phone* pieces of Steve's original iPhone pitch are still there, the defining aspect of the iOS success story is its *internet communicator* capabilities, which you are about to dive into with iOS app development using Xcode. In this first chapter, my goal is to make sure you are informed, prepared, and excited to begin developing for the iOS platform. We'll be covering a wide variety of topics, including:

- A developer's responsibilities
- Working on a team
- An overview of the Xcode 8 suite of tools

- Understanding the Model-View-Controller paradigm
- Signing up for an Apple Developer Account

So without any further delay, let's go!

A developer's responsibilities

Before we get into anything too technical, let's go into a little detail about what an iOS developer does. It's obvious that we'll be doing a lot of coding, but that's not the whole story! As a developer, you might be responsible for many different technical aspects of a project depending on the team structure, which we'll get into shortly. But for now, we'll take a look at the general items that end up on a developer's to-do list.

As we walk through the next few sections, don't be alarmed if you find yourself a little lost. Everything discussed here is explored in much more detail in this book, but for now we're going to jump right in and learn through immersion. By introducing you to terms in a meaningful context, you should hopefully have a good idea of how they relate to each other before we explore them individually.

Pre-production

Every project starts with an idea; that's the easy part. Unfortunately, you're not the idea person, but the one in charge of execution. In the pre-production phase of a project, your responsibilities are to take an idea and translate it from wishful thinking into a plan of action.

The first thing that usually happens after brainstorming is that you'll write out a list of features that the application will have. Using your programmer's point of view, you want to break down the idea into all of the technical components that you can.

As you become more experienced it will become easier to know what to plan for, but as a general rule of thumb you will only want to focus on the core features of your app here. What features are needed for a minimum viable product? Again, experience here will help you figure out how deep you should go into your plan, but once you have a good idea of what you will be doing, it's time to move ahead.

Project setup

Now, before you can even write one line of code, you first have to set up your development environment. For most projects, this means creating a new Xcode project and setting up your preferred method of source control.

When setting up a new project, it's important to refer back to the technical plan you made during pre-production to help inform your decisions. Are you going to be using any of the Xcode project templates? Where will your repository be located? Is there anyone else on the team that needs access to the source code? Does the app need any services enabled? Are there pre-existing code libraries that you need to import for your project?

It will be your job to make sure that Xcode and any other necessary tools are configured properly and optimized for the job ahead. Once you've got all of the setup out of the way, it's finally time to start writing some code!

Development

When the application is in active development, it is your time to shine. In this phase you'll be having the most fun, but you'll also have the most responsibilities.

When developing an application, you'll be writing code to handle both the data model and the user interface of the program. You'll also be using storyboards in Xcode to layout the screens of an application. A lot of your time will be spent with these two tasks to create new view controllers that add or change features in your app.

In addition to building the software, you will need to do routine project maintenance. This means that you should be frequently checking in with source control and reviewing other programmers' code additions. You will also be writing unit tests to make sure your code is functioning as expected. On top of all of that, you will be debugging and optimizing your code.

While development can take weeks, months, even years to get to a *finished* state, the market can't wait that long! Usually, once your app has all of its core features implemented and tested, you will polish it up and release it to the world to get feedback.

Deployment

When a new feature is complete, or when a predetermined milestone is hit in a project, you need to then get your app into the hands of people who actually want to use it!

For you, this means several things. First, you'll want to create a release build of the application that removes any *debug* features that an end-user doesn't need. Then you'll be responsible for packaging that build up and putting it somewhere that others can access it; if you're still beta testing, a platform like **TestFlight** might make sense, or if you have a finished, tested build, it's time to get ready for the App Store.

Working on a team

In the previous section, we started to touch on what a developer can be expected to do over the length of a project. More importantly, though, we should also be able to see how even with all of those responsibilities there are still many things unaccounted for! Who is designing the layout of the screens we are building? Who is creating the assets that we will be using in our app? Who is keeping everything on schedule?

While we will be taking a *lone wolf* approach to development as we learn throughout this book, the real world of software development doesn't work that way. As a developer, you are just one of many roles on a team. Depending on the size of the team, you may even be splitting the technical responsibilities among several other people. Let's take a look at the other project roles you may interact with while making an app.

 Remember: every team is different! You may never encounter a team in your career where the roles resemble the descriptions below. (But I highly doubt that!)

Designers

If you think of the developer as the person who deals with the *How* of a project, the designer is the person who actually determines the *What*. Designers are responsible for developing what the application looks like, and the content that is inside of it. They will often approach problems from both a psychological and aesthetic point of view, trying to tie the two together to create an experience that is seamless and intuitive.

When working with a designer, communication is key. You are both trying to solve the same problems, but from very different angles; it is common to not understand where the other person is coming from. But remember, the success of the project depends on your cooperation. Taking a moment to explain a technical limitation (or to listen to feedback about your implementation of their design) will not only help avoid similar problems in the future, but will also promote trust within the team.

Other programmers

In addition to designers, the other role you will be spending the most time with is…
more programmers. While some small projects can get by with a single programmer,
it is much more likely that you'll be working with at least a few other programmers.
With multiple programmers on one team, you'll be split up in all kinds of ways.
Sometimes you will be evenly split between different major features. Other times
each developer might be in charge of different tasks (build master, unit tests, etc.).
It all depends on the needs of the project and the size of the team.

While there won't be as much of an understanding barrier between other coders
as there might be with designers, there are still plenty of issues that can arise from
working with other developers. It is common for every programmer to have his or
her own unique style of coding, but when working on a team it is important to have
at least some ground rules so that everybody can understand everyone else's code.

Sometimes, you will also be working with developers who might not be as
experienced in a topic as you are (or maybe you will be the inexperienced one!). In
those cases, it's still important to be patient and help those people understand what's
going on. Teams thrive on trust, and you never know what that person might be able
to teach you down the line.

Project managers

A project manager's job is pretty self-explanatory. They need to make sure that
everyone on the team is making progress towards whatever goal has been set.
Perhaps more than any other role, the project manager can come in many different
shapes and sizes. Every company, every team, every *project* even will approach the
management of a project differently.

Many teams these days use some form of *agile* development, but the implementation
varies greatly. Generally, the goal of an agile team is to work in short bursts called
sprints that last for a week or two. During each sprint you'll be working on only a
handful of tasks, with the intention of lightweight and rapid iteration.

On these kinds of teams, the project manager might be a dedicated person, or
even a hierarchy of individuals responsible for leading small feature teams.
Whatever arrangement you find yourself in, it's important to work with your
project manager (or project management software) to make sure that your
progress is being tracked properly.

Investors

An investor is one of the people (or perhaps the only person) who has a financial stake in your project. Investors could range from parents, to clients, to venture capitalists. The important thing is that they have put up some amount of cash to fund the project, and are most likely expecting to get a return on that investment.

Depending on your seniority in a team, or the type of project you're working on, you may or may not ever have to deal directly with an investor. While every investor you have to deal with is guaranteed to be very different from the last, it's always important to treat them with respect and honesty (unless the honesty will compromise the respect!). Remember, they're the ones putting food on your table.

The Xcode 8 toolset

At this point, we've taken a pretty good look at a lot of the general things that an iOS developer does during a project, and how they work with a team. So, with all of that out of the way, let's take a tour of the main event: Xcode 8 (and friends!).

We'll be taking a much deeper look at Xcode in the next chapter (*Chapter 2, Welcome to Xcode*), so we'll mostly be skimming through the big pieces here to get an understanding of how they all fit together.

Xcode

Xcode is Apple's full IDE (integrated development environment) for building software for any Apple platform. First used for Mac OS X development, then expanded for iOS, watchOS, and tvOS, if you're making apps for Apple hardware you're using Xcode. Luckily, it's chock full of features, easy to use, and looks great:

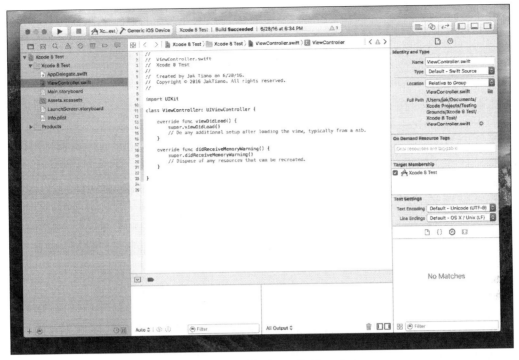

Figure 1.1: The main Xcode application window

Xcode has several primary features. As an IDE, it uses a custom `.xcodeproj` file format to manage all of the code, asset, and configuration files that you create and import. It also has a fully-featured source code editor that is optimized for Objective-C and Swift languages, including file presets made for macOS/iOS development, and built-in documentation viewing. Finally, Xcode compiles your code and makes it easy to deploy the resulting packages to simulators, test devices, and even the App Store.

There's no reason to go any deeper than that for now, since the rest of this book is about doing exactly that. However, I would like to introduce you to some other major tools that are hidden within the Xcode application that you will be seeing again later.

If you'd like to actually see where these tools reside for yourself, first navigate to the Xcode.app (most likely in your Applications folder). Then right-click on the icon and select **Show Package Contents**. Then, navigate to **Contents | Applications**, and **Contents | Developer | Applications** to see the hidden apps we are about to explore. And don't worry! We'll have much easier access to them from within Xcode, so there's no need to remember how to find them like this.

iOS and watchOS simulator

The iOS and watchOS simulators are small applets that make it easy to test the applications you make without needing a dedicated testing device. With the variety of screen sizes now available on iOS devices, the chances are slim that you will own one of every size to test on; luckily, the simulators make it easy to check your app's layout on every screen size:

Figure 1.2: The iOS and watchOS simulator windows

The Apple watch is also a relatively new product. Leading up to its launch (and shortly after), limited availability of Apple Watches made it near impossible to get a hold of one for testing. Even now, it isn't nearly as ubiquitous as an iPhone, and not every developer has access to a real device. Finally, sometimes your devices are preoccupied, and you just need to test some code!

Prior to Xcode 7, to test an app on a real device required a paid Apple developer license. For many students or hobby developers, the simulator was their only way of running the apps they made without paying for the full license. In 2015, however, Apple revamped the way their developer accounts work, and building to your device no longer requires a paid account.

Instruments

When creating an app, you spend most of your time dealing with high-level concepts, like the sequential logic of a function, or the layout of a screen. At some point, though, it is important to get a better understanding of how your app works under the hood:

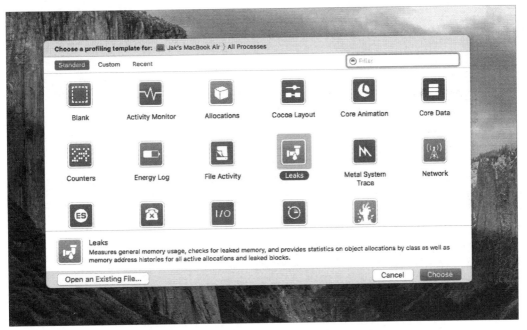

Figure 1.3: The Instruments application's template chooser

Instruments is an analysis and profiling tool that can help you do just that. It is made to help you understand how your application's processes are running on the CPU to help you reproduce hard to find logic errors, patch memory leaks, and stress test different parts of your app.

Application Loader

Application Loader is a small application that ships with Xcode with the sole purpose of uploading data to the App Store servers. In the standard workflow of iOS development, managing the App Store side of things can usually be taken care of with iTunes Connect in conjunction with Xcode directly:

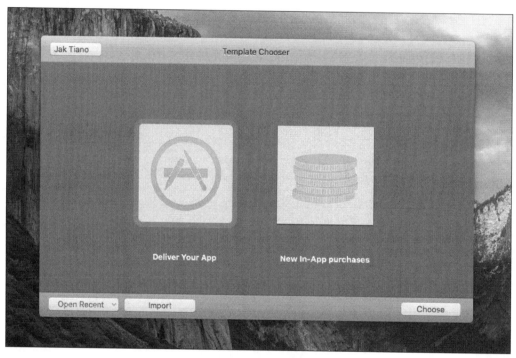

Figure 1.4: The Application Loader template chooser

However, some people prefer to use Application Loader to upload app binaries and in-app-purchase content. Essentially, they accomplish the same tasks, but Application Loader tends to be a bit clearer.

Understanding Model-View-Controller (MVC)

Developing any type of software requires logical thinking and strong problem-solving skills. However, programmers have been building software for decades, and have collectively encountered and solved a great number of the common problems encountered when writing code.

As time has passed, some of the best solutions to common problems that have been developed and shared are in the form of *patterns*. On a granular level, there are design patterns that are used to solve common problems at the object or multi-object level. As an example, the *Singleton* pattern describes a class that may only have one instance, with a global access point. Since it isn't a specific set of instructions for any given language (remember, it's just a pattern), the Singleton pattern can be implemented in many different languages, as is the case with most design patterns.

In addition to solving smaller issues with design patterns, programmers have also developed many patterns concerned with outlining how an entire program should be structured; these are called *architectural patterns*. At the core of Cocoa Touch, Apple's native API for building apps for iOS, is the architectural pattern called **Model-View-Controller**.

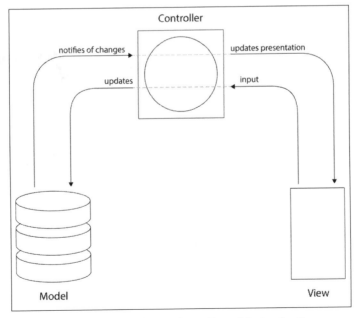

Figure 1.5: The Model-View-Controller architectural pattern

The pattern is pretty simple to understand: the code of an MVC program is separated into a data layer (the model), a user presentation layer (the view), and a third layer that connects the two halves (the controller). This allows for a very logical separation of functionality in your code.

 Cocoa Touch is based on the original Cocoa, which is the API that Apple built for programming OSX apps. There is a very fascinating history behind Smalltalk, Objective-C, NeXTSTEP, and how all of that led to OSX and ultimately iOS. Since it won't be covered in this book, I hope you will research and understand these technologies that led to the modern iOS development environment.

Since it is foundational to the underlying technology of Apple's development frameworks, using MVC when building your applications is pretty much mandatory, and enforced at every turn. As we explore Xcode and Swift, you'll see the idea of MVC everywhere: CoreData is how you can design your model; Storyboards are quite literally where you create views; UIKit has many types of built in view controllers. In time, we'll cover all of these individually and in depth, but for now let's make sure we have a firm grasp on the basics of Model-View-Controller.

Model

At the very core of an application is its data. In a music app, that would be the music files and associated metadata. In a contacts app, it would be a database of your saved contacts. In Twitter, it's the tweets. You get the idea. The model of an application is all about how you represent and manipulate that persistent data.

Let's use the contacts app as an example, and assume that the database of contacts is stored locally on your device. The model for that data would need to do several things. There needs to be a way to load contact information from the database into an object in code. There should also be ways to modify and save that data, for times when a user might want to change a contact's information, or add a new contact altogether. Finally, the model needs to be able to tell a controller when any of the contact data has changed:

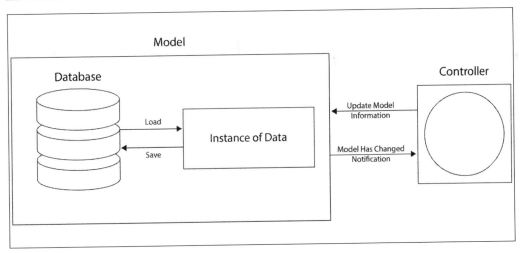

Figure 1.6: How the model functions and interacts with a controller

While the first capability (having a container to load data into) is an internal feature of the model, the other two capabilities are essential exposures needed for the model to communicate with the controller. The controller will be capable of sending updated information to the model, which needs to be able to receive that data, format it correctly, and save it back to the database. Likewise, the model needs to let the controller know when its data has changed, so that the controller can react accordingly.

This creates a clean, separated relationship; the controller sends simple data to the model and handles general update events, while the model takes care of all the saving, loading, manipulation, and formatting.

View

While the model is taking care of the raw data, the view is in charge of what is actually being seen by the user. Continuing the example of a contact management app, let's take a look at how the view might be handled:

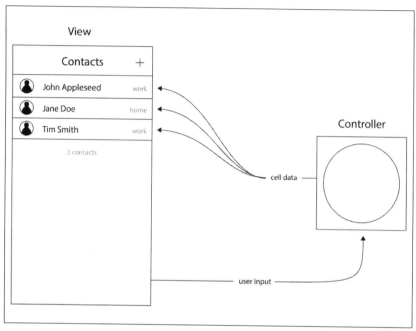

Figure 1.7: The view of a contacts app, shown interacting with a controller

Here, we can see that the view is showing the user some nicely formatted contacts. On the left is a round portrait of the person, followed by their name, and less important on the right is a greyed out word that signifies if the contact is for that person's home or work information. You can also see that the controller is sending the view the information to display, and that the view is relaying any user input back to the controller.

What's powerful about decoupling your view from all of the other application logic is that you can rapidly iterate how your app looks and feels, without having to worry about breaking any of the important logic underneath. It also keeps the amount of data needed in your model to a minimum. For example, our model has no idea that the portrait image will be cropped to a circle, or what size the font needs to be on a contact's name. The view keeps track of everything related to presentation, often in a way that is highly reusable.

Controller

We've seen how the controller works independently with both the model and the view and we've got a pretty good idea of how everything works together, but let's look at a little bit more of a detailed big picture to really see what the controller is doing:

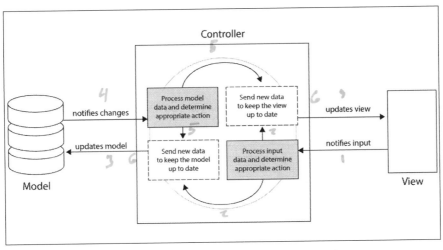

Figure 1.8: How the controller ties everything together

Looking inside the controller, you can see that we've elaborated a bit on what's going on. You'll notice that the controller is capable of receiving notifications from both the model and the view, and then make decisions based on those notifications. It is also capable of sending updated information back to the model and the view.

 As you'll see later in the book, a controller can (and often does) do a lot more than just listen for changes. It is also responsible for setup tasks, supplementary logic, and pretty much anything else that doesn't fit in the model or view.

This cycle repeats for the duration of the controller's existence. Listen for changes. Process notifications. Update appropriate objects. Listen for changes. Process notifications. Update appropriate objects. It's a very elegant solution that keeps your code decoupled while still making it easy for changes on both sides to be properly dealt with throughout the application.

However, this diagram shows a very generic representation of controller logic. Often when developing an app, you'll write many unique controllers that all need custom logic, and each handle things a little differently. At each controller's core though, you'll find that they all need to implement this functionality in some way.

MVC on the web

Now, we've spent some quality time with the theory of the Model-View-Controller software architectural pattern, but I find the best way to learn is through examples. So let's take a quick look at how MVC is used on an Internet browser, something most people use every single day:

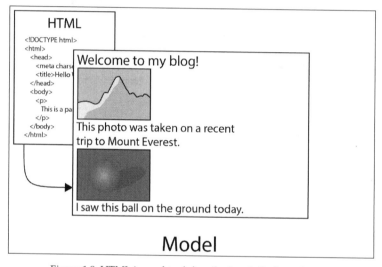

Figure 1.9: HTML is used to define the "model" of a web page

One of the most interesting parts of how the web works is that it has several different languages, and each one handles a different function. HTML is a markup language that defines the content of a web page. This means that HTML defines our model. There usually shouldn't be any formatting in an HTML file, so viewing one directly will be an unformatted jumble of source text and images. In *Figure 1.9*, you can see how the HTML document contains the data for the website title, along with images and captions:

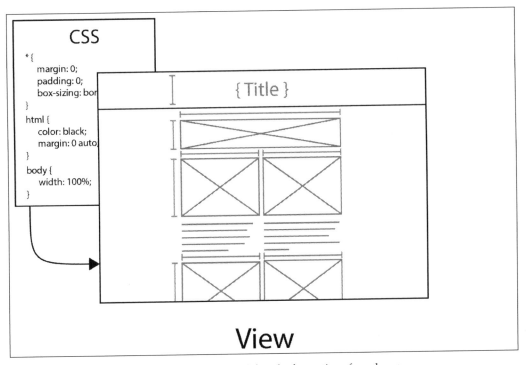

Figure 1.10: The CSS files define the formatting of a web page

Separate from HTML is a *style sheet* language called **CSS**. CSS knows nothing about the data in your HTML files, and is only responsible for defining the visual rules for how HTML elements will be displayed. It determines things like the height and widths of different elements, color information, and rules for how text should be displayed. This would make CSS in charge of our view. In *Figure 1.10*, you can see how the CSS file results in a basic layout of a web page, such as position and size information. However, all of the content is blank, to reinforce that it does not know anything about the content that will be displayed:

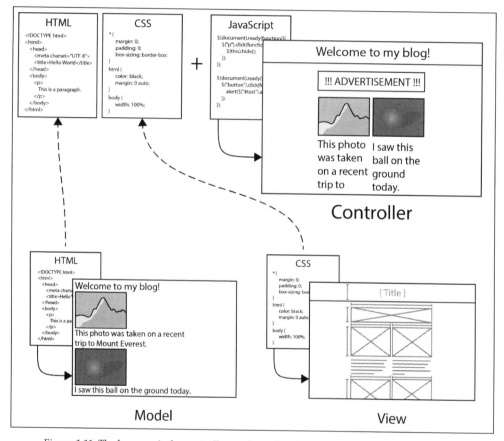

Figure 1.11: The browser is the controller, and uses JavaScript to implement additional logic

Finally, we have the browser itself, which loads both the HTML data and the CSS rules to give us the final rendered page. The browser uses a third language, JavaScript, to dictate its behavior. It can receive input events like clicks and key-presses, and listens for changes in the model. It can then respond to these events with JavaScript callbacks. Our browser is our controller.

If you're well versed in coding the web, you'll know that there is a lot more than this going on behind the scenes. There are many other languages and technologies that keep the modern web afloat, but we're simplifying it for educational purposes.

Hopefully, looking at MVC through a piece of software you are already familiar with has given you a stronger grasp of these concepts, in addition to giving you a bit of insight into how the web works! Now let's jump back to iOS and put everything together.

MVC on iOS

As I alluded to earlier, Xcode and the entire iOS toolset and APIs are built around the concepts of Model-View-Controller. I'd like to point out a few of the more obvious ways in which the concepts are enforced, but as you read through the book and eventually go out to explore and learn on your own, keep an eye out for all of the ways that MVC is present:

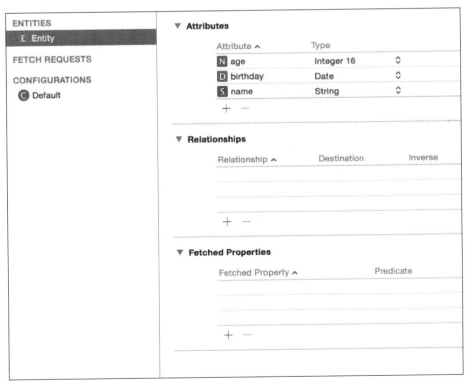

Figure 1.12: A sneak peek at the CoreData model editor in Xcode 8

As we've been doing, let's start with the model. Usually when working on an iOS application, your goal is to represent some kind of data. Sometimes it is a small amount of simple data, like in a weather application, and you can just retrieve it from the web on demand each time you load the app. Other times, you'll be storing and processing large amounts of data, usually in some type of database.

The simple cases don't require too much thought, but there are some great features in Swift that we'll cover in *Chapter 3, Introduction to Swift 3*, that make simple models easy to code, and easy to use.

For the more complex scenarios, there is CoreData, which is essentially an Apple-developed solution for building data models. CoreData is built into iOS, and a visual CoreData model editor is built right into Xcode (see *Figure 1.12*). This means that implementing a complex data model is fast, easy, and native to the development environment. We'll talk more about CoreData in *Chapter 9, Working with Core Data*:

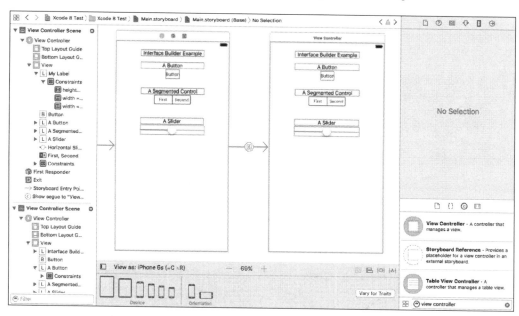

Figure 1.13: Interface builder lets us create the views for iOS apps

Next, let's talk about views. When we talked about a web browser in the last example, we looked at how CSS dictates the appearance of a web page. On iOS, there's an even better way to build out our visual layouts: Interface Builder (see *Figure 1.13*). As the name implies, Interface Builder allows us to directly drag and drop UI elements in a visual **What-You-See-Is-What-You-Get (WYSIWYG) editor.** We can move things around, set different properties, and then even set constraints that allow us to dictate how they should look when the screen changes orientation, or when displayed on different screen sizes. This means that building views is done in a way that makes the most sense: visually. We'll be covering Interface Builder in *Chapter 4, Using Storyboards, Auto Layout, and Size Classes*.

So now we've discussed how to build models and views for iOS apps, and we haven't even talked about coding yet! That's a bit of a lie though, since there is a little more programming than was mentioned in the model section, but still! If we think about how MVC works, though, this should make sense. Models and views are mostly things that need to be defined; all of the action happens in the controller.

On iOS, controllers are usually implemented by creating a sub-class of a UIViewController, a class built into the UIKit framework. We could talk about UIViewControllers for hours (and in fact, we will throughout the rest of the book), so for now just know that this is where you will be doing a good chunk of your coding: handling input events, updating the views, and running supplementary logic.

Becoming a registered developer

Before we can get full access to all of the tools we'll need throughout the book, we're going to have to enroll in the Apple developer program. There are two options we can choose here: we can sign up with a free account, or we can pay the $99/year fee to become a fully licensed Apple developer.

Which account do you need?

The free account will be good for those just starting out, as it provides access to a handful of important features. You have full access to the Xcode developer tools, in addition to beta releases of new versions of Xcode. You'll also have access to the developer forums, where you can chat with other developers about issues you might be facing. Most importantly, however, is that you can test your apps on a real device.

The $99 account gives you everything else. This includes access to betas of new versions of iOS, all of the app services that Apple provides (iCloud, Game Center, and so on), and of course the ability to publish your app to both TestFlight and the App Store.

For most of this book, you will be able to get by just using a free account. However, there will be some parts of chapters (in addition to the entire chapter about distribution) where you will need a paid account to be able to follow along. So, let's get you set up with this one last thing before we embark on our journey!

Registering a free developer account

Signing up for a free developer account couldn't be simpler. First, make sure you have an Apple ID. If you already have an iCloud or iTunes account, you probably already have one. If you'd like to create a separate Apple ID for development, you can do that at `https://appleid.apple.com/`, although it isn't really necessary.

Once you have determined what Apple ID you want to use for your developer account, head over to `http://developer.apple.com/membercenter`, and log in with those Apple ID credentials. You should end up on the following screen:

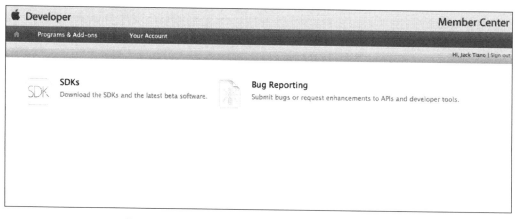

Figure 1.14: The iOS developer member center home page

If so, you're done! In the next chapter, we'll be covering everything you need to know about getting your account set up with Xcode.

Registering a paid developer account

Registering a paid developer account is quite a bit more tedious. When you sign up for a paid account, there are legal and financial formalities involved since you will be able to sign contracts and sell digital products on the App Store worldwide.

To begin the process, start from where the previous section left off. Make sure your Apple ID is set up properly, and log in at http://developer.apple.com/ membercenter. Once you've done that, click on the **Join the Apple Developer Program** area at the bottom of the page (the arrow in *Figure 1.14*), and then the **Enroll** button in the upper-right corner on the next page.

Follow the instructions and fill out the information that it asks for throughout the signup process. Finally, you'll have to pay the $99 fee, and submit your application. The application usually has to go through a review period before you are approved.

Once you're approved, congratulations! You're now officially licensed to create and sell iOS, watchOS, and even Mac OS X apps on all of Apple's App Stores! All you have left to learn is… everything else.

Summary

Whew! Take a deep breath, because that was a lot of information. We touched on many different subjects, but hopefully you are now in the right mindset to begin your journey. Let's do a quick review of everything we learned in this chapter. First, we discussed a developer's responsibilities throughout a normal product lifecycle. Next, we outlined how a team might look, and how a developer would interact with the different roles. Perhaps one of the most important topics that we covered in this chapter is the Model-View-Controller architectural pattern for building software. Lastly, we looked at setting up an **Apple Developer Account**.

In the next chapter, we'll be taking a much deeper look into Xcode. You've already seen and read about bits and pieces of Xcode, but now we'll be walking through all of the major features, and getting a feel for navigating through the program. As we're exploring, keep in mind the topics of this chapter, especially MVC, and see if you can figure out how they manifest throughout Xcode.

Onwards!

2
Welcome to Xcode

For the uninitiated, developing for the iOS platform can seem a little daunting. There are so many aspects to think about when building an application: interface layout, backend data manipulation, managing code libraries and documentation, creating and releasing builds — the list goes on and on.

As you probably know by now, Xcode was built to let you perform all of these tasks in a single, consistent application. It is a true **integrated development environment (IDE)**. However, with so many features and capabilities, it can take a while to learn all of its tricks. In this chapter, we'll be walking through the basics and getting you on course to be an Xcode master. Topics we'll cover include:

- Setting up Xcode and new projects
- Navigating the sections of the Xcode application
- Configuring a project
- Understanding resource files
- Using the editor to modify source files
- Creating a `Hello world` applet

By the end of this chapter, you'll be able to create and configure a new project, create/import/edit source files, and build your project to a simulator or device.

Getting started

Before we can jump in and get our hands dirty, there are a few things we need to do. We'll start off by installing Xcode and looking at where you can access beta versions of the software when they're available. Then we'll get set up with the developer accounts we made in *Chapter 1, Overview of iOS Development*. Finally, we'll look at setting up a new project.

Installing Xcode

Really? A whole subtopic on installing an application? It does seem a little silly, but you'll find that when working with development environments there is a lot more going on than a traditional consumer-facing application. For that reason, we'll take a little time to make sure that everything is installed properly.

In this book, we'll be working with Xcode 8. In order to make things as simple as possible, Apple distributes the latest version of Xcode through the **Mac App Store** (**MAS**). When new versions of iOS are released (10.0, 10.1, 10.2, and so on), Xcode will be updated through the App Store, bundled with the latest SDK.

To install the latest stable version of Xcode, visit the MAS, search for Xcode, and click **Install**. During the download and installation, make sure that you allow Xcode to install any additional components, especially the **Command-Line Tools**. These tools are important to the backbone of Xcode, and it's necessary to make sure they are installed:

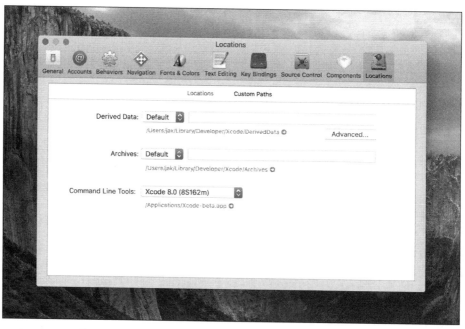

Figure 2.1: Ensuring the command-line tools are installed properly

A quick way to make sure the command-line tools are installed is to open Xcode, navigate to the menu bar item **Xcode | Preferences**, then click on the **Locations** tab all the way to the right. At the bottom of the window, you should see a drop-down menu for **Command-Line Tools**. If it is filled in, like in the previous screenshot, everything should be working properly.

Great! Everything should be installed and running smoothly now. However, as a developer it will be your job to make sure your apps are up to date when new versions of iOS launch to the public. In order to let developers check for bugs and add support for new features, Apple frequently releases beta versions of Xcode on their developer portal. This way you'll be a few months ahead of major releases, and your app can be up to date and bug free on the day that everyone else gets the new OS.

> Apple frequently rearranges their developer portal to make it easier to navigate, so while these instructions are valid at the time of writing, you might have to do a little improvising if things have moved. It's also worth noting that there isn't always a current beta; if you don't see one, they just might not have one.

To download Xcode betas, you won't be able to use the Mac App Store. You'll have to navigate to the Xcode developer portal at `https://developer.apple.com/xcode/download/`. If there is a beta version available, it will be near the top of the page. Here is an example from the Xcode 8 beta page:

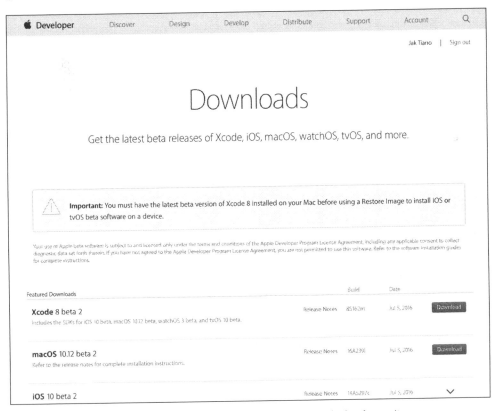

Figure 2.2: The Xcode download portal on the Apple developer site

Remember though, we're using Xcode 8! If there is an Xcode 9+ beta by the time you read this, it might be fun to poke around, but make sure you are on 8.x for the rest of the book so that everything lines up. (Most of what you learn in this book will most likely apply to Xcode 9 and higher, though.)

Adding your developer account

Once you have Xcode installed, there's still one more thing you have to do to complete the initial setup. When I first started using Xcode (version 3.0), managing your developer account was a real pain. You had to create provisioning profiles and register App IDs manually on the developer portal, and then download and import certificates into Xcode. Luckily, pretty much the entire process is now automated and integrated into Xcode itself; all we have to do is log in to our developer account from inside Xcode:

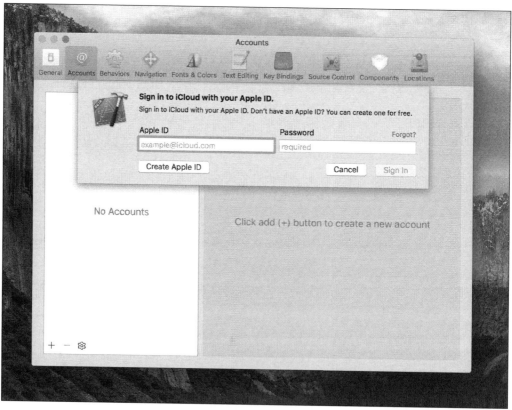

Figure 2.3: Logging in to our developer account from the Xcode 8 account preferences

First, launch Xcode. You should see the **Welcome to Xcode** dialog box, with options to start a new playground or a new project. What we want to do is navigate to the menu bar item **Xcode | Preferences**, and then in the resulting window click on the second tab, labeled **Accounts**. Then click on the little **+** button in the lower-left of the window and select **Add Apple ID**. Then simply type in the Apple ID and password you used to register your account... and that's it! Xcode will now take care of all provisioning profiles and App IDs automatically!

A note on provisioning profiles and signatures:

Provisioning profiles are what Xcode uses to *sign* your application's executable file; a valid signature is required to load and run an app on an iOS device. This makes it so that it is very hard to install malware on a device, but it also causes a lot of headaches for new developers. If you ever run into errors that have to do with signatures, there are tons of threads all over the Internet that can help you figure out your specific problem.

Creating a new project

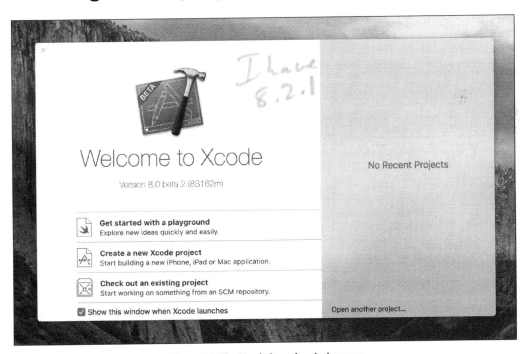

Figure 2.4: The Xcode launch splash screen

Now we're installed, logged in, and ready to roll. Launch Xcode (or just click on the icon in your dock) to bring up the **Welcome to Xcode** dialog again. On the right will be a list of recent projects you've opened. Since this is the first time you've opened Xcode, yours will most likely be empty. In *Figure 2.4*, you can see how my most recent projects fill that space. On the left are three options: **Get started with a playground**, **Create a new Xcode project**, and **Check out an existing project**. We'll get to all of these options in time, but for now, go ahead and select **Create a new Xcode project**.

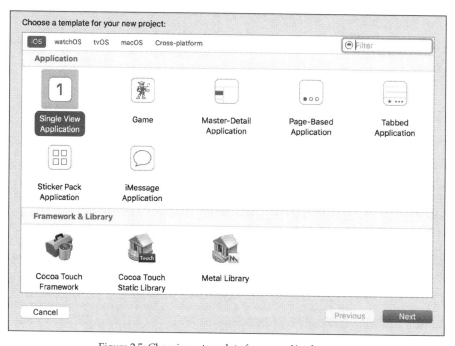

Figure 2.5: Choosing a template for a new Xcode project

In the next dialog, you can choose a template. On the left, you can select the platform and category for the template, and on the right you can choose a specific template. For the most part, we'll be sticking to the **iOS | Application** category, and more times than not we'll be working with a **Single View Application** template. This template is as close as you can get to a *blank project*. The second most useful template here is the **Game** template, which allows you to create a new SpriteKit, Metal, or OpenGL project. This would otherwise be very difficult to manually set up from a **Single View Application**. If you're interested in what the other templates do, you can read a description at the bottom of the window by clicking on each one. But for our purposes, we'll be selecting **Single View Application**, and then clicking **Next**.

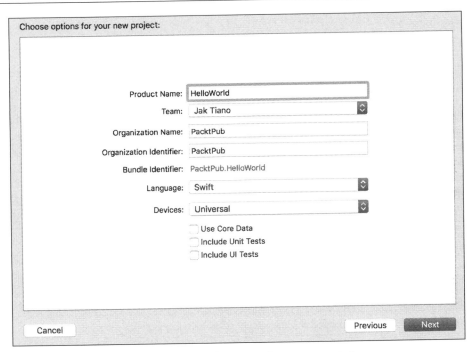

Figure 2.6: Setting the options for our new project

The next screen is our final piece of setup. In the first text field, you can give your project a name. I've named this project **HelloWorld**, because it's fitting and I'm uncreative, but you can name it anything you like. It's worth noting that while you can have spaces in your name, it's usually best practice to avoid them, as I did. Below the **Product Name** is a dropdown for the **Team** being used: this is your Apple Developer account (for me, it's my name).

The second text field is for the **Organization Name**. Here you should type in either your own name or the name of the company you are working for. This will usually be the same as your team name, though I'm using PacktPub here because this book is being published by Packt Publishing.

The third text field, **Organization Identifier**, is a bit more complicated. When publishing to the App Store, every app needs a unique bundle ID. To ensure this, Apple encourages a reverse-domain-name format for IDs. This means that you would use your company (or personal) website domain name, since every domain is unique and has one owner. You would then use the format of *domainExtension. domainName.productName.*

In *Figure 2.6*, you can see I used the website of this book's publisher packtpub.com, but I reversed it to read com.packtpub. If you don't own a website, you can put anything in there, but before you publish to the app store it's a good idea to buy a domain and use that.

Underneath that text field, you can see some grey static text that represents your final bundle identifier. You'll see it uses your reverse-domain **Organization Identifier**, with your **Product Name** appended to the end.

The next option is a drop-down menu to select the programming language for the project you're starting. You can choose from Swift or Objective-C, but in this book we will be sticking exclusively to the new Swift programming language, so keep Swift selected.

Below that is another dropdown that lets you select the devices you are building for. You can choose to build only for iPhone, only for iPad, or create a Universal build for all devices. Xcode now has so many features that make it easy to create universal builds, so we'll be using that option exclusively in this book, so again, leave it selected.

The last three options are checkboxes that enable certain features. Each one is self-explanatory, and sets up your project with the files needed to use each given feature. Later in the book there is a chapter dedicated specifically to using **Core Data**, and another chapter covering both **Unit Tests** and **UI Tests**. For now, we don't need any of these features so leave them all unchecked and click **Next**.

The next and final screen is a standard OS X dialog box to choose where to save your project. When you save, Xcode will create a root folder with the name you gave your project, so you don't need to create a new folder for the project. I use a folder called Xcode Projects in my Documents folder, but where you save it is up to you. Once you've selected a location, click **Create** in the lower right of the window, and we've finished creating our project.

Navigating Xcode

Now that we've finally made it into the software, let's take a look around. You'll notice that there are a lot of subsections in the application window, along with a handful of toolbars and buttons. To make sense of everything that's going on, we're going to break things down into different areas. Before we begin, in the top-right corner of the application window should be three grouped buttons. Make sure they are all blue and active by clicking on them. This will make all of Xcode's shelf areas visible:

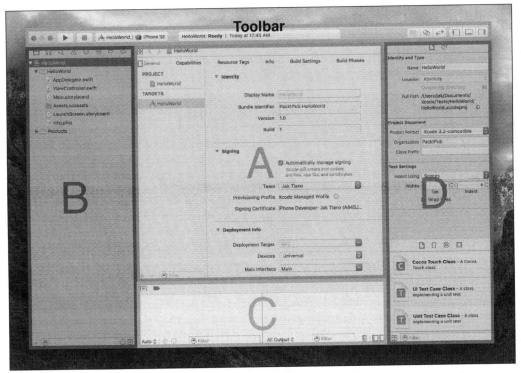

Figure 2.7: A breakdown of the main components of the Xcode application window

At this point, your window should look similar to the preceding screenshot. I've broken down the full window into four separate sections: section **A is the editor view**, section **B is the navigator sidebar,** section **C is the debug area,** and section **D is the utilities sidebar**. At the very top is the **Toolbar**; we'll be using the buttons on the far right of the toolbar very frequently throughout the next few sections. Each of these separate sections has its own characteristics and functionalities, so let's dive into each one individually.

Editor

The editor is the main part of the application window, and is the only area you cannot hide. Xcode's editor window is equipped to handle many different file types. A little later on in the chapter we'll discuss the most common and important file formats that Xcode can use, but the one thing they all share is that you can modify them in the editor window. The most common uses of the editor are to write source code and build out application views. Since the editor is the main stage, we'll cover it in much more detail in the next section.

Navigator sidebar

The navigator sidebar (labeled as area **B** in *Figure 2.7*) is used for a large amount of tasks. You'll find that it is indispensable during development, and that it will be the second most used part of Xcode after the editor.

The initial mode of the navigation sidebar is just that: a project navigator view that lets you navigate and select any of the files in your project. However, if you look along the top of the sidebar, you'll see eight small icons. Clicking each icon changes the functionality of the navigator sidebar. Let's take a look at the most common modes.

The first icon, as already mentioned, is the project navigator. It lets you go through the folders and files that make up your project, and clicking on a file will open it in the editor view. You can also right-click on files or folders in the project navigator to add, modify, or delete them.

> **Navigator shortcuts**:
>
> To jump quickly between the different navigators, you can use the shortcuts *command + 1* through *command + 8*, respective to their position in the toolbar. You can hide the navigator completely with the shortcut *command + 0*.

The third icon (the magnifying glass) is the find navigator. Simple and straightforward, it's used to find anything you might be looking for in your project. It also has *find and replace* functionality built in, in addition to being able to change the scope of a search.

The fourth icon (the warning sign) is the issue navigator. When your code has warnings or errors, they will show up here. A yellow warning icon will let you know something is wrong, but your code will still compile and run. A red error icon means something is broken, and must be fixed for the app to be compiled. Clicking on an error or warning in the issue navigator will bring you to the source of the issue in the editor, making it easy to find the issues.

The sixth icon (it almost looks like a sandwich) is the **debug navigator**. When you are testing your app on a device or a simulator, the debug navigator will show you important metrics, such as CPU and memory usage. We'll cover a lot more of the debugging features in *Chapter 14, Debugging an iOS Application*.

You can click through the other icons and explore what they do, but for the most part they are used less frequently than the rest.

All the way at the bottom of the navigator sidebar is a filter. Different from the find navigator, this is used to filter the contents of the navigator itself. For example, head back to the project navigator and type in `view`. You should see the project hierarchy filtered to only show `ViewController.swift`. You can see how this will be useful when projects get larger.

Debug area

The debug area (labeled as area C in *Figure 2.7*) is located along the bottom of the window when active. To show the debug area, you can click the middle button on the right-most grouping of buttons on the toolbar, or use the keyboard shortcut *command + shift + Y*.

The debug area is split into two sections: the variables view on the left and the console on the right. The variable view is useful when stepping through breakpoints and inspecting the values of variables. The console is where all of your print statements will display, along with any other errors that output to the console.

If you don't understand these terms, that's okay. Like the debug navigator, we'll take a much deeper dive into the debug area and its many functionalities in *Chapter 14, Debugging an iOS Application*.

Utilities sidebar

The utilities sidebar (labeled area D in *Figure 2.7*) is located on the right side of the screen when active. Again, you can use the buttons on the very right of the toolbar to show this sidebar, this time with the third button all the way on the right.

The utilities sidebar is split into two sections, top and bottom. The top is a context-sensitive utilities drawer. Like the navigator sidebar, there are icons along the top that change to different functionality tabs. Since it is context-sensitive, the available tabs will change depending on the type of file that is currently active in the editor. The most use that the top section will get is when editing storyboard files. We'll cover these in more detail when relevant throughout the book.

The bottom half of the utilities sidebar is a drag-and-drop object library. The first tab lets you create new files by dragging them into the project navigator. The second tab lets you drag predefined code snippets to your source code. The third tab is the object library for Interface Builder, where you can drag items such as buttons, sliders, and text fields into your view. On the bottom of the utilities sidebar is a filter for the object library, just like in the navigator sidebar.

Exploring the editor

Now we have a pretty good idea of what all the different parts of the Xcode window do and how they work together. We covered the two sidebars and the debug area in a good amount of detail, but now let's take a closer look at what the main editor can do.

Standard editor

Let's take a look at some of the different configurations for the editor. In your navigation sidebar, you can see a list of files. Right now, the HelloWorld project file is selected. Clicking on a file will make that the active file and open it in the editor. Select the ViewController.swift file and you'll see the editor change to show the source code:

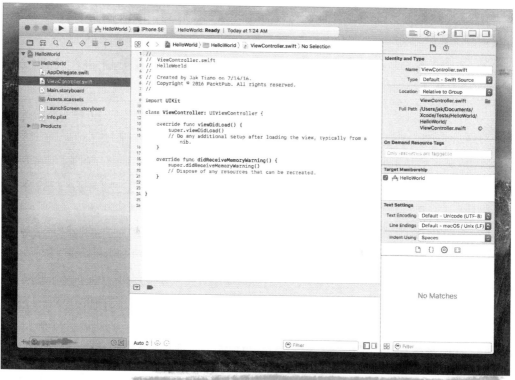

Figure 2.8: The editor view when a .swift file is active

You'll also notice that at the very top of the editor window is a hierarchy bar view starting at the root project (the blue icon), going through folders and files, ending at No Selection. If you click your cursor around at different points in the source file, you'll see that No Selection changes depending on where the cursor is, always being the closest scoped coding block.

For example, if you click at the end of `super.viewDidLoad()` on line 14, the cursor will move inside of `func viewDidLoad()`, and the hierarchy will show you that `viewDidLoad()` is the current method selected. If you click on the `viewDidLoad()` text in the hierarchy bar, you'll see a list of all the classes and methods in the file. Right now we only have two methods, but when your classes get bigger, this is an easy way to quickly navigate through a source file to find a function.

To turn on line numbers in Xcode, go to **Xcode | Preferences | Text Editing**, and check off the first box labeled **Line numbers**.

Next, let's take a look at how the editor responds to some other file types. Just under `ViewController.swift` in the navigation sidebar is `Main.storyboard`. Select that file and see how the editor changes completely (it may take a second or two to load). This is the Interface Builder editor window, and this is where we'll be creating our views:

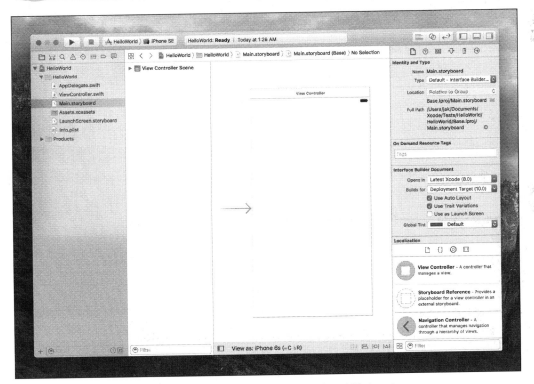

Figure 2.9: The editor view when a .storyboard file is active

Underneath `Main.storyboard` is `Assets.xcassets`, which is an asset catalog file. Select that file and again take note of how the editor adapts. Right now, the only item in the asset catalog is the application's icon. If you click on the item named **AppIcon**, you can see all of the different versions of the icon that the asset needs:

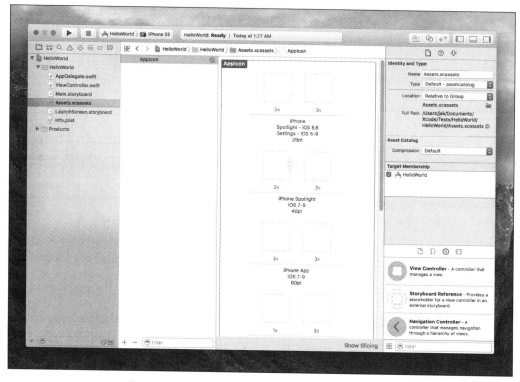

Figure 2.10: The editor view when a .xcassets file is active

One of the most useful features of the Xcode editor is the ability to access documentation right from your source code. To try this out, head back to `ViewController.swift`. This class is already partially filled out by default, so there is some code in here that we might not understand. For example, on line 14, this function calls another function in its superclass named `viewDidLoad()`. To see what this does, press and hold the option key; you'll see that your cursor turns into a crosshair. While still holding down option, drag the crosshair over that `viewDidLoad()` function and you'll see the crosshair turn into a question mark. Click on `viewDidLoad()` and a documentation popup will appear:

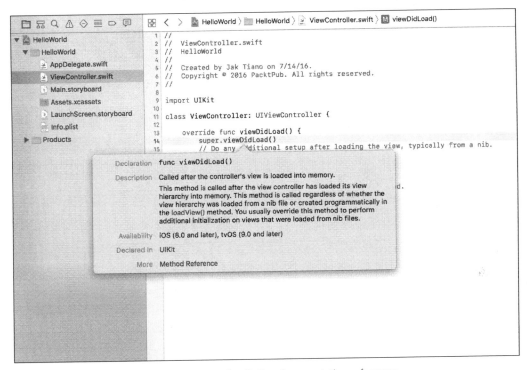

Figure 2.11: Example of inline documentation references

Assistant editor

We've been using the top-right-most grouping of buttons on the Xcode toolbar to show and hide all of the secondary areas, but the group of buttons to their left are just as important. Unlike the secondary area toggles, which can all be turned on and off independently, this set of buttons (which look like a paragraph, two circles, and two arrows) toggle the editor mode, and only one can be active at a time. The default mode (the paragraph icon) is the standard editor which we have been using up to this point. The second icon (two circles) is called the assistant editor. Click on the middle button, and let's see what happens:

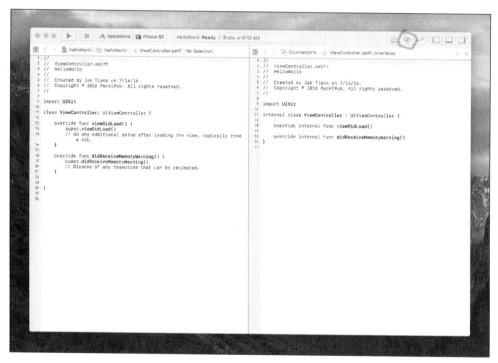

Figure 2.12 The main editor window in assistant editor mode

Whoa! It split our editor in half! (I also hid all of the secondary areas to make it easier to read, but you're free to leave them open.) On the left side of the screen is our original `ViewController.swift` file, and on the right hand side is… something else? By default in Xcode 8 what you should be seeing here is the *Interface* view of your `swift` class. Since Swift doesn't have header files, this is a sort of simulated header file for your `swift` class, so that you can see all of your functions and variables without worrying about the implementation of those methods. You'll notice that it's read-only, and that you can't make any edits on the right side of the screen. (If you've never used Obj-C or C++, don't worry about what a header file is.

However, that's not all the assistant editor can do! If you look at the top of the assistant (right) side of the editor, you'll see a different type of hierarchy bar. If you click on the part that says **Counterparts**, you'll see a ton of other categories of related files that are automatically determined by Xcode. Since this is an empty project, there really isn't much here. At the top, you can see that there is an option for a manual mode, so if you really want to open two arbitrary files next to each other, this would be the way to do it.

So this is cool and all, but it's really not that useful to us. Not so fast! Let's see what happens when we open the `Main.storyboard` file:

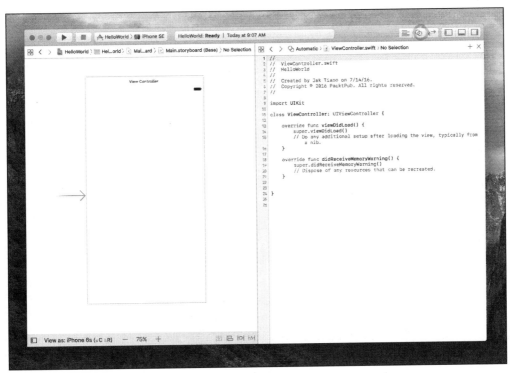

Figure 2.13: The assistant editor being used with a storyboard file

Now this is convenient! On the left side of the screen, we can see the visual representation of our view, and on the right side of the screen we can see the code for our controller. Remember how we talked about the Model-View-Controller, and how the controller needs to update the view? With this setup, we'll be able to build our view alongside our controller, and connect things back and forth with the code. This will be one of the most important uses of the assistant editor, and we'll be back soon to put it to use.

Version editor

Back to the buttons on the toolbar. The third button (the two arrows) toggles the last mode of the editor, known as the version editor. I'm only touching on it now as a formality, because if you click it in your current project you'll get a **No Editor** message on the other side of the screen. This is because the version editor helps you see changes in a file that is under version control, which we haven't enabled on this project. We'll spend a lot more time with the version editor, and version control in general, in *Chapter 5, Taking Advantage of Source Control in Xcode*.

Understanding project settings

Now that you have a good understanding of navigating Xcode on your own, let's head back to the file that was open when we first started our project. In the project navigator, this is the very topmost file; it has a blue icon, and is named the same as your project:

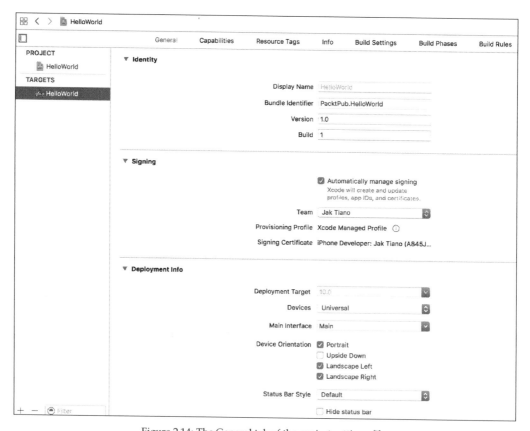

Figure 2.14: The General tab of the project settings file

This file represents your project's settings. There are a lot of important sections in the project settings file that you'll have to interact with in pretty much every project, from app icons, to iCloud capabilities, to custom compiler settings. In this section, we're going take a tour of the most commonly used parts of the project settings file.

Project targets

Like many of the other windows we've explored, you'll notice that the editor for the project settings is split into two columns. On the left, you can see the projects and targets in your app, and on the right are the actual settings. Let's look at the left sidebar for now.

The **PROJECT** heading seems pretty self-explanatory, but what is a target? Let's take a quick detour to understand this.

Essentially, a target is a set of instructions needed to create a single build. It describes for the compiler what all the source files are, the build settings, and any resources or frameworks to include. In our current project, we only have one app target, which will build an iOS app. However, if wanted to also make a build for the Apple Watch, we'd need to create and configure a new app target (actually, we'd need a few). We'll be trying that later on in the book!

Sometimes you can even create a single Xcode project that builds to iOS and OS X, like with SpriteKit. In that case, you could have all of your game's SpriteKit logic and assets shared, but have the platform specific interface code separated. Then in your app targets, you could specify which source files to use, and make sure each one builds for a different platform. Then you'd have a single project that shares assets to build for two completely different platforms!

What's important to understand for now is that each target has its own settings. So in this sidebar, you'll need to select each build target and configure each one separately. When you create a new target, you'll be selecting from presets so they'll be heavily pre-configured, but it's important to comb through yourself and make sure they are set up properly.

Generally, you won't really be changing a lot of the project's settings; what you're actually configuring are the project's **TARGETS** settings. Go ahead and click on the `HelloWorld` project under the Project heading on the sidebar. Notice how there's a lot less going on here? Now let's go back to the **HelloWorld** app target and take a look at what we can do here.

The General tab

Along the top of the editor view for the project settings file is a row of different tabs for groups of configuration options. The **General** tab gives you the ability to set some, well, general settings for your app. Most of this page isn't very dangerous, and it's a good idea to run through it before starting to write any code.

Starting at the top, we have the **Identity** section. In here, you'll see the **Bundle Identifier** we gave our project during setup. If you messed it up, the good news is that you can change it here! This might be useful if you get a new website while making an app, or change its name part way through development. We've also got some text fields to set the **Version** and **Build** numbers. We're going to leave these at 1.0 and 1, respectively, but if you were working on an update to an existing app, this is where you would set that information.

After the **Identity** section is the Signing area. By default, you should have the **Automatically Manage Signing** checkbox enabled. This makes Xcode take care of all code signing responsibilities. Make sure your *team* is selected from the dropdown. If you are registered as an individual developer, this should be your name.

The next section is called **Deployment Info**. This section allows you to change settings regarding the way the app will run on a device. The first item is the **Deployment Target**, which means the *lowest* version of iOS that the app will run on. Right now it's set to 10.x, and we're going to leave it there, but in a real-world environment, you will almost always need to target older devices. The next option is **Devices**, which is the same option we set when creating the project. Next is **Main Interface**, which lets you choose the default storyboard file to use when your app is loaded. By default, it is set to `Main.storyboard`, but if you wanted to create a new storyboard file you could make it the default here. The next four checkboxes for **Device Orientation** will either enable or disable those orientations for your app. For example, if you only left portrait checked, the app wouldn't auto-rotate to any other orientation. The next option, **Status Bar Style**, lets you change the visual style of the status bar, while the last two checkboxes, **Hide status bar** and **Requires full screen**, explain themselves.

Below the deployment settings is a small section where you can set up your **App Icons and Launch Images**. Earlier, when we were in the `Assets.xcassets` file, we saw that we had an `AppIcon` asset in there. You can add as many icon assets as you want, and this first drop-down menu lets you pick which one you want to use for the actual app icon. The next two options have to do with the launch screen for your app. By default, the launch screen is determined by the contents of `LaunchScreen.storyboard`, a file in the root of your project. If you wish to use images instead of a storyboard, you can click the **Use Asset Catalog** button, and if you want to change the storyboard that is used, you can select it from **Launch Screen File**.

The last two sections let you import embedded binaries and link frameworks and libraries. We won't be using these features right now, but if you wanted to include a framework that someone else has built, you could use the little **+** buttons in the lower-left corner of these sections to add them to the target's build resources. We'll start covering this in *Chapter 8, Exploring Common iOS Frameworks*.

The Capabilities tab

When building an application, sometimes you want to tap into some iCloud or system services to make your app work better with the Apple ecosystem, or just provide a better experience for the user. Since having all of these services on by default would waste a ton of resources, you need to manually enable the capabilities you want to use in your app. You can do this from the **Capabilities** tab, found next to **General** in the navigation tab bar along the top of the editor:

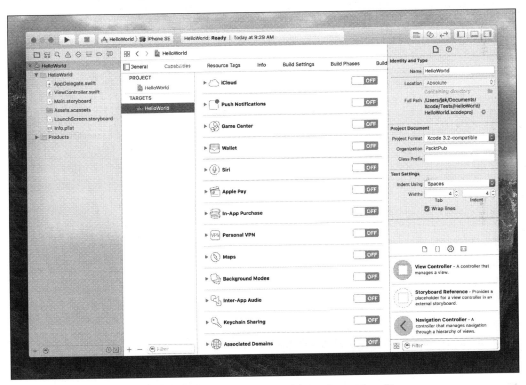

Figure 2.15: The Capabilities tab of the project settings file

Here, you can see a list of the many capabilities that you can enable for your app. By clicking on the drop-down arrow to the left of each icon, you can get a good idea of what each service does. To enable a capability, just flip the switch on the right side of that capability's row. Some common capabilities you might use are the **iCloud**, **Push Notifications**, **Game Center**, and **In-App Purchase** capabilities.

The Info tab

We've looked at a ton of settings for our project and targets so far, but there are always more miscellaneous settings than can ever be fit into a predetermined menu! For those settings, we have the **Info** tab. The first section is all we're concerned with, titled **Custom iOS Target Properties**. As the name implies, this is where we can set custom properties for the app target we are currently editing:

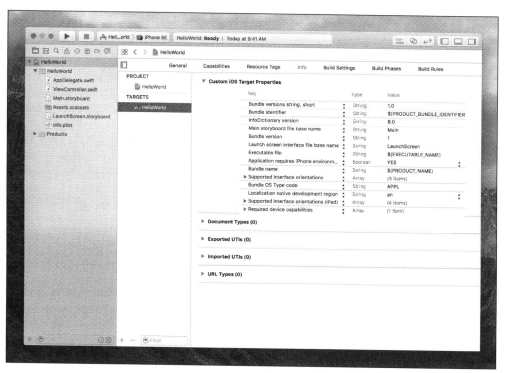

Figure 2.16: The info tab of the project settings file

This section uses a key-value dictionary to set the value for different settings. You can see that there are a handful of custom properties already in the dictionary, and some are even borrowing from other parts of our target settings; for example, the `Supported interface orientations` item is just pulling from the **Deployment Info** section of the **General** tab.

If you select any of the fields in the list, you'll see **+** and **−** buttons appear in the center. If you click the **+** button, it will create a new entry beneath it. You'll see that it will bring up an autocomplete form to select one of the many custom properties you can set. We aren't actually going to set a custom property right now, so you can go ahead and click the **−** button on that new entry to delete it.

There are far too many custom properties for it to make any sense to talk about them here. What's important is that you know where they are and how to modify them.

Creating and managing files

So far on our tour of Xcode we've been looking at and fiddling with all of the files that were automatically created when we started the project. Now we're going to take a look at the different types of resources that are used in a typical Xcode project and how to create, import, and manage them.

Resource types

While the number of resource types that Xcode can handle is quite large, there are only three resource types that you'll need to know about for most use cases. These are the Swift file, the Storyboard, and the Asset Catalog. We've already seen an example of all three resource types, but before we continue we should get a better understanding of what they are used for and how they work.

A Swift source file is a text document that contains source code written in the Swift programming language. Normally, you'll have one class per file, but you can technically declare as many classes, structs, and so on in a source file as you like. We'll discuss the Swift programming language at length in *Chapter 3, Introduction to Swift 3*.

A Storyboard file is a special resource type that defines an application's views, which you can edit visually. A Storyboard file is edited with a drag-and-drop editor called Interface Builder, and also allows you to visually connect UI elements to code blocks in your view controller. We'll discuss Storyboards at length in *Chapter 4, Using Storyboards, Auto Layout, and Size Classes*.

An Asset Catalog is an organized collection of asset resources. These can be images, text files, you name it! Anything your app uses as an asset can be stored and recalled from an asset catalog. There are even some great features you can use with an asset catalog to optimize your app by making sure that only the relevant resources are downloaded on the device you are using. We'll learn a lot more about asset catalogs (and optimization in general) in *Chapter 15, Optimizing Your App*.

Creating new resources

In Xcode, there are several ways to create a new resource file. The quickest and most useful way to create a new file is with the keyboard shortcut *command + N*. This will immediately bring up the new file dialog box:

Figure 2.17: The new file template dialog box

This should look familiar, since it follows the same format as the new project template chooser. On the left you can see the categories, with the resource types on the right. Selecting a broad category on the left (such as iOS, shown in the image) will show you all available resource types for that category. You can also select a more specific category to show only the relevant resource types. For testing purposes, select a **Swift File** and click **Next**.

You'll be asked to give the file a name, and choose a location to save it. Type in `TestClass` as the file name, and save it to the folder with the same name as your project. Click **Create** to finish the process.

You'll notice that Xcode will immediately bring the new file to the focus in the editor, and that it was given some comments at the top describing the file, and a single line of code that reads `import Foundation`. Depending on what file was selected in your project navigator, Xcode may have placed the new file in a strange place in your folder hierarchy. You can drag it to a better location, but instead, let's explore a different way to create a file. Select the `TestClass.swift` file in the project navigator and press *command + delete* to delete the file. When prompted, click **Move to trash**.

This time, instead of using a keyboard shortcut, right-click on the folder in your project navigator that has the same name as your project. For me, that would be the `HelloWorld` folder. In the drop-down menu that pops up, select **New File...**

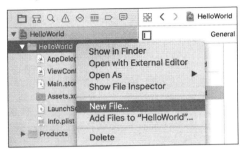

Figure 2.18: Creating a new file by right-clicking in the project navigator

You'll be presented with the same resource type choosing dialog. Again, choose a Swift file, name it `TestClass.swift`, and save it in your project folder. This time, no matter what file was selected in the project navigator, or what folder you saved the actual file to, the new resource will show up as a child of the folder you right-clicked on in the beginning. Let's look at one more way to create files, so this time right-click on `TestClass.swift`, select **Delete**, and again click **Move to trash**. If you select **Remove Reference**, the file will still exist on the disk, but just won't show up in your project:

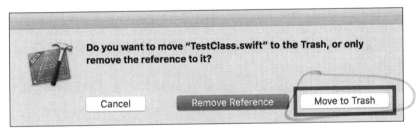

Figure 2.19: Moving to trash versus removing the reference when deleting a file

The third way to create a new resource is a more visual way that's more suitable for people who are uncomfortable with keyboard shortcuts. First, make sure your Utilities sidebar is open and that the bottom section is set to the first tab, the `File Template Library`. A shortcut to bring up this menu is *control + option + command + 1*. Now, scroll down until you see the Swift file icon. Click and drag the icon from the file template library over to the project navigator, into the desired place in the file hierarchy:

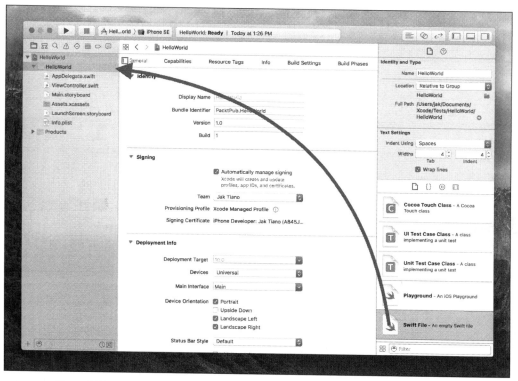

Figure 2.20: Dragging a Swift file template from the file library into the project navigator

This time, when you let go, you only need to give the file a name and a location, since you already chose the type. Just hit **Cancel**, since we've already gone through this process a few times and we don't really need this file.

It's up to you which way you want to create new files. No one way is the best solution, as long as the method you choose is the fastest and easiest for you.

Importing existing files

Sometimes, you'll have a preexisting file that you need to add to your project. Just dragging a file into the project's folder in Finder won't let the Xcode project know that the file is actually part of the project. To import a file into your project, you need to explicitly let Xcode know to add an existing file. Let's try this out.

First, select `ViewController.swift` in the project navigator. We're going to press the *delete* key, but this time we are going to select **Remove Reference**. What we've done is delete Xcode's awareness of the file, but not the file itself. The file is still in our project folder in Finder, but Xcode doesn't know about it anymore. Now we can pretend that the `ViewController.swift` file was obtained from some other source, and see how we can add this file to our project. To do this, right-click on the yellow folder with your project name in the project navigator. From the drop-down, select `Add Files to (PROJECT NAME)`:

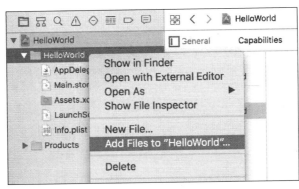

Figure 2.21: Adding files to your project by right-clicking on a destination folder

The next screen should be a file-select window. The file-select window should start in the project's root folder, so the `ViewController.swift` file should be visible. Click on it to select it as the file to add to the project. On the bottom of the file select window, click the Options button; this will give you more control on the file you are about to import. If you're adding the file from a location other than your project folder (for example, your `Downloads` folder), then checking **Copy items if needed** will make a copy of the resource and make sure it's in your project folder. We'll cover the `Added` folders options shortly. At the bottom, you can select which targets the file should be added to, so if you're working in a project with multiple targets you can make sure it's set up properly from the start.

Click on **Add**, and you're done; the file is now properly imported into your project.

Groups and folders

As you noticed when importing that file, there was an option for determining how folders are imported into your Xcode project: as **Groups** or **Folder References**. These two different methods of organization, while similar, have some important distinctions that are important to understand when organizing and managing your Xcode project's files:

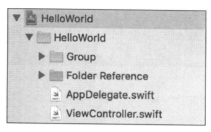

Figure 2.22: Highlighting the visual difference between a group (yellow) and a folder reference (blue)

A group, which shows up as a *yellow* folder icon in Xcode, exists only within Xcode itself. When thinking about how Xcode manages all of our file resources, we know that it stores references to files on your disk. What a group does is make a *group* of these file references. That means that each individual file has its own reference, and that the group folder that it is inside is strictly for visual organization only. If you move files around inside a folder on your disk, it won't affect how the group in Xcode displays them. In fact, when your project is built, all the contents of your groups get dumped into a single directory. The benefit of this is that you can select which target each file belongs to, which you cannot do with a folder reference.

A folder reference, which shows up as a *blue* folder icon in Xcode, is fairly straightforward. Instead of having many references to files on your disk, a folder reference is simply a reference to the containing folder. The benefit of not keeping track of the child files is that moving them around on your disk is automatically reflected. So, basically, a folder reference just points at a folder on your disk, and relays the contents to make them visible in Xcode. Unfortunately, this means that you can either have a whole folder as part of a target, or not. You can't pick and choose which files are part of which targets. You also must specify explicit file paths if a file is inside a folder reference, since it retains its structure in a build.

While being wary of the pitfalls, know that groups are usually the best tool for the job.

Creating builds

When the time comes to actually build your project, you'll find there are a number of features and options to think about. Later in the book we'll take a look at creating distribution builds, but for now let's look at what it takes to understand the basics, and get development builds on our devices.

Build and run

First, let's discuss the only part of the Xcode window we haven't looked at yet: the main toolbar. Earlier we used the buttons on the right side of the toolbar, but we haven't looked at what's happening on the left:

Figure 2.23: The build options and commands in the upper left of the Xcode toolbar

The four buttons along the top (from left to right) are the build and run button, the stop process button, target selection, and platform selection. With these buttons, you can run most of the development builds you'll need.

To test this, let's run our project on the iPhone SE simulator. First, click on the platform selection button. You'll find that it's not a button, but a drop-down menu that allows you to select a target platform. Select the **iPhone SE** option. We won't be needing it at the moment, but the target selector is also a dropdown that lets you choose the target you wish to build.

 In the next step, your computer might ask you if you wish to enable developer mode on your computer. Make sure to click **Enable** and enter your password.

Now that our target and platform are set, all we need to do is click the build and run button. This will build our app, launch the simulator, and then deploy and run the app. It might take a little time for the simulator to launch, but you should end up with a white screen on the simulator:

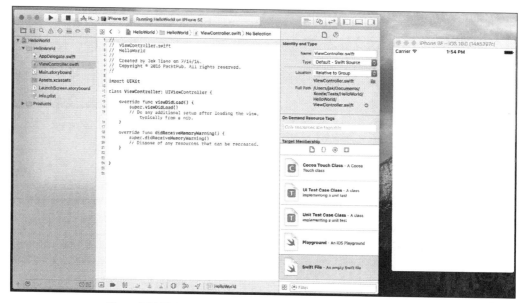

Figure 2.24: This is what your project and simulator should look like

Great! It doesn't look like much, but that's because the project is empty; our app is indeed running on the simulator. Now, to stop running the application, you can press the stop process button.

To speed up this process, you can use the keyboard shortcut *command + R* to build and run your project, and *command + .* to end the process.

Running on a device

The simulator is great on occasion, but most of the time we are going to want to test our apps directly on our devices. Luckily, Xcode makes this dead simple.

First, make sure your device is eligible (running the most recent version of iOS) and plugged into your computer. After a few moments, you should see your device name show up in the platform selection dropdown in the toolbar, at the top of the list.

Resolving device issues:

If you have any issues, go to the menu bar and select **Window | Device**, then find your device and see whether there are any issues with using it for development. You should be able to use information on this screen to search the Web for solutions.

Then, select your device from the platform selector. Before you run, make sure your device is unlocked if it has a passcode, since the passcode lock will prevent code from being deployed to the device. Finally, to run your project on your device, just press the build and run button, or use the shortcut (*command + R*). After a few moments of building and deploying, you should have your blank white screen properly running on your device!

Applying the basics

At this point, we've covered all of the basic features of the Xcode IDE that you need to know to start doing some real work. Throughout the rest of the book, we'll be taking closer looks at many different aspects of the editor.

However, before we move on, let's put our new knowledge to the test, and put everything together to create our first **Hello World!** iOS application. This little application will have a single button that writes text on the screen.

Setting up the workspace

The current project that we've been playing around with throughout this chapter should still be a blank project. As long as you were able to get the blank white screen to show up in the simulator when we were building in the last section, there's no need to create a new project. If you'd like though, you can start afresh by following the exact same instructions from the beginning of the chapter to create a new project.

Once we have a project to work with, let's get the workspace set up for the task at hand. For this project, we are going to want to see both our `Main.storyboard` file and our `ViewController.swift` file at the same time; sounds like a job for the assistant editor mode. Earlier in the chapter, we looked at how this is useful for developing a view and a controller simultaneously, and that's exactly what we're going to do here. Select the `Main.storyboard` file and then enter assistant editor mode, and your project window should look something like this:

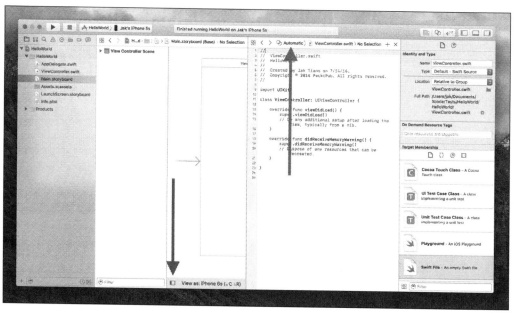

Figure 2.25: Configuring the assistant editor for development

We've got our storyboard on the left and our `ViewController.swift` on the right. However, as you can see in *Figure 2.25*, my storyboard has a sidebar on the left taking up a lot of space. The blue arrow is pointing to a little icon that will hide the sidebar. If your sidebar was already hidden, you can click the same button to show it, but make sure you end up leaving it hidden for now.

Another possible issue you might run into is that the file on the right is a file other than our `ViewController.swift` file. Remember from earlier that there are different ways to display the second file in the assistant editor. To fix this, the red arrow is pointing at the drop-down menu that lets you select a file. From that dropdown, select **Automatic** and you should be all set.

Now, just drag the center divider of the assistant editor to make sure the full Interface Builder view is visible. One final thing: on the **Utilities** sidebar, set the object library in the lower half to the third tab (or just press *control + option + command + 3*). If your final window looks like *Figure 2.26*, we're good to go:

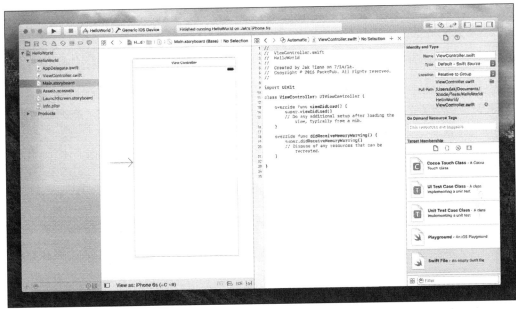

Figure 2.26: The overall look of our application window after being set up for development

Creating the model, view, and controller

This title is a little misleading because this app will be so simple that it doesn't have any data, and therefore doesn't need a model! However, it's best to still think of separating your apps into these three categories when developing them, and most apps *will* have models. So with the model *taken care of*, let's move on to the view.

For this application, we are only going to have a button that, when pressed, will make text appear. In iOS terms, we need a **UIButton**, which we can press, and a **UILabel**, which can display text. To add these to our view, all we have to do is drag them from the object library into our storyboard.

We've already used the object library to create new files, so you should be somewhat familiar with how it works. Again, make sure the third tab is selected in the object library, since this is where the interface builder objects are. You can scroll through the library looking for a **Button** and a **Label**, or you can use the search bar at the bottom to find them quicker:

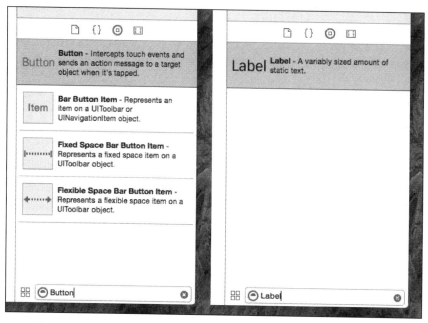

Figure 2.27: Using the search bar in the object library to find interface elements

Once you find each object in the library, just drag it out into the storyboard. We need one of each element. Place the label towards the upper left of the view, and the button beneath it. If you double-click on the button, you should be able to edit the text; set it to say **Press Me**. Next, do the same with the label, but type in `Hello World!`

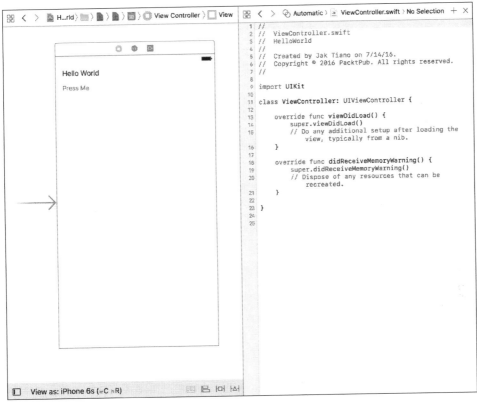

Figure 2.28: Our simple, completed storyboard

Very simple, but this is our finished view! With our *model* and our view both complete, all that remains is the controller. Our controller is going to need to have control over our label so that it can change the text inside of it, and it is also going to need to know when the button has been pressed.

Xcode has two really great features that make connecting storyboards and Swift files really intuitive. These are called **IBActions** and **IBOutlets**, where the **IB** stands for **Interface Builder**. An action is related to an event that happens in the view, and an outlet is a reference to an object in the view. So using these definitions, we want to create an IBOutlet for our label, and an IBAction for when the button is clicked.

Let's start by making an outlet for our label. Press and hold the *control* key on your keyboard, and then click and drag from the label into your Swift file. You should have a blue line connection from the label in your view to a line in the code:

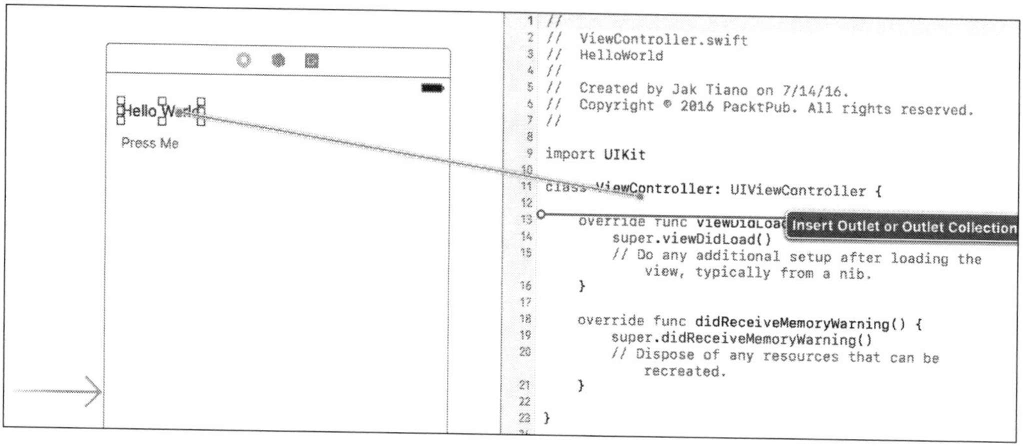

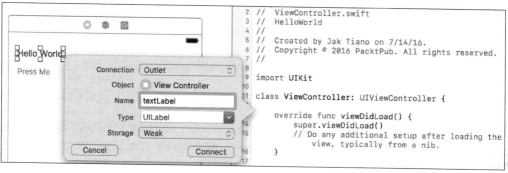

Figure 2.29: Control dragging from the label in the storyboard to the code in the controller

In *Figure 2.29*, you can see that there is a horizontal blue line in the Swift file, which represents the line that code will be generated. Make sure it's below the class definition, and above the `viewDidLoad()` function, on just about line 12. When you let go, you'll be greeted with a new dialog box to set up the `IBAction` or `IBOutlet`:

Figure 2.30: Configuring the label outlet

Make sure the **Connection** is set to `Outlet` and give the outlet the name of `textLabel`. Click **Connect** and you should see that Xcode generated a line of code for you. The code that it generated is a variable that allows you to access that text label in your view controller's code. Isn't that awesome? All we've done so far is click and drag a few times, and we have objects on screen that we can manipulate.

Now let's make an `IBAction` for when the button is clicked. Just like making an outlet for the label, press and hold control and then drag from the button into the Swift file:

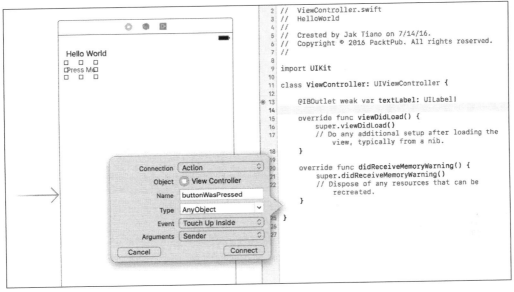

Figure 2.31: Configuring the button action

This time, set the connection type to **Action**, and give the action a name of `buttonWasPressed`. Click **Connect**, and you'll see that this time it generated a whole function! Now we've connected everything from our storyboard, so our controller has all the information it needs from the view. That means it's time to move on to our last step: writing the few lines of code that make everything work!

The first thing we want to do is make sure the label has no text in it when the application starts. That way, it only appears once we press the button. To do this, we're going to want to place a line of code in the `viewDidLoad()` function that erases the text. Here's what the final function should look like:

```
override func viewDidLoad() {
    super.viewDidLoad()
    textLabel.text = ""
}
```

You can see that we're able to access the label in our view using the `textLabel` outlet that we created earlier.

Finally, we need to change the text when the button is pressed. It should be pretty obvious that we'll be using the `buttonWasPressed()` IBAction function we made earlier, and we'll be using a very similar line of code to the one we used to clear out the text. This is what the final `buttonWasPressed()` function should look like:

```
@IBAction func buttonWasPressed(sender: AnyObject) {
    if textLabel.text == "" {
        textLabel.text = "Hello World!"
    } else {
        textLabel.text = ""
    }
}
```

Stepping through this code, we can see that we first look to see if the label is blank. If it is blank, we change it to say `Hello World!`, but if it isn't empty, we set it back to blank. That way, each time we press the button, it will toggle back and forth between on and off. And remember, this function will be automatically called whenever the button is pressed. That means our controller, and thus our entire app, is finished!

Testing our work in the simulator

You're welcome to try this on your device, but for now, select the iPhone 6 Simulator from the platform selector, and then build and run your project. You should see the button that says **Press Me!** and when you click it, the text `Hello World!` should appear above it! When you press it again, it should disappear:

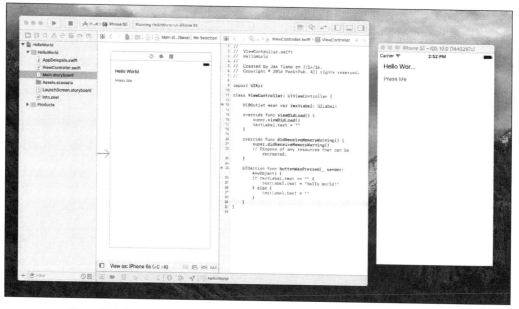

Figure 2.32: An overview of our finished project, and the app open in the simulator

And that's it! We've built our first little app for iOS. It's not much, but we've taken our first step on this journey. It only gets better from here!

Summary

In this chapter, we learned how to find our way through the sometimes intimidating interface of Xcode. We broke down all the different sections, learned about the many different toolbars and editors, and tested our knowledge by building a simple iOS app! We should now have a really good idea of what different parts of the application are called, and we even have a few handy keyboard shortcuts to speed things up.

In the next chapter, we'll be taking a little break from Xcode and diving headfirst into the world of Swift programming. We'll start from the beginning, looking at how variables and functions work in Swift, but quickly work our way up to some of the powerful and unique features the language has to offer, such as optional types, closures, and generics. We'll also take a look at the new features that Swift 3 has to offer, such as error handling and protocol extensions.

Introduction to Swift 3

For a long time, developing applications on an Apple platform meant you had to know how to use Objective-C. It is a quirky language, but it has adapted over the years to be a powerful tool for application development and was tied to the core of the Cocoa and Cocoa Touch frameworks.

As everyone knows by now, Apple changed the game in 2014 when they introduced Swift, an entirely new and modern language meant to carry app development into the next few decades.

Looking back, it's easy to see why a new language was necessary. Swift cleaned up a lot of long-standing problems with Objective-C, and has enabled Apple to really blow open their development platforms. Since Swift launched in 2014, we've seen a huge addition of functionality to iOS, and two entirely new development platforms with watchOS and tvOS. It is clear: Swift is here to stay.

In this chapter, we'll be getting through as many of the big, important features of Swift as we can. The goal is to get you up to speed with the language and get a feel for how it works. We'll be using it throughout the rest of the book, but within the context of developing an actual app. For now, let's learn the basics! We'll be covering the following topics:

- Using Swift playgrounds in Xcode 8
- Data types, optionals, variables, and collections
- Functions and control flow
- Using classes, structs, and enumerations
- Closures, protocols, class extensions, and error handling

That may look like a lot to cover, but trust me when I tell you that Swift is an absolute blast to learn, and even more fun to use. Let's go!

Discovering playgrounds

When Apple first introduced Swift, they created an interactive book where developers could read about the new language and actually use the language all in one document. It was built on top of a new feature in Xcode 6 called **playgrounds**. The idea behind the playground was that it was a good place to learn and experiment with the new language, without having to worry about setting up test projects in Xcode.

Throughout this chapter, we're going to be using playgrounds as we learn about and play with Swift. However, always try to keep them in mind, since they can be an invaluable tool for rapid prototyping when working on your own projects.

Setting up a playground

One of the things that makes playgrounds so powerful in Xcode is that they are not a part of a project, but are just individual files. This makes using them extremely straightforward. You don't have to worry about project settings or dependencies; you can just jump in and start playing.

To create a new playground, let's open up Xcode. Previously, we learned how to create a new project from this screen, using the second option. This time, we're going to just select **Get started with a playground**:

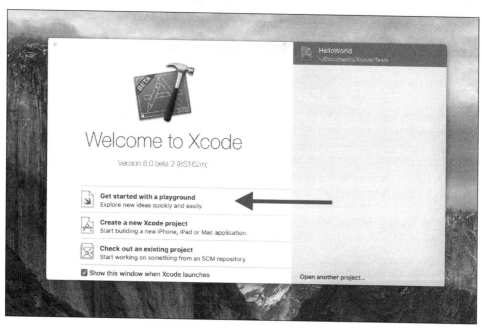

Figure 3.1: Creating a new playground from the Xcode startup screen

As with setting up an Xcode project, there is some minor configuration to be done. In the next window, set the name of the playground to `LearningSwift`, and make sure the platform is set to iOS. If your screen looks like the following one, we're good to go:

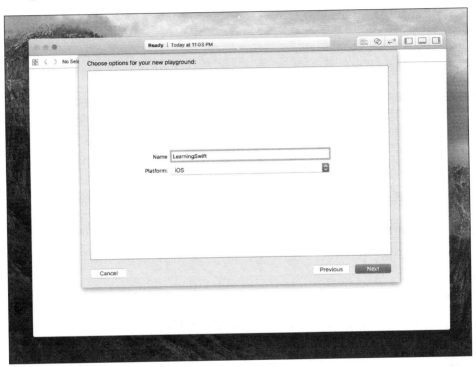

Figure 3.2: Configuring a new playground environment

You'll be asked to choose where to save the file next. I created a `Playgrounds` folder, inside my `Xcode` folder, inside my `Documents` folder (`Documents` | `Xcode` | `Playgrounds`), but you may save it wherever you wish.

> Just because they don't require a project, that doesn't mean you can't have a playground inside a project. When working in a normal Xcode project, you can always press *command* + *N* (to create a new file), select a playground file, and save it inside your project.

Now that we're set up, let's take a look around the playground. You'll notice that it is very similar to the standard Xcode window we already know, but with fewer buttons. We still have our editor mode toggles, and our sidebar toggles in the upper right of the window, but that's about it.

You'll notice that there's no build and run button. That's because in a playground, the code is automatically being run as you type. On the right side of the editor window is a large grey area. As your code is being run, the output of each line of code is being shown in this area as shown in *Figure 3.3*:

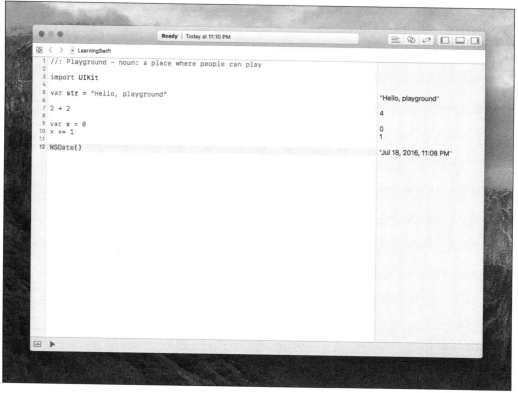

Figure 3.3: The results of each line are displayed to the right of the code editor

On the left, you can see I wrote a few sample lines of code. On line 7, I wrote `2 + 2`, and then on the right you can see that the playground evaluated that line to the value of `4`. Underneath that, I created a variable called `x`, and incremented it by one. The last line I created an instance of the `NSDate` class, and in the grey sidebar you can see the current date information stored inside it.

Anyhow, those examples are just to illustrate how the playground's editor window is set up. You write code on the left and the results are displayed on the right.

Using previews

Being able to see how something works so quickly and easily is an extremely valuable tool. However, playgrounds don't stop with the line evaluation previews that we just looked at. There are many custom visualizers to help you understand your code better. Let's take a look at a few of the most useful of these previews.

Sometimes when writing code, you'll want to see how something changes over time. This can be real time, as in seconds, or maybe just the number of iterations a loop has run through. In these cases, Swift playgrounds have visual data graph previews that make it easy to see how values have changed over time. To test this out, replace the code in your playground with the following:

```
var time: Float = 0
var position: Float = 0

while time < 1.0 {
    position = time*time
    time += 0.05
}
```

This short snippet of code tracks two things: a `time` variable that we increase linearly until it reaches 1.0, and a speed value that is calculated as the elapsed time squared. If you've spent some time with math or physics, you might be able to mentally picture how these two values relate to each other.

Luckily, computers make it so that we rarely need to use our brains at all anymore, and we can have Xcode visually show us what is going on:

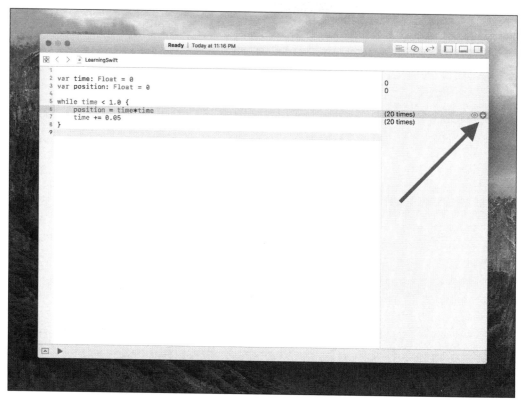

Figure 3.4: The plus button enables the results view in a playground

If you hover over any of the evaluation previews on the right, you will get two little icons along the right side of the window: a quick look eye, and a + sign which turns on the **results view**. The quick look button will let you quickly display the visual preview, and the plus sign will display the visual preview inline with your code. Click the results view button (+ sign, see *Figure 3.4*) for both of the calculations inside our `while` loop, and you'll be greeted with a beautiful visualization of the data:

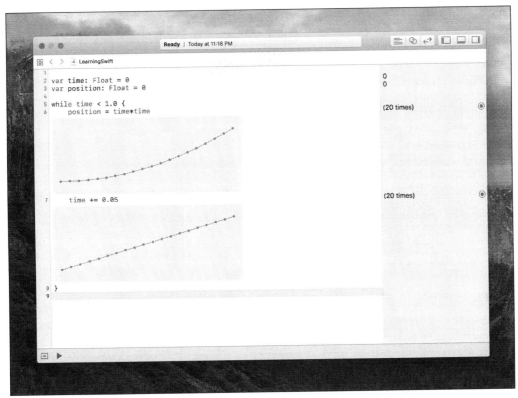

Figure 3.5: The results view shows a graph of our values over time

Now, regardless of our math background, we can easily see how these two values increase over time! This can be extremely useful depending on what you're programming. I've used it to visually check how interpolation functions work, and you could also use it to look at animation curves. Basically, anytime you need to visualize data, this is a fantastic way to do it.

Let's throw a little more code at our playground. Copy the following lines into your playground:

```
import UIKit

var view = UIView(frame: CGRect(x: 0, y: 0, width: 100, height: 100))
view.backgroundColor = UIColor.red()
view.layer.borderColor = UIColor. green().cgColor

view
```

Dosnt like (), or [handwritten annotation]

This time, we are prototyping a custom view for an app, so we use `import UIKit` at the top. Then we create our view by initializing it with a frame that is `100` points by `100` points. Then we change the background color to red and the border color to green. This should be a little easier to visualize in our heads, but let's click the results view button (plus sign) that is next to that last view that we tacked on:

```
import UIKit

var view = UIView(frame: CGRect(x: 0, y: 0, width: 100, height: 100))
view.backgroundColor = UIColor.red()
view.layer.borderColor = UIColor.green().cgColor

view
```

Figure 3.6: Visualizing the view we programmed using the results view button

We can see our view is about 100px square, and that it is red, but what happened to the green border that we set? Well, we actually need to set the width of the border if we want to see it, since it defaults to a width of 0. Luckily, in our playground it's very easy to add or change code and immediately see the visual changes:

```
import UIKit

var view = UIView(frame: CGRect(x: 0, y: 0, width: 100, height: 100))
view.backgroundColor = UIColor.red()
view.layer.borderColor = UIColor.green().cgColor
view.layer.borderWidth = 8.0

view
```

Figure 3.7: The updated view code now shows the green border

There we go! Now we have our red background and green border. Naturally, you can try out the results view button on all kinds of things and see what works and what doesn't, but it's an extremely helpful feature to test visual objects and to visualize data.

Resources, pages, and rich comments

Before we move away from playgrounds, it's worth going over three features that make playgrounds a lot more useful, especially as living documentation or learning tools. These three features are resources, pages, and rich comments.

Resources

The ability to have resources in playgrounds really expands what you can do with them. The most obvious use case here is that you can now use images in a playground. In the resources folder of Chapter 3, I've included a file named wink.png. To add this to your playground, first open the navigator sidebar (shortcut: *command + 1*). Then drag wink.png into the resources folder of your playground. Now you can access that file in your playground. To try this out, copy the following code into your playground:

```
import UIKit

var winkImage = UIImage(named: "wink")
```

If you open the results view for the second line where you create the wink image, you'll see that it loaded the file just fine!

Pages

The next feature, pages, is pretty self explanatory. With this feature, you can now add multiple pages to your playgrounds. To create a new page, go to **File | New | Playground Page**, or use the shortcut *command + option + N*:

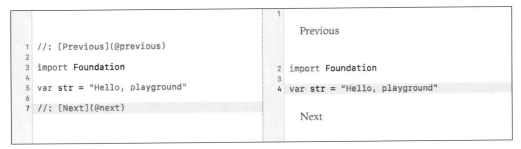

Figure 3.8: Special code comments (shown on the left) create previous and next buttons (shown on the right)

If you open the new page you created, you'll see some strange comments at the top and bottom (the left side of *Figure 3.8*). These are actually part of the rich comments system we'll talk about next, but their function is to let you navigate between pages. To switch out of edit mode, you'll need to go to **Editor | Show Rendered Markup** from the menu bar. You should now be able to click the **Next** and **Previous** buttons to navigate through pages (right side of *Figure 3.8*). The **Next** and **Previous** buttons will cycle you through the pages based on their order in the navigation side bar (*command +1*). Play around with this and see what you can do!

Rich comments

Now that we've taken a peek at what rich comments can do, let's understand them a little better. In normal Swift code, comments are used to make notes or clarify parts of your code. In a playground, however, we can use rich comments to create visually appealing blocks of text that can make a playground look more like an interactive textbook. Combining these rich comments with pages and resources, you can make some amazing coding tutorials or training programs to teach others how to use your Swift code.

To begin using rich text commenting, you're going to make a standard Swift comment, which is a `//` at the beginning of a line, followed by a colon (`:`). The end result should look like this `//:`. You can also make a multi-line rich comment by using `/*:` at the beginning of the comment, and `*/` at the end.

Once you've started either a single or multi-line comment, playgrounds use the Markdown syntax to format the text. You can read all about Markdown online, but here is an example of a Markdown formatted comment:

```
/*:
This is a header
================

Here is some sample text that describes this page in our playground.

* this is a list item
* this is another list item

_Below is some code_

    func main() {
        let x: Int = 0
    }

This is the **end** of the header.
*/
```

If you paste this somewhere in your playground while in raw markup mode, then enable rendered markup (**Editor | Show Rendered Markup**), you can see that it translates visually to this comment:

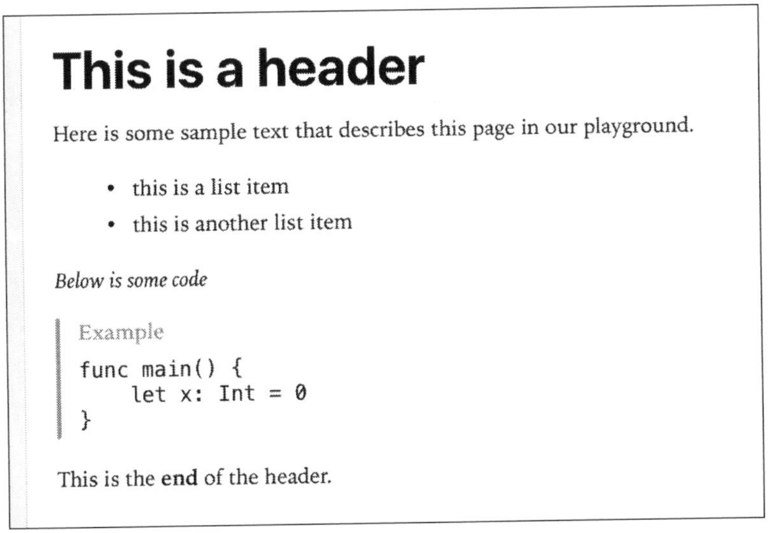

This is a header

Here is some sample text that describes this page in our playground.

- this is a list item
- this is another list item

Below is some code

```
Example
func main() {
    let x: Int = 0
}
```

This is the **end** of the header.

Figure 3.9: Some examples of using Markdown to create rich comments

There's a lot more to learn about Markdown, but there are better places to read about it than here. Go online and do some research, then see what you can create in a playground using pages and rich comments!

Understanding Swift basics

Like any new programming language, Swift has its quirks. But as with most languages, the building blocks are pretty simple and straightforward. In this section, we're going to start with the features of Swift that nearly every programming language has, so that you can get a feel for how it works. If you've never used any programming language before then there may be some terms you are unfamiliar with, but I suggest you read through and look those up as you read along.

Before you start, open up a fresh playground and code along as you read!

Data types, constants, and variables

If you break down how software works to the lowest level of granularity, all that really ever happens is that data on your computer is written, manipulated, and moved. When you go up a level of granularity and look at the source code for that software, you'll see a lot of data structures, classes, and functions, but all of these are just efficient and readable vessels for chunks of code that create, manipulate, and save data.

Data types

So as it would seem, creating and manipulating data is pretty important. Let's take a look at some of the most common built-in data types in Swift by defining some constants:

```
let integer: Int           = 0
let floatingPoint: Float   = 0.0
let string: String         = "Hello"
let boolean: Bool          = true
```

Starting from the top, we have an integer (`Int`), then a floating point number (`Float`), then a string (`String`), and finally a Boolean value (`Bool`). You'll notice all of the built-in types are capitalized, which may be a little strange if you're coming from Objective-C.

Constants

While we're here, let's take a look at how a constant is defined in Swift:

```
let constantName: DataType = {Value}
```

First, we use the `let` keyword to signify that we are defining a constant. The next part is our constant's name, which we will use to reference it, followed by a colon. After the colon we define the data type of our constant, and finally we set it equal to its default value. Go to your playground and try to define some of your own constants using the data types we just looked at. (This example won't work: `DataType` is not a real data type! Replace that with a real data type, such as `Int` or `String`).

Variables

Since Swift has a strong focus on speed and safety, the use of unchanging constant values is encouraged as frequently as possible. However, we know that won't always be possible, and in cases where a value needs to change we use a **variable**. Defining a variable is exactly the same as defining a constant, but instead of using `let`, we use `var`:

```
var variableName: DataType = {Value}
```

Now we can manipulate and rewrite the value of this variable as much as we need!

One of the most important features of the Swift programming language is that it is type safe. This means that all of the constants and variables you define must have a type, or else the code won't even compile. In these past few examples, we've defined our variables and constants with **explicit** types, meaning we wrote the type right next to them to make sure the compiler knows about it. But the Swift compiler is very smart and can also figure out a type by its context, therefore giving it an **implicit** type. Here's an example:

```
var value1: Int = 0
var value2 = 0
```

On `value1`, we explicitly state that the variable is of the type `Int`. On `value2`, we just set an un typed value to `0`, but the compiler knows that `0` is an integer and deduces that `value2` must be an `Int`. This is called **type inference**. This will usually make more sense when instantiating objects later on, since it's more readable:

```
var myView = UIView()
```

Here, it's very clear that `myView` will be of the type of the `UIView` class (we'll get to classes soon enough):

```
var value1, value2, value3: String
```

You can also declare several variables on one line, and even use emojis as a variable name! (Although, it's really only useful as a novelty; I don't recommend using emojis in real-world code.)

Optionals

One of the most powerful features of Swift is the way that it handles the absence of a value. So far, we've been using data types that are guaranteed to have a value; later on we'll see how the compiler will require those data types to have a value before an object is finished initializing. This means that you are guaranteed that a variable will have a value, which makes your code safer and less prone to failure.

However, sometimes it's important that a variable doesn't have a value at all. There are many parts of the Cocoa Touch framework that are built around the idea of an object being `nil`, which in Objective-C means that there is nothing there. Swift takes this concept a step further by requiring that you plan ahead and let the compiler know which variables are capable of not having a value. Because of their functionality of being able to have or not have a value, these are called **optionals:**

```
var normalInt: Int = 0
var optionalInt: Int?
```

The `normalInt` variable is declared as a standard `Int`, and assigned a value of `0`. However, the `optionalInt` is defined as the type `Int?`. The question mark signifies that a value may or may not be present. Since it's optional, we don't assign it a value, and that's okay. Now we have an issue, though: we have a variable running around our code with no value! What happens if we try to use it? Let's see:

```
normalInt = optionalInt
```

If we tried to do this, we'd get a compiler error! That's because the compiler isn't sure if there is a value inside `optionalInt`, and it really, really doesn't want the code to crash when it runs. To use an optional value, we have to check if there is a value inside or not; this is called **unwrapping**. Here's how we would unwrap an optional:

```
if let unwrappedInt = optionalInt {
    normalInt = unwrappedInt
}
```

The `if let` statement is a special type of `if` statement which checks whether an optional has a value. In this case, it checks to see whether `optionalInt` has a value, and if it does it assigns the value to `unwrappedInt`, which you can then use inside the brackets. However, if `optionalInt` didn't have a value, the code would be skipped. You can also unwrap multiple optional values at once if they are all needed.

That would look like this:

```
var normalString: String = ""
var optionalString: String?

if let unwrappedInt = optionalInt, unwrappedString = optionalString {
    normalInt = unwrappedInt
    normalString = unwrappedString
}
```

(handwritten annotation: let)

Here, the two unwrapping conditions are separated by a comma, and the `if` branch will only be executed if both values can be unwrapped.

With a normal optional value, you can force it to be unwrapped using an exclamation mark:

```
normalInt = optionalInt!
```

However, this can be dangerous, because you are overriding the compiler and telling it that you are sure that the optional value definitely has a value. If you're wrong, the code will crash at runtime. As scary as that sounds, sometimes you are sure.

In cases where a value needs to be assigned after the `init` function, but will always have a value once it's assigned, you can declare a variable as an **implicitly unwrapped** optional. This means that you can use the variable like a normal variable, without unwrapping it with an `if let` statement. To do this, simply declare the variable as such:

```
var implicitlyUnwrappedInt: Int!
```

So, instead of using the question mark to denote a standard optional, we use an exclamation mark to show that it should be treated as unwrapped. To use it, we can just do the following:

```
normalInt = implicitlyUnwrappedInt
```

You can also at any time set an optional value back to being empty by assigning it to the value `nil`:

```
optionalInt = nil
```

This has just been a brief introduction to optionals in Swift, but we'll be encountering them throughout the book and using them in many different ways.

Collection types

With an understanding of how to use simple data types, let's now take a look at the different kinds of collection built into Swift. The two most commonly used types of collection are arrays and dictionaries. Both of these are native to the Swift language.

Arrays

An array in Swift is a simple ordered collection of values of a certain type. If you want your array to be immutable, meaning you can't add/remove/change values, then you define it with a `let` keywords. To make it mutable (changeable), define it with `var`:

```
let immutableArray: [Int] = [1, 2, 3]
var mutableArray: [Int] = [Int]()
```

In this example, you can see that the immutable array is initialized with default values of 1, 2, and 3, and that it is of the type `[Int]`. The square brackets around a data type let the compiler know that it is an array, and not just a single value. Beneath that, we did something similar, but instead of giving the `mutableArray` starting values, we just initialized a new empty array of integers to use later. Using what we learned about type inference in the last section, we could also let the compiler figure out the types and shorten these declarations to the following:

```
let immutableArray = [1, 2, 3]
var mutableArray = [Int]()
```

Let's take a look at some of the basic functionality of a Swift array. Adding an element to the end of an array looks like this:

```
mutableArray.append(1)
mutableArray.append(2)
mutableArray.append(3)
```

The contents of the array would now look like this: [1, 2, and 3], and if you're typing this into a playground, you should be able to see that in the results sidebar. To remove the last element, you can use dot-syntax to call a function on the array:

```
mutableArray.removeLast()
```

You can also use dot-syntax to access the properties of the array, such as `count` the number of elements the array contains:

```
mutableArray.count
```

Or you can even access a Bool value to let you know whether the array is empty or not:

```
mutableArray.isEmpty
```

You can access elements in an array by using subscript syntax, where you put the index of the element you are looking for in square brackets after the array variable, like this:

```
mutableArray[0]
```

There is plenty more to learn about the Swift arrays, but this should be enough to get us started. Feel free to experiment and look through Apple's documentation.

Dictionaries

A dictionary is a collection where every value has a key that can be used to retrieve it. So as an example, if I put the number 05401 in a dictionary with the key zipCode, then later I would ask for zipCode and it would return 05401:

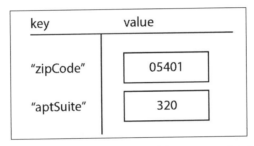

Figure 3.10: Dictionaries use keys which have an associated value

This has many use cases when developing software, and usually has the benefit of being easily human-readable. Let's take a look at how to create a dictionary:

```
var myDict = [String: Int]()
```

Here, we created an empty dictionary called myDict, where it uses a String as its key, and stores an Int value. Again, the two parentheses show that we are creating a new object here. To add a value for a key, or to access the value at a key, you can use subscript notation like with an array, but instead of an index you use the key:

```
myDict["example"] = 12345
let test = myDict["example"]
```

In the first line, we are creating a new entry in the dictionary with a key of example and assigning its value as 12345. In the second line, we retrieve the value stored at the key example and assign it to our test variable. The test variable will now store the value 12345. Again, there is a lot more to know about the Swift dictionary, but this should be enough to get you started.

Conditional statements

With a solid understanding of the different ways to represent data in Swift, we need to now look at the ways that we can control the execution of our code.

if statement

Starting with conditional statements, let's look at how Swift handles a standard if statement:

```
let condition = true

if condition {
    // condition was true
} else if !condition {
    // condition was false
} else {
    // this would honestly never happen
}
```

At the top, we just declare a simple Boolean called condition and set it to true. Remember, Swift is using type inference to determine that the condition is a Boolean value. The first line of the statement uses the if keyword, followed by the condition, and finishes with a set of curly braces to wrap the branch.

The things to note about Swift's implementation is that parentheses around the condition are not required, but the curly braces always are. In some languages, they are unnecessary for single-line code branches, but in Swift they are mandatory.

Underneath the first if statement is an else if statement. Like other languages, if an if statement's condition is not met, it will fall through to any number of else if statements before terminating at an else statement. So for example, if our condition Boolean was set to false, the first if would fail and the else if condition would pass (Swift uses the exclamation mark to invert a conditional expression/Boolean, like many other languages). Since a Boolean can only be true or false, our final else statement would never realistically be hit, and is only there to show you what it looks like.

guard statement

Similar to the if is the **guard** statement. The primary difference is that if a guard statement's condition is true, code continues after the braces, instead of inside. The primary use case for a guard is to exit code early. In this way, the guard statement is a way of saying *make sure these conditions are true before we continue*:

```
let age = 25

guard age > 0 else {
    // invalid age!
    return
}
```

In this example, we have an age variable. Then we use guard to ensure that the age is greater than 0, since that would be invalid. If the condition fails, then the code block inside the else is executed. There must always be an else statement for a guard.

You can also use guard to unwrap optionals:

```
guard let myInt = optionalInt, myString = optionalString else {
    return
}
```

Sometimes this makes more sense than using if let and only using those unwrapped optionals inside the scope of if let.

switch statement

In addition to the if/guard conditionals, we also have the switch statement. The switch takes a value, matches it against cases until it finds a match, and then executes the code block pertaining to that case:

```
let value = 1

switch value {
case 0:
    print("value was 0")
case 1:
    print("value was 1")
case 2:
    print("value was 2")
case 3, 4, 5:
    print("value was between 3 and 5")
default:
    print("value was some number")
}
```

In this example, the value that the `switch` statement is considering is an integer, `1`. It then checks against each case until it finds one that matches. You'll notice one case has multiple matching conditions, separated by commas. If no matches are found, the default case will be executed.

Unlike some other languages, there is no implicit fall-through with cases in a Swift `switch` statement. That means that you don't need to use `break` to end a case. In addition, a `switch` case must be exhaustive, meaning that every possible value is represented. If there are too many values for that to make sense, a `default` case must be specified at the end.

Loops

Swift implements many of the standard types of loop found in most programming languages, such as `for`, `for-in`, `while`, and `repeat-while`. Similar to conditional statements, they don't require parentheses for their input, but are otherwise comparable to other C-like languages.

for loop

In Swift 3, the old C-style `for` loop has been deprecated. Now, our only option is to use the `for` loop, which is a very powerful alternative. This is how we can use a `for-in` loop to run a piece of code 5 times:

```
for var i = 0; i < 5; i++ {
    // loop code
}
```

Like most implementations, you have the first expression that runs before the loop starts, the second expression which is the condition for the loop to run, and the third expression that runs on the completion of the loop.

for-in loop

However, in Swift the `for-in` loop is a very powerful alternative. Here is that same loop above, but using the `for-in` method:

```
for i in 0..<5 {
    // loop code
}
```

This is much easier to read, since you can see that you are incrementing through a range from 0 to 5, not inclusive (0...5 would be inclusive). Using for-in with collections is even easier:

```
var sum = 0
var values = [0, 1, 2, 3, 4, 5]
for value in values {
    sum += value
}
```

Here we declare a small array of integers for testing purposes, named values. Then, in the for-in, we ask it to loop through every element in the values array, and give us access to those elements through the name value. Then we add them to our sum variable. This makes for-in much simpler to use, and much easier to read than a standard for.

while loop

The while loop is a very basic loop. At the top is a condition that evaluates to true or false, and the loop will run forever until the condition is no longer true. We used one earlier in the chapter, but let's take another look:

```
var time: Float = 0
var position: Float = 0

while time < 1.0 {
    position = time*time
    time += 0.05
}
```

Here, our condition is that the loop will continue until the time is over one second. When working with while loops, it's important to make sure that the condition can be changed from inside the loop. If, for example, we were not increasing the time variable, the condition would never be false, and the loop would run forever and crash our program.

repeat-while loop

Finally, we have the `repeat-while`, which is the same as the `while` loop, except that it runs through its code *before* it checks the condition:

```
var x = 0

repeat {
    x += 1
} while x < 0
```

In this example, the condition is always `false`, but since it is a `repeat-while`, the code in the loop will run a full cycle before it checks the condition and exits the loop.

Functions

Now we know how to define data, check conditions, and loop through logic, but we're missing one final, major piece: functions. Functions are used to group code into logical actions, and Swift makes writing and calling functions very easy. Let's jump right into functions by taking a look at one:

```
func findAverage(value1 v1: Int, value2 v2: Int) -> Float {
    let sum = Float(v1 + v2)
    return (sum/2.0)
}
```

We'll break this down piece by piece.

First, the `func` keyword means that you are beginning a function declaration.

Next, we have the name of the function, which in this case is `findAverage`.

Inside the parentheses, we have two parameters separated by a comma. Each parameter follows the format `externalParameterName localParameterName: Type`. So in this case, when calling the function, you will see `value1` and `value2`, but inside the function we refer to the parameters by their short names, `v1` and `v2`.

After the parentheses, we have an arrow (made of the dash and less than signs) and finally the return type of the function. We then use curly braces to contain the logic of the function.

Functions can also have no parameters or return types:

```
func doNothing() {
    return
}
```

They can also have default parameter values:

```
func someFunction(parameter1: Int = 0) {}
```

Or they can have a variable number of parameters:

```
func someOtherFunction(parameters: Int...) {
    for param in parameters {
        // do something
    }
}
```

Calling a function is very straightforward. Here are some examples of a function declaration and then its invocation:

```
// declaration
func findAverage(value1 v1: Int, value2 v2: Int) -> Float {...}


// invocation
findAverage(value1: 3, value2: 5)



// declaration
func someOtherFunction(parameters: Int...) {...}


// invocation
someOtherFunction(parameters: 1,2,3,4,5)
```

You'll notice that in the both examples, when we call the function, we label the parameters inside the parentheses. The names we use here are the external parameter names. The name is followed by a colon and then the actual value. In the second example, there was a variable number of possible parameters, as indicated by the ellipsis in the function declaration. When we called the function, we just passed it as many values as necessary.

Every function you use, whether written by you or another developer, is going to be different. We'll get plenty of exposure to many different kinds of function over the course of the book, but this should be enough of a primer to get us started.

Comments and printing

Before we move on, there are just a few other minor features that we should discuss. When writing code, there are many, many instances where you are going to want to make some notes in your code or test things. Two of your most valuable tools are making comments and printing text to the command line.

Throughout this chapter, I've been using comments to act as notes throughout my code. We also briefly talked about them when talking about rich comments in a playground:

```
// they look like this


/*
They can also look like this
when they span multiple lines
*/
```

To make a single line comment, you can use the double-slash, //, to cancel out all code for the rest of the line. To be more specific, you can use the open and close comment symbols, /* and */, to select a certain range for your comment, which can span multiple lines. Here are some examples that show how you can comment only parts of lines of code:

```
var i: Int // = 0

var j /* : Int */ = 0
```

Comments can be tremendously useful, not only to explain what your code does, but to turn off a line of your code without having to delete it, then retype it again when you realize it wasn't the problem. The quickest way to comment out a line of code in Xcode is to highlight a line you want commented and use the keyboard shortcut *command + /*.

I've also snuck a few `print` statements into this chapter before now. A `print` statement is a function that takes a `String` as an argument and then prints that string out to the console. If you remember from *Chapter 2, Welcome to Xcode*, the console is found in the debug area. Using `print()` is a good way to test parts of your code by printing out variable contents, or just checking to see if parts of your code have been hit:

```
var pi = 3.14159
print("The value of Pi is \(pi)")
```

You can also use string interpolation (as seen above) to print out non-string variables. To insert a numeric value into a string, use the backslash character followed by opening and closing parentheses, \( ), and put your variable inside the parentheses.

Creating classes, structs, and enums

So now we've covered the building blocks of programming in Swift. Our next step is to understand how to put these pieces together in an object-oriented programming environment. To do that, we're going to need to learn about classes, structs, and enumerations in Swift.

Classes

Classes in Swift are composed of properties and methods (functions). Let's jump right into an example:

```
class MyClass {

    var myInt: Int
    var myFloat: Float

    private var myOptString: String?

    init () {
        myInt = 0
        myFloat = 0
    }

    func generateString() -> String {
        myOptString = "\(myInt) \(myFloat)"
        return myOptString!
    }

}
```

On the first line, you see the beginning of the class declaration, beginning with the `class` keyword, followed by the class name. Class names in Swift should always be capitalized. The rest of the `class` declaration is inside a set of curly braces.

At the top of the class, we declare our properties, in this case `myInt`, `myFloat`, and `myOptString`. You'll notice that `myOptString` is set to private. By default, properties are `internal`, so `myInt` and `myFloat` will be accessible from other classes.

In Swift, source code is separated into modules. Here is the definition from Apple's documentation:

A module is a single unit of code distribution – a framework or application that is built and shipped as a single unit and that can be imported by another module with Swift's import keyword.

The **internal** access keyword means that it can be accessed only from that module. Usually, you can think of it as **public**, but in Swift **public** means it can be accessed from outside of its defining module as well.

Under our property declarations, we have our `init()` method. This method is called when the class instantiates a new object. In Swift, it is mandatory to give all properties a value by the end of the `init()` method. If you cannot assign a value to a property until after the `init()` method, it should be an made an optional property since it will take on the default value of `nil`. Since our first two properties are not optionals, they are initialized in our `init()` function.

Finally, below our `init()`, we declare our class's methods. In this case, there is only one method, which creates a string out of our two numbers, saves that to a private property, and returns the result.

Now let's take a look at a simple inheritance scenario in Swift:

```
class MySubclass : MyClass {

    var myDouble: Double

    init(doubleValue: Double) {
        myDouble = doubleValue
        super.init()
    }

    override func generateString() -> String {
        super.generateString()
        myOptString! += " \(myDouble)"
        return myOptString!
    }

}
```

Again, on the first line we begin the `class` declaration with the `class` keyword. This time, since we are creating a subclass, we write the new class's name followed by the parent class and separated with a colon.

As with our parent `class` declaration, we have our property declarations at the top, followed by our `init()`, and finally our methods. In this class, we only declare one additional property and inherit the other three.

In Swift, **private** properties are inherited by subclasses, which isn't always the case in other languages.

Now let's look at how `init()` has changed. You can see that in this `init()` we are passing in a parameter, which will be the initial value of the `myDouble` variable. You can also see that at the bottom there is the line `super.init()`, which initializes the superclass.

In Swift, we call methods (public functions in other classes) and access properties using dot syntax. In this example, **super** is a keyword that refers to the object's superclass (in this case `MyClass`), and we call its `init()` function.

The most important thing to note about this initializer is that the order in which we do things is important. In a Swift initializer, a class must always initialize all of its own properties before its superclass does so. That's why we assign a value to `myDouble`, and then call `super.init()`. It's also worth noting that we can't customize our properties until after our superclass initializes everything. So first we initialize all properties, then pass off responsibility up the class hierarchy, then once the scope comes back to the class we can do further setup.

Finally, let's take a look at the new method in our subclass. Here you'll see a new keyword, **override**. This means that we are rewriting the functionality of a function from our superclass. The functionality of the original function (`generateString`) was to generate a string from its two properties, but now we have a new property to add to that string. You can see that we also call the superclass's implementation of this function from inside our new version. So first we let the original version do its thing, then add our new data to the end, and finally return our result.

Now let's look at how we could use this object:

```
let myObj = MySubclass(doubleValue: 2)
myObj.myFloat = 3.14
myObj.myInt = 33
```

Here you can see how initializers work in practice. Since `init()` isn't a standard method, we don't call it like other methods or functions. Instead, we use the class name followed by parentheses, which contain our arguments. Here we are passing in the value of 2 to initialize our `myDouble` value, then we set some public variables as we like:

```
let str = myObj.generateString()
```

This is how we could use our `generateString()` method to get a description of the values in our object. If you're in a playground, you'll see that the `str` constant contains a value of `33 3.14 2.0`.

Again, this is just a very rough overview of classes in Swift, but we'll be using them extensively throughout the rest of the book, so we'll be pros by the time we're finished.

Structs

Structs are similar to classes, but with limited functionality. In most cases, you'll be using structs to create a custom data type that can store related information in a single, easily digestible package.

The important difference between a struct and a class is that a struct is a *value type*, which means that its values are copied when assigned or passed to a function. Here is an example:

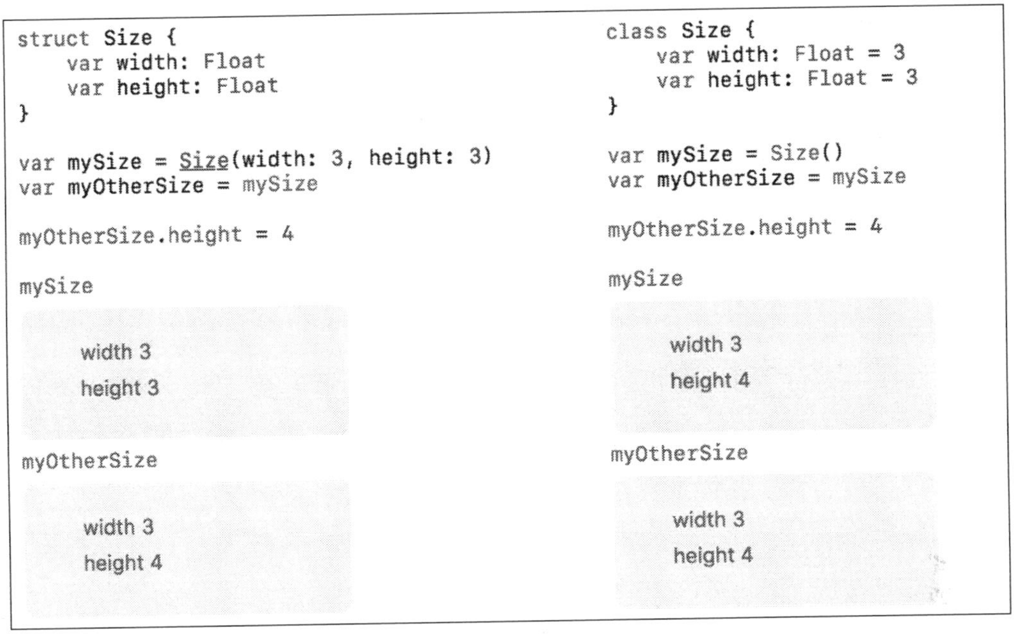

```
struct Size {                          class Size {
    var width: Float                       var width: Float = 3
    var height: Float                      var height: Float = 3
}                                      }

var mySize = Size(width: 3, height: 3) var mySize = Size()
var myOtherSize = mySize               var myOtherSize = mySize

myOtherSize.height = 4                 myOtherSize.height = 4

mySize                                 mySize


    width 3                                width 3
    height 3                               height 4



myOtherSize                            myOtherSize


    width 3                                width 3
    height 4                               height 4
```

Figure 3.11: The playground results view shows the difference between a class and a struct

In *Figure 3.11*, you can see that on the left I define a new **struct** called Size, which has a width and height property. Then I create an instance called mySize, and a second instance called myOtherSize which is assigned from mySize. On the right, I do the exact same thing except with a class.

Since a struct copies values, myOtherSize is a completely new set of data, and when I change one of the values, the other one doesn't change. You can see on the left that mySize still has its initial values of 3 and 3, where myOtherSize has the modified value of 4 for its width.

With a class, a reference to an object is passed around, so when we modify the width of myOtherSize as a class (on the right), you see the mySize object also changes. That's because they actually point to the *exact same data*, whereas the struct creates new, separate copies.

As mentioned earlier, structs are usually best used for modeling information that is just a set of simple data types. If it needs special behaviors or inheritance, you should probably be using a class.

Enumerations

An **enumeration** (**enum**) is a very powerful tool in Swift. Since the language focuses on being thorough and specific, an enum is a great way to create a new data type that has a finite number of possible values. This lets the compiler know ahead of time what the possible values can be so that it can protect against issues.

For example, since `switch` statements must have exhaustive cases, the compiler knows every possible value of an enum, and can make sure every possible value is accounted for with a case.

Let's take a look at how we would create a new enum:

```
enum Season {
    case spring
    case summer
    case fall
    case winter
}
```

Just like with classes and structs, we begin with a keyword, this time **enum**, followed by the type name and a set of curly braces. However, with an enum, we want to be defining a set of possible values that the type can be set to, which we do using the **case** keyword followed by the value.

To use an enum, we use dot syntax:

```
let favoriteSeason = Season.fall
let leastFavoriteSeason: Season = .summer
```

You can see in the first example that we set our `favoriteSeason` equal to `Season.Fall`. The type `Season` is inferred. However, in the second example, we can see that if the type is explicitly stated, the Swift compiler knows that we are dealing with a `Season` enumeration, and lets us use a shorthand to access its values by omitting the enum's type name.

If you've used enums in some other language, such as Objective-C or C++, you'll notice that in Swift there is no backing type or value behind our cases. That's because enums in Swift aren't redefined integers, as in other languages. We can, however, give an enum a backing value, and we're not limited to integers:

```
enum Season: String {
    case spring = "Spring"
    case summer = "Summer"
    case fall = "Fall"
```

```
        case winter = "Winter"
}

let favoriteSeason = Season(rawValue: "Fall")!
print(favoriteSeason.rawValue)
```

Modifying some of our code from earlier, we've now given all of our seasons a backing value of the type String. Note the differences in the `enum` declaration, how we can now initialize an enum value by using its `rawValue`, and how we can also access the raw value later.

Using important Swift features

We've now covered the basics of Swift, in addition to the building blocks we need to create robust classes and organized data with structs and enums. With these tools, you'd be able to accomplish some great things, but there are a few other important features of Swift that can save you a lot of time, and help you squeeze out even more performance from your code. In this last section, we are going to introduce closures, protocols, class extensions, and Swift's error handling features.

Closures

We've already talked about functions, where we can take a chunk of code and turn it into a reusable command. However, in Swift there is another way to achieve that kind of functionality (no pun intended): closures. Using closures is a great way to pass a chunk of code (sometimes called a block) into a function as an argument, and they're commonly used as completion or error handers. Let's take a look at an example:

```
// defining a simple closure
let myClosure: () -> Void = {
    print("Hello from this closure!")
}

// executing a simple closure
myClosure()

// using closure like a variable
someOtherFunction(closure: myClosure)
```

In the first part, we create a closure in a way that is similar to declaring a variable, and also similar to declaring a function. We start out with a `let` (or `var`) keyword followed by the name of the closure. Then we declare the closure's type, which is composed of the closure's input and output type signature. Here we see that the type is `() -> Void`, meaning it has no parameters, and a `void` return type. Finally, we set the closure equal to a code block surrounded by curly braces.

Below that, you'll see that executing a closure looks exactly the same as calling a function. The fun part, however, is what else we can do with a closure. At the bottom you can see that we're passing our closure into another function, like a variable. That's because as long as we don't use the `()` at the end of the closure's name, it behaves just like a variable.

Let's take a look at a closure with a more interesting type signature:

```
let convertIntToFloat = { (value: Int) -> Float in
    return Float(value)
}


let myNewFloat: Float = convertIntToFloat(6)
```

The first thing you might notice here is that we don't define the type signature like we did in the first closure; Swift can infer the type here as well! To define parameters and return types in a closure, we begin the closure with the `() -> ()` pattern followed by the **in** keyword. On the left side of the `->` arrow, we put our parameters inside parentheses in the same format we do for a function declaration. On the right side of the arrow, we do the same for our return value types, although with a single return type we don't need parentheses.

Closures (and functions) can return multiple values using something called a **tuple**. A tuple is a grouping of several values into a single value. A tuple can be defined as follows:

```
let myTuple: (Float, Int) = (3.14, 33)
```

The two (or three, or four, and so on) values in a tuple don't have to be the same type. You'll see them fairly frequently when coding in Swift, and I encourage you to play around with them in a playground!

So, looking at this new closure, we can see that the first line reads `(value: Int) -> Float in`. We can tell that the closure takes one parameter, an `Int` named `value`, and returns a `Float`. Then in the example below that, we see that when we execute the closure we pass it an integer, and assign the result to a `Float`.

Closures are used extensively throughout iOS frameworks, so you'll be seeing them quite often. We could probably spend a whole chapter just looking at the many forms they can take, but we need to keep moving on so we can start making apps!

Protocols

Since you'll be making a lot of subclasses of common objects when developing for iOS apps in Swift (such as UIViewControllers), class hierarchies need to be as streamlined as possible. Sometimes, you need to ensure that a class is equipped to perform a certain task, but class inheritance doesn't really make sense or the object already inherits from another object. In these instances, you can use what is called a **protocol**.

As you might be able to guess, a protocol is a set of instructions that a class must adhere to. It is similar to a class, except instead of programming functionality into a protocol, you only describe what variables and methods need to be implemented; it's up to the actual class that adopts the protocol to give them definitions. Here's an example:

```
protocol MyProtocol {
    var value: Float { get set }
    func someMethod(someParameter: Float) -> Int
}

class MyClass : MyProtocol {
    var value: Float = 10

    func someMethod(someParameter: Float) -> Int {
        return Int(value * someParameter)
    }
}
```

First we define a new protocol just like a class, but with the **protocol** keyword. Inside the curly braces, you can see some minor differences. First, we describe a property by assigning it a type, and determining if it should have a getter and/or setter. Then we describe a function using only the method signature; there is no implementation given for this method.

Later on, we make a simple class that adopts our new protocol. You'll notice that it looks very similar to the way we specify a parent class. Inside the body of our class, you can see that we actually have to redefine the properties and methods of the protocol since there was no real inheritance involved. If you don't implement all of the properties and methods exactly as described in the protocol, the compiler will complain.

While it is a very useful tool, and you can certainly create your own protocols, most beginners will usually spend a lot of time implementing protocols that exist in iOS frameworks. Here's an example of one of the most common cases:

```
Class MyViewController: UIViewController, UITableViewDataSource {…}
```

Here you can see that we are creating a new subclass of `UIViewController` named `MyViewController`, but we use a comma after `UIViewController` to show that we are also adopting the `UITableViewDataSource` protocol. In fact, we can inherit from a class and adopt many protocols at once by continuing to separate them with commas.

Class extensions

Sometimes you come across a situation where you need something to have a bit more functionality. In some cases, it might make sense to create a subclass, but in Swift there is a smarter and cleaner way to achieve the same result. With extensions, you can add functionality to any type, even to a class that isn't part of your source code. Specifically, in Swift 2 and Swift 3, we can extend classes. There's not much else to say, so let's look at how this works:

```
class BoringClass {
    var boringInt: Int = 0
    var moreBoringInt: Int = 0

    func add() -> Int {
        return boringInt + moreBoringInt
    }
}
```

First we have a `BoringClass`, which stores two values and a single function that adds the two values together. Now let's imagine that we didn't write that `BoringClass`, so we couldn't add functionality directly. Instead we could *extend* the class, like so:

```
extension BoringClass {
    func subtract() -> Int {
        return boringInt - moreBoringInt
    }
    func multiply() -> Int {
        return boringInt * moreBoringInt
    }
    func divide() -> Float {
```

```
        if moreBoringInt != 0 {
            return Float(boringInt / moreBoringInt)
        } else {
            fatalError("tried to divide by zero")
        }
    }
}
```

Now our class is decidedly less boring, and much more functional.

While class extensions are certainly useful, you can extend a lot of other things as well. For example, we can even extend an `Int`:

```
extension Int {
    var inches: Int { return self }
    var feet: Float { return Float(inches / 12) }
    var yards: Float { return feet/3.0 }
    var miles: Float { return feet/5280 }
}

let distance = 3392
print(distance.inches)   //   3,392
print(distance.feet)     //   282.0
print(distance.yards)    //    94.0
print(distance.miles)    //  0.0534
```

While extensions can be amazingly useful, you should always think about all the ways to solve a problem and choose the best fit for the job. Sometimes it *is* just better to use a subclass.

Error handling

When building an application for use in the real world, sometimes there are errors that will occur at runtime which are *okay*. For example, if you tried to modify a message that had been deleted since that page had last refreshed, or if a network connection is lost while transmitting a file. These are the kinds of error that you can't prevent from a programming standpoint, so instead you just need to know how to react and alert the user. For these instances, we can use the error handling functionality built into Swift.

Before you can handle an error, you need to be able to define it. In Swift, there is an empty protocol called `ErrorProtocol` that you can use to denote that some value represents an error and can be used for error handling. Adding the `ErrorProtocol` protocol to an `enum` allows you to create some very simple and descriptive error types for the problems you may encounter.

Let's say that we're making a class that models a coffee machine. The user can press a button that will brew them a cup of coffee, but we need to make sure that we are prepared for cases in which the machine cannot complete the task. We'll create an `enum` that stores all the possible cases for failure:

```swift
enum CoffeeMachineError: Error {
    case NotEnoughWater
    case NotEnoughGrounds
    case ReplaceFilter
}
```

So, here we've defined a new enum called `CoffeeMachineError`, which adopts the protocol `Error`:

```swift
class CoffeeMachine {
    let groundsNeededPerCup: Float = 0.1
    let waterNeededPerCup: Float = 0.33

    var grounds: Float = 10.0
    var water: Float = 10.0

    func brewCup() throws  {
        guard grounds > groundsNeededPerCup else {
            throw CoffeeMachineError.NotEnoughGrounds
        }

        guard water > waterNeededPerCup else {
            throw CoffeeMachineError.NotEnoughWater
        }

        grounds -= groundsNeededPerCup
        water -= waterNeededPerCup
        print("coffee is brewed")
    }
}
```

Here, we've modeled the rest of the coffee machine; it knows how much coffee and water it needs to brew a cup, the current levels of those supplies, and a function that attempts to brew.

In this example, we use a throwing function to handle errors. At the end of the brewCup function declaration, you'll see that we wrote throws instead of a standard return type. This means that the function has the ability to throw an error. You'll also see that we use the guard keyword that we looked at earlier in the chapter. Here it makes a bit more sense, since we are saying *guard against this undesirable condition occurring; otherwise, complain.* As long as the code makes it through all of the guards there won't be a problem, but if the guards get upset they can throw an error.

So this is what it would look like to call this function that might throw an error:

```
let coffeeMachine = CoffeeMachine()

do {
    try coffeeMachine.brewCup()

} catch CoffeeMachineError.NotEnoughWater {
    print ("Please refill the water container")

} catch CoffeeMachineError.NotEnoughGrounds {
    print ("Please add more coffee grounds")

} catch CoffeeMachineError.ReplaceFilter {
    print ("Please replace the filter")
}
```

To handle the errors that can be thrown, we use a do-catch statement, and call our throwing function with a try statement which is placed in the do block. We need to use try to call our function because of the fact that it might return an error. If it completes successfully, our code will carry on outside of the do-catch statement.

In order to handle an error, we need to catch them. After the _ block that we wrote here, we have a separate catch statement for each of our possible errors. If one of those errors is caught, it will execute the code in that branch. In this example, we are just printing to the console, but in theory we could require user input or actually fetch new materials, whatever will best resolve the error.

Summary

In this chapter, we sprinted through the Swift programming language and learned all of the basics we need to start creating our own iOS and watchOS applications. First we took a look at Xcode playgrounds, before we jumped into Swift itself, where we covered the basic data types, optional values, collections, control flow, and functions. Once we had the basics down we took a look at classes, and the related structs and enums. We finished by getting an overview of some common and powerful Swift features such as closures, protocols, extensions, and error handling.

In the next chapter, we take one of our final steps toward being able to create our first app: understanding how to use storyboards, size classes, and auto layout. This is where we'll learn all about the view portion of MVC. We'll be creating layouts, understanding how things adjust on different screen sizes, and creating future-proof interfaces that can adapt for devices that don't exist yet!

4
Using Storyboards, Auto Layout, and Size Classes

As we've progressed through our journey so far, it's been difficult to separate the different pieces of app development. We've already looked at how the model, view, and controller interact in a theoretical way, and we've explored some of the tools in Xcode that we can use to manipulate them.

In the previous chapter, we took a deeper look at Swift, the language we will use to define our models and write our controller logic. Now, while we've already looked at how to use some of the basic functionality of storyboards and Interface Builder, it's time to understand the systems at play when developing views for our iOS applications: storyboards, Auto Layout, and size classes.

In this chapter, we will cover:

- Mapping screen flow with storyboards
- Storyboard segues
- The view hierarchy
- Auto Layout constraints
- Using size classes to create flexible interfaces

Storyboards

Back in *Chapter 2, Introduction to Xcode IDE*, we had a brief encounter with a storyboard file. We dragged some interface objects out of the object library, connected them to our ViewController's code, and moved on. In this section, we are going to take a look at the big picture of what is happening in a storyboard file, and really understand its namesake. However, before we can get to that, we're going to have to start a new project!

Getting started

Let's open Xcode and create a new project. Select the **Single View Application** from the **iOS | Application** section of the project template chooser, and match your settings with *Figure 4.1*:

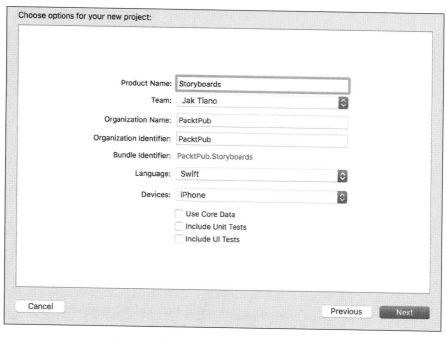

Figure 4.1: Setting up our storyboards test project

Click **Next**, find a place to save your project, and complete the creation of a new project. Once your project is created, make sure your **Team** is set from the drop-down menu in the **Signing** section of your project settings. This needs to be set correctly in order for you to test the app on your device later:

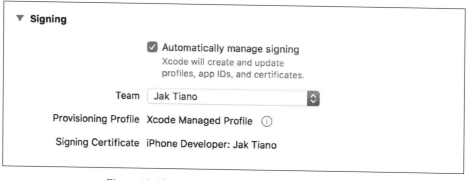

Figure 4.2: The team option should be set to your name

Now, let's head over to the main storyboard file and make sure it's ready for us to play with. First, we'll shrink our navigator sidebar (on the left edge of the editor) by dragging the edge in a bit to make more room for the editor window in the center. Then we'll do the same with the utility sidebar on the right. Let's also make sure the debug area is hidden (remember: *command + shift + Y* will hide/show the debug area).

In your Utility toolbar, make sure the top section is set to the fourth tab, the attributes inspector (*option + command + 4*), and the bottom section is set to the third tab, the object library (*control + option + command + 3*).

The last step is to either maximize or full screen your Xcode window; we'll be working with a lot of visuals in this chapter, so we're going to need as much screen real estate as we can get!

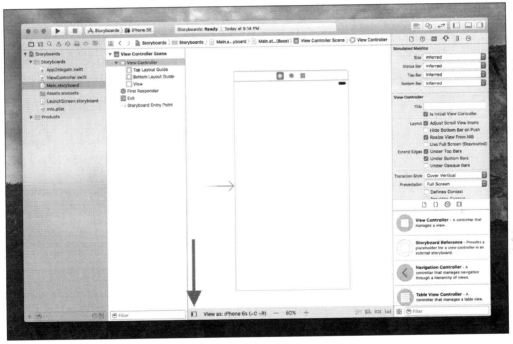

Figure 4.3: Our Interface Builder window; highlighted button closes the document outline

When you've done all this, your window should look something like *Figure 4.3*. Click the icon at the red arrow in *Figure 4.3* to close the document outline sidebar; we won't need that until later, when we cover the view hierarchy. Now we're all set up and good to go!

View controllers and screen flow

When you think of the word *storyboard*, what comes to mind? Usually the word refers to a literal board where a story is planned out for a movie, comic book, or TV episode. Artists and writers will come together and pin a bunch of sketches to a wall to quickly visualize how a story should play out and interact, while being able to add new ideas, shuffle the order, and throw out the things that don't work.

When using a storyboard file in Xcode, we have the same functionality. We can plan out the many different screens that our application will be composed of, and quickly mock-up and edit them. Instead of boarding a story here, we're boarding out the application's screens, so I like to call this stage *screen flow* planning. Let's take a look at how this works.

 As we explore storyboards, Auto Layout, and size classes for the rest of the chapter, we're going to be building out the views for a timer application.

We're going to be building a timer application in this chapter, so before we begin, let's take a second to think about what we want to accomplish. The built-in timer in the iOS clock app is pretty bare bones. Every time we wish to run a timer, we must manually set the number of hours and minutes. In our solution, we think it would make sense to give the user some presets on the main screen for added convenience. We also need to make sure the user can input a custom time, otherwise there would be very limited functionality. Finally, they'll need to be able to see the timer counting down.

By my count, I think we'll need three different screens: a main screen with shortcuts, a screen to set a custom timer, and the actual timer view itself.

Let's begin by zooming out on our storyboard view. We're going to be dragging in a few more screens, so we're going to need the extra space. To zoom out on your storyboard, you can hold option and scroll in and out, or use the plus and minus buttons at the bottom of the editor window. If you have a trackpad, you can also use the pinch gesture to zoom in and out.

 As a new feature in Xcode 8, storyboards can be fully edited at any zoom level; in older versions you would have to be fully zoomed in to edit view controllers.

Now that we're zoomed out, let's drag in two more view controllers from our object library, which is in the bottom half of our utility sidebar. Your storyboard should now look similar to this image:

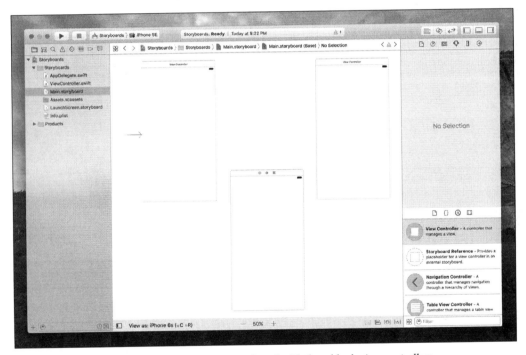

Figure 4.4: Our zoomed out storyboard with three blank view controllers

Next, we're going to want to name our view controllers so we can differentiate between them. To name a view controller, you can click on the little yellow circle on the top of the view to select the view controller, and then from the Attributes Inspector (the fourth tab on the top half of the utility sidebar), you can set the **Title** of the view controller (see *Figure 4.5*). Let's name the top-left one **Selection View Controller**, the top-right one **Timer View Controller**, and the bottom one **Custom Time View Controller**:

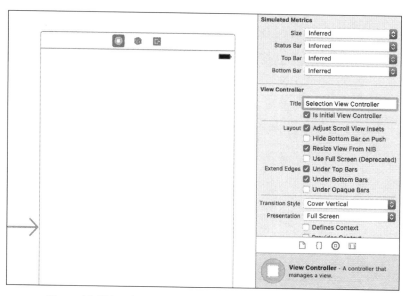

Figure 4.5: Using the Attributes Inspector to name a view controller

Now that we've got all of our screens in the storyboard and named, we should go in and flesh them out a bit. To zoom back in on your storyboard, you can double click on one of the view controllers. Let's start with **Selection View Controller**.

First, let's drag four buttons into our view controller. Three of these will be our timer presets, and the fourth will let the user create a custom timer. Double-click on each button to edit the text, and name them `Preset 1`, `Preset 2`, `Preset 3`, and `Custom`.

Now let's give them a bit of a style by changing some of the attributes for each button in the Attribute Inspector. If you click and drag a selection box over all four buttons, you can edit them all at once. Near the top of the Attribute Inspector, change the **Font** to size `18` by using the arrows next to the font size. Next, we'll change the font color to white, by changing the **Text Color** attribute directly beneath the font size attribute. Then, scroll down to the **View** section of the Attribute Editor and change the **Background** attribute to an accent color of your choice; I chose a nice purple. At this point, you should have something that looks similar to this:

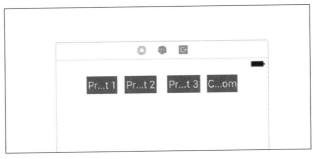

Figure 4.6: Some loosely styled buttons

You'll notice that when we increased the font size, the text grew too large for the bounding rectangle of our buttons. Next, we're going to make our buttons bigger so our words should be visible again soon enough. To modify our buttons' sizes, we need to switch to the Size Inspector, which is the fifth column in the utility sidebar (*command + option + 5*). Select all of the buttons again, then go to the Size Inspector and set their widths and heights to 128. Finally, stack the boxes vertically along the left side of the screen so you have something similar to the following figure:

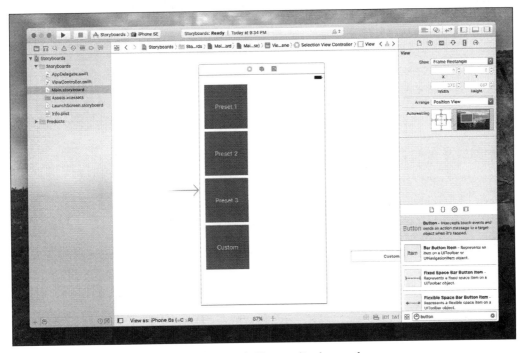

Figure 4.7: Our large, styled buttons lined up on the screen

We'll be tweaking the layout more later on, so that's good enough for now! Time to move on to our next view, the **Custom Time View Controller**, which should be below the **Selection View Controller** that we just finished. In this view, drag in three labels, and three stepper controllers (remember that you can search the object library at the bottom of the sidebar).

The labels are going to be where we show the hours, minutes, and seconds of our custom timer, and the steppers are going to be used to increment those values. Finally, drag in two buttons, which will be used to confirm and cancel our timer.

Using what we learned on the last view controller, set the three labels to use the same accent color for their text **Color** attribute, set their font size to 32, make the text center aligned, and give them the names Hours, Mins, and Secs. Then use the Size Inspector to set their sizes to 90 width and 40 height.

For the three stepper controls, set their **Tint** attribute (under the **View** section) to be the same accent color.

With our two buttons, name one Confirm and the other Cancel. Next, we will set the width to 150 and the height to 50. On our Confirm button, set the background color to our accent color, and the text color to white, and for the Cancel button, just set the text color to our accent color.

Once everything is styled visually, you can lay everything out as shown in *Figure 4.8*:

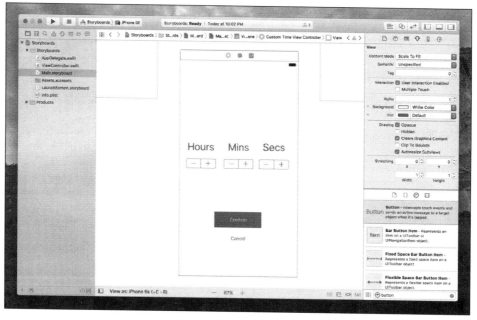

Figure 4.8: The final layout for the Custom Time View Controller

Now we just need to lay out our final view, the **Timer View Controller**. This will be the simplest of our controllers, and will actually be very similar to the **Custom Time View Controller**. In fact, you can just select all of the elements in our **Custom Time View Controller**, copy them (*command + C*), and paste them (*command + V*) into the **Timer View Controller**. Then, just select and delete all of the stepper controls. Finally, change the `Confirm` button text to say `Pause`, and our last view controller is finished!

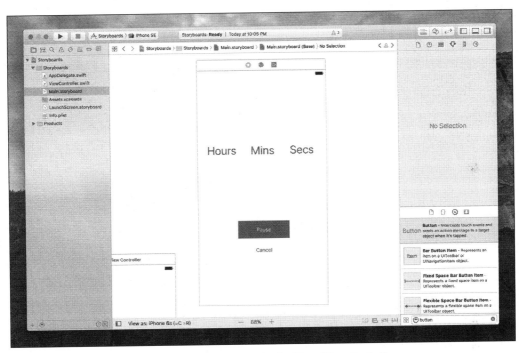

Figure 4.9: Our final layout for the Timer View Controller

Great! We've gone through our storyboard and fleshed out each screen of our application. If you zoom out on your storyboard now, you'll see all the screens of your app, planned out. But hold on a minute… it's a little difficult to see what's going on here. How do we know when one screen moves to another, and which ones can go where? The answer lies with segues.

Understanding segues

In any given iOS app, you will constantly be transitioning to different screens that serve a variety of functions. In our app, we have a quick launch view controller, a detailed timer setting view controller, and a data viewing view controller. A segue is how we define the transitions between those view controllers.

Let's create our first segue now. Zoom in on your storyboard, and make sure the `Custom` button in your **Selection View Controller** is visible, along with any part of the **Custom Time View Controller**. Much like several other Interface Builder actions, hold down the *control* key, then click and drag from the `Custom` button to the **Custom Time View Controller**, and release:

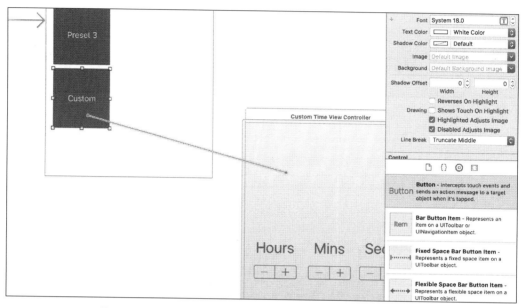

Figure 4.10: Creating a segue from a button to another view controller

When you release the mouse button, you'll be given a drop-down menu where you can choose the type of segue you'd like to create. Select **Show**, and then you'll see the segue appear connecting the two view controllers together.

Repeat this process for each of the pre-set buttons, but instead of connecting them to the **Custom Time View Controller**, connect them to the **Timer View Controller**, since they don't need to be set up. Finally, connect the `Confirm` button in the **Custom Time View Controller** to the **Timer View Controller**.

Your storyboard should now make a lot more sense:

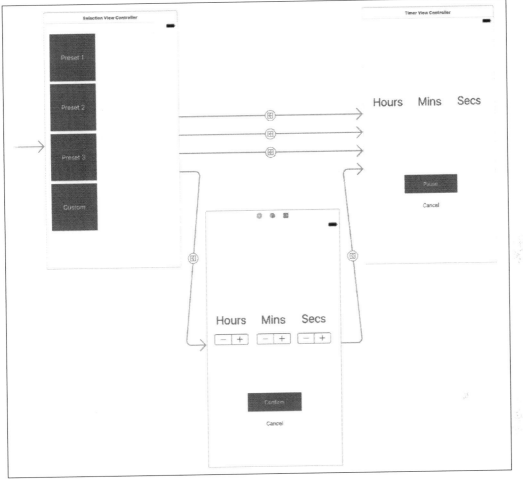

Figure 4.11: Our storyboard is visualizing our application segues

Our app now has all of its forward-moving segues in place, but what about our Cancel button that will bring us backwards? To move backwards through our view controller hierarchy, we are going to use a special type of transition called an **unwind segue**. To do this, we're going to need to add a little code.

Open the `ViewController.swift` file in your project. Then, replace the code in that class with the following code:

```
import UIKit

class ViewController: UIViewController {

    override func viewDidLoad() {
        super.viewDidLoad()
    }

    @IBAction func unwindToSelection(sender: UIStoryboardSegue) {

    }
}
```

You'll notice that the main difference with this code is that we added the `unwindToSelection()` function, which defines an unwind segue that we'll use shortly.

If you followed along with the book, your **Selection View Controller** should be the view controller that you started out with, which means that it is already linked with the `ViewController.swift` class. If **Selection View Controller** has a little arrow next to it in the storyboard, you should be fine. If not, first drag that arrow from the view controller that does have it onto **Selection View Controller** (this sets it as the initial view controller). Then, go to the Identity Inspector in the utility side bar (*option + command + 3*), and set the *custom class* property of **Selection View Controller** to **View Controller** (this lets Xcode know what code is associated with that view in the storyboard). Finally, make sure the other two view controllers do not have a custom class set.

Now that we've added this function, head back to the storyboard file. On our **Custom Time View Controller**, we're going to connect the `Cancel` button to the unwind segue we just created. To do this, you want to control drag from the `Cancel` button not to a different view controller, but to the **Exit** icon at the top of its own view controller:

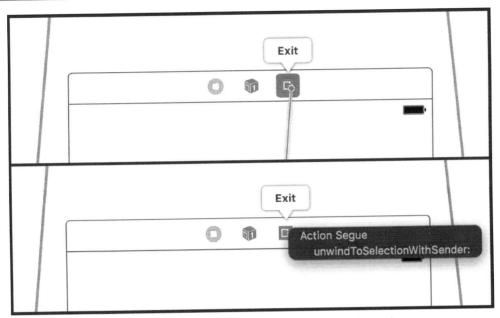

Figure 4.12: Control-dragging to the exit icon will show the unwind segue

Then from the dropdown, select `unwindToSelection:`, the unwind segue we created in the `ViewController.swift` class. This will make the view hierarchy unwind to the view controller where that segue was created, which in this case would be our **Selection View Controller**. Do the same thing for our `Cancel` button in **Timer View Controller**, and then all of the segues for our project are complete!

Now, let's just run this on the iPhone 6s simulator to test our work, and check it out!

Auto Layout

Now let's try it out on some other devices, like the iPhone SE simulator! But... hmm, this isn't right. All of our hard work is spilling outside the edges of the screen! We can't see all of the UI elements we added to our view controllers! What's going on?

If you take a look at the view controllers that we were populating in our storyboard, you'll notice that at the bottom of the editor it says that it was specifically laid out for the iPhone 6s. How does our view controller know how to adjust for different sized screens?

The bad news is that it doesn't know how to do that by default. The good news is that we have **Auto Layout** to solve this very problem. Auto Layout is a constraint system that lets us set rules for how all of our interface elements should be positioned, and with some clever thinking we can make sure our views can adjust for any size screen.

The view hierarchy

Before we get into constraints, let's go back and take a look at the view hierarchy that we minimized earlier. To bring that back up, click the same button you used to hide it in the lower left corner of the storyboard editor window, or use the menu bar option **Editor | Show Document Outline**:

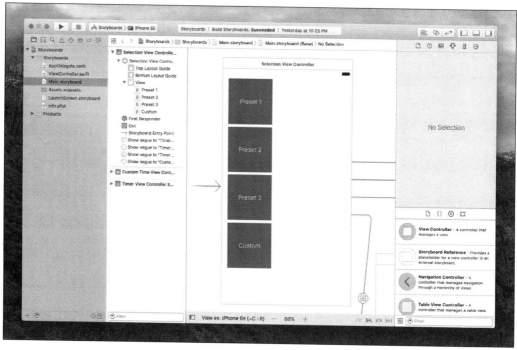

Figure 4.13: The Xcode window with the document outline visible in the storyboard editor view

Taking a quick look at the document outline, you can see that the storyboard document is split up into different *scenes* for each view controller. Each scene has a number of objects (like the segues we created), but what we are interested in is the view hierarchy attached to the view controller object. All of the UI elements that we added to our view controllers are visible in this hierarchy, with their name defaulting to whatever their text says. If the object doesn't have text associated with it (like the steppers, for example), you can assign your own name to the object by selecting the list item in the view hierarchy and pressing *return* (or *enter*).

It's also important to understand that the view hierarchy is just that: a hierarchy. Objects can have children and parents, as denoted by the grey triangles which step down into the hierarchy. The objects are also drawn in the order they are listed in the hierarchy; if you have an element that is on top of another element when it should be behind it, rearrange their order in the view hierarchy to fix the draw problems.

Finally, once we start adding constraints to our UI elements, they will show up as children of their associated views in the hierarchy. This can make it easy to see ownership of constraints, and quickly identify errors.

Constraints

The powerhouse behind Auto Layout is the constraint system. Constraints can either be position or size constraints. Position constraints are *owned* by the parent of the object and enforced on the child, where size constraints are *both owned and enforced* by the object that they describe. Let's get our hands dirty with some constraints to see how they work.

We'll start with **Selection View Controller**. Before we start laying out constraints, we want to mentally plan out what we are going to do. Right now, we've got a stack of squares along the left side of our screen. What we want to do is have a stack of equal-height buttons that fills the entire screen, with some margins around each button so that they don't overlap. This means that the height and width of every button can vary depending on screen size, but the margins should remain constant.

This is actually a fairly straightforward problem to solve. We can set all of the margins at once for all four buttons, and then add an `Equal Heights` constraint to make sure the heights are distributed evenly. Now that we have a plan, let's add these constraints.

First, let's select all of the elements that we want to constrain. Remember, we can do this in the storyboard, but we can also select them in the view hierarchy too. Once they're selected, we can start using the Auto Layout menus:

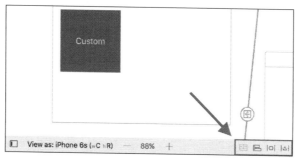

Figure 4.14: The Auto Layout menu icons

At the bottom right hand side of the storyboard editor window is a row of four icons. They are the **Stack**, **Align**, **Pin**, and **Resolve Auto Layout Issues** menus. The most useful buttons for us are the pin and resolve issues buttons, and right now we're going to open the Pin menu (the third icon):

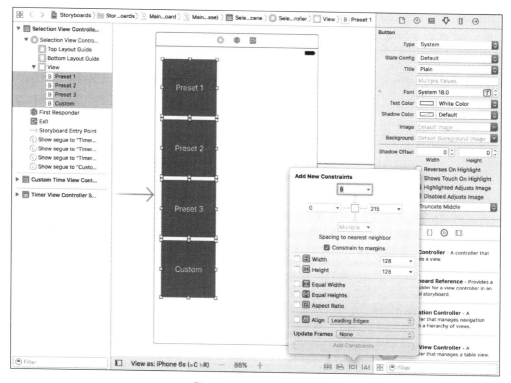

Figure 4.15: The Pin menu

Inside the Pin menu, you'll see a lot going on. At the top, you have a bit of a visual constraint setting system, with a bunch of strut toggles, checkboxes, text fields, and dropdowns. The bottom half is a bit easier to read, since it just has checkboxes. Let's decode the top part of the Pin menu, since that's what we need to use:

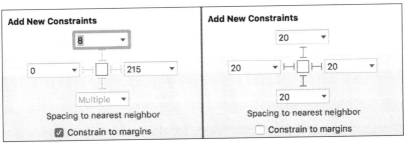

Figure 4.16: Before and after we set up our constraints using the top-most part of the Pin menu

This top part of the Pin menu is where you can set spacing constraints. These constraints will let you say how many points of space there should be between an object and its nearest neighbor in any direction. We want all of our buttons to have an even 20 points of spacing in all directions, so we fill that in for every direction.

 You can see that near the bottom, it clarifies the neighbor spacing with the text **Spacing to nearest neighbor**. If you want to set a spacing constraint relative to a different object other than the nearest neighbor, you can use the drop-down menu on the value you wish to adjust, and select that object from the list.

Next, you'll want to make sure that you click on all the red struts that extend from the white square out to the values. Activating the red strut is what tells Auto Layout that you want to create a constraint in that direction; only specifying a value will not create a constraint if the red strut isn't lit.

Finally, we are going to uncheck the box that says **Constrain to margin**. When that box is checked, it will be positioning elements based on screen margins, not the actual boundaries of the screen. But, in our case we are trying to set our own margins, so we are going to ignore the defaults. (Remember that all four buttons in the storyboard should be selected).

Once your spacing constraints are set, we just need to check the box on the bottom half that says **Equal Heights**. You might want to try setting the constraints without **Equal Heights** first, just so you can see why it's important, then undo the constraints and apply them correctly.

Before you click the **Add Constraints** button at the bottom of the Pin menu, you'll want to set the **Update Frames** drop-down option to `All Frames in Container`. If you skip this step, you will apply the constraints, but none of your buttons will move, instead opting to complain about how they are not positioned according to their constraints.

In this case, you can manually update their frames to fit their constraints by selecting the buttons and using the keyboard shortcut *option + command + =*:

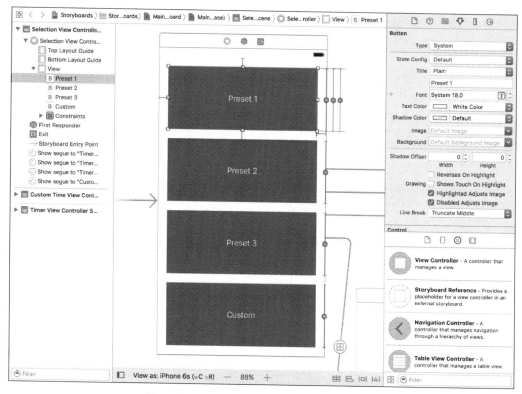

Figure 4.17: Our fully constrained View Controller

Great! We fully constrained our first view controller, and have no issues. If you try running this in the simulator now, you'll have no issues. Try running it in several different sized simulators, like the iPhone SE and the iPhone 7 Plus; it works perfectly in both!

Let's move onto the **Timer View Controller**. On this screen, the size of the elements is important, and not fluid like in the **Selection View Controller**. Right away, you should select all of the elements and constrain their widths and heights from the Pin menu, by checking the **Width** and **Height** boxes. This will make it so the widths and heights cannot change. This time, however, don't update the frames when you apply the constraints, since we still need to set more constraints for our elements to be in the right place.

Next, we're going to use the Align menu (the icon to the left of the Pin menu). Select the objects in the center of the view controller (the `Mins` label, and our two buttons), and then open the Align menu:

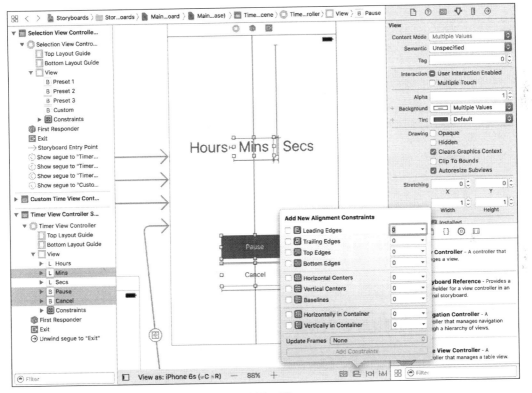

Figure 4.18: The Align menu

Here, you can see all of the alignment constraint options for UI elements. For now, we are just going to center these three objects horizontally in their container, which is the view. Check that box, and add the three constraints.

To finish this view controller, we just need to apply some final spacing constraints. Select all three time labels and apply a 150-point constraint to the top edge of the view. Then select just the Mins label and apply a 10-point constraint on the left and right side, making sure that they are using the nearest neighbor (being the Hours and Secs labels). Finally, on the Cancel button, apply a 100-point constraint on the bottom, and a 10 point constraint on the top, which will anchor it to the bottom of the view, and then pin the Pause button on top of it.

Once all of these constraints have been implemented, you should be able to select all of the elements and press the *option + command + =* to update all of the frames:

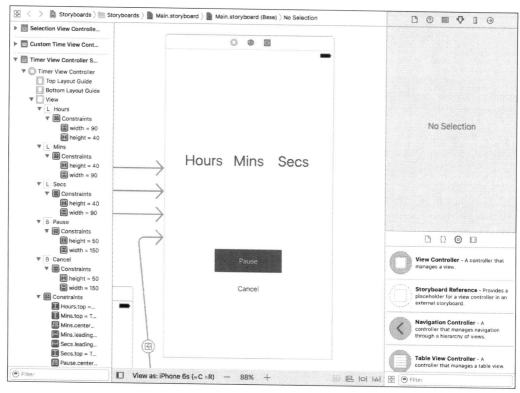

Figure 4.19: The final layout for the Timer View Controller

Beautiful! Again, try testing this on different simulators to see how the design works across multiple screen sizes. Now, since the last view controller, **Custom Time View Controller**, is so similar to this one, I think you can handle it on your own! Make sure to plan ahead of time how you want to handle the stepper elements.

If you can't figure it out on your own: apply all of the same constraints as you did for the **Timer View Controller**, then horizontally center the center stepper, give all steppers a 30-point top constraint, and finally add 10-point constraints to the left and right of the center stepper.

Resolving issues

Sometimes when creating constraints, you'll run into issues with Auto Layout. For the most part, an issue will arise when two constraints conflict, or when constraints are missing and Auto Layout does not have enough information to determine an element's position:

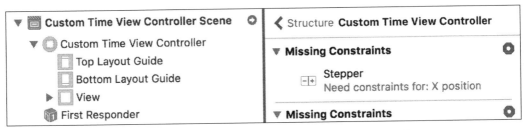

Figure 4.20: Examples of Auto Layout issues in the document outline

When this happens, you'll get a bunch of red marks everywhere, and a little red arrow next to your scene in the document outline. If you click on the red arrow, Auto Layout will walk you through the errors, and present your options for dealing with the issues.

Size classes

So now we've built out all of our views in our storyboard, connected them with segues, and set constraints using Auto Layout, and everything is perfect! Or... is it? If you've tried to rotate your phone into landscape, you may have noticed that everything is decidedly *not* perfect. Our constraints don't hold up particularly well when the screen becomes so wide and short.

But what should we do? It would be nearly impossible to come up with a set of constraints that are so robust that they work in all sizes and orientations that a device can come in. Luckily, there is one last feature that solves this very problem: **size classes**.

Size classes are a way to group constraints into categories that are general enough that you don't have to design for each individual device, but specific enough to change rules depending on the heights and widths of a device. The biggest use case for size classes are for when you switch between landscape and portrait modes, or when you use multitasking views on the iPad in iOS 10.

Devices, orientations, and size classes

New in Xcode 8 is the ability to work directly with device sizes. In earlier versions of Xcode you would have to work with general size class shapes like squares and rectangles, which forced you to always think about the general shape of a size class, and not a specific layout for a given device. Now we have a much better visualization in interface builder, *and* a great tool for working with size classes–the best of both worlds. Let's see how it works:

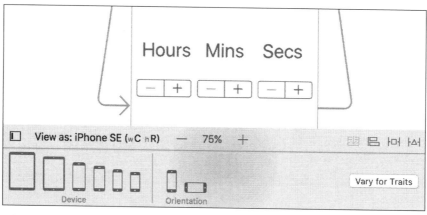

Figure 4.21: The device selection bar at the bottom of the interface builder editor window

First, click on the **View as: {Device Name}** button on the bottom of the window. This should open up a tray full of devices, as shown in *Figure 4.21*. Clicking on all of the devices on the left half of the tray will change the physical size of the interface builder view controllers to match the size of those devices. Likewise, you can use the orientation buttons to switch between the different orientations for all devices.

While this is a fantastic visualization tool, the most important piece of information for us right now is the text in parenthesis next to the device name (in *Figure 4.21* it reads (**wC hR**) where C stands for **Compact** and R stands for **Regular**). This is letting us know that the current device at the specified orientation has a certain width and height size class. Both the horizontal and vertical size classes can have a value of Compact and Regular. So using the example from *Figure 4.21* the iPhone SE has a width size class of Compact and a height size class of Regular.

Here's an interesting note: all iPhones have compact widths in both orientations with one exception–the iPhone 6s Plus is so big that when in landscape, it has a Regular width. Keep this in mind when developing landscape views for the iPhone.

Once you know the size class of the device and orientation you are targeting, we're ready to put them to work.

When you click on the **Size Class Selection** button, you'll be greeted with a grid that lets you visually select the size class that you want to work with (see *Figure 4.22*), along with a description of the types of devices it covers. Since we want to fix our constraints for landscape mode, we want to find the right size class that covers iPhones in landscape mode. After some quick searching, it looks like we want to choose the `Any Width, Compact Height` size class.

Size classes in action

Now that we know how to find our size classes, it's time to edit our constraints. Let's work on the biggest issue: the Custom Time View Controller. *Figure 4.22* shows what it looks like right now on the iPhone 6s in landscape mode:

Figure 4.22: The Custom Time View Controller in landscape before using size classes

Everything is overlapping! The issue here is that in portrait mode we have more vertical space to work with than we do in landscape. If you look at the size classes for the two different orientations, you'll see that we go from a Regular height to a Compact height. To fix this issue, we're going to want to implement some special constraints for the hC size class.

To begin, make sure you have selected the landscape iPhone 6s device (technically, any configuration with a hC size class will work). Next, click on the button on the far right of the device bar that says "Vary for Traits" as shown in the figure 4.21. It will ask you which traits you would like to make variations for, and in this case we want to check off variations for the height class. Once we check off the height checkbox, the device bar will turn blue, letting you know that you are now editing constraints for specific size classes:

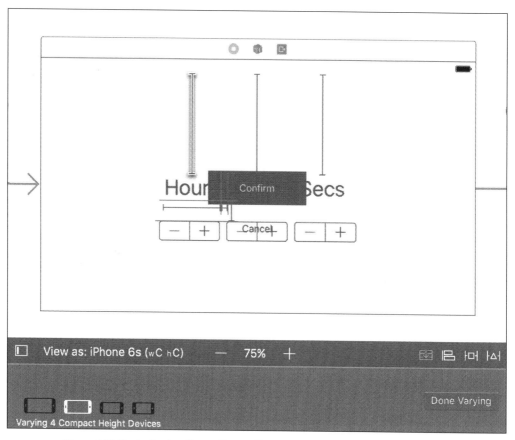

Figure 4.23: Beginning to edit our Custom Time View Controller for the hC size class

In the device bar in *Figure 4.23* we can see that four devices are visible, namely all four iPhone sizes in landscape. This is letting us know which devices are being affected by the varying traits.

To modify a constraint for the current size class, hover over the little blue strut for a second until it *pops* out, and then double click on it. Let's start with the constraint that pins the **Hour** label to the top of the screen. First click on the **Hour** label, then hover and double click on the top pin constraint and you should see something similar to *Figure 4.24*.

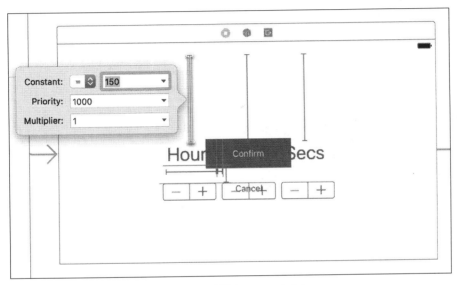

Figure 4.24: Editing a constraint

We'll change the constraint constant from 150 to 30; this will make it hug the top of the screen much tighter. Next we'll do the same for the top pin constraints for the other two labels. After those are finished, we'll do the same for the bottom pin label on the **Cancel** button, also setting the **Constant** to 30.

With those changes, we have fixed our landscape layout, and we can click the **Done Varying** button in the device bar to lock in our modifications.

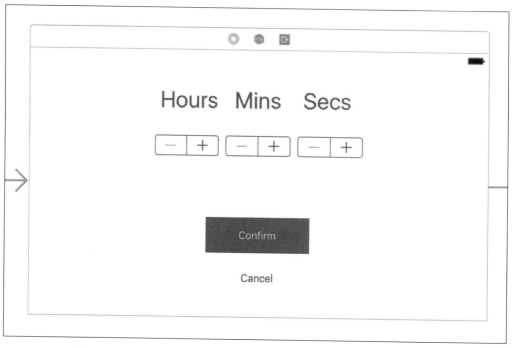

Figure 4.25: Our finished landscape view for the Custom Time View Controller

Now, when switch between portrait and landscape mode in the device bar, you should see how the layouts are correct in both modes (see *Figure 4.25* for the final landscape layout). Everything looks much better now! To get another perspective on what we just did, select the top pin constraint on the **Hours** label again, and then look at the inspector sidebar.

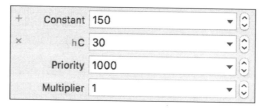

Figure 4.26: The added constant value for the Compact height size class

Looking at *Figure 4.26*, we can see that underneath the default constant value there is another constant defined with an **hC** next to it. This means that when the size class is hC, the new value will override the default. If you wanted to, you could manually add new constants for different size classes using the plus button next to the constant field. In fact, you can set override values for any attributes in the inspector that has a plus sign next to it. This means you can change things like font size and background color based on size classes too.

For a final challenge to test your new skills, go ahead and try to fix the Timer View Controller without looking at the instructions for the Custom Time View Controller we set up. For an even bigger challenge, see what you can do for some of the iPad layouts!

Once you've done that, you should finally have a completely working app in both portrait and landscape across all iPhone models!

Summary

We just survived a crash course through the world of storyboards, Auto Layout, and size classes. We learned how to map our screen flow with storyboards, and how to connect view controllers with segues. Then we set up a system of constraints to intelligently scale our UI depending on both size *and* orientation. It's a bit daunting and a lot to take in, but Auto Layout is just one of those things that takes time and practice to get good at. Try mocking up some apps with placeholder UI elements, and setting up constraints as practice!

In the next chapter we'll be learning how to set up, integrate, and master Git source control in Xcode 8.

5
Taking Advantage of Source Control in Xcode

In the field of software development, the size of a project can range from one person coding away on his or her laptop, in his or her free time, to hundreds or thousands of developers spread out across the world working 40 hour weeks. Unfortunately, as a team gets larger, the chance of issues increases dramatically. Files may get corrupted while being sent from one developer to another; hardware failures may cause teams to lose weeks, or even months, of progress; coders may modify the same file at the same time, resulting in issues down the line. On teams of any size, a good source code management system can save you from all of these headaches.

In Xcode, we'll be taking advantage of a source control (or version control) system called **Git**. We'll take a look at the features of Git, learn how it interfaces with Xcode, and set up an account on a website called GitHub that allows us to save our projects online. To be more specific, in this chapter we'll be covering:

- What is Git, and how is it used?
- Creating an Xcode project with Git
- Working with remote repositories on `https://github.com/`
- Using version control features built into Xcode

Before we get started, I just want to offer some words of encouragement. Git (and version control systems in general) can be a little complex and overwhelming to understand, especially at first. Don't worry if it doesn't click right away, or if you think it clicks but you can't get it to work immediately. It will come with practice!

Understanding version control

The purpose of this chapter is to make sure you understand how to manage your project in a way that makes it easier to roll back changes in your code when things go wrong, and to facilitate collaboration with other coders. It would be easy to jump right into Xcode and start playing with the features that let us accomplish these goals.

However, it will be much more rewarding if we take a little time up front to learn the basics of Git, the underlying technology for Xcode's version control functionality. Technically speaking, Git is a **distributed version control system**, but before we unpack what that means, we should take a look at what a *generic* version control system might look like.

There are many version control solutions that have been created for software development, but most of them can be boiled down into a set of functionality that you see in *Figure 5.1*:

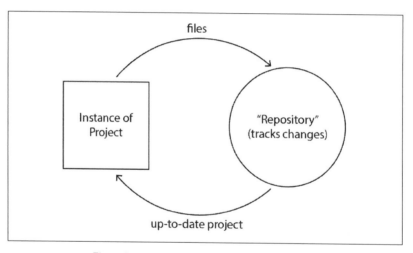

Figure 5.1: A generic approach to version control

On the left, we have the instance of our project that we are working from. This is sometimes referred to as a *working directory*, or a *working copy*, and is usually local to your machine.

Then, from your working directory, you can send your files to the repository on the right, which tracks the changes you made to the files. If you're working with other people, the repository makes sure that what you changed doesn't interfere with changes that someone else has made. If there are *conflicts*, you'll have to solve them before your work can be added to the repository. This helps to prevent two people from overriding each others' changes.

Finally, the repository will update your working directory with any changes that aren't present, so that the working directory is fully up-to-date. Obviously, if you are the only person using the repository, this won't really happen.

Let's say you have your project at a stable point, but you accidentally ruined a big chunk of your code, and it no longer compiles. It happens sometimes! The power of a version control system is that you can just **revert** to an earlier *version* of your project, like hitting a giant undo button that works on everything! If you also use a remote repository (meaning that it lives somewhere other than your physical computer), then you can also guard against losing your work when hardware is damaged or lost:

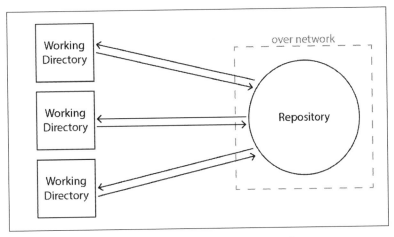

Figure 5.2: Client-server model of version control systems

A lot of version control systems follow a client-server model, meaning that developers have their own machines (clients) which then send all of their files over a network to a central repository (server). The server repository manages all of the changes made by everyone that contributes, and acts as a gatekeeper. This system works fine, but over the years has proven to not meet the demands of every type of project.

Introduction to Git

Let us jump back a bit and look at the definition of Git: a distributed version control system. Differing from the client-server model, there doesn't have to be a central repository with Git. In fact, every local copy is also a full repository, complete with versioning information. The repositories then sync up with each other:

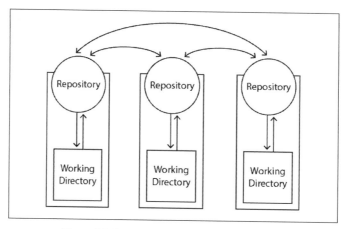

Figure 5.3: Git model of repository management

With repositories set up this way, each user has complete access to the entire project history, and because everything is local on their drive they can perform repository operations very quickly.

Now that we have a big-picture idea of how Git manages everything, let's look at what's going on in one of those rectangles on a user's local machine:

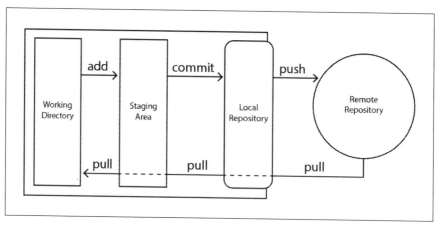

Figure 5.4: The anatomy and functions of a Git repository

First, we have our **Working Directory** where we are editing our project files. In Xcode, this will be all of our source code files, and other project resources like storyboards. Once we have decided that we've accomplished a task and that our code is in good standing, we want to begin the process of making a record of our changes.

To begin this process, we need to **add** the desired files to the **Staging Area**. This lets Git know that it should make a record of those changes. Often, all of the files that have been changed will be staged automatically, but sometimes you want to be a little pickier with what will be added. Once we've added all of the desired files to the staging area, we can **commit** them to our **Local Repository**.

When you commit to your local repository, you are creating a snapshot of your project at that point in time, and creating an official record of all the changes that have occurred since the last time you made a commit. If you're working alone, this is the final step, but if you're working with others (or just also storing your project on a remote server for backup purposes), then you also need to **push** your repository to the **Remote**. This sends your local repository and all of its changes to the remote repository.

However, if you want to push to a remote repository, then before any of this process takes place you must **pull** down from the remote. This is to ensure that you have the latest work from the remote repository and it gives you a chance to resolve conflicts before sending your work over. If you don't pull the latest version of a remote before pushing your work (or if someone else pushed their work before you could), then your push will be rejected, and you must pull and merge again before being allowed to push. So to put it simply: first *pull*, then *stage*, then *commit*, and finally *push*.

And that's really all you have to know for now about Git! There is way more to learn, and you can read whole books about it, but this should be enough information to begin putting it to use in your Xcode projects.

Setting up Git in Xcode

Now that we have some theory under our belts, let's put it to good use. In this section, we are going to learn several ways to get an Xcode project set up with version control. Let's launch Xcode and get to work!

Creating a local repository

To begin, create a new project in Xcode. Choose a **Single View Application**, and give it any name you like. Make sure your settings look like mine do in *Figure 5.5*:

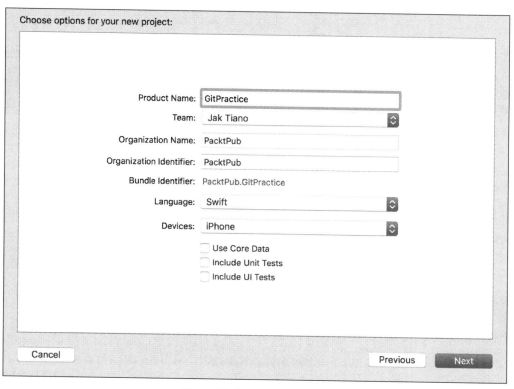

Figure 5.5: Our project settings

Once that's done, click **Next**, and choose a folder to save your project. Before you finish creating your project though, take notice of the checkbox at the bottom of the dialog box (see *Figure 5.6*):

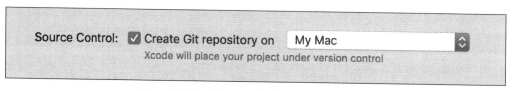

Figure 5.6: The Git setup checkbox on a new project

You want to make sure you check the box so that Xcode will automatically configure the project folder that it creates as a Git repository. Now, you can click **Create** and enter your new project.

 If you run into any issues with Git from this point on, you should double check that you installed the command-line tools for Xcode. Head back to the beginning of *Chapter 2, Welcome to Xcode*, to see how we installed them. It's possible that you don't have Git installed properly on your machine.

You'll notice that not much is visibly different. In fact, our project looks exactly the same as all of the new projects we've created previously! Despite this, our project is now completely under Git version control.

As a test, let's head over to the ViewController.swift file. Inside the viewDidLoad() function, let's add a comment to the bottom of the function that just says //test. Now check out the file navigator sidebar: next to our ViewController.swift file name, there should be a little M. This means that Xcode detected a change in that file, and has automatically flagged that file to be staged when we commit later on (the M means the file has been *modified*).

And that's all there is to it! We've set up a new project with a Git repository, and made sure that it's working. Let's look at a few other ways to get set up before moving on.

Adding Git to an existing project

Sometimes, you'll start a project without setting up a Git repository, like we just did. There are several ways to get an unversioned project set up with Git. We're going to look at two ways to do this: using Xcode itself, and using the command line.

First, create another new Xcode project with the exact same settings as the last one, except name this one GitPractice2a, and make sure *not* to check the box that creates a Git repository.

Now, with the project open, all we have to do is go to the menu bar item **Source Control**, and select **Create Working Copy...** from the dropdown, and in the resulting dialog box click **Create**:

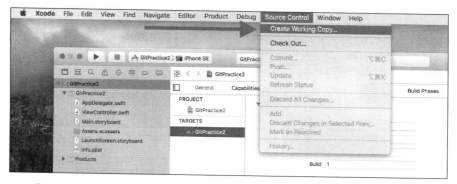

Figure 5.7: Create Working Copy... will turn your project folder into a Git repository

If you go back and modify a file, you should see the M appear, letting you know that Git is properly set up!

At some point, you're going to have to bite the bullet and learn how to use Git from the command line. Why not start early? Now we're going to do the same thing that Xcode just did for us, but manually using command-line tools in **Terminal**.

First make yet another new project, this time named GitPractice2b (and *don't* check off the Git box!), then launch the Terminal app. The easiest way to do this is by searching your computer with Spotlight by pressing *command* + space button, and then typing in **Terminal**, and selecting the application:

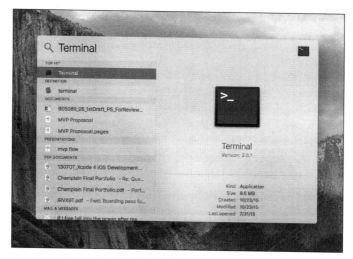

Figure 5.8: Using Spotlight to open the Terminal app

Once we're in the terminal, we want to navigate to the folder that we want to turn into a Git repository. If you've never used the command line before, this might be a little strange, so here's a shortcut: type in cd (which means *change directory*), followed by a space character. Then, from a **Finder** window, drag the root folder of your Xcode project into the **Terminal** window and release it. It should place the file path of that folder into your command line as text!

At this point, your **Terminal** window should look something like in *Figure 5.9* (keeping in mind that your file path will be different):

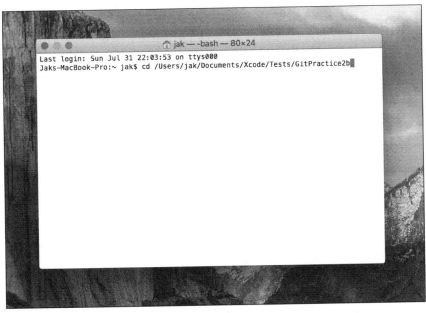

Figure 5.9: A change directory command in the Terminal app

Press *enter* on your keyboard to execute the command and change your command line's scope to that of the Xcode project folder. If it worked, the beginning of your current line should be something like this: {ComputerName}:GitPractice2b {User}$, where each piece in curly brackets matches your settings.

Now that we're inside our project folder, we want to turn it into a Git repository. Luckily, that's very simple! Type in the command git init, press *enter*, and we've done it!

However, that's not all we have to do. We also want to perform our first commit, so that our repository has a starting point. If we think back to the diagrams from earlier though, you'll remember that we need to stage our files before we commit anything. Since all of the files begin as *unversioned*, we want to add all of the files to the staging area. The command is pretty straightforward: `git add`. We also need to specify which files should be added, but in this case we can just add a `.` to the end of the command to tell it that we want all the files. So, our final command should read `git add .` then press *enter*.

To make sure that we added all of our files to the staging area, use the command `git status` to see what changes are set to be committed. If your `git status` command gives you results that look like *Figure 5.10*, that means you successfully added all of the files to the staging area:

Figure 5.10: The files were successfully staged

To make our initial commit, we are going to use the `git commit` command. When making a commit, we always need to include a message describing what we did. To add this commit message, we'll use the `-m` flag, followed by our message in quotes. The final command should look something like this:

```
git commit -m "Initial commit"
```

Finally, type `exit` into your Terminal window, hit *enter*, then quit.

 If you accidentally only typed `git commit` and hit *enter*, Terminal will launch `vi`, a command line text editor and force you to write a commit message. First press the *I* key to enter *insert mode*, then type a small commit message. Next, press *esc*, followed by *:wq*, then press *enter*. Don't worry about it… just remember to use the `-m` flag to make a commit message from the standard command line. Now your Xcode project should be under Git version control.

Head back to Xcode where our project should now be under version control. Xcode is a little slow, though, so you'll need to quit Xcode and then relaunch the project for it to notice the new Git properties of our project. Once you do that however, you'll notice that we get our little M's when we modify and save files. Success!

Using a GitHub hosted repository

For this last part, we're going to use a remotely hosted Git repository. To do this, we're going to use a free service called GitHub. GitHub is one of the most popular Git hosting services in the industry, and it's a great resource for collaborative coding.

Go ahead and register an account on GitHub now if you don't already have one (`https://github.com/`). Once your account is all set up, create a new repository and set it up so that it looks like the one as follows:

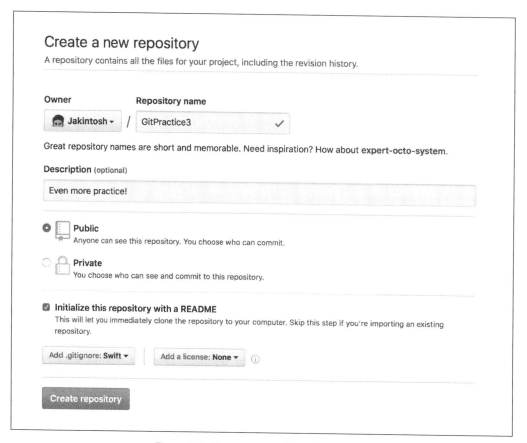

Figure 5.11: Creating a new GitHub repository

You'll notice that there is a new element here that we haven't yet talked about: a
.gitignore file. A .gitignore file is a hidden file in your Git repository that tells
the repository to ignore certain files. There are many reasons why you wouldn't want
to place some files under version control, and the .gitignore is where you list those
files. When creating a new repository on GitHub, you can chose from a bunch of
premade .gitignore files, and you can see that I chose one that is made for Swift:

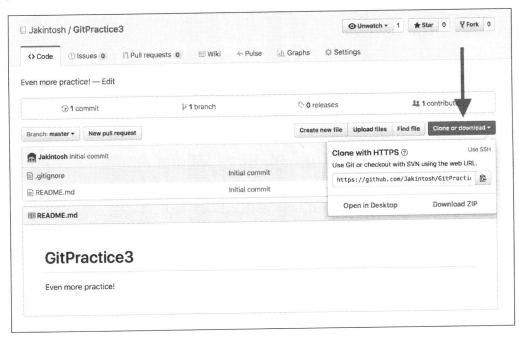

Figure 5.12: Finding the repository link on GitHub

Once you've configured the repository, hit the green **Create Repository** button to finish creating it. Now you should be brought to the repository's page. We want to find the link to the repository so that we can access it in Xcode. If you click the green **Clone or download** button (*Figure 5.12*) on the repository overview page, you should see a link to the repository. Make sure you select the *HTTPS* version of the link, before copying it to your clipboard:

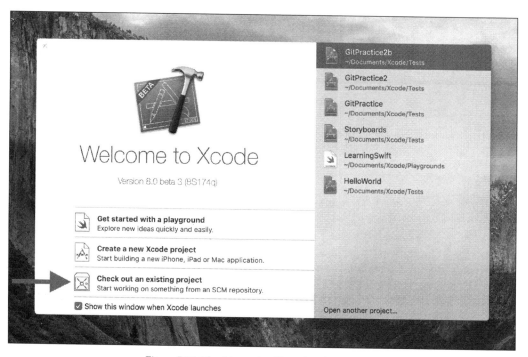

Figure 5.13: Checking out a Git project from Xcode

Back in Xcode, let's go to the startup window, and select the **Check out an existing project** button (*Figure 5.13*). This will allow us to use the link we copied from GitHub to access our repository straight from GitHub. In the checkout window, paste in the link from GitHub, click on the **Next** button, and select a location to save the project. This will download the repository, but since it's empty, we still need to create the Xcode project that will go in it:

Figure 5.14: Pasting the link from GitHub to check out the project from Xcode

One last time, let's create a new project (single view application) named GitPractice3, and save it into the folder that we just pulled down from GitHub. In the last step, the checkbox should be greyed out, letting you know that the folder is already a Git repository. Click **Create**, and you're finished!

We've now covered many different ways to configure a new or existing project to use Git. Now let's see what we can do with it in Xcode!

Using version control in Xcode

Now that we know what Git does, and have a project all set up with a local Git repository, in addition to a remote Git repository hosted on https://github.com/, let's take a look at the version control tools built into Xcode.

Pull, push, and commit

In the last section, we left off with a newly created project in our freshly cloned local repository. We never staged or committed any of our new files to our repository that we pulled down, so let's use this opportunity to look at how we use commit from within Xcode.

To begin a commit, press *option + command + C* on the keyboard, or navigate to **Source Control | Commit** in the menu bar. Once you do that, you'll see the commit window:

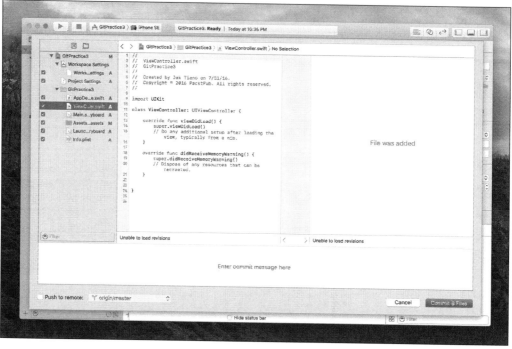

Figure 5.15: The commit window in Xcode

On the far left is the staging area. Each file that is eligible to be staged will have a checkbox next to it, and if you wish to add it to the commit you are about to make, you need to make sure the box is ticked.

On the right side of the window is a split-view of the selected file's *new* version on the left half, and the *last committed* version on the right half. In this case, all of the files are new, so there's nothing to see on the right half.

On the bottom is a text box where you can enter a commit message. Remember, a commit message is *necessary*, and Xcode won't let you finish a commit without writing a message in the box.

Finally, on the lower left hand side, is a checkbox that lets you automatically **push** your work to a remote repository, after it commits to the local repository.

For now, let's write `Added new project` as the commit message, and then click the `Commit {X} Files` button to commit our changes.

Now that we've committed to our local repository, we want to push our changes up to our remote repository on GitHub. Thinking back to our charts earlier in the chapter, we remember that before we can push, we need to make sure we pull from the remote first. To pull, we can use the shortcut *option + command + X* or navigate to **Source Control | Pull**:

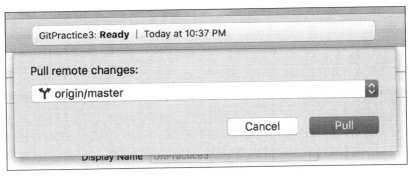

Figure 5.16: Selecting which branch to pull

Before you pull, you have to select a branch to pull from; right now, we only have the master branch, but more on that later. Click **Pull**, and you should be notified that your local repository is up to date. Now we're ready to push our changes back up to the remote.

Navigate to **Source Control | Push** in the menu bar, then click **Push** on the dropdown that appears. Before it finishes the push, you will probably be asked for your GitHub user name and password. Enter these in the dropdown and press **OK**, and you'll see your push go through!

If you head back to `https://github.com/` and look at the page for your repository, you can see that the changes we just made are reflected there. Pretty neat, huh?

The version editor

Remember back in *Chapter 2, Welcome to Xcode*, when we were exploring the different editor modes? There was the standard editor which we use all the time, and there was the assistant editor which we've used on occasion so far. But now, it's finally time to check out the third tab: the version editor. To quickly switch to the version editor, use the shortcut *option + shift + command + enter*.

The name of the version editor is pretty self-explanatory: it lets you edit a file while looking at its version history, and seeing the differences. Try opening up `ViewController.swift` and start writing some blank test functions to see how it works:

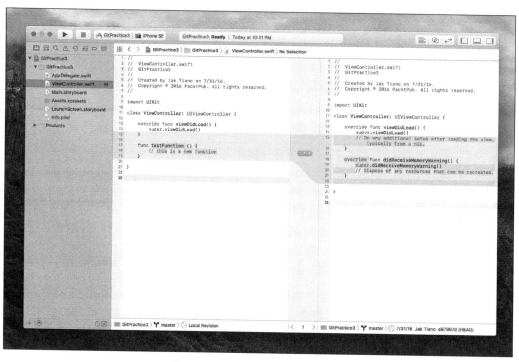

Figure 5.17: The version editor in use

The version editor does its best to show you where parts of the code have been added or deleted since the last commit. You can also go to the bottom of each split editor window and select which revision you want to be viewing, to compare the file to several different versions of itself. You can also click on the dropdown that appears in the middle of a change to discard that change if you realize that the change was made by accident or in error.

At the bottom of the middle bar between the two versions is a timeline button. Click it, and you'll be given a graphical timeline that will let you scrub through all of the commits over the life of the project to find a previous version of the code. If you find that something has been broken, you can use this feature to go back through code to find an older version that still works.

Creating and merging branches

The last feature that we're going to look at in this chapter is one of Git's most powerful. When working on a large project with other developers, it's important to have a stable codebase. But sometimes, you need to add big new features that may hurt the stability of your code for a little while. In situations like these, you can create a **branch** from your *master* copy of the project, and work on the new feature without worrying about breaking the main application. After a while, once the feature is complete and the stability has returned, you can merge the branch back in with the master copy. Let's look at how we would do this.

We're going to create a new branch where we can make some new test functions for our app. To do this, navigate to the **Source Control** menu-bar item, then select your working copy, and click **New Branch**:

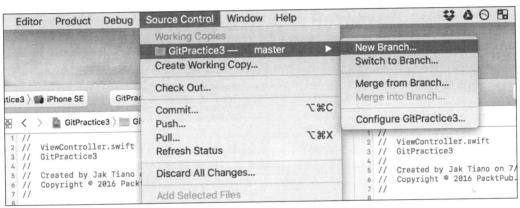

Figure 5.18: Creating a new branch in Xcode from the Source Control menu

Once you select **New Branch...**, give the branch a name (no spaces). We'll call our branch **New-Test-Functions**. Now that we've got a new branch, we can go around and make changes to our code without worrying about breaking anything in the *master* branch.

To test this out, let's go back to `ViewController.swift`, and make a couple test functions. Change out your `ViewController` class so that it contains this code:

```
class ViewController: UIViewController {

    override func viewDidLoad() {
        super.viewDidLoad()
    }

    func testFunction1 () {
        print ("test 1")
    }
}
```

```
func testFunction2 () {
    print ("test 2")
}
}
```

Now commit the code (*option + command + C*) to the `New-Test-Functions` branch. If you go back to the **Source Control** menu-bar item, then select your working copy again, but this time choose **Switch to branch**, you can jump back to the master and see that it's just how you left it.

In the real world, this means that if you are hard at work on version 2.0 of a product, but a small bug is found in the previous version, you can save your work, jump back to the old version to patch the bug, and then go right back to the new branch and resume work on 2.0.

Now to wrap this all together, let's merge our `New-Test-Functions` branch back in with the master. Head to the **Source Control** menu-bar item, then select your working copy again, and this last time choose the **Merge from branch** option. When given the option, choose the `New-Test-Functions` branch to merge from. You will be brought to the branch merge window:

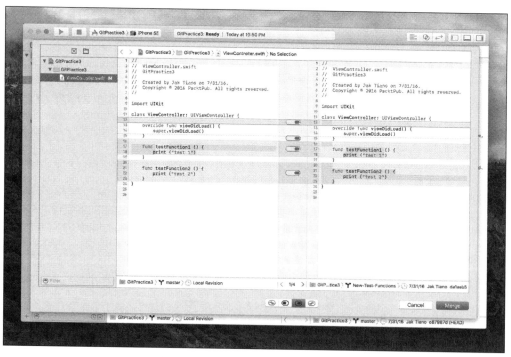

Figure 5.19: The branch merge window

The branch merge window is very similar to the commit window, but instead of the commit message area, it has some toggles. On the left side of the window is a list of all the files that need to be merged together. If you click on a file, it will show you the *final* version of the file on the left, and the branch's version of the file on the right. The toggles along the bottom allow you to choose how each individual difference is merged.

Remember, the file on the left is how the file will end up after the merge. Make sure that the left hand side is how you want the resulting file to be!

Once you have gone through every file and selected all the correct points for merging, you can hit the **Merge** button in the lower right part of the window. That's it! You created a new branch, switched between branches, and merged it back into the master branch.

Summary

In this chapter, we covered a lot of material. We learned about what version control is, how Git differs from other solutions, and what its strengths are. We created new Git repositories for our Xcode projects in several different ways, including using the command line, and then we made a GitHub account and set up a remote repository. Finally, we spent some quality time with the version control features built into Xcode, and used our knowledge of Git to commit, push, and pull changes to our local and remote repositories.

In the next chapter, we'll be putting to the test everything we've learned so far in this book: it's time to make our first real app.

6

Building Your First iOS App

For the last five chapters, we've been covering many different aspects of iOS development. We've learned how to navigate Xcode, we've explored the basics of Swift 3, and we've practiced creating storyboards for apps. We've even looked at responsible ways to manage a project with source control. There's not much left to procrastinate about: it's time to make our first app.

We've got all the skills we need to build out the model, views, and controllers of a real iOS application. Now, we're going to use all of these skills together to create a simple note-making application called **Snippets**. Let's break it down. In this chapter we're going to:

- Breakdown an app idea into a feature list
- Create a plan for app development
- Develop model code for the application
- Lay out the app in a storyboard
- Build and connect our view controllers
- Deploy the app to our devices

That's a lot of ground to cover! However, you'll notice that most of these things we've done already. As we learn how to break down our app into a feature list and a development plan, we'll see that building an app isn't really so hard. Let's go!

Pre-production

As much fun as it would be to just dive in and start writing code, things usually go a bit smoother if we spend a little time thinking about what we are about to do. First, we're going to go on a mental journey through using the app to determine all of the features that will be present in the finished product. Then we're going to consult a designer (that's going to be me) to determine what the app will look like, and collect any assets we might need. Finally, we're going to break that feature list down into a development plan that gives us an idea of the actual tasks that will need to be completed to deliver each feature.

Assembling a feature list

As I mentioned earlier, the app we're going to create is a notes-style application called Snippets. The core feature of the app is that it lets the user make little *snippets* of life to save for later, which consist of text or images, or maybe later even web links or audio. Then the user can scroll through their snippets in reverse chronological order. Down the line, we might end up with a product that resembles the popular organization software *Evernote*, or maybe it will evolve into a private journaling app.

Notice how I said it *might* end up some way, and it will *maybe* have certain features. When developing software in a lean, agile manner, it's often best not to think too far ahead. Right now, we have our big goal: create an app that lets users take little notes. But once we show the app to potential users, they might have a completely different idea of what they like about our app, and we might pivot our development goals to meet the needs of the customer.

To avoid spending a lot of time developing features that we might remove from our app, we use a strategy that has us build an **MVP**, or **minimum viable product**. That means that in our v1.0 feature list, we only want to build the most basic and essential features of our app, so that we can test them and see what people like. So with that in mind, let's nail down our intended experience.

When a user opens our app, there should be a very clear and simple way to create a new snippet. Creating a new snippet is going to be an *urgent* task for the user; there will usually be some time pressure as they try to capture a moment or thought as quickly as possible. When they tap the button that creates a new snippet, there needs to be a way to select if they are making a **Text snippet** or a **Photo snippet**, which are going to be the two post types we allow in our MVP. If the user selects text, they should be able to type in text and save. If they select photo they should be able to take a square photo with the camera and save. All posts should save the date and time they were created.

So far, our feature list for snippet creation looks like this:

- New snippet button
- Snippet-type selection menu
- Text snippet data entry
- Photo snippet data entry
- Log date posts were made

Now, the other half of this app is the ability to view the timeline of our snippets. Similar to apps like Twitter or Tumblr, we want to be able to infinitely scroll through all of our snippets in reverse chronological order, meaning we've got the newest snippets at the top of the screen. Each snippet should show the content data along with the date and time the snippet was created.

Let's append the new features we need, and look at our final list:

- New snippet button
- Snippet-type selection menu
- Text snippet data entry
- Photo snippet data entry
- Log date posts were made
- Display a list of scrollable snippets
- Snippet displays content and timestamp

Alright! We've got seven features to implement to hit our v1.0 features goal. Now let's explore what the app should look like when completed to help guide our development plan.

Visual design

So we've got a solid feature list nailed down for our v1.0 release. At this point in the process, we're going to get a simple pre-visualization of the app from a designer. We'll give them our feature list, and see what kind of ideas they come back with.

In this case, I've taken it upon myself to do a really quick mockup of what our app should look like given our features and restrictions. Since design isn't the main focus of this project, it's a bit on the safe side, but it should give us a good idea of what we're shooting for, and the kinds of view controllers we'll have to be developing.

Let's take a look at the visual designs in *Figure 6.1* and get acquainted with some common iOS UI elements:

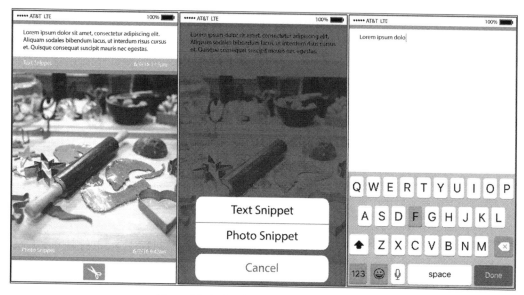

Figure 6.1: A visual target for v1.0 of Snippets

In our first screen, we have a customized `UITableView`. `UITableViews` are used in almost every iOS application, since they are the best way to present *tables* (or *lists*) to a user. This might be a list of options in the settings application, or a *list* of tweets in a Twitter client. In Snippets, we're going to use a `UITableView` to show a scrollable timeline of our individual snippets.

In the second screen, we can see a popover set of options that will show up when we press the **New Snippet** button. This is called a `UIAlertController`, which lets the user know that their input is needed to continue. Here, we're using an `Action Sheet` style where the actions come up from the bottom of the screen, but alert controllers can also display information in a floating window in the center of the screen.

Finally, on the third screen, we're using a modal view controller that will slide up from the bottom of the screen to allow you to create a new snippet. In this image, we're using a `UITextField` to input text, but we'll also allow the use of a `UIImagePickerController`, which lets the user take or add a picture.

We've now got a list of features, and a visual target for our app. Now we just have to put together our development plan and we'll be ready to start coding!

Creating a development plan

In the world of software development, you'll hear about many different project planning methods. With names like *Scrum* and *Kanban*, they can seem daunting and foreign to novice developers who just want to code! There's no reason to become deeply educated in a specific project planning philosophy this early, because every team that you end up working on is going to operate a little differently.

However, there are a few concepts that are proven to be effective, and we're going to apply them loosely to create our development plan. Most teams in software have adopted an *agile* method of development. Agile development refers to the fact that projects are not planned from 0-100% at the beginning, but are instead highly iterative endeavors. Earlier, we went over the idea of a *minimum viable product*. The MVP is a product of this iterative thinking: we haven't planned out the entire app all at once, since we're just going to build our core features and then see if people like them.

Another common feature of these agile development methods is that they focus on delivering features for the user, instead of creating functionality we think we need as a developer. For example, we as developers might say, "This week, I am going to program a database management system. However, when we think from the end user's perspective, we get a different idea of our development priorities. The user might say, "I'd like to be able to view my posted photos" (this is commonly referred to as a *user story*). Now, when focused on delivering that feature to the user, you will have more direction on what your database manager will need to do, and which aspects are most important to develop first. To summarize, agile development tends to be *user-centric*.

Finally, we want to take our user-centric features and break them down into smaller tasks. To keep our project lean and agile, these tasks should be as clear and granular as possible; a single task should not take more than an hour or two, and sometimes much less.

So now, with an understanding of how we want to manage this project, let's create a development plan for `Snippets`. Earlier, we created a feature list that looked like this:

- New snippet button
- Snippet-type selection menu
- Text snippet data entry
- Photo snippet data entry
- Log date posts were made
- Display a list of scrollable snippets
- Snippet displays content and timestamp

This is a great start for our set of user stories, but we'll need to do a little clean up so that everything makes sense under our new guidelines:

- "I want to be able to create a new snippet"
- "I want to select the type of snippet I am creating"
- "I want to enter text when creating a snippet"
- "I want to attach a photo to a snippet"
- "I want to scroll through my snippets"
- "I want to see the date a snippet was made"

Perfect! Now we have a list of user-centric features that describe everything a user wants to do with our MVP application. The last step is to break these stories down into tasks. The more projects you work on, the better you'll get at mentally breaking down stories, so for now I'll just show you how my final task list ended up:

- **Story**: "I want to be able to create a new snippet"

  Tasks: Create a model class for bare-bones `SnippetData`; create a toolbar with a button that, when pressed, creates new `SnippetData` and adds it to an array

- **Story**: "I want to select the type of snippet I am creating"

  Tasks: Append the `SnippetData` model to allow for Text and Photo types; create an alert controller that allows the user to select the type of `Snippet` that is created

- **Story**: "I want to enter text when creating a snippet"

  Tasks: Create a new subclass of `SnippetData` that represents the `TextSnippet`; create a new view controller with a `UITextField` that saves the text input in the `TextSnippet`

- **Story**: "I want to attach a photo to a snippet"

  Tasks: Create a new subclass of `SnippetData` that represents the `PhotoSnippet`; create a new view controller with a `UIImagePickerController` that allows the user to take a picture and save the data to the `PhotoSnippet`

- **Story**: "I want to scroll through my snippets"

  Tasks: Add a `UITableView` to our first scene, with two prototype cells for the `TextSnippet` and the `PhotoSnippet`; program the view controller to display the information from our data array in our `UITableView`

- **Story**: "I want to see the date a snippet was made"

  Tasks: Append our base `SnippetData` to hold a date; when a snippet is created, save the current date to our data model; add a `UILabel` to our prototype cells to hold date information, and assign the text in our view controller

Whew! By my count, that's 13 individual tasks that we need to complete to reach our MVP. That's not so bad! Hopefully you can see how much easier it will be to move quickly through our project once we have a clear direction of where we are going. It's an important step in every project.

Throughout the rest of the chapter, we're going to be working through each story, task by task. If you ever get stuck, the completed project can be found in the `Resources` folder for *Chapter 6, Building Your First iOS App.*

At this point, you've created several new Xcode projects, so I trust that you can create a new project called **Snippets** using the Single View Controller template (iPhone device target, Swift language). Make sure you enable Git, like we went over in *Chapter 5, Taking Advantage of Source Control in Xcode.*

Finally, it's time to code.

New snippet

Our first story is "I want to be able to create a new snippet". For this feature, we have two tasks:

- Create a model class for bare-bones `SnippetData`
- Create a toolbar with a button that, when pressed, creates new `SnippetData` and adds it to an array

For the first task, we are going to create a simple Swift struct that will hold the data for our snippet. There won't be a whole lot going on here! For the second task, we'll be going into our storyboard and adding some UI elements, then adding some code for our button to execute when pressed. Remember, the goal is just to have a button create a new instance of a data structure, nothing more.

SnippetData model

Current task: Create a model class for bare-bones `SnippetData`.

For the time being, we're not really sure what is going to go into our `SnippetData` model. Looking at our project specs, we know that we're eventually going to want to store text, photos, and timestamps, but for now we just know that it will be a struct, and that we need to create a new one when we press a button. For that reason, the implementation we go with at first may surprise you.

First, create a new Swift file (*command + N*), and call it `SnippetData.swift`. Then, inside the file, we're going to create the `SnippetData` struct, like so:

```
struct SnippetData {

    init() {
        print ("new snippet created")
    }

}
```

If that's not bare-bones, then I don't know what is! We declare a struct called `SnippetData`, and then we tell it what to do when we create a new instance of it using the `init` function. In this case, we put in a simple `print` statement that will write to the console when a `SnippetData` struct is created, so we can see if our code is working properly. And that's it. Seriously. We'll add to the data model over the next few user stories, but that's all we need for now.

New snippet button

Current task: Create a toolbar with a button that, when pressed, creates new `SnippetData` and adds it to an array.

Now that we've built out the model side of this feature, we need to implement the view and controller. Let's start with the view.

Head over to your storyboard and drag a toolbar onto the screen from the object library (*control + option + command + 3*). We're going to want it anchored to the bottom of our view, so we're going to use a little bit of Auto Layout magic.

First, select the toolbar, and then from the pin constraints (lower-right of the storyboard window, shaped like an **H** with a square in the middle) give it left, right, and bottom margins of 0. Uncheck the box that says **Constrain to margins** so that it is 0 pixels from the edge of the screen, not the margins. Then select the **All frames in container** option from the **Update Frames** dropdown, and hit **Add Constraints**. You can always refer back to *Chapter 4, Using Storyboards, Size Classes, and Auto Layout,* to review Auto Layout, if you feel a little lost.

Now we want to add a button to the middle of our toolbar. To do this, we aren't going to use Auto Layout to position the button, but a special form of bar button item called **Flexible Space**. In the object library, search for `flex` and you should see it immediately. Drag two of them onto our toolbar. Then, find a `Bar Button Item` in the object library, and drag it in between the two flex space items. Change the text of the bar button item to say `New`:

Figure 6.2: Our toolbar with flexible space items and a New bar button item

Try running the project in the simulator to make sure all of our layout constraints are working. If they are, the toolbar should be situated nicely along the bottom of the screen, with our `New` button centered in the middle.

Now that our view is complete, it's time to create the controller. Open the Assistant Editor (*option + command + return*), and make sure that our `ViewController.swift` file is in the assistant view. Hold the control key and drag from our `New` button into our view controller file, then release. Set the connection type as **Action**, and give it the name `createNewSnippet`.

If you remember from earlier, this creates a new function in our view controller that gets called when the user presses the button:

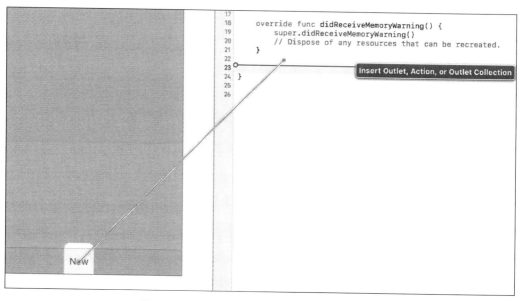

Figure 6.3: Creating an IBOutlet for the New button

You should now see a function stub that looks like this:

```
@IBAction func createNewSnippet(_ sender: AnyObject) {
}
```

All we have left to do is to create a new `SnippetData` struct when the button is pressed, and store it in an array. At the top of our `ViewController` class, we'll declare a new array of `SnippetData` as such:

```
var data: [SnippetData] = [SnippetData]()
```

Then, inside our `createNewSnippet()` function, we'll add two lines of code to create the new data, and then save it into our array. Our final `ViewController` should look like this:

```
import UIKit

class ViewController: UIViewController {

    var data: [SnippetData] = [SnippetData]()
```

```
override func viewDidLoad() {
    super.viewDidLoad()
}

@IBAction func createNewSnippet(sender: AnyObject) {

    let newSnippet = SnippetData()
    data.append(newSnippet)
}

}
```

You can see that we created a new instance of `SnippetData` and assigned it to a `newSnippet` variable, and then we append it to our data array.

When you run this in the simulator, you should see that when you press the `New` button on the toolbar, you get a console output that says **new snippet created**, just like we wrote in the `init` function.

And that's it! Our first user story is completed. We have successfully made a button that creates a new `SnippetData`. Only five more stories to go. Before we move on, make sure to commit (*option + command + C*) your changes to your Git repository now that you've completed a user story, and give it a good description describing the work you did.

Select snippet type

Our next story is "I want to select the type of snippet I am creating". The tasks are:

- Append the `SnippetData` model to allow for Text and Photo types
- Create an alert controller that allows the user to select the type of snippet that is created

For this feature, we're going to expand on our `SnippetData` model to include the ability to have a type using an enum. Then we're going to create and present an alert controller to the user that allows them to choose a type. Finally, we're going to update our view controller to respond to the different options the user can select, and create the correct type of data.

Update SnippetData model

Current task: Append the `SnippetData` model to allow for Text and Photo types.

When we created our `SnippetData` model, it was a very simple Swift struct that didn't hold any data. Now we want to add a *type* property to the struct so that it knows what kind of data it is holding. We're going to create an enum to describe the possible types that can exist for our `SnippetData`, and use a `String` as a backing type for our enum. This means that our enum will be built on top of `String` values. Let's add this enum to our `SnippetData.swift` file:

```swift
enum SnippetType: String {
    case text = "Text"
    case photo = "Photo"
}
```

At the top, we declared a new enum called `SnippetType`, and then said that it is built on top of the `String` class. This syntax is similar to the way we use inheritance in Swift, which makes sense, since, in a way, we are inheriting and writing on top of a string. Inside the enum, we define two possible cases, `Text` and `Photo`. We then assign a `String` value to our cases, which is the backing (or *raw*) value of that case.

Then, inside our `SnippetData` struct, we add a new property to hold our new `SnippetType` information, and update the initializer to take an argument for the type:

```swift
struct SnippetData {

    let type: SnippetType

    init ( snippetType: SnippetType ) {
        type = snippetType
        print ("\(type.rawValue) snippet created")
    }
}
```

At the top of our struct, we declare `type` with the `let` keyword, which means it is a constant. This makes sense because, once we initialize a snippet, its type should never change. Then, in our `init` function, we updated it to accept a parameter for our `SnippetType`, and then we assign the parameter value to our `type` constant.

Finally, you'll see that we changed our `print()` function. We replaced the word `new` with the expression `\(type.rawValue)`. If you remember from earlier, the `\()` syntax allows us to splice data values into a string. In this case, we are inserting the `rawValue` property of our `type` enum. Remember how, when we created our `SnippetType` enum, we assigned each case a *backing value*? That is the `rawValue` we're using here. So if we create a new `SnippetData` with the type `SnippetType.Text`, then our `type.rawValue` will equal the `Text` string we assigned in our enum, and it will print out `Text snippet created` when it is initialized.

Now our `SnippetData` model has the capability to support multiple types. Let's enable our user to select which type they want to make.

Create an alert controller

Current task: Create an alert controller that allows the user to select the type of snippet.

In our basic pre-visualization of the app, we saw that we were using an action sheet with a few options that let the user select the type of snippet they were creating. Now we're going to walk through the process of creating an action sheet like that using the `UIAlertController`.

Since we want to give the user this option after pressing the new button, we're going to delete the code we have in our `createNewSnippet()` function, and replace it with some new code that presents an action sheet. Let's take a look:

```
@IBAction func createNewSnippet(_ sender: AnyObject) {

    let alert = UIAlertController(title: "Select a snippet type",
message: nil, preferredStyle: .actionSheet)
    let textAction = UIAlertAction(title: "Text", style: .default) {
(alert: UIAlertAction!) -> Void in
        self.data.append(SnippetData(snippetType: .text))
    }
    let photoAction = UIAlertAction(title: "Photo", style: .default) {
(alert: UIAlertAction!) -> Void in
        self.data.append(SnippetData(snippetType: .photo))
    }
    let cancelAction = UIAlertAction(title: "Cancel", style: .cancel,
handler: nil)

    alert.addAction(textAction)
    alert.addAction(photoAction)
```

```
    alert.addAction(cancelAction)
    present(alert, animated: true, completion:nil)
}
```

First, we create a new UIAlertController, and initialize it with a title and a preferred style of .actionSheet. The title property is what goes at the top of the action sheet and describes what the alert is for, while the message property is for giving more detail. Since our alert is pretty simple, we don't need both, so we set the message to nil.

 UIAlertController is also used to show you alerts in the middle of the screen, so if you set the preferred style to .alert, it will take that form. Try it out!

Next, we create new UIAlertActions. These are going to be the actual options that the user can select from the action sheet. The first two UIAlertActions are very similar, since they are both used to create a new Text snippet and Photo snippet, respectively.

When creating a UIAlertAction, we need to pass in three things: a title, a button style, and a completion handler. The title is the text on the button, the style is the formatting of the button, and the completion handler is the code that runs when the button is pressed.

```
let textAction = UIAlertAction(title: "Text", style: .default) {
(alert: UIAlertAction!) -> Void in
    self.data.append(SnippetData(snippetType: .text))
}
```

For our text/photo actions, we pass in the title, set the style to .default, and then use what's called a *trailing closure* tacked on to the end. Inside the completion handler closure are two parts: the definition of the parameters being passed into the closure, and the body of the closure.

The first part is the (alert: UIAlertAction!) -> Void in line, which tells the closure that we are passing in a parameter named alert that is the type of an explicitly unwrapped optional UIAlertAction, and returns Void (nothing).

In the body of our completion handler we have the following line:

```
    self.data.append(SnippetData(snippetType: .text))
```

Here we are initializing and appending a new `SnippetData` struct to our data array. We use the new initializer we wrote for our `SnippetData` struct, and let it know that its snippet type is `.text`. In our photo action completion handler, we'd write `.photo`.

 Also notice that we have to write `self.` at the beginning of the line. In a closure, we need to be explicit about the scope, so by letting the closure know exactly what we're talking about with `self.data`, it can capture the scope of the function and use it later on whenever the completion handler is run.

Further down, you'll see our `cancelAction` is a little different. Since our cancel button doesn't really do anything, we can pass in `nil` for the completion handler, instead of using a trailing closure like the other actions.

Finally, we add all of our `UIAlertActions` to our `UIAlertController` by writing `alert.addAction( UIAlertAction )` for each action. Then we present our `UIActionController` like this:

```
presentViewController(alert, animated: true, completion:nil)
```

This presents our alert controller to the user.

And that's it! Build and run the project on the simulator, and try out our new type selection. In the debug area, you'll see that the console now says `Text snippet created` and `Photo snippet created`, depending on which button you press. Before we move on to the next user story, remember to commit your changes to the local Git repository now that we've finished a story and the project is stable.

Text snippet implementation

The next user story is "I want to enter text when creating a snippet". The tasks we need to complete for this feature are:

- Create a new subclass of `SnippetData` that represents the `TextSnippet`
- Create a new view controller with a `UITextField` that saves the text input in the `TextSnippet`

Now it's time to start building out useful snippet-creation tools. Right now we spawn some empty `SnippetData` structs, but there's no user data in there. First we're going to add to our `SnippetData` struct to allow it to hold user data, and then build an interface that allows the user to enter and save the data.

Update SnippetData model

Current task: Create a new subclass of `SnippetData` that represents the `TextSnippet`.

So far, our data model doesn't do much aside from hold a type identifier. Now we want to create a subclass of our data model that gives us the ability to store information for our text data. There's only one problem… you can't subclass a struct. You can only subclass a class (makes sense, doesn't it?).

So, while a struct will usually serve you well when creating an application's data model, it's not going to work for us here. Luckily, all we have to do to change our struct to a class is just swap the keyword. Here's our newly upgraded `SnippetData` class:

```
class SnippetData {
    let type: SnippetType

    init ( snippetType: SnippetType ) {
        type = snippetType
        print ("\(type.rawValue) snippet created")
    }
}
```

Like I said, not a huge change. Now that it's a class, we can create a subclass called `TextData`. We're going to add a new property to hold a string, and give it a new initializer. Here it is:

```
class TextData: SnippetData {
    let textData: String

    init ( text: String ) {
        textData = text
        super.init(snippetType: .text)
        print ("Text snippet data: \(textData)")
    }
}
```

At the top, we define the new class as a subclass of `SnippetData` by using the colon. Then, we add a new `textData` property, which is a string. Then we create a new initializer that takes a string as an argument, which will be stored inside. Inside the initializer, we also call our super class's initializer, which is the `SnippetData` initializer. Since we know that a `TextData` class will always be of `SnippetType` `.text`, we can just pass that to the super class. Finally, we just print out the string so we can check to see if it worked later on.

Now our model is updated and ready to hold some string data.

`SnippetData.swft`:

```
import Foundation

enum SnippetType: String {
    case Text = "text"
    case Photo = "photo"
}

class SnippetData {
    let type: SnippetType

    init ( snippetType: SnippetType ) {
        type = snippetType
        print ("\(type.rawValue) snippet created")
    }
}

class TextData: SnippetData {
    let textData: String

    init ( text: String ) {
        textData = text
        super.init(snippetType: .text)
        print ("Text snippet data: \(textData)")
    }
}
```

Text entry view controller

Current task: Create a new view controller with a `UITextField` that saves the text input in the `TextSnippet`.

Next on our list is to create a new view controller that allows us to actually enter text and save it to a new `TextData` object. This task has a few subtasks related to it. We need to do the following:

- Create a new `TextSnippetEntryViewController` class
- Set up a `UITextView` in a new view controller in our storyboard
- Update our initial `ViewController` class to present the `TextSnippetEntryViewController`.

Let's start with creating a new Swift file (*command + N*) named
`TextSnippetEntryViewController.swift`, and then create a new class with the
same name, that inherits from `UIViewController`. We'll also need to import UIKit
at the top of the file. Then, we're going to use a class extension to implement the
`UITextViewDelegate` protocol to keep our code neat and compartmentalized:

```
import Foundation
import UIKit
class TextSnippetEntryViewController: UIViewController {

    override func viewDidLoad() {
        super.viewDidLoad()
    }

    extension TextSnippetEntryViewController : UITextViewDelegate {
        func textViewDidEndEditing(textView: UITextView) {

        }
    }
}
```

So again, at the top, we declare the new class as a subclass of `UIViewController` by
using the colon, then below that we create an extension to implement the protocol.
We're going to be adding a `UITextView` later on, so we need to make sure the class
implements the `UITextViewDelegate` protocol. We are also adding a function stub
that will be called when the text view finishes editing, which is a part of that protocol
. There's not much more we can do in our Swift file until we do some work in our
storyboard, so let's move over to our `Main.storyboard` file now.

From the object library, drag in a new view controller. First, we need to change the
class of the view controller to reference the new class we just made. Click on the little
yellow view controller icon on top of the VC in the storyboard (it's a yellow circle
with a white square) to select the VC. Then, go to the identity inspector (*option+
command + 3*) and change the **Class** attribute to `TextSnippetEntryViewController`:

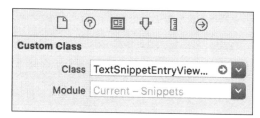

Figure 6.4: Changing the custom class of the view controller in a storyboard

Directly underneath the **Custom Class** section is the **Identity** section. Here, we're going to set the Storyboard ID to `textSnippetEntry`. Later, we'll use this ID to move to this view controller via code. I think it's time to add a little color to the project, so click inside the new view controller to select the view, then set the background color to a nice orange, like in our pre-visualizations (and while you're at it, set our old view controller's background color to the same color). To set the color, go to the attributes inspector on the right sidebar (fourth column, or *option + command + 4*).

Next, drag a `UITextView` (note: *not* a `UITextField`) onto the new view controller. Go to the pin menu to set the Auto Layout constraints. Again, uncheck the **Constrain to margins** checkbox, then set the top to `8`, the bottom to `20`, and the sides to `0`. Set the update frames dropdown to `All`, and add the constraints. It should now fill most of the screen, leaving a little room at the top and bottom.

Next, we need to tell the `UITextView` that our view controller is going to be its delegate. Hold the control key and click on `Text View`, then drag to the view controller icon, like in the following image. Then select `delegate` from the **Outlets** dropdown:

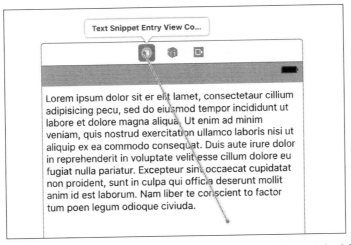

Figure 6.5: Control-dragging from our text view to the view controller to set the delegate

Before we leave the storyboard, we need to create an outlet to our `UITextView` in our view controller class. To do this, enter the assistant editor (*command + option + return*), make sure our `TextSnippetEntry...` class is visible in the assistant view, then control-drag from the `UITextView` into the top of our `TextSnippetEntry...` class. Name the outlet `textView`:

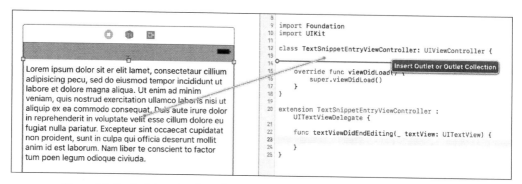

Figure 6.6: Control dragging from the text view to the view controller to create an outlet

Now that everything is set up in our storyboard, let's go back to `TextSnippetEntryViewController.swift` to finish adding the view controller logic. We need this view controller to do a few things. First, it needs to immediately present the keyboard. Then we need a button that completes text entry. Finally, we need to dismiss the view controller when text has finished editing.

The first part is very simple. In iOS, there is something known as the *responder chain*. Basically, it lets the app know which part of the app is directly responding to input events. In this case, we want our `Text View` to be the first responder, which will bring up the keyboard. To do this, we just have to write `textView.becomeFirstResponder()` in our `viewDidLoad()` function. Now, once the view controller loads, it will automatically bring up the keyboard:

```
override func viewDidLoad() {
    super.viewDidLoad()
    textView.becomeFirstResponder()
```

Next, we want to allow the user to tell the app they are done entering text. To do this, we are going to add a toolbar above our keyboard that has a `Done` button. When finished, it will look like this:

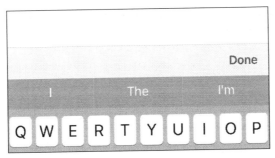

Figure 6.7: A keyboard accessory toolbar with a Done button

We're going to build this toolbar using code. Create a new function in our view controller called `createKeyboardToolbar()`, which returns a `UIView`. The function will look like this:

```
func createKeyboardToolbar () -> UIView {
    let keyboardToolbar = UIToolbar(frame: CGRect(x: 0, y: 0, width:
UIScreen.main.bounds.width, height: 44))

    let flexSpace = UIBarButtonItem(barButtonSystemItem:
.flexibleSpace, target: nil, action: nil)
    let doneButton = UIBarButtonItem(barButtonSystemItem: .done,
target: self, action: #selector(doneButtonPressed))
    keyboardToolbar.setItems([flexSpace, doneButton], animated: false)

    return keyboardToolbar
}
```

In the first line, we create a new `UIToolbar` and give it a width that is equal to the screen width, and a height of 44. Next, we create a few new `UIBarButtonItems` to put on our toolbar. If you remember from earlier, we used a `Flexible Space` bar button item to center our `New Snippet` button. Here, we create one through code and call it `flexSpace`. Then we create a `Done` button, which has a target of `self` and a selector called `doneButtonPressed`. This means that when someone presses our `Done` button, it will look for a function called `doneButtonPressed` on the target object of `self`. Finally, we add the bar button items to our toolbar, and return it.

The `doneButtonPressed` function needs to undo what we did at the beginning of the view controller. The opposite of `becomeFirstResponder()`, we'll be using `resignFirstResponder()` to let the `TextView` know that it's no longer being interacted with. The function should look like this:

```
func doneButtonPressed() {
    textView.resignFirstResponder()
}
```

Now that we've built a functional toolbar, we need to add it to our keyboard. To do this, we'll be using the `inputAccessoryView` property of our `UITextView` in the `viewDidLoad()` function. Our final `viewDidLoad()` should now look like this:

```
override func viewDidLoad() {
    super.viewDidLoad()
    textView.inputAccessoryView = createKeyboardToolbar()
    textView.becomeFirstResponder()
}
```

It assigns the keyboard toolbar, and then tells the `TextView` it is the first responder, bringing up the keyboard. Then, when you tap the **Done** button on the top of the keyboard, the keyboard is dismissed.

Once the keyboard is dismissed and the user has finished editing text, we want to dismiss the view controller and return to the main screen. This is as easy as one line of code in the function stub we created earlier in our `UITextFieldDelegate` extension:

```
func textViewDidEndEditing(textView: UITextView) {
    dismiss(animated: true, completion: nil)
}
```

Since we set our view controller to be the delegate of our `UITextView`, the text view will call specific functions in our view controller during certain events. Those functions are outlined in the `UITextViewDelegate` protocol, which our view controller implements. The `textViewDidEndEditing(textView: UITextView)` function is one of those functions, and is called when the text view leaves edit mode.

> Using delegate protocols is pretty common in iOS, and this won't be the last time we use one in this book. If you forget what a protocol is, you can go back and brush up on the features of Swift in *Chapter 3, Introduction to Swift 3*.

Now, when our view controller is presented, it will automatically present the keyboard with a toolbar on top, and when you press the Done button the keyboard will be dismissed, and then the view controller itself will be dismissed. All we have left to do is connect this view controller to our initial view controller and grab the text data.

Let's head back to the original view controller. First, we want to change what happens when we select the text option from our snippet type action sheet. We're going to change it so that it only calls a single (new) function called `createNewTextSnippet()`. Our definition for our `textAction` in the `createNewSnippet()` function should now look like this:

```
let textAction = UIAlertAction(title: "Text", style: .default) {
(alert: UIAlertAction!) -> Void in
    self.createNewTextSnippet()
}
```

Now we have to actually write that `createNewTextSnippet()` function. The function will instantiate our `TextSnippetEntryViewController`, then set it up, and finally present it:

```
func createNewTextSnippet () {
    guard let textEntryVC = storyboard?.instantiateViewController(wi
thIdentifier: "textSnippetEntry") as? TextSnippetEntryViewController
else {
        print("TextSnippetEntryViewController could not be
instantiated from storyboard")
        return
    }

    textEntryVC.modalTransitionStyle = .coverVertical
    present(textEntryVC,animated:true, completion:nil)
}
```

The first line we instantiate a new view controller using a storyboard ID (remember that from earlier?). We're also using a `guard` statement here, so that if our instantiation fails, we can catch the issue and write out the error to the console, and assume that our `textEntryVC` is valid throughout the rest of the function.

Then, we set up the `textEntryVC`. First we set its `modalTransitionStyle` to `.coverVertical`, which makes it slide up from the bottom when presented. Finally, we just present the view controller!

If you build and run, you can press the `New` button, select `Text`, enter text into the text field, press `Done`, and return to the main screen. Awesome! However, you'll notice we don't have anything being written to the command line confirming that we created a new `TextData` object! Let's fix that.

Head back to the `TextSnippetEntryViewController.swift` file. We are going to create a new property, but the type of the property is going to be a *closure*. To do this, add the following line to the top of the class:

```
var saveText: (_ text: String) -> Void = { (text:String) in }
```

Here, we're creating a new closure, called `saveText`, that takes one `String` parameter called `text`, and returns nothing. Then we are giving it a default value of a closure with no body. Now, go down to the `textViewDidEndEditing()` function, and just before we dismiss the view controller, we're going to execute our closure and pass in our UITextView's text:

```
func textViewDidEndEditing(textView: UITextView) {
    saveText(textView.text)
    dismiss (true, completion: nil)
}
```

That's great, but what exactly is this doing? Right now, nothing. We've got an empty closure, *but* the closure is now taking the text from our `TextView` as an input. All we have to do is modify the body of our closure to use that text to create a `TextData` snippet object, which is exactly what we're going to do.

Go back to our `ViewController.swift` file, to our `createNewTextSnippet()` function. Just below the line where we set the `modalTransitionStyle`, we are going to redefine the body of the other view controller's `saveText` closure:

```
textEntryVC.modalTransitionStyle = .CoverVertical
textEntryVC.saveText = { ( text: String ) in
    let newTextSnippet = TextData(text: text)
    self.data.append(newTextSnippet)
}
```

As you can see, we modified the body of the closure to use the input to create a new text snippet, and save it to our data array! There are other ways to accomplish this task, but we took this route to see an interesting way that closures can be used to accomplish our goals.

Now if you build and run, when you enter text and hit done, the closure we just wrote will be executed and a new `TextData` object will be created with the contents of the `UITextView`, and it will be saved.

Another story completed! Commit your work (*option + command + C*), and let's move on. (You can also remove the *lorem ipsum* placeholder text from the text view in the storyboard, if you haven't done so already.)

Here's the current state of our view controllers, if you are having any issues:

TextSnippetEntryViewController.swift:

```swift
import Foundation
import UIKit

class TextSnippetEntryViewController: UIViewController {

    @IBOutlet weak var textView: UITextView!

    var saveText: (_ text: String) -> Void = { (text:String) in }

    override func viewDidLoad() {
        super.viewDidLoad()

        textView.inputAccessoryView = createKeyboardToolbar()
        textView.becomeFirstResponder()
    }


    func createKeyboardToolbar () -> UIView {
        let keyboardToolbar = UIToolbar(frame: CGRect(x: 0, y: 0,
width: UIScreen.main.bounds.width, height: 44))

        let flexSpace = UIBarButtonItem(barButtonSystemItem:
.flexibleSpace, target: nil, action: nil)
        let doneButton = UIBarButtonItem(barButtonSystemItem: .done,
target: self, action: #selector(doneButtonPressed))
        keyboardToolbar.setItems([flexSpace, doneButton], animated:
false)

        return keyboardToolbar
    }

    func doneButtonPressed() {
        textView.resignFirstResponder()
    }
}
extension TextSnippetEntryViewController : UITextViewDelegate {

    func textViewDidEndEditing(_ textView: UITextView) {
        saveText(textView.text)
        dismiss(animated: true, completion: nil)
    }
}
```

ViewController.swift:

```swift
import UIKit

class ViewController: UIViewController {

    var data: [SnippetData] = [SnippetData]()



    override func viewDidLoad() {
        super.viewDidLoad()
    }

    @IBAction func createNewSnippet(_ sender: AnyObject) {

        let alert = UIAlertController(title: "Select a snippet type",
message: nil, preferredStyle: .actionSheet)
        let textAction = UIAlertAction(title: "Text", style: .default)
{ (alert: UIAlertAction!) -> Void in
            self.createNewTextSnippet()
        }
        let photoAction = UIAlertAction(title: "Photo", style:
.default) { (alert: UIAlertAction!) -> Void in
            self.data.append(SnippetData(snippetType: .photo))

        }
        let cancelAction = UIAlertAction(title: "Cancel", style:
.cancel, handler: nil)

        alert.addAction(textAction)
        alert.addAction(photoAction)
        alert.addAction(cancelAction)
        present(alert, animated: true, completion:nil)
    }

    func createNewTextSnippet() {
        guard let textEntryVC = storyboard?.instantiateViewController(
withIdentifier: "textSnippetEntry") as? TextSnippetEntryViewController
else {
            print("TextSnippetEntryViewController could not be
instantiated from storyboard")
            return
        }
```

```
textEntryVC.modalTransitionStyle = .coverVertical
textEntryVC.saveText = { ( text: String ) in
    let newTextSnippet = TextData(text: text)
    self.data.append(newTextSnippet)
}

present(textEntryVC,animated:true, completion:nil)
    }
}
```

PhotoSnippet implementation

Now that we've added text snippets, let's allow the user to create photo snippets. This user story says "I want to attach a photo to a snippet". The associated tasks are:

- Create a new subclass of SnippetData that represents the PhotoSnippet
- Create a new view controller with a UIImagePickerController that allows the user to take a picture and save the data to the PhotoSnippet.

Just like our last story, we're first going to update our data model to support the new snippet we are creating. Then we're going to build another data entry view controller, but this time it will let the user take a picture. Don't worry, though; it might be easier than you think.

Update SnippetData model

Current task: Create a new subclass of SnippetData that represents the PhotoSnippet.

For our photo snippet, we'll be creating another subclass of the SnippetData class. However, instead of holding a String property, it's going to hold a UIImage. To start, head over to our SnippetData.swift file, and add a new import to the top of the file, underneath the existing Foundation import:

```
import Foundation
import UIKit
```

This allows us to use the UIImage class in our new data structure. Next, create a new class below our TextData class called PhotoSnippet:

```
class PhotoData: SnippetData {
    let photoData: UIImage
```

```
init ( photo: UIImage ) {
    photoData = photo
    super.init(snippetType: .Photo)
    print ("Photo snippet data: \(photoData)")
}
}
```

This should look almost exactly like our `TextData` class, except we are replacing most of the instances of the word `Text` with the word `Photo`, for obvious reasons. Like I said earlier, the most important change is that we are now storing a `UIImage` instead of a `String`.

PhotoSnippet data entry

Current task: Create a new view controller with a `UIImagePickerController` that allows the user to take a picture and save the data to the `PhotoData` snippet.

With our data model updated, we now need to create a way for the user to take a photo and save it. To do this we are going to use a `UIImagePickerController`, which is a very convenient class that allows us to let the user take a picture or select a photo from their library. Because `UIImagePickerController` inherits from `UIViewController`, we don't even need to create a new view controller class of our own!

To get started, let's go to our base view controller class, `ViewController`. `swift`. Like in the last section, we are going to be adding an extension to our `ViewController` class to handle a delegate protocol so that it can implement some callback functions of the `UIImagePickerController`. Let's update our class declaration to include the necessary extension below the main class:

```
extension ViewController : UIImagePickerControllerDelegate,
UINavigationControllerDelegate {

}
```

Here, we added `UIImagePickerControllerDelegate` and `UINavigationControllerDelegate`, to a `UIViewController` class extension. While we won't be using any Navigation Controller delegate functions, we still need to include it, since `UIImagePickerController` inherits from `UINavigationController`.

At the top of our class, we are going to create a new instance of the image picker so that we can use it throughout our code. Just below the line where we initialize our array of `SnippetData`, we'll add our image picker:

```
var data: [SnippetData] = [SnippetData]()
let imagePicker = UIImagePickerController()
```

Then, we need to assign its delegate, so it knows which object is responsible for handling the functions that it is delegating. In this case, we are just going to handle the delegate functions right here in our `ViewController` class, so we'll assign the image picker's delegate in the `viewDidLoad()`. Our updated `viewDidLoad()` function should now look like this:

```
override func viewDidLoad() {
    super.viewDidLoad()
    imagePicker.delegate = self
}
```

Great! Now we have created a new `UIImagePickerController`, and set up our `ViewController` class to be its delegate. Next, let's create a `createNewPhotoSnippet()` function, much like we did with the text snippet. Then, in our `photoAction` completion handler, we'll have it call the new function:

```
let photoAction = UIAlertAction(title: "Photo", style: .default) {
(alert: UIAlertAction!) -> Void in
    self.createNewPhotoSnippet()
}
```

As for the `createNewPhotoSnippet()` function itself, it needs to perform two tasks: set up our image picker, and present the view controller:

```
func createNewPhotoSnippet () {
    guard UIImagePickerController.isSourceTypeAvailable(.camera) else
{
        print ("Camera is not available")
        return
    }

    imagePicker.allowsEditing = true
    imagePicker.sourceType = .camera

    present(imagePicker, animated: true, completion: nil)
}
```

At the top of the function, we use another guard statement to check if the camera source type is available. If the camera is unavailable (for example, if you try to run this in the simulator), then our code can print out the issue, and return gracefully.

Then, we do some basic setup on our image picker. First, we set `allowsEditing` to `true`, which lets the user crop the photo they take into a square. Then we set the `sourceType` of our image picker to `camera` (other source types include the user's photo library, or the user's saved photos). Finally, we present the Image Picker View controller.

Before we can use the camera, however, we need to add some information to our app's `Info.plist` file. When the device asks the user if it can use the camera, it needs some text to show the user so they know *why* the camera is being used. To add this, select the `Info.plist` file from the project navigator. Add a row by hovering over an existing row, and clicking the little plus-button that shows up. For the key, write **Privacy - Camera Usage Description** (it should autocomplete). Then for the description, you can write whatever you like—I wrote **Snippets needs to access the camera to create photo snippets**.

Key		Type	Value
▼ Information Property List		Dictionary	(14 items)
Localization native development region	⇕	String	en
Executable file	⇕	String	$(EXECUTABLE_NAME)
Bundle identifier	⇕	String	$(PRODUCT_BUNDLE_IDENTIFIER)
InfoDictionary version	⇕	String	6.0
Bundle name	⇕	String	$(PRODUCT_NAME)
Bundle OS Type code	⇕	String	APPL
Bundle versions string, short	⇕	String	1.0
Bundle version	⇕	String	1
Application requires iPhone environment	⇕	Boolean	YES
Launch screen interface file base name	⇕	String	LaunchScreen
Main storyboard file base name	⇕	String	Main
Privacy - Camera Usage Description	⇕ ⊕ ⊖	String	Snippets needs to access the camera to create photo snippets.
▶ Required device capabilities	⇕	Array	(1 item)
▶ Supported interface orientations	⇕	Array	(3 items)

Figure 6.8: Adding a camera privacy usage description to our app's info file

At this point, you should be able to run the project on your device (with a camera!), and see the `UIImagePickerController` in action. Tap the `New` button, then select `Photo`, and a familiar image-taking interface should slide up, allowing you to take a picture. *Make sure to allow the app to access the camera when prompted*! Now all that is left to do is to implement a `delegate` function that tells the app what to do with the pictures that we take:

Figure 6.9: Snippets asking for permission to use the camera.

Inside our class extension, we're going to implement a function that will be called when we finish taking our picture. As part of the image picker delegate protocol, it will be called automatically:

```
func imagePickerController(_ picker: UIImagePickerController,
didFinishPickingMediaWithInfo info: [String : Any]) {
    guard let image = info[UIImagePickerControllerEditedImage] as?
UIImage else {
        print("Image could not be found")
        return
    }

    let newPhotoSnippet = PhotoData(photo: image)
    self.data.append(newPhotoSnippet)

    dismiss(animated: true, completion: nil)
}
```

The first thing we do is use another `guard` statement to make sure we can find a valid edited photo from our image picker. To find the image, we're looking inside the `info` array that the function is passed, which contains a handful of information.

 When dealing with delegate protocols like this, it's best to check out the Apple documentation to see what is going on inside. That's how we learn about what functions exist to implement, and what might be inside something like the "info" array we used previously.

After we make sure that we have a valid image, we create a new photo snippet by initializing it with said image. Then, we add the photo snippet to our data array. Finally, we tell the image picker that it can be dismissed.

If you try running the app again, you'll notice that when you finish taking the photo, the app will write out the console, letting us know that we created a new PhotoData object. Success!

Hopefully you've seen how powerful classes can be hidden throughout the iOS SDK. It took significantly less effort to take, crop, and save a picture than it did to enter and save some text in the last part.

Again, make sure to commit your work (*option + command + C*) before moving on. Here's the new code we added to ViewController, in case you have any issues:

```
class ViewController: UIViewController,

    var data: [SnippetData] = [SnippetData]()
    let imagePicker = UIImagePickerController()

    override func viewDidLoad() {
        super.viewDidLoad()
        imagePicker.delegate = self
    }


    @IBAction func createNewSnippet(_ sender: AnyObject) {

        let alert = UIAlertController(title: "Select a snippet type",
message: nil, preferredStyle: .actionSheet)
        let textAction = UIAlertAction(title: "Text", style: .default)
{ (alert: UIAlertAction!) -> Void in
            self.createNewTextSnippet()
        }
        let photoAction = UIAlertAction(title: "Photo", style:
.default) { (alert: UIAlertAction!) -> Void in
            self.createNewPhotoSnippet()
        }
        let cancelAction = UIAlertAction(title: "Cancel", style:
.cancel, handler: nil)

        alert.addAction(textAction)
        alert.addAction(photoAction)
        alert.addAction(cancelAction)
        present(alert, animated: true, completion:nil)
    }


    func createNewPhotoSnippet() {
        guard UIImagePickerController.isSourceTypeAvailable(.camera)
else {
```

```
        print ("Camera is not available")
        return
    }

    imagePicker.allowsEditing = true
    imagePicker.sourceType = .camera

    present(imagePicker, animated: true, completion: nil)
  }

}

extension ViewController : UIImagePickerControllerDelegate,
UINavigationControllerDelegate {

    func imagePickerController(_ picker: UIImagePickerController,
didFinishPickingMediaWithInfo info: [String : Any]) {
        guard let image = info[UIImagePickerControllerEditedImage] as?
UIImage else {
            print("Image could not be found")
            return
        }

        let newPhotoSnippet = PhotoData(photo: image)
        self.data.append(newPhotoSnippet)

        dismiss(animated: true, completion: nil)
    }
}
```

Scroll through snippets

All this time, we've been building out our data model and adding ways to input new information. However, we still can't see any of the snippets we've been making! Now it's time to actually let the user see what they've been saving.

The next story is "I want to scroll through my snippets". The tasks that we need to complete are:

- Adding a UITableView to our first scene, with two prototype cells for the TextSnippet and the PhotoSnippet

- Programming the view controller to display the information from our data array in our UITableView

To satisfy our user story, we're going to use a `UITableView`, which allows us to scroll through cells of data. We're also going to create our own custom cells (called *prototype* cells) to define a distinct look for both the Text and Photo type cells. Then, we are going to populate the table view with data from our data array.

Create prototype cells

Current task: Add a `UITableView` to our first scene, with two prototype cells for the `TextSnippet` and the `PhotoSnippet`.

The first part of this story has us building out custom views to display the snippet data we've been creating. As we just discussed, we'll be using a `UITableView` with prototype cells. The table view is a special type of view that will manage and display a list of data cells that the user can scroll through. However, in order to use a table view, we are going to once again use a protocol.

Head over to `ViewController.swift`, and let's add yet another extension to implement a protocol:

```
extension ViewController: UITableViewDataSource {

}
```

The new protocol that we added is `UITableViewDataSource`, which lets the table view know which object is responsible for telling it what its data is. In the next task we will actually implement some of that protocol's functions, but for now we just need to let the class know that it implements that protocol.

Let's go back to `Main.storyboard`. On our initial view controller (the one with the `New` snippet button), we're going to add a **Table View** (*not* a Table View Controller) from the object library. Just drag it out to the center and resize it so the sides touch the edges of the screen, the top touches the bottom of the status bar, and the bottom touches the top of the toolbar.

Now we're going to use Auto Layout to configure our table view. Select the table view, and then go to the pin menu. On the top area, we're going to set constraints for all four sides. Again, first uncheck the box that says **Constrain to margins**, then set all four sides to `0`. Remember to click on the little red lines next to the numbers to create that constraint. Then set **Update frames** to `All`, and click **Add Constraints**.

Now that our table view is in our view and set up with Auto Layout, we want to set up its data source. Earlier, we set our ViewController class to implement the UITableViewControllerDataSource protocol, so we want to let our new table view know that ViewController will manage its data source. To do this, control-drag from the table view up to the view controller icon on the top of our view controller:

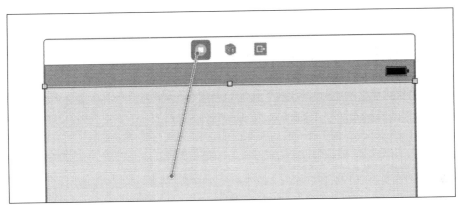

Figure 6.10: Control-dragging from the table view to the view controller to set the data source

When you let go, it should show two outlets: delegate, and data source. Select the dataSource outlet to connect the two objects together.

To finish up with the table view itself, select the table view and check out the Attributes Inspector (*option + command + 4*). In the second section, you should set the **Separator** attribute to None. This will get rid of the little lines that show up between each cell. Finally, scroll down toward the bottom to the View category. Change the background color to Clear color. This will let us see through to the orange background color of the app.

Next, it's time to create our custom cells. Before we create the visual parts, we're going to need some very simple custom classes to back them up. Create two new files (*command + N*), and name the first one TextSnippetCell, and the second PhotoSnippetCell. In each file, we're going to create a very simple subclass of the UITableViewCell, which is the default cell type in Table View:

TextSnippetCell.swift:

```
import UIKit

class TextSnippetCell: UITableViewCell {

    @IBOutlet var label: UILabel!

}
```

PhotoSnippetCell.swift:

```
import UIKit

class PhotoSnippetCell: UITableViewCell {

    @IBOutlet var photo: UIImageView!
}
```

In each subclass, we're only adding one interface builder outlet, which will point to the UI element where we'll be displaying our data.

Back in the storyboard, we are going to create the two cells that represent the classes we just made. In the object inspector, search for the UITableViewCell, and drag two into our table view:

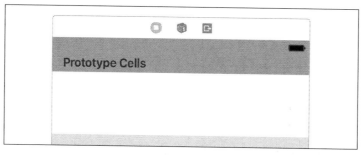

Figure 6.11: Two blank table view cells in our table view

Right now, each of these cells represents the standard UITableViewCell, but we have to assign them a custom class type using our new TextSnippetCell and PhotoSnippetCell classes. Let's set up the text cell first.

Select the first cell, then go to its Identity Inspector (*option + command + 3*). In the Custom Class section, set its class to TextSnippetCell. Now the prototype cell knows that it is actually of the class TextSnippetCell. Next, go to the Attributes Inspector, and change the Identifier attribute to textSnippetCell. This is unrelated to the class, but we'll be using it later as an ID to reference the type of cells we want to use.

Next, we'll follow the same instructions as above, but for the second prototype cell. Instead, we'll set the class to PhotoSnippetCell, and the identifier to photoSnippetCell.

Now it's time to add custom UI elements to our cells, so that they can display our user data. Drag a UILabel out onto our top (text) cell, and a UIImageView onto our bottom (photo) cell.

For the `UILabel`, in the Attributes Inspector, set the `Lines` attribute to 0. Setting **Lines** to 0 allows the label to have as many lines as it needs without a cutoff. We need this, since our users are allowed to write as much text as they want. Our `UILabel` needs to grow to accommodate the user's text.

To finish setting up the `UILabel`, we need to configure its Auto Layout constraints. These are going to be pretty simple. Select the label, and go to the **Pin** menu. At the top, enable all four directional constraints, and set them all to 0. This time, you can leave the **Constrain to margins** checkbox enabled, since we actually want to use the margins this time. Set **Update Frames** to `All` and press **Add Constraints** to finish setup. Our `UILabel` is now complete.

Basically, what we did was anchor the height of the table view cell to our label. As more lines are added to the label, the cell will expand, since its edges are constrained to the label's edges.

Next we'll set up the `UIImageView` in our photo cell. The photo doesn't need any attributes changed, so we can get right to setting the auto layout constraints. From the **Pin** menu, we are once again going to set all four directional pins to 0, and we're going to *uncheck* the **Constrain to margins** box, since we want the image to stretch to the edge of the screen. This time, we are also going to use the **Aspect Ratio** constraint further down, so check that off as well. Now set **Update Frames** to `All` and press **Add Constraints** to set the constraints.

There are still more constraints to add, however! Select the image view again, and go to the `Align` menu (directly to the left of the `Pin` menu). Here, we're going to add **Horizontally in Container** with a value of 0, and **Vertically in Container** with a value of 0. Set **Update Frames** to `All` and press **Add Constraints** to set the constraints.

So far what we've done is tell the image view to expand all the way to the edges of its containing cell, and to stay centered vertically and horizontally. However, what we want is for the image to be perfectly square, and stretch the cell to be as tall as it is wide.

That's where the aspect ratio constraint comes in. If the pin constraints are pulling our image view to the edges of the cell, but the image is then forcing itself to be the same height as its width, it will stretch the cell out vertically, too. For this to work, we need to set the aspect ratio constraint to be `1:1`. Find the aspect ratio constraint in the document outline (underneath our image view), and then in the Inspector set its multiplier to `1:1`:

Figure 6.12: Finding the aspect ratio constraint in the document outline (left); setting its multiplier (right)

If everything went well, your constraints should be all set up now! However, it's worth noting that the cell height won't automatically update live in your storyboard, so the image will go off the bottom of the cell. When you run the app later, though, everything will be fine!

Now that all of our Auto Layout is set up, we have one last thing to do: we need to connect the outlets in our `TextSnippetCell` and `PhotoSnippetCell` to our storyboard. Click on the `textSnippetCell` object in the document outline, and then navigate to the Connections Inspector (*option + command + 6*). Find the `label` outlet in the **Outlets** section, then click and drag from the circle onto the label in the cell to connect them:

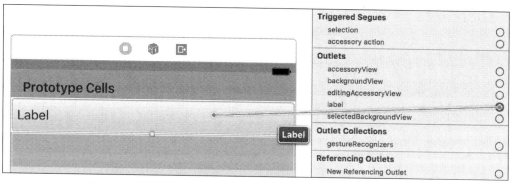

Figure 6.13: Connecting the label outlet to the UILabel in the storyboard

Do the same with the photo cell and its `photo` outlet with the image view:

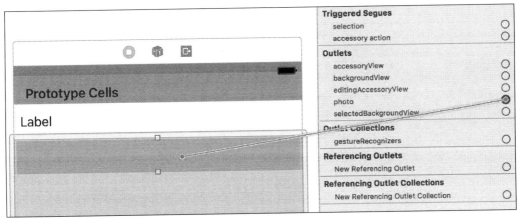

Figure 6.14: Connecting the photo outlet to the UIImage in the storyboard

And now our views are fully configured!

Populate table view

Current task: Program the view controller to display the information from our data array in our `UITableView`.

With our custom table view cells configured, we now have to set up the table view's data source. The prototype cells we built in our storyboard were just visual blueprints for cells. When our application is running, the table view will ask its data source to tell it what information it should present to the user. The data source is responsible for choosing what type of cell to use, and what data to fill those cells with.

Let's open up the `ViewController.swift` file, since that is the class that is our table view's data source. First, we're going to need a reference to our table view, so at the top of the class, add an `@IBOutlet` for the table view, like so:

```
@IBOutlet weak var tableView: UITableView!
```

Then, in `Main.storyboard`, use the assistant editor to connect the outlet to our table view:

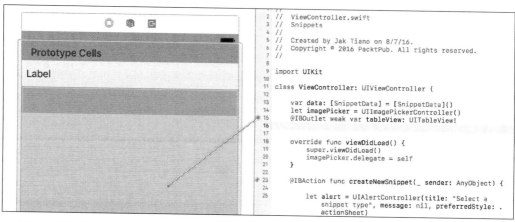

Figure 6.15: Dragging from the IBOutlet in the view controller into the storyboard to make a connection

Now, in our `viewDidLoad()` function, we can set some properties on our table view. Right now, if you were to run the app, the cells on the table view wouldn't expand vertically to match the content. That's because by default, `UITableViewCells` have a standard height of 44 points. You can set a custom height in the storyboard, but we don't want a single custom height, we want a *dynamic* height based on the content. We have to tell the table view that we want that behavior:

```
override func viewDidLoad() {
    super.viewDidLoad()
    imagePicker.delegate = self

    tableView.estimatedRowHeight = 100
    tableView.rowHeight = UITableViewAutomaticDimension
}
```

In our `viewDidLoad()` function, we added two lines; the first one gives the table view an estimated height (this mostly just has to not be 0), and the second line tells the table view that the row height will be automatic. Now our table view will let Auto Layout dynamically resize each cell based on the content and our Auto Layout constraints.

Next, we are going to implement some functions from the UITableViewDataSource protocol class extension that we added a little while ago. The functions that we are going to add are as follows:

```
func numberOfSections(in tableView: UITableView) -> Int {

}

func tableView(_ tableView: UITableView, numberOfRowsInSection
section: Int) -> Int {

}

func tableView(_ tableView: UITableView, cellForRowAt indexPath:
IndexPath) -> UITableViewCell {

}
```

The first function needs to return an Int that tells the table view how many sections it will have. A section in a table view is used to group different parts of the table (think about the Settings.app), and each section can have a header. In our app, we are just going to have one big section with no header, so we're just going to return 1:

```
func numberOfSections(in tableView: UITableView) -> Int {
    return 1
}
```

The second function tells the table how many rows are in a given section. Since we only have one section, we don't have to take into account which section it is asking about; we only have to return a single value. Since our table is going to store all of our snippets, the number of rows will be equal to the number of snippet data objects we have. That means it's as simple as returning the length of our data array:

```
func tableView(_ tableView: UITableView, numberOfRowsInSection
section: Int) -> Int {
    return data.count
}
```

At this point, our table knows how many sections and rows it has. Now it just needs to know what goes in each cell. For that, we're going to use the last function, tableView(cellForRowAtIndexPath:). This function gives us an index, and asks for us to give it a cell.

Before we look at the code, let's talk about how this will work. We're going to use the index to ask our data array what data is at that index. Then we're going to check what type of data it is, and then configure a new cell based on that information:

```swift
func tableView(_ tableView: UITableView, cellForRowAt indexPath:
IndexPath) -> UITableViewCell {

    let cell: UITableViewCell

    let sortedData = data.reversed() as [SnippetData]
    let snippetData = sortedData[indexPath.row]

    switch snippetData.type
    {
    case .text:
        cell = tableView.dequeueReusableCell(withIdentifier:
"textSnippetCell", for: indexPath)
        (cell as! TextSnippetCell).label.text = (snippetData as!
TextData).textData

    case .photo:
        cell = tableView.dequeueReusableCell(withIdentifier:
"photoSnippetCell", for: indexPath)
        (cell as! PhotoSnippetCell).photo.image = (snippetData as!
PhotoData).photoData
    }

    return cell
}
```

Let's start from the top. First, we declare a cell that will be a UITableViewCell. We don't assign it a value just yet. Then, underneath that, we *sort* our data. Since we want our table view to list our snippets in *reverse* chronological order, we need get the reversed version of our data array. Now that we have a sorted data array, we ask for the specific data at the specified row. (Note how this functions passes in an indexPath value as a parameter.)

Once we have the specific data that we are making a cell for, we need to know what kind of data it is, so we can create the right kind of cell. To do that, we use a switch statement with the snippetData's type, which is an enum. Then we make two cases, depending on if the type enum was .text, or .photo.

In the case that the type was `.text`, we want to create a cell using the `textSnippetCell` prototype cell from our storyboard. To do that, we call the function `dequeueReusableCell()`, and pass in the `String` identifier for the prototype cell we want to use.

 UITableView is smart, and doesn't create and delete new table view cells all the time. Instead, it only has a handful of cells that it reuses as cells go off the screen, and new ones come on screen. Imagine if we had tens of thousands of pieces of data... we'd run out of memory trying to create that many cells! So when you use `dequeueReusableCell()`, you are actually just asking the table view for an already existing and available cell of the right type.

After we dequeue the cell, we want to take the text from our data, and put it into the label in our cell. However, since `cell` thinks it is a `UITableViewCell` class, and `snippetData` thinks it is a `SnippetData` class, we need to *cast* the data to the appropriate subclass:

```
(cell as! TextSnippetCell).label.text = (snippetData as! TextData).
textData
```

We tell the `cell` that it should be read as a `TextSnippetCell`, and the `snippetData` that it should be read as a `TextData` object. Then we can access their properties, because the compiler knows what type they are. The exclamation point (`!`) forces the cast, otherwise we'd end up with an optional value.

Underneath all that, we just do the same thing, except for the photo cell. Here we use the cell identifier `photoSnippetCell`, and then cast `cell` as `PhotoSnippetCell` and `snippetData` as `PhotoData`. Also, instead of setting the label's text property in the cell, we are setting the image property of the `photo` (which is a `UIImageView`).

At the end, we just return the cell.

If you were to build and run on your device and create a new snippet... nothing happens. Where is our snippet? Well, our table view has a data source, but it doesn't know when to load the data from the data source. Naturally, it tries to load the data when the app starts, but in our case there's no data yet.

Luckily, this is a quick fix. We want to refresh the data whenever one of our popover view controllers is dismissed. To do this, add this function to the class, near the top (under `viewDidLoad()` is a good place for it):

```
override func viewWillAppear(_ animated: Bool) {
    tableView.reloadData()
}
```

The `viewWillAppear()` function is called just before the view controller becomes visible to the user, making it the perfect time to tell our `tableView` to reload its data.

Build and run the project now, create a new snippet... and it works! We can now create as many snippets as we want, and scroll through them. Our app is almost complete! Remember to commit your work (*option + command + C*), and now let's move on to our final user story.

Snippet dates

Our last story is a pretty simple one: "I want to see the date a snippet was made". To do this, we're going to have to accomplish the following tasks:

- Appending our base `SnippetData` to hold a date
- When a snippet is created, saving the current date to our data model
- Adding a `UILabel` to our prototype cells to hold date information, and assign the text in our `view` controller

This should be a fairly straightforward feature to add, especially since we set up the rest of our code pretty neatly. Let's get to it.

Update SnippetData model

Current task: Append our base `SnippetData` to hold a date.

First, let's make a quick update to our data model, in `SnippetData.swift`. In our base class of `SnippetData`, we want to add a new property called `date`, of the type `Date`. We then also need to update all of our initializers to accept a value for the date, and we then assign that date to our `date` property. Here is the updated source code for our data model, with the changed lines highlighted:

```
class SnippetData {
    let type: SnippetType
    let date: Date
```

```swift
    init ( snippetType: SnippetType, creationDate: Date ) {
        type = snippetType
        date = creationDate
        print ("\(type.rawValue) snippet created at \(date)")
    }
}

class TextData: SnippetData {
    let textData: String

    init ( text: String, creationDate: Date ) {
        textData = text
        super.init(snippetType: .text, creationDate: creationDate)
        print ("Text snippet data: \(textData)")
    }
}

class PhotoData: SnippetData {
    let photoData: UIImage

    init ( photo: UIImage, creationDate: Date ) {
        photoData = photo
        super.init(snippetType: .photo, creationDate: creationDate)
        print ("Photo snippet data: \(photoData)")
    }
}
```

Simply enough, our updated data model is complete.

Save data to model

Current task: When a snippet is created, save the current date to our data model.

Next, we need to actually assign the current date to our data when we create it. Luckily, this is also pretty easy. If you create a new Date object with no arguments, it will default to storing the current date. So a simple line like this will give you the current date:

```swift
let now = Date()
```

Taking this into account, we need to go into our `ViewController.swift` file, find the two places where we create our new `TextData` and `PhotoData` objects, and update the initializers to pass in the current date. In the `createNewTextSnippet()` function, we are going to change this line:

```
let newTextSnippet = TextData(text: text)
```

... to this:

```
let newTextSnippet = TextData(text: text, creationDate: NSDate())
```

Since `Date()` creates a new instance of an `Date` object with the current date, we can just create it and pass it into our `TextData` object at the same time.

Now, if we go down to our `imagePickerController( didFinishPickingMediaWithInfo: )` function where we create our `PhotoData` object, we can update it in a similar way:

```
let newPhotoSnippet = PhotoData(photo: image, creationDate: Date())
```

Now both of our snippet data structures are aware of the date they were created, and we just need to give them a place to be seen in our cells.

Update view and controller

Current task: Add a `UILabel` to our prototype cells to hold date information, and assign the text in our view controller.

This is the last task we need to complete to finish our MVP, so let's jump to it!

To show the user the date the snippet was created, we're going to create a little date bar underneath our main content view in each snippet using a new `UIView` and a `UILabel`. Open `Main.storyboard`, and let's get to work on the `textSnippetCell` first.

To begin, we're going to delete the bottom constraint on our label in the `textSnippetCell`. That's because we're going to add a new view underneath the label, and constrain it to that instead. To delete that constraint, click on the label and then from the Size Inspector (*option + command + 5*), double click the constraint that goes from the *bottom margin to Superview*:

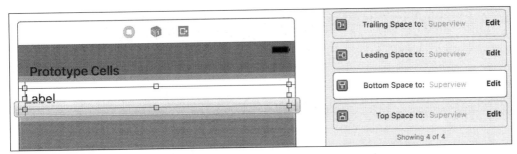

Figure 6.16: Selecting the bottom constraint from the Size Inspector

This should highlight the constraint in the **Document Outline**, where you can then delete it by pressing the *delete* key (remember, you can show the document outline from the **Editor** menu on the menu bar).

Next, from the object library, drag in a UIView into the text snippet cell prototype. From the Attributes Inspector, set the background color of the view to Light Gray. Then, from the **P**in menu, turn off Constrain to margins and set the following constraints: **Left:** 0, **Bottom:** 0, **Right:** 0, **Height:** 24. Set it to update the frames, and click **Add Constraints**. Resize our big label so that its bottom is above our gray view (If the cell is too small, you can select the cell from the **Document Outline**, then from the **Size Inspector** increase the height to around 80 points):

Figure 6.17: Our new gray view along the bottom of the cell, with the label resized without overlap

Now select the label again, and go to the **Pin** menu. Turn off **Constrain to margins**, and set a new bottom margin constraint with a value of 8. This will set the bottom of the label relative to the top of our gray view. Set it to update frames, and click **Add Constraints** (see *Figure 6.17*).

Finally, drag a new UILabel out from the object library and onto our grey view so that it becomes a subview. Then, with the new label selected, go to the **Pin** menu to set up the Auto Layout constraints. Turn off **Constrain to margins**, then set **Left:** 8, **Bottom:** 0, **Right:** 8, **Top:** 0. Set it to update frames, and click **Add Constraints:**

Figure 6.18: The final layout for the text snippet cell

Now, select the new label again, and from its Attributes Inspector, set the font color to white. And with that, our date footer is complete.

 At this point, we should set up the same date footer on our photoSnippetCell, but due to the size of the cell and the way the interface builder works, the Auto Layout constraints are very difficult to set up, especially for a novice. So instead, we'll continue on without doing so; but in the final project that is included with this chapter, you can see how the photo cell looks with the date footer.

Our view is set up, but we still need to let the backing class know that the new label exists. Open the `TextSnippetCell.swift` file, and add a new line to the class:

```
class TextSnippetCell : UITableViewCell {
    @IBOutlet var label: UILabel!
    @IBOutlet var date: UILabel!
}
```

Then, back in the storyboard, select the `textSnippetCell` in the **Document Outline**. Open the Connections Inspector (*option + command + 6*) and connect the new `date` outlet to the date label in our cell by dragging from the circle to the label:

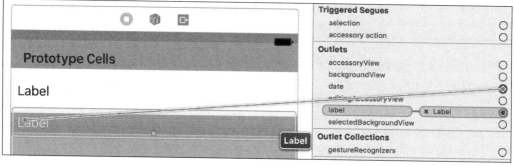

Figure 6.19: Connecting the date label outlet to the new label in the storyboard

And with that, we now have a code outlet to access our date label. The last thing we need to do is assign the text to our date label when we create the cell in our `ViewController`.

Open `ViewController.swift`, and navigate to the `tableView( cellForRowAt: )` function. Here we want to accomplish two things: we want to format the date stored in the `Date` to something readable, and then we want to assign the string to our date label.

Just above our `switch` statement, put these three lines of code:

```
let formatter = DateFormatter()
formatter.dateFormat = "MMM d, yyyy hh:mm a"
let dateString = formatter.stringFromDate(snippetData.date)
```

Here, we are creating a `DateFormatter`, which lets us create a custom way of formatting a date string. Then, we create a date string by telling the formatter to format a string with the date from our snippet data.

Then we just need to assign the date string to our date label's text field. Inside our `switch` statement, in the case for our `.Text` snippet type, add this line to the bottom of our cell set up code:

```
case .Text:
    cell = tableView.dequeueReusableCellWithIdentifier . . . .
    (cell as! TextSnippetCell).label.text . . . .
    (cell as! TextSnippetCell).date.text = dateString
```

Now our cell should display the date in the date label we created! Build and run the project to check that this is the case.

> At this point, you can commit your work (*option + command + C*). If you want, you can try to figure out how to set up the photo cell with the same date footer. If you can't figure it out (it is hard, so don't feel bad if you can't!), then you can look at the finished project to see how it looks on the photo cell.

And that's it! We've successfully completed every user story we laid out at the beginning of the chapter, and we've built an entire MVP for an app that allows the user to create multiple types of snippets, and then view them in a reverse chronological order timeline. It's a little rough around the edges, but it works, and we can get it in users' hands to see what they like and dislike.

> If you had any trouble during this chapter, you can look at the final project included with this chapter to see how your project may have differed. Look through the source code and storyboards to see if you can solve any problems you may have had. If it all worked okay, then great job!

Summary

This was quite the ride! We walked through every step, from app idea to visual development to project planning, all the way through six user stories, and ended up with a functioning minimum viable product. Now we get to keep testing and building on this app for the remainder of the book!

In the next chapter, we're going to take a look at multitouch and gestures. We'll learn about some fun ways to integrate those touch features into the next version of Snippets.

At this point in the book, we've reached a bit of a turning point. We've made a functioning app! The training wheels are off! But that also means we're going to stop spending so much time discussing how to do some things. From now on, I'm going to assume you know what the different areas of Xcode are called, so I won't give you the keyboard shortcut every time we navigate to a new area. I'm also going to assume that you know how to create a new storyboard outlet, and link a storyboard element to a code class.

If these things still seem unfamiliar to you, feel free to review the first five chapters of the book now, since we're going to be putting all of this knowledge to use simultaneously from here on out.

7
Integrating Multitouch and Gestures

When the iPhone was first released in 2007, the world of consumer electronics was accustomed to the resistive touchscreen, which required the use of a stylus and was limited to a single contact point. Because of these limitations, the multitouch capabilities of the original iPhone were a major selling point, and its operating system (now in its tenth iteration) was built around the idea of finger-based touch and gestures.

As the smartphone industry has evolved, all phones have moved toward this model of interaction. Capacitive touchscreens and gesture-based navigation is standard. With the exception of 3D touch in the 2015 iPhone models, the topic of multitouch hasn't changed since its inception.

However, as a developer, it is still your job to understand these aspects of app development. In this chapter, we're going to cover the following topics:

- The human interface guidelines for gestures in iOS
- Adding gestures to your app from the storyboard
- Adding gestures through code
- Setting up 3D touch shortcuts

For the beginning of this chapter, we're going to take a little break from our app, Snippets, and focus on how and when to use gestures. Since our app has plenty of built-in gesture control from using the UITableView, we'll be working in a new project to experiment, before coming back and adding 3D touch shortcut support to Snippets.

Human interface guidelines – gestures

When we use software, we expect it to act a certain way based on convention. When we see something that looks like a button, we expect to be able to tap it, and for some event to happen when it is tapped. Part of this comes from the fact that some methods of interaction are universally intuitive, and have been established for a long time. However, most application development environments come with a set of **Human Interface Guidelines (HIG)**, which outline the intended look, feel, and use of the software being created.

Apple, famous for its strict policies over design, has a very thorough set of HIG available for developers that make it easy to understand how they expect your software to function. While the full set of documentation covers many aspects of app interactions, we're going to focus on the standard gestures and what users expect from them.

Standard gestures

When using a touch screen device, there are only a handful of basic, intuitive gestures that a user can perform. These basic gestures are based on physical metaphor, and so most people have an expectation of how an app should react to their input. The gestures, as outlined in Apple's HIG, are as follows:

- **Tap**: The simple single tap is used to select items, or press buttons. The tap is the most widely used gesture in the entire operating system and can almost always be thought of as a *do something* gesture. When tapping on an element, the user will almost always expect something to happen. If an element would normally perform an action, but the action can't happen when the user taps it, there should at least be a visual indication that the tap was received.

- **Double Tap**: The double tap gesture is used to *focus* and *un-focus* on elements. Usually, the double tap will zoom to fill the screen with the double tapped area, as in web browsers, or mapping applications. When applicable, a second double tap will zoom back out to the default view.

- **Drag**: When the user places their finger down on the screen and moves it around, it is referred to as a drag. Dragging is primarily used to move the view vertically and horizontally. For example, in our app `Snippets`, the `UITableView` automatically uses the drag gesture to let you scroll up and down. In web browsers and map views, you can drag both vertically and horizontally to move the view in all directions. This gesture can also be referred to as a *pan*.

- **Flick**: Similar to the drag gesture, a flick is a drag that is executed quickly. Unlike a drag, a flick has momentum associated with it when the user finishes the gesture. That means that the movement of the view can continue after the user stops touching the screen, allowing them to flick quickly through lists.

- **Swipe**: A swipe gesture has several use cases. In a table view, it can bring up the `Delete` button on a cell. In apps with navigation controllers, swiping from the side of the screen can navigate back through the navigation stack. On an iPad, four fingers swiping up allow you to switch apps. Swiping is one of the most versatile gestures in iOS, and thus doesn't have much of a standard use. However, swiping is usually used to *move* objects on screen to reveal new information.

- **Pinch**: The pinch gesture is almost always used to zoom in and out. The most logical uses are again in web browsers, and map views, but it can be used in any situation where you might want to change the scaling of objects on screen.

- **Shake**: The shake gesture is unique, since it doesn't use the screen at all, and only uses the accelerometer data. The shake gesture is used throughout iOS to initiate an undo or redo action.

While all of these gestures are possible on a touch screen, when using `UIKit` (classes with the `UI` prefix, like `UITableView`) there's a good chance that you will get this functionality for free. Since Apple wants to make sure that their gestures are consistent, most of these `UI` classes have gestures built right in, like how `UITableView` in our app already supports tapping, dragging, and flicking automatically.

Usage guidelines

When implementing support for these basic gestures, Apple has several recommendations, or *usage guidelines*, for how these gestures should behave to maintain consistency.

The most important rule that should be followed is that you should *never associate different actions to these standard gestures*. No matter how intuitive you might think it would be to swap one of these gestures with a different activity, users of iOS software expect a standard method of interaction, and even the slightest changes can confuse users.

Second, *try not to create alternate gestures that perform the same tasks as one of the standard gestures*. This will also confuse users who might not understand why a certain task is now being completed in a different way.

Third, *complex gestures should only be used to expedite tasks, and should not be the only way to perform a given action.* While you as a developer might not understand why someone would go out of their way to perform a task when they could just use a custom gesture, it is still important to provide alternative ways to accomplish tasks.

Finally, *it is usually not a great idea to create new custom gestures at all.* Obviously there are exceptions to this rule, especially if you're making a game. However, if you are making a custom gesture to perform a task, you should really consider why it is necessary and if there are other ways to implement the feature.

With a good understanding of what the standard set of gestures are, in addition to the usage guidelines set forth by Apple, we are now in a good place to start learning how to implement these gestures in a development environment.

How gestures work

So far, we've discussed the *theory* of gestures: what they consist of, what they are expected to do, and how to use them. However, we should also take a little bit of time to understand how they work in *practice*. Even though you'll see that a lot of the basic gestures have an abstracted implementation provided by Apple, it's worth understanding how they work below the surface.

To understand the technical side of gestures, we need to first take a look at how the view hierarchy interprets touches. At the top of the inheritance chain is the simple `UIView` class. Essentially, `UIView` is a rectangle that can draw itself to the screen. However, it can also receive touch events. A `UIView` class contains a `userInteractionEnabled` property, which lets the view know whether it can receive touch information.

If interaction is enabled, `UIView` is alerted every time a touch begins, moves, and ends inside of it. You can actually override the methods that handle these events in any `UIView` subclass with `touchesBegan(_ touches: Set<UITouch>, with Event event: UIEvent?)`, `touchesMoved (_ touches: Set<UITouch>, with Event event: UIEvent?)`, and `touchesEnded (_ touches: Set<UITouch>, with Event event: UIEvent?)`.

In the very early days of iOS programming, app developers had to override those methods manually and track the movement of touches to identify gestures. As you can imagine, every developer had different ideas about how to implement those gestures, and functionality varied from app to app, breaking the consistency of interactions. It was also difficult to reuse gestures because you had to program the gesture recognition right into the `UIView` subclass.

To solve these issues, Apple created a UIGestureRecognizer class. This class provides those same touchesBegan() (and so on) methods, but decouples them from a specific view. This means you can write your gesture code once, and then attach the recognizer to different views. To make it even easier, Apple also provided subclasses for most of the basic gestures; UITapGestureRecognizer, UISwipeGestureRecognizer, and UIPinchGestureRecognizer are some examples.

For the next two sections, we'll be looking at the ways that we can implement these UIGestureRecognizer classes into an app. Using these provided gesture classes means that adding gestures is not only quick and easy, but consistent with the way Apple (and users!) expect the gestures to behave.

Adding gestures from the storyboard

So far, we've seen how to add interface elements to a storyboard, and then how to add constraints to keep the elements in their correct place. However, we can also add and configure gestures in our storyboard, and for simple gestures this can be quite powerful. In this section, we are going to add a double tap gesture to an image that will flip it upside down.

Before we get started, let's create a little test project for us to explore gesture input. Create a new Single View Application Xcode project (Swift/Universal), and name it Gestures. Don't bother creating a git repository for it. Before we start working, you'll also want to add the wink.png file in the resources folder of this chapter to your project folder, and then add the file to the Xcode project (*option + command + A*).

Setting up the storyboard

As per usual when working with the storyboard, we are going to implement most of our functionality without having to write any code.

To start, go to the storyboard and drag an image view onto our view controller. From the Attribute Inspector, set the image to wink.png. Give it a size of 200 x 200, add a width constraint, and then a 1:1 aspect constraint. Finally, give it a vertical center and horizontal center constraint, and we should have a square, centered image to play with.

Next, we're going to add a gesture to our storyboard. In the object library, search for tap, and you should see the UITapGestureRecognizer. Drag the gesture from the library onto the image view; this will create a link between the two.

Before we move on, remember earlier when we talked about how `UIView` has a `userInteractionEnabled` property? Well, while most default to `true`, `UIImageView` is set to `false` by default. That means that our gesture isn't going to receive touch information. To change this, go to the `Attributes Inspector`, and check the box that says **User Interaction Enabled**, as shown by the red arrow in *Figure 7.1*:

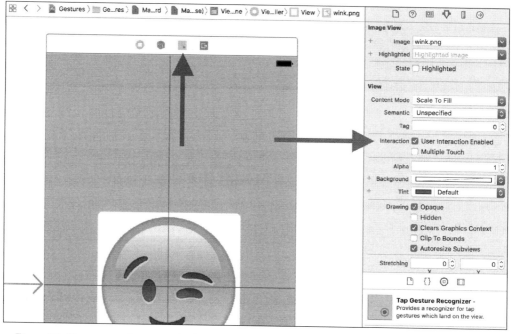

Figure 7.1: Blue arrow – the gesture in the storyboard; Red arrow – the User Interaction Enabled property

Next, we want to configure the gesture itself. If you look at the top of the view controller, you'll see a new icon that represents our tap gesture (the blue arrow in *Figure 7.1*). Like we said before, gesture recognizers are reusable, so they aren't added to specific views but to the view controller itself.

Click on the tap gesture icon in the view controller icon bar; you'll see its properties show up in the `Attribute Inspector`. Since we want to configure the tap gesture to be used as a double tap, we set it to recognize 2 **Taps** from 1 **Touch**:

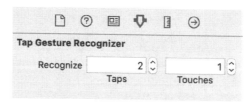

Figure 7.2: Configuring the tap gesture from the Attribute Inspector

The last step in the storyboard is to link up our objects to our view controller code. Go into the `Assistant Editor` view and create an `@IBOutlet` for the `UIImageView` with the name `imageView`. We are also going to create an `@IBAction` for the gesture. Just like creating outlets or actions for `UI` elements, you can control drag from the `tap` gesture icon into the view controller code:

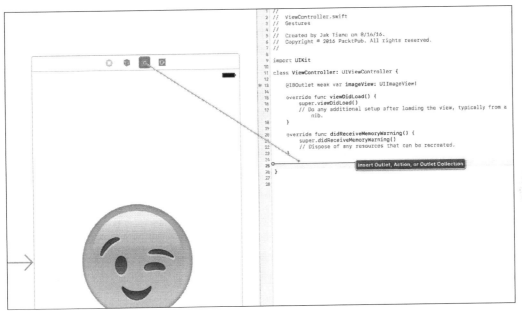

Figure 7.3: Control-dragging from the gesture in the storyboard to our ViewController.swift file

Here, you'll want to create an action named `flipImage`. This is the function that will be called when the gesture is recognized. With that, the double tap gesture is completely set up in the storyboard, and we just need to write a little code to actually make the image flip.

Flipping the image

If you build and run the app on your device, you'll see the wink image in the middle of the screen. We've set up the gesture, but when you double tap on the image nothing happens! Let's add a little functionality so we can see that our gesture is working properly.

First, we're going to add two properties to the top of our view controller class, a `UIImage` and a `Bool`:

```
var image = UIImage(named: "wink")
var flipped: Bool = false
```

The image stores a reference to the same wink image that we used in the storyboard, which we'll need when we flip the image later. The Boolean will be used to keep track of the state of the image.

Then, inside the `flipImage()` function, we are just going to switch the `Bool` to the opposite of its current state:

```
@IBAction func flipImage(sender: AnyObject) {
    flipped = !flipped
}
```

All that's left is to change the image when the `Bool` value changes. To do this, we're going to use a cool feature of Swift that lets us run some code whenever a value of a property is changed. Let's update our `flipped` property to look like this:

```
var flipped: Bool = false {
    didSet {
        if flipped {
            let temp = UIImage(cgImage: image!.cgImage!, scale: 1.0,
                orientation: .downMirrored)
            imageView.image = temp
        } else {
            imageView.image = image
        }
    }
}
```

After the property declaration, we'll add a set of brackets and then define a code block that runs after the property's value changes using the `didSet` keyword. Inside, we'll check to see if `flipped` is `true`, and if so, we change our the image of `imageView` to be the flipped version of the image. Otherwise, we use the standard one.

So now when we double tap the image, we flip our `flipped Bool`, which then automatically changes the image in our `UIImageView`. Build and run on your device, and then double tap the `wink` image to see our gesture recognizer in action.

Here's all of the code for the view controller. Look how much we accomplished with such a small amount of code:

```
import UIKit

class ViewController: UIViewController {

    @IBOutlet weak var imageView: UIImageView!
    var image = UIImage(named: "wink")
```

```
    var flipped: Bool = false {
        didSet {
            if flipped {
                let temp = UIImage(cgImage: image!.cgImage!, scale:
                    1.0, orientation: .downMirrored)
                imageView.image = temp
            } else {
                imageView.image = image
            }
        }
    }

    override func viewDidLoad() {
        super.viewDidLoad()
    }

    @IBAction func flipImage(_ sender: AnyObject) {
        flipped = !flipped
    }
}
```

Adding gestures from code

While implementing gestures from the storyboard is a simple and visual way to set up gestures, sometimes you'll need to get into the details and create them purely with code. In this section, we're going to look at how to do just that, by adding a pinch gesture recognizer that allows us to scale our image up and down.

Creating a gesture through code

The first thing we're going to need to do is create a property to hold our gesture. Since the gesture is going to be created outside of initialization, we are going to have to make it an implicitly unwrapped optional value (remember, that is shown with the exclamation mark after the variable name).

Here's a quick refresher on optional values in Swift:

First, there's a standard variable, which *must always* contain a value:

```
var view: UIView
```

Then, there's an optional variable, which *may or may not* have a value:

```
var view: UIView?
```

This means we need to *unwrap* the value every time we use it, to make sure there is a value inside, using the `if let` syntax:

```
if let unwrappedView = view { /* do something */}
```

Finally, an *implicitly unwrapped optional* value, which tells the compiler that there is definitely a value inside, means we don't need to unwrap it:

```
var view: UIView!
```

In our `ViewController.swift` file at the top of our class, create the property like so:

```
var pinchGesture: UIPinchGestureRecognizer!
```

Next, we have to create the gesture recognizer itself. When using the storyboard, you'll remember that the gesture recognizer didn't belong to any specific view, and was instead shown at the top of the view controller. Behind the scenes, the storyboard knows how to register and unregister the gesture recognizer with its associated views, since issues can occur if a gesture recognizer is connected to a view that gets deleted. Now, however, we're going to have to do this manually.

To do this, we are going to use the `viewWillAplear()` and `viewDidDisappear()` functions that are inherited from the `UIViewController` class. These are called (quite obviously) just before a view is presented, and then just after it is dismissed from the user. This is the perfect time to create and destroy gestures, since the views still exist, but the user can't see them:

```
override func viewWillAppear(_ animated: Bool) {
    super.viewWillAppear(animated)

    pinchGesture = UIPinchGestureRecognizer(target: self, action:
#selector(ViewController.pinch(_:)))
    view.addGestureRecognizer(pinchGesture)
}
```

In the `viewWillAppear()` function, we first call our superclass's implementation to make sure everything executes properly. Then, we create a new `UIPinchGestureRecognizer`, passing in the target object that will handle the gesture (`self`), and the method that will be called on that object. The `#selector` operator is a way of specifying that we're passing a function, in this case `ViewController.pinch(_:)`. Finally, we tell our view to add our pinch gesture:

```
override func viewDidDisappear(_ animated: Bool) {
    super.viewDidDisappear(animated)

    view.removeGestureRecognizer(pinchGesture)
    pinchGesture = nil
}
```

In the `viewDidDisappear()` function, we'll be doing the same thing in reverse. Again, first we call the superclass's function. Then we remove the gesture from the view, before setting the `pinchGesture` to `nil`. At this point, we've configured and managed the lifetime of our pinch gesture.

Reading the gesture data

Now that our gesture is set up, we want to process the data that it provides. In the last part, we registered the gesture to call a function called `pinch(_:)`. Now, we need to create that function and process the data.

The first thing we need to do is create some variables to track the scale that we get out of the gesture. Create these variables at the top of the file:

```
var lastScale: CGFloat = 1;
var currentScale: CGFloat = 1;
```

We'll update the `lastScale` value at the end of each cycle so that we can use it in the next frame. Then, we'll assign the new scale to the `currentScale` value, and ultimately use that to set the size of our image. Now let's create the `pinch` function itself:

```
func pinch(_ pinch: UIPinchGestureRecognizer) {

    if (pinch.state == .began) {
        lastScale = 1
    } else if (pinch.state == .changed) {
        let delta = pinch.scale - lastScale
        currentScale += delta
        lastScale = pinch.scale
    }
    print(currentScale)
}
```

The most important part of this function is that we're taking in the actual pinch gesture as an argument. First, we ask the gesture what state it's in; if it just started, we reset the `lastScale` variable, and if it changed we update the scale. To do that, we get the `delta` (change) of the scale by subtracting the last scale from the current scale. Then we add the `delta` to the current scale, and then update the last scale. Finally, we print out the current scale.

If you build and run, then pinch on the screen, you can see the scale changing in the console. Now we have our scale data, and we're ready to apply the scale to our image.

Changing the scale of our image

To change the size of our image, we're going to leverage the power of auto layout. The image is already locked to the center of the screen, and is forced to maintain a `1:1` aspect ratio. Therefore, all we have to do is modify its width constraint, and it will automatically make all the necessary adjustments.

To do this, we'll create a new property to store the starting width of our image:

```
var startWidth: CGFloat = 0
```

Then, we'll implement the `viewDidAppear()` function, where we'll grab the initial value. We need to use `viewDidAppear` instead of `viewWillAppear`, because the image view won't be properly sized yet inside the `viewWillAppear` function:

```
override func viewDidAppear(_ animated: Bool) {

    startWidth = imageView.frame.size.width
}
```

Here, we're setting the `startWidth` to be the width of the frame of `imageView`.

Before we move on, we're going to have to make it so that we can access the width constraint on our image view so we can update it. In the `Main.storyboard` file, find our **Image View** in the document outline, and then select its `width` constraint:

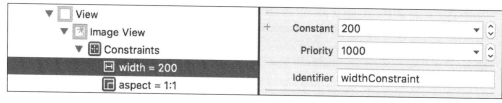

Figure 7.4: Selecting the width constraint, and giving it an identifier string

With the width constraint selected, find the `Identifier` field in the `Attribute Inspector`, and set it to `widthConstraint`. This string will be used as an ID so we can find this constraint in the next step.

Next, we're going to write a function that actually handles updating the constraint. Back in the `ViewController.swift` file, add a new function to our class:

```
func updateImageSize() {
    for constraint in imageView.constraints {
        if constraint.identifier == "widthConstraint" {
            constraint.constant = startWidth * currentScale
            break
        }
    }
}
```

First, we start running a `for` loop that looks for every constraint in our image's `constraints` array. Then for each constraint, we check to see if its identifier is `widthConstraint`, which we just set in the last step. If it's the correct constraint, we update the constraint's constant value to equal our starting width multiplied by our current scale, then we break out of the loop.

Great! Now we've got a function that will update our image's constraints, and therefore its whole size! We'll need to call this function every time we change the scale, so let's call it right at the end of our `pinch()` function:

```
func pinch(pinch: UIPinchGestureRecognizer) {
    if (pinch.state == .Began) {
        lastScale = 1
    } else if (pinch.state == .Changed) {
        let delta = pinch.scale - lastScale
        currentScale += delta
        lastScale = pinch.scale
    }
    updateImageSize()
}
```

If you build and run, you'll see that when we pinch in and out, our image grows and shrinks. Try double tapping the image, and you'll see it still flips in place too!

Here's the final look at our new (slightly more code heavy!) `ViewController` class:

```
class ViewController: UIViewController {

    @IBOutlet weak var imageView: UIImageView!
```

```swift
    var pinchGesture: UIPinchGestureRecognizer!
    var image = UIImage(named: "wink")
    var flipped: Bool = false {
        didSet {
            if flipped {
                let temp = UIImage(cgImage: image!.cgImage!, scale:
                    1.0, orientation: .downMirrored)
                imageView.image = temp
            } else {
                imageView.image = image
            }
        }
    }

    var lastScale: CGFloat = 1;
    var currentScale: CGFloat = 1;
    var startWidth: CGFloat = 0


    override func viewDidLoad() {
        super.viewDidLoad()
    }

    override func viewWillAppear(_ animated: Bool) {
        super.viewWillAppear(animated)

        pinchGesture = UIPinchGestureRecognizer(target: self, action:
#selector(ViewController.pinch(_:)))
        view.addGestureRecognizer(pinchGesture)
    }

    override func viewDidAppear(_ animated: Bool) {

        startWidth = imageView.frame.size.width
    }

    override func viewDidDisappear(_ animated: Bool) {
        super.viewDidDisappear(animated)

        view.removeGestureRecognizer(pinchGesture)
        pinchGesture = nil
    }
```

```swift
func pinch(_ pinch: UIPinchGestureRecognizer) {

    if (pinch.state == .began) {
        lastScale = 1
    } else if (pinch.state == .changed) {
        let delta = pinch.scale - lastScale
        currentScale += delta
        lastScale = pinch.scale
    }
    updateImageSize()
}

func updateImageSize() {
    for constraint in imageView.constraints {
        if constraint.identifier == "widthConstraint" {
            constraint.constant = startWidth * currentScale
            break
        }
    }
}

@IBAction func flipImage(_ sender: AnyObject) {
    flipped = !flipped
}
}
```

If you're up for a challenge...

Now that you've seen how to set up these gestures both with code and the storyboard, see if you can use Apple's documentation to use other gestures and come up with your own functionality! I recommend trying to use the `UISwipeGestureRecognizer`.

Creating 3D Touch app shortcuts

One of the coolest new features of the 2015 models of iPhones (iPhone 6s and 6s+) is their *3D Touch* capabilities. In this section, we're going to take a look at how to implement the new `Quick Action` app shortcuts in our app, `Snippets`. We're going to create two shortcut actions that allow us to create both a text snippet and photo snippet by using a hard press on the app icon.

> Unfortunately, as of this writing, Apple only allows 3D touch capabilities in their iOS 10 simulator if you have a force touch trackpad built into your mac laptop, or a new magic trackpad. This means that unless you have a physical 3D Touch-capable device or a force touch trackpad, you won't be able to test the code in this section. You can (and should!) still follow along and learn how to add this functionality for the future.

For this section, you'll want to open up the `Snippets` Xcode project that is in the *Chapter 6, Building Your First iOS App*, `resources` folder (since the project in current chapter will have the completed code from the *end* of this section). The project in the `resources` folder will have the finished auto layout constraints, just in case you weren't able to get the date bar to work on the photo snippet at the end of *Chapter 6, Building Your First iOS App*.

Setting up Info.plist

To let our app know about the possible shortcuts it can perform, we're going to have to add some information to our `Info.plist` file.

To get there, select the Xcode project in the `Project Navigator` sidebar (the blue file at the top), and then click on the **Info** tab along the top of the editor window:

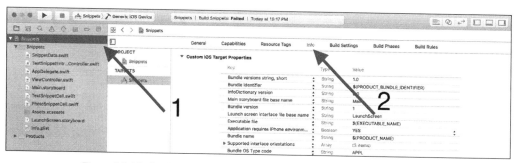

Figure 7.5: Navigating to the Info.plist file from the Xcode project settings file

This file is used to define certain capabilities and other assorted information about your application. Right now, we're going to add some new elements to the property list that describe the 3D touch shortcut actions.

First, we need to add a new row to the list. To do this, hover over any of the existing rows and click the **+** button that shows up near the middle to create a new row below it. In the **Key** column of the new row, type `UIApplicationShortcutItems`. In the **Type** column, set the type to `Array`.

Now we want to add two items to the array. To do this, *first* click the arrow next to the row to make it drop down, even though there are no elements yet. Now when you press the plus button on that row, it will create *child* elements within the array, instead of *new* elements below it. Do this twice to create two children, and then change their types to `Dictionary`:

Key		Type	Value
Bundle versions string, short	⬍	String	1.0
Bundle identifier	⬍	String	$(PRODUCT_BUNDLE_IDENTIFIER)
InfoDictionary version	⬍	String	6.0
Main storyboard file base name	⬍	String	Main
Bundle version	⬍	String	1
Launch screen interface file base name	⬍	String	LaunchScreen
Executable file	⬍	String	$(EXECUTABLE_NAME)
Application requires iPhone environm...	⬍	Boolean	YES
▼ UIApplicationShortcutItems	⬍	Array	(2 items)
▼ Item 0		Dictionary	(3 items)
UIApplicationShortcutItemType		String	com.PacktPub.Snippets.createPhotoSnippet
UIApplicationShortcutItemIconType		String	UIApplicationShortcutIconTypeCapturePhoto
UIApplicationShortcutItemTitle		String	New Photo Snippet
▼ Item 1		Dictionary	(3 items)
UIApplicationShortcutItemType		String	com.PacktPub.Snippets.createTextSnippet
UIApplicationShortcutItemIconType		String	UIApplicationShortcutIconTypeCompose
UIApplicationShortcutItemTitle		String	New Text Snippet
▶ Supported interface orientations	⬍	Array	(3 items)
Bundle name	⬍	String	$(PRODUCT_NAME)
Bundle OS Type code	⬍	String	APPL
Privacy - Camera Usage Description	⬍	String	Snippets needs to access the camera to create pho
Localization native development region	⬍	String	en
▶ Required device capabilities	⬍	Array	(1 item)

Figure 7.6: What our finished Info.plist file should look like

In both the *children* items (`Item 0` and `Item 1`), create *three* children of their own, all of type `String`. These three children should have the following keys: `UIApplicationShortcutItemTitle`, `UIApplicationShortcutItemIconType`, and `UIApplicationShortcutItemType`. The first element will be the text displayed in the shortcut, the second element will be the icon that is used, and the third element will be used as an ID in our code to process which shortcut was used.

`Item 0` will describe our `New Photo Snippet` action. In the first element, the `ItemTitle` element, type `New Photo Snippet`. This will be the exact text displayed when the user sees the shortcut options. Next, for the `ItemIconType` element, we're going to use the `UIApplicationShortcutIconTypeCapturePhoto`, which is a built-in system icon that looks like a camera. Finally, for the `ItemType` element, type `com.PacktPub.Snippets.createPhotoSnippet`. You'll notice that this is our app's bundle identifier, followed by `createPhotoSnippet`, which describes our action.

In `Item 1`, we're doing very similar work. The title will be `New Text Snippet`, the icon type will be `UIApplicationShortcutIconTypeCompose`, and the item type will be `com.PacktPub.Snippets.createTextSnippet`.

At this point, if you build and run the app *on a 3D touch-capable device*, you should be able to force press on the app icon and see our shortcuts! See the following image if you don't have a 3D touch device to test for yourself:

Figure 7.7: 3D touch shortcuts on the Snippets application icon

If you do have a 3D touch device and you're not getting the same results, you should go back and double check all of your spelling. There's no code hinting in the `Info.plist` file, and everything is *very* sensitive to proper spelling. Check the earlier image that shows the final `.plist` file to make sure the parenting is correct, and don't forget that you can compare to my finished chapter project in the resources folder for this chapter. Once everything is spelled and parented correctly, you should get the same results as the image above when you force press the app icon.

Handling shortcuts in the app delegate

Next, we're going to journey into another unexplored part of our Xcode project: the `AppDelegate.swift` file. What is the app delegate? Essentially, it is the highest level of control over your app. The app delegate is where you take care of launching, entering, and exiting the app, in addition to other functionality, like handling shortcuts.

First, let's lay some groundwork for what we need to do. Create an empty function stub at the top of the `AppDelegate` class, like so:

```swift
func handleShortcut(shortcutItem: UIApplicationShortcutItem) {

}
```

This first function, `handleShortcut()`, is where we're going to write the logic to determine what shortcut was executed, and what to do about it. This next function is part of the `UIApplicationDelegate` protocol, and will get automatically called when we launch the app from the shortcut menu. For now, we just need to implement this function, and call our `handleShortcut()` function from there:

```
func application(_ application: UIApplication, performActionFor
shortcutItem: UIApplicationShortcutItem, completionHandler: @escaping
(Bool) -> Void) {
    handleShortcut(shortcutItem)
}
```

Inside our `handleShortcut()` function, we receive a `UIApplicationShortcutItem` object. This object contains the string we wrote in our `Info.plist` file for each shortcut, so we're going to process that string to see which shortcut to run.

In order to reduce the possibility of spelling errors, we're going to use an `enum`. At the top of the class, create a new `enum` called `ShortcutItems`, which uses `String` as a backing type:

```
enum ShortcutItems : String {
    case newText = "com.PacktPub.Snippets.createTextSnippet"
    case newPhoto = "com.PacktPub.Snippets.createPhotoSnippet"
}
```

Now, as long as we spelled everything properly here, we no longer have to write out these strings again. Instead, we can access them by writing `ShortcutItems.NewText.rawValue`. Remember, accessing the `rawValue` of an `enum` gives you its backing data.

Inside our `handleShortcut()` function now, we can use a `switch` statement to process the shortcut command. We'll be using `shortcutItem.type` as our `switch` condition (this is the input string), and then we'll create a case for each of our `ShortcutItem` types. We'll also need a default case, which we'll leave blank:

```
func handleShortcut(shortcutItem: UIApplicationShortcutItem) {
    switch shortcutItem.type {
        case ShortcutItems.newText.rawValue:

        case ShortcutItems.newPhoto.rawValue:

        default:
            break
    }
}
```

So, now we've got a place to write some code depending on which shortcut was called, but what do we do with it? Well, if we used the `text` shortcut, we want to start a new text snippet automatically, and the same for a `photo` shortcut. But how do we do this? Luckily, there's already code to do this in our `ViewController` class: we have `createNewTextSnippet()` and `createNewPhotoSnippet()` functions already there! Let's look at how to call those functions.

In the app delegate, we have access to our application's window (`UIWindow`), which in turn has a root view controller. In this case, the root view controller is our `ViewController` class. Here's an example of how we'd get access to the `ViewController` from the app delegate:

```
let vc = self.window!.rootViewController as! ViewController
```

Here, we are accessing our window (and forcefully unwrapping that optional), then accessing its `rootViewController`. Then, we (forcefully) cast the `rootViewController` to our `ViewController` class type, since we know that it is that type. This lets the compiler know about our class specific functions like `createNewTextSnippet()`.

Now that we've got a reference to our view controller, we just call the function we want to use:

```
vc.createNewTextSnippet()
```

Let's put this in the context of our `handleShortcut()` function:

```
func handleShortcut(_ shortcutItem: UIApplicationShortcutItem) {
    switch shortcutItem.type {
        case ShortcutItems.newText.rawValue:
            let vc = self.window!.rootViewController as!
    ViewController
            vc.createNewTextSnippet()

        case ShortcutItems.newPhoto.rawValue:
            let vc = self.window!.rootViewController as!
    ViewController
            vc.createNewPhotoSnippet()

        default:
            break
    }
}
```

And that's how simple it is! When we open our app from the shortcuts that we made, it will automatically open inside the correct snippet creation view controller.

Unfortunately, there's a big issue here. What happens if the user was already in the middle of creating a new snippet, then left the app for some reason without finishing their entry. Then they forgot about it, and later tried to create a new snippet from a shortcut. What happens?

Actually, right now nothing would happen. Our root view controller wouldn't be able to present a new snippet creation controller, because the existing snippet creation controller would have control over the view. But that's not great either; users might think the shortcut is broken.

Here's what we want to happen: if the user launches from a shortcut, but the app is already in the middle of creating a new snippet, we should present the user with an alert that asks if they want to continue the old one, or erase it and start a new one.

To begin, we want to check the status of the app when the shortcut is called in the `application(....)` function. To do that, we're going to check to see if our root view controller has presented a view controller on top of it. Let's look at the code and go through it:

```swift
func application(_ application: UIApplication, performActionFor
shortcutItem: UIApplicationShortcutItem, completionHandler: @escaping
(Bool) -> Void) {
    let vc = self.window!.rootViewController!
    if vc.presentedViewController != nil {
        let alert = UIAlertController(title: "Unfinished Snippet",
message: "Do you want to continue creating this snippet, or erase and
start a new snippet?", preferredStyle: .alert)
        let continueAction = UIAlertAction(title: "Continue", style:
.default, handler: nil)
        let eraseAction = UIAlertAction(title: "Erase", style:
.destructive) { (alert: UIAlertAction!) -> Void in
            vc.dismiss(animated: true, completion: nil)
            self.handleShortcut(shortcutItem)
        }

        alert.addAction(continueAction)
        alert.addAction(eraseAction)
        vc.presentedViewController!.present(alert, animated: true,
completion: nil)
    } else {
        handleShortcut(shortcutItem)
    }
}
```

First, we create a reference to our root view controller named `vc`, for future reference. Next we check to see if `presentedViewController` of `vc` exists by checking if it's not `nil`. If there is no presented view controller on top, then in the `else` we just handle the shortcut as normal. However, if there *is* a presented view controller, then we create a new alert view.

We give the alert a title and message describing that there is an unfinished snippet, and then create two buttons: one which lets the user continue editing the old snippet, and one that deletes the unfinished snippet and continues creating the new snippet they expected from the shortcut. It's important to note that the `eraseAction` has its style set to `.destructive`, which gives it the red coloring.

The continue action has no completion handler, since it essentially just lets the user continue editing the old snippet without changing anything. The erase action *does* have a completion handler though, because it needs to tell the root view controller to dismiss whichever snippet creating view is on top, and then finally tell the app delegate to call `handleShortcut()`.

At the bottom of the `if` statement, we finish setting up the alert, and then present it to the user:

Figure 7.8: A user attempting to create a new snippet while a photo snippet was already being created

However, we have one last issue to solve here. If this alert is presented while the `TextSnippetEntryViewController` is on screen, the text field will lose its first responder status, and `textViewDidEndEditing()` will be called, triggering it to save unwanted data. To fix this, we want to make sure that data is only saved when we press the `Done` button.

In the `TextSnippetEntryViewController.swift` file, create a new `Bool` variable at the top of the class, named `shouldExit`, and set the default to `false`:

```
var shouldExit = false
```

Then, below in the `doneButtonPressed()` function, set the `shouldExit` variable to `true`:

```
func doneButtonPressed() {
    shouldExit = true
    textView.resignFirstResponder()
}
```

Finally, in the `textViewDidEndEditing()` function, first check that the `Done` button was pressed before saving data:

```
func textViewDidEndEditing(_ textView: UITextView) {

    guard shouldExit else { return }

    saveText(text: textView.text)
    dismiss(animated:true, completion: nil)
}
```

Now, our save code will only run when we press the `Done` button, not for any other reason that the text might finish editing. This should be a lesson: try to make sure your code is built keeping in mind that other circumstances may trigger the same function, especially when working with protocols and delegates.

But now we're really done! You can leave the app in any state when you exit, but we have a graceful way to handle our shortcuts when we re-enter the app. And again, now that we've added a new feature, don't forget to commit your work (*option + command + C*).

Summary

In this chapter, we took a crash course on touch. We looked at the expected uses of the common set of multitouch gestures in iOS, and then learned how to implement them in an app from the storyboard, and purely with code. Then we went back to our app `Snippets` and added some really useful 3D Touch app icon shortcuts. While doing that, we learned a bit more about the `Info.plist` file, and got introduced to the App Delegate, and even learned how to clean up some old code to fit with a new feature.

Next, in *Chapter 8, Exploring Common iOS Frameworks*, we're going to get introduced to some of the more common Apple-provided frameworks, and we will also see how to apply them to our `Snippets` application. We'll be reviewing some `UIKit` (which we've been using a lot of!), and getting acquainted with the `CoreLocation` and `Social` frameworks.

8

Exploring Common iOS Frameworks

Up to this point in the book, we've been focused on learning about the different aspects of iOS development, and then applying those concepts to sketch out the rough features and interactions of an app. Now that we've built our app up to a pretty decent point, let's take some time to explore the kinds of functionality that we can add to our app using some of the commonly used frameworks built into the iOS SDK.

In the last two chapters, we've been using the framework UIKit almost every step of the way. In this chapter we'll take a deeper look at this essential iOS framework, in addition to learning about the CoreLocation and the Social frameworks. We will cover the following topics:

- What is a framework, and how do we use them?
- The basics of UIKit
- Using CoreLocation to integrate location data
- Using the Social framework to share content with social media

Frameworks

Before we get to coding, it's important that we talk about what a framework is, and how we use frameworks in iOS programming.

What is a framework?

When writing software, you'll find that you need to do the same things in almost every project. On a lower level, iOS itself handles a lot of the most fundamental functionality, like drawing pixels to the screen, or connecting to wireless networks.

However, as we move to higher levels of functionality we start to see the need for reusable sets of code, but only around certain types of functionality. These *reusable, (mostly) self-contained blocks of code that focus on specific functionality are called frameworks.*

For example, if we want to work with the photos on a user's device, we'd have to create the functionality to load the user's photos, build an interface to view the photos, allow the user to edit and save photos, and so on. In cases like this, we can create a *framework* which does all of these things, and then import that framework in any project that needs to access photos. In fact, Apple has already created `Photos.framework` for these exact needs.

When using a framework in this way, we reduce the amount of code we have to write. However, most of the time you won't even be writing your own frameworks; the iOS ecosystem is very mature, and Apple (along with third-party developers like Facebook) provide many frameworks for us to use. To get a sense of how many frameworks are included in the standard iOS SDK, check out Apple's overview at this link:

```
https://developer.apple.com/library/ios/documentation/
Miscellaneous/Conceptual/iPhoneOSTechOverview/iPhoneOSFrameworks/
iPhoneOSFrameworks.html.
```

Linking frameworks in a project

Now that we have a basic understanding of what framework are, we need to learn how to use them in practice. As a quick test, create a new Xcode project; the settings don't matter, since we won't be using it for more than a minute or so:

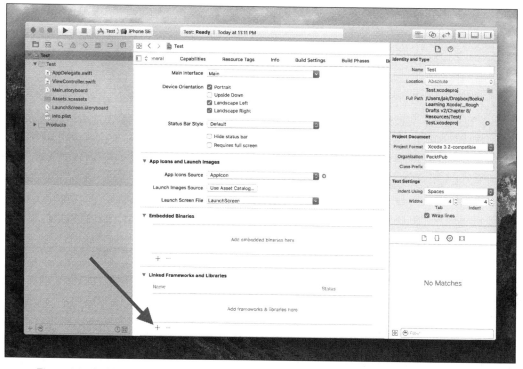

Figure 8.1: The blue arrow points to the button that allows you to add a framework to your project

First, on the **General** tab of our project settings, scroll to the bottom to see the section labelled **Linked Frameworks and Libraries**. You should see that by default, no frameworks are included, but if you click the plus button at the bottom (*Figure 8.1*), you can add frameworks to your project. For this example, let's choose the same **Photos.framework** from our earlier example. You should now see that the photos framework has been linked to our project (*Figure 8.2*):

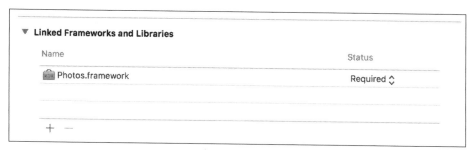

Figure 8.2: Choosing Photos.framework from the drop-down list adds it to our Linked Frameworks

Now, we're ready to use the framework in our code, so head over to the `ViewController.swift` file. In order to use the classes and functions inside `Photos.framework`, we need to include it in this file. To do so, we just write this at the top of the file:

```
import Photos
```

That's right; we've been importing frameworks many times throughout the book already, though we've mostly been sticking to the foundation and `UIKit` frameworks.

Now that we've linked `Photos.framework` to our app, and imported the framework into our `ViewController.swift` file, we are free to use any of the functionality found within the photos framework.

And that's it! We've linked and imported a framework. Feel free to delete this test project before we move on to more fun with frameworks.

Understanding UIKit fundamentals

At this point in the book, we've heard a lot about `UIKit`. We've seen it at the top of our Swift files in the form of `import UIKit`. We've used many of the UI elements and classes it provides for us. Now it's time to take an isolated look at the biggest and most important framework in iOS development.

In this section we're going to be talking about mostly concepts rather than concrete code examples. Since we've been using `UIKit` throughout the whole book (and will continue to do so), I'm going to do my best to elaborate on some things we've already seen, and give you new information that you can apply to what we do in the future.

Application management

Unlike most other frameworks in the iOS SDK, `UIKit` is deeply integrated into the way your app runs. That's because `UIKit` is responsible for some of the most essential functionalities of an app.

It provides the event handling for user input (like touch and gestures), which we covered in depth in the last chapter. It also manages your application's window and view architecture, which we'll be talking about next. It also drives the main run loop, which basically means that it is executing your program.

The UIDevice class

In addition to these very important features, UIKit also gives you access to some other useful information about the device the app is currently running on through the UIDevice class.

> Using online resources and documentation: Since this chapter is about exploring frameworks, it is a good time to remind you that you can (and should!) always be searching online for anything and everything. For example, if you search for UIDevice, you'll end up on Apple's developer page for the UIDevice class where you can see even more bits of information that you can pull from it. As we progress, keep in mind that searching the name of a class or framework will usually give you quick access to the full documentation.

Here are some code examples of the information you can access:

```
UIDevice.current.name
UIDevice.current.model
UIDevice.current.orientation
UIDevice.current.batteryLevel
UIDevice.current.systemVersion
```

Some developers have a little bit of fun with this information: for example, Snapchat gives you a special filter to use for photos when your battery is fully charged. Always keep an open mind about what you can do with data you have access to!

Views

One of the most important responsibilities of UIKit is that it provides views and the view hierarchy architecture. We've talked before about what a view is within the MVC programming paradigm, but here we're referring to the UIView class that acts as the base for (almost) all of our visual content in iOS programming. While it wasn't too important to know about when just getting our feet wet, now is a good time to really dig in a bit and understand what UIViews are, and how they work both on their own and together.

Let's start from the beginning: a view (UIView) defines a rectangle on your screen that is responsible for output and input, meaning drawing to the screen and receiving touch events. It can also contain other views, known as subviews, which ultimately creates a view hierarchy. As a result of this hierarchy, we have to be aware of the coordinate systems involved. Now let's talk about each of these three functions: drawing, hierarchies, and coordinate systems.

Drawing

Each `UIView` is responsible for drawing itself to the screen. In order to optimize drawing performance, the views will usually try to render their content once and then reuse that image content when it doesn't change. It can even move and scale content around inside of it without needing to redraw, which can be an expensive operation.

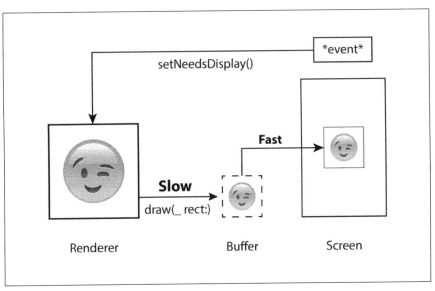

Figure 8.3: An overview of how UIView draws itself to the screen

With the system's provided views, all of this is handled automatically. However, if you ever need to create your own `UIView` subclass that uses custom drawing, it's important to know what goes on behind the scenes. To implement custom drawing in a view, you need to implement the `draw(_ rect:)` function in your subclass. When something changes in your view, you need to call the `setNeedsDisplay()` function, which acts as a marker to let the system know that your view needs to be redrawn. During the next drawing cycle, the code in your `draw(_ rect:)` function will be executed to refresh the content of your view, which will then be cached for performance.

A code example of this custom drawing functionality is beyond the scope of this book, but discussing this will hopefully give you a better understanding of how drawing works, in addition to giving you a jumping off point should you need to do this in the future.

Hierarchies

Now let's discuss view hierarchies. In earlier chapters, when we would use a view controller in a storyboard, we would drag UI elements onto the view controller. However, what we were actually doing is adding a subview to the *base view* of the view controller. And in fact, that base view was a subview of the UIWindow, which is also a UIView. So though we haven't really acknowledged it, we've already put view hierarchies to work many times.

The easiest way to think about what happens in a view hierarchy is that you set one view's parent coordinate system relative to another view. By *default*, you'd be setting a view's coordinate system to be relative to the base view, which is normally just the whole screen. But you can also set the parent coordinate system to some other view, so that when you move or transform the parent view, the children views are moved and transformed along with it:

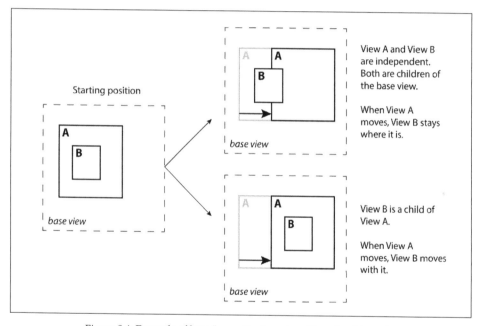

Figure 8.4: Example of how "parenting" works with a view hierarchy

It's also important to note that the view hierarchy impacts the draw order of your views. All of a view's subviews will be drawn on top of the parent view, and the subviews will be drawn in the order they were added (the last subview added will be on top). To add a subview through code, you can use the `addSubview()` function. Here's an example:

```
var view1 = UIView()
var view2 = UIView()
view1.addSubview(view2)
```

Finally, we briefly touched on this in the last chapter, but this is a good time to reiterate that touches are processed depending on their order in the view hierarchy. The top-most views will intercept a touch first, and if it doesn't respond it will pass it down the view hierarchy until a view does respond.

Coordinate systems

With all of this drawing and parenting, we need to take a minute to look at how the coordinate system works in `UIKit` for our views. The origin (0,0 point) in `UIKit` is the top left of the screen, and increases along X to the right, and increases on the Y downward. Each view is placed in this upper left positioning system relative to its parent view's origin.

 Be careful! Other frameworks in iOS use different coordinate systems. For example, `SpriteKit` uses the *lower* left corner as the origin.

Each view also has its own set of positioning information. This is composed of the view's frame, bounds, and center. The frame rectangle describes the origin and the size of view relative to its *parent view's* coordinate system. The bounds rectangle describes the origin and size of the view from its *local* coordinate system. The center is just the center point of the view relative to the parent view.

When dealing with so many different coordinate systems, it can seem like a nightmare to compare positions from different views. Luckily, the `UIView` class provides a simple `convert(point: to:)` function to convert points between systems.

Try running this little experiment in a playground to see how the point gets converted from one view's coordinate system to the other:

```
import UIKit

let view1 = UIView(frame: CGRect(x: 0, y: 0, width: 50, height: 50))
let view2 = UIView(frame: CGRect(x: 10, y: 10, width: 30, height: 30))
view1.addSubview(view2)

let pointFrom1 = CGPoint(x: 20, y: 20)
let pointFromView2 = view1.convert(pointFrom1, to: view2)
```

Hopefully you now have a much better understanding of some of the underlying workings of the view system in UIKit. Try to keep this in mind as we continue to work with UIKit throughout the rest of the book.

Documents, displays, printing, and more

In this section, I'm going to do my best to introduce you to the many additional features of the UIKit framework. Descriptions of these features could take up a whole chapter each, so I won't be covering them in depth. The idea is to give you a better understanding of what is possible with UIKit, and if anything sounds interesting to you, you can go off and explore these features on your own.

Documents

UIKit has built-in support for documents, much like you'd find on a desktop operating system. Using the UIDocument class, UIKit can help you save and load documents in the background, in addition to saving them to iCloud. This could be a powerful feature for any app that allows the user to create content that they expect to save and resume working on later.

Displays

On most new iOS devices, you can connect external screens using HDMI. You can take advantage of these external displays by creating a new instance of the UIWindow class, and associating it with the external display screen. You can then add subviews to that window to create a second screen experience for devices like a big-screen TV. While most consumers don't ever use HDMI connected external displays, this is a great feature to keep in mind when working on internal applications for corporate or personal use.

Printing

Using the `UIPrintInteractionController`, you can set up and send print jobs to `AirPrint` enabled printers on the user's network. Before you print, you can also create PDFs by drawing content off screen to make printing easier.

And more!

There are many more features of `UIKit` that are just waiting to be explored! To be honest, `UIKit` seems to be pretty much a dumping ground for any general features that were just a bit too small to deserve their own framework. If you do some digging in Apple's documentation you'll find all kinds of interesting things you can do with `UIKit`, like creating custom keyboards, creating share sheets, and custom cut-copy-paste support.

Using CoreLocation.framework

With today's *always on, always tracking* social media apps, using and tracking the user's location has become a standard feature of many apps. In this section we're going to explore a new framework from the inside out, by jumping straight to coding. This framework is `CoreLocation`, which as the name might imply is going to give us the tools we need to access location services on a user's device.

We're going to be switching back to our `Snippets` application and adding the functionality for the user to attach their current location to a new snippet when they create it. You can continue to work from your old `Snippets` project, or if you had any problems with yours you can grab the final version from the resources folder of this chapter, because again, the folder will have the finished work from this chapter.

[Before we get started, make sure to link `CoreLocation.``framework` to your `Snippets` project like we did in the test project earlier in the chapter.]

Setting up CoreLocation permissions

Apple has always trumpeted iOS's security and respect for user privacy. Before iOS 8, the first time your app tried to access location services, an alert would show up for the user asking them if it was okay to enable location services. However, in iOS 8 and newer, the developer is now responsible for explicitly asking the user for permission to use location services. Before we can access user location data we'll have to do that ourselves, so let's get to it.

There are two types of authorization that we can ask for: *when in use* and *always* authorization. These should be pretty self-explanatory. *When in use* authorization allows us to access location services when the app is active and being used, while *always* lets our app use location data even when it is running in the background. It can be tempting to just ask the user to *always* access their location, but some users may wonder why you need access to that information, or be worried about battery life and deny your request.

> Here's a tip/warning: if a user denies your request to access location data the first time you ask, the only way for them to change this is to manually go into the settings app and change the toggle for your app. It is very important that you gain the user's trust before asking, since their denial of your request may very well be the last chance you get to ask for permission.

To give the user a good idea of why we need location data in the first place, we can include a description of what location data is being used, for that will be included in the permissions prompt. This is where we'll start with our own permissions setup. Open the `Info.plist` file like we did in *Chapter 7, Integrating Multitouch and Gestures*, and add a new row using one of the + buttons. Set the key to `Privacy - Location When In Use Usage Description`, and set the value to `Adds location information to a new snippet when it is created`.

What we're doing here is letting the app know that when location permissions of the type *when in use* are requested, the user should be given our description string so they know why the location is needed.

Next, we're going to head over to the `ViewController.swift` file and add the code that actually asks for permissions. At the top of the file, add a new import for `CoreLocation`:

```
import CoreLocation
```

Now we can create an instance of `CLLocationManager`, which is what we are going to use to ask for permissions, and later on use to actually get the user's location. Inside the class, near the top with the other properties, create a new property for the location manager:

```
var data: [SnippetData] = [SnippetData]()
let imagePicker = UIImagePickerController()
let locationManager = CLLocationManager()
@IBOutlet weak var tableView: UITableView!
```

We're also going to need to add yet *another* class extension to our `ViewController` class extension to implement a protocol, this time the `CLLocationManagerDelegate` protocol. Our class declaration should now look like this, at the bottom of the file:

```
extension ViewController: CLLocationManagerDelegate {

}
```

Now, we need to actually set the delegate of our `locationManager` to the view controller object, so it knows what object should be handling location requests. In our `viewDidLoad()` function, we'll add a new line to set the delegate:

```
override func viewDidLoad() {
    super.viewDidLoad()
    imagePicker.delegate = self
    locationManager.delegate = self

    tableView.estimatedRowHeight = 100
    tableView.rowHeight = UITableViewAutomaticDimension
}
```

Our location manager should be all set up at this point, and we've added a description string to the `Info.plist` file. All that we have to do now is request permission to use location services. To do that, we're going to create a small function that first checks to make sure we're not already authorized, and then asks the user if we can use location services *when in use*. Let's create a function in the main class body called `askForLoacationPermissions()`:

```
func askForLocationPermissions () {
    if CLLocationManager.authorizationStatus() == .NotDetermined {
        locationManager.requestWhenInUseAuthorization()
    }
}
```

Here, we first check to make sure the authorization status is `Not Determined` (because if it is already determined, then we don't need to do anything). If the status is undetermined, then we tell the location manager to request *when in use* authorization, which will tell the system to present an alert to the user using the description we provided in `Info.plist`.

Finally, we need to call this function on startup, so we'll put this at the bottom of our `viewDidLoad()` function:

```
override func viewDidLoad() {
    super.viewDidLoad()
    imagePicker.delegate = self
    locationManager.delegate = self

    tableView.estimatedRowHeight = 100
    tableView.rowHeight = UITableViewAutomaticDimension

    askForLocationPermissions()
}
```

If you build and run the app now, you should be greeted with a permissions box like so:

Figure 8.5: Snippets will now ask the user if it can access their location, using the description from Info.plist

If this didn't work, then aside from double checking your code is correct, make sure that everything in the `Info.plist` file is correct. If the system can't find a valid description key in the `Info.plist` file, it will ignore your request for permissions! Your entry should look like this:

Privacy - Camera Usage Description	String	Snippets needs to access the camera to create photo snip	
Localization native development region	String	en	
Privacy - Location When In Use Usage Description	String	Adds location information to a new snippet when it is creat	

Figure 8.6: The correct Info.plist entry for location usage permissions (the last row)

Again, make sure that the key says `Privacy - Location When In Use Usage Description`, and the type is set to `string`. Spelling mistakes in the value string don't matter, since it will just be displayed to the user as is, but double check the key is spelled correctly.

Alright! It should be a given that you press **Allow** on that alert window. Now that our app is authorized to access location data, it's time to move on to the exciting parts.

 If you (or the user) denies permission, you (or they) will need to reinstall the app, or go to the `Settings.app` to manually change the location permissions.

Getting the user's location

To obtain the user's location, we're going to need to do a few things. First, we need to set the parameters for our location manager. Then, we need to tell it to start updating the user's location. Finally, we need to handle both successful and unsuccessful update cases.

To start, let's go back to our `viewDidLoad()` function and set some properties for our `loactionManager`, highlighted as follows:

```
override func viewDidLoad() {
    super.viewDidLoad()
    imagePicker.delegate = self
    locationManager.delegate = self
    locationManager.desiredAccuracy = kCLLocationAccuracyBest
    locationManager.distanceFilter = 50.0

    tableView.estimatedRowHeight = 100
    tableView.rowHeight = UITableViewAutomaticDimension

    askForLocationPermissions()
}
```

First, we set the desired accuracy to a constant called `kCLLocationAccuracyBest`, which sets the desired accuracy of the location manager to its highest setting. After that, we set the distance filter to `50.0`. The distance filter tells the location manager how far away from the previous location the user must move in order to update the location (in meters). So in this case we are letting the location manager know that when the user moves `50` meters or more, it should update their location.

Next, we need to tell the location manager to start updating the user's location. To add functionality to the location manager, we're going to start working with the delegate pattern again. We're going to add these delegate methods to the `CLLocationManagerDelegate` class extension we made earlier.

> Remember, the delegate pattern uses a *protocol* to define a set of functions that a class should implement. Then, the object calls those functions in its linked delegate object, which implements the protocol. Here, the `CLLocationManager` object has a delegate that follows the `CLLocationManagerDelegate` protocol, which is the `ViewController` class.

First, we'll implement the `locationManager` (`didChangeAuthorizationStatus:`) delegate function:

```
func locationManager(_ manager: CLLocationManager,
didChangeAuthorization status: CLAuthorizationStatus) {

    if status == .authorizedWhenInUse {

        locationManager.startUpdatingLocation()

    }

}
```

This function is called in two different scenarios: when the location manager first starts up, and again if the authorization status is ever changed while running. That means that the first time our app starts up this function will be called. In that case, the status will *not* equal `.authorizedWhenInUse`, so the location manager will not start updating.

However, once the user gives the app permission to use the location, the function will be called again, and this time it will start updating. Then, every other time you start up the app, the authorization status will still equal `.authorizedWhenInUse`, and location updates will begin immediately.

Now that the location manager has been told to start updating its location, it will do so based on the parameters we set earlier (every time a change of 50 meters is detected). It's up to us to handle these update events with more delegate functions, one to handle a successful location update, and one to handle an error.

First, we'll implement the `locationManager(didFailWithError:)` function:

```
func locationManager(_ manager: CLLocationManager, didFailWithError
error: Error) {
    print("Location manager could not get location. Error: \(error.
localizedDescription)")
}
```

This gets called when the location manager cannot get a proper location due to an error. To keep things simple, we're just going to print to the console that an error occurred, along with the description of the error. In a final production app, we'd want to handle these errors a bit more elegantly, but this is fine for testing.

Next, we'll actually handle what happens when the location update is successful, with the `locationManager (didUpdateLocations:)` function:

```
// main class
var currentCoordinate: CLLocationCoordinate2D?

// CLLocationManagerDelegate extension

func locationManager(_ manager: CLLocationManager,
didUpdateLocations locations: [CLLocation]) {
    if let currentLocation = locations.last {
        currentCoordinate = currentLocation.coordinate
        print("\(currentCoordinate!.latitude),
        \(currentCoordinate!.longitude)")
    }
}
```

At the top of our main (non extension) class we're going to declare a new variable, which is an optional `CLLocationCoordinate2D` type. This data type stores a latitude and longitude coordinate, and we're going to use it to keep track of the most recent coordinate the app has detected.

Then back in the extension, we implement the location update handler. Inside our location update handler, we are being passed in an array of the locations that have been processed, with the most recent location at the end. We use the *if let* syntax to unwrap the optional value from the end of the array (`locations.last`) into `currentLocation`. Since the `locations` array may be empty, the `.last` property returns an optional value that we must unwrap. If we are successful in unwrapping the optional value, we then pull the coordinate out of the `currentLocation`, and use it to update our `currentCoordinate` variable. Now, at any point in our code we can access the `currentCoordinate` property to get the most recent valid coordinate.

Following that (in the highlighted code), I made a `print` statement that outputs the latitude and longitude coordinate to the console so you can see how that works. At this point, you can build and run the project on your device. If you see the latitude and longitude coordinates in the console (*shift + command + C*), everything worked! Feel free to delete the highlighted print statement.

Adding location data to Snippets

Okay, so we've imported the `CoreLocation` framework, gotten permission to use location services, and set up a location manager that updates the most recent location coordinate of the device; now it's time to bring it all back into our `SnippetData` model! In this case, we are just going to add the location information as metadata to the data model. Later on we may choose to do something fun with it, like display it on a map or find nearby points of interest to display on the snippet, but for now it will live only as data.

First, let's open up our `SnippetData.swift` file, and make some amendments to our base data type, `SnippetData`. Before we begin, remember to `import CoreLocation` at the top of the `SnippetData.swift` file.

```
class SnippetData {
    let type: SnippetType
    let date: Date
    let coordinate: CLLocationCoordinate2D?

    init ( snippetType: SnippetType, creationDate: Date,
    creationCoordinate: CLLocationCoordinate2D? ) {
        type = snippetType
        date = creationDate
        coordinate = creationCoordinate
        print ("\(type.rawValue) snippet created on \(date) at
        \(coordinate.debugDescription)")
    }
}
```

At the top of the `SnippetData` class, we'll add a new `CLLocationCoordinate2D?` property to hold the optional coordinate data. Then, we'll pass that data in through the `init` function, and we'll assign it in the body. Finally, we'll add the coordinate data to our debug `print` statement so we can check to see if it worked later.

Now that the base type is updated, we need to update the text and photo types to also add the coordinate into the `init` functions:

```
class TextData: SnippetData {
    let textData: String
    init ( text: String, creationDate: Date,
    creationCoordinate: CLLocationCoordinate2D? ) {
        textData = text
        super.init(snippetType: .text, creationDate:
        creationDate, creationCoordinate: creationCoordinate)
        print ("Text snippet data: \(textData)")
    }
}
class PhotoData: SnippetData {
    let photoData: UIImage
    init ( photo: UIImage, creationDate: Date,
    creationCoordinate: CLLocationCoordinate2D? ) {
        photoData = photo
        super.init(snippetType: .photo, creationDate:
        creationDate, creationCoordinate: creationCoordinate)
        print ("Photo snippet data: \(photoData)")
    }
}
```

Here, you can see that we updated the `init` functions for both data types to also include the `creationCordinate` parameter at the end, and that they both pass that data into the initializer for their super class (`SnippetData`). Now we can pass in a coordinate to any of our `SnippetData` classes, so let's go update our `ViewController`, which is where we are actually creating this data!

In the `ViewController` class, we create new `SnippetData` objects in two different places: the `createNewTextSnippet()` function, and the `imagePickerController(d idFinish…:)` function:

```
func createNewTextSnippet () {
    guard let textEntryVC = storyboard?.instantiateViewController(wi
    thIdentifier: "textSnippetEntry") as? TextSnippetEntryViewController
    else {
        print("TextSnippetEntryViewController could not be
    instantiated from storyboard")
        return
    }
```

```
        textEntryVC.modalTransitionStyle = .coverVertical
        textEntryVC.saveText = { ( text: String ) in
            let newTextSnippet = TextData(text: text, creationDate:
    Date(), creationCoordinate: self.currentCoordinate)
            self.data.append(newTextSnippet)
        }


        present(textEntryVC,animated:true, completion:nil)
    }
```

In `createNewTextSnippet()`, we have to update the line where we create a new
`TextData` object. You can see at the end of its initializer that we are passing in the
`currentCoordinate` property that we created and updated in the last section:

```
    func imagePickerController(_ picker: UIImagePickerController,
    didFinishPickingMediaWithInfo info: [String : Any]) {
        guard let image = info[UIImagePickerControllerEditedImage] as?
    UIImage else {
            print("Image could not be found")
            return
        }


        let newPhotoSnippet = PhotoData(photo: image, creationDate:
    Date(), creationCoordinate: self.currentCoordinate)
        self.data.append(newPhotoSnippet)

        dismiss(animated: true, completion: nil)
    }
```

Again, in the `imagePickerController(didFinishPickingMediaWithInfo:)`
function, we are going to update the initializer of the `PhotoData` object with
the same `currentCoordinate` parameter.

Now, we've updated our data model to support coordinate data and we updated our
controller to track location and pass the data into our data model. If you build and
run the app, you should see that when you create a new snippet the console should
output the coordinate that the snippet was created at(*Figure 8.7*):

```
Text snippet created on 2016-08-20 20:38:19 +0000 at
Optional(__C.CLLocationCoordinate2D(latitude: 44.486323026981658, longitude:
-73.210722059079643))
Text snippet data: hello world
```

Figure 8.7: The debug output when creating a new snippet with location data

And that concludes our crash course on CoreLocation! Like I said earlier, now that we've added location information to our data model, later on we can come back and do all kinds of fun things with it. For now, I think we've demonstrated a basic way to integrate some location data in an application. Commit your work, and let's move on.

Using Social.framework

When building an app where the user generates their own content, it is usually a good idea to include the ability for them to post what they've made to an external social media service. Luckily, Apple has integrated some of the most popular social media services (like Facebook and Twitter) right into iOS. In this section, we're going to get our feet wet with the Social.framework, and let users post their snippets straight to Twitter.

 Again, before we get started, link the Social.framework to your Snippets project so that we can use the social APIs included within.

Setting up the views

The first thing we'll need to do to post our snippets to Twitter is to add a new button to the actual snippets for the user to press. We'll be adding a Tweet button to the right side of the grey bar that sits at the bottom of each snippet. Let's open up Main.storyboard and get started:

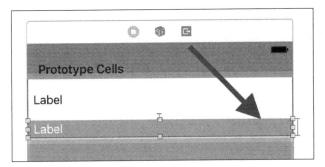

Figure 8.8: The Tweet button added to the right of the grey bar on the text snippet

First, drag a button from the object library onto the grey bar of the text snipp
Set the text to read `Tweet`, then set its color to our orange color. Finally, add
Vertically constraint, and a **Right Edge Pin** constraint set to `10`.

Next, we're going to do the same thing for the grey bar on our photo snippe
However, due to strange auto layout constraints, our grey bar is not visible
off the bottom of the screen! We're going to have to take a leap of faith here, and set
this up blind. If we make it to the other side, we will be auto layout ninjas!

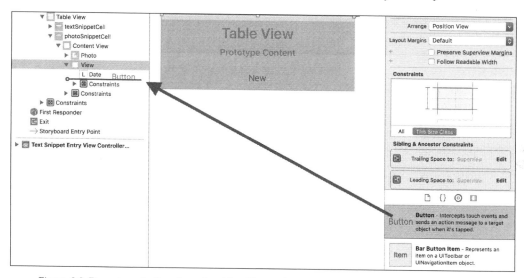

Figure 8.9: Dragging a button from the object library directly into the storyboard document outline

Here's what we need to do:

1. Drag a button from the object library straight onto our photo cell's grey bar
   view in the *document outline* (see preceding image).

2. Select it from the document outline and set its color and name property in the
   Attribute Inspector.

3. While still selected in the document outline, use the **Align** and **Pin** menus to
   set the same Auto Layout constraints (`Vertical Center/Right Pin 10`).

If you build and run and then create a photo and text snippet, you should see two identical grey bars (*Figure 8.10*)! If the photo one didn't come out right, try following the instructions again until it does. Once it works, you are officially an auto layout master.

Figure 8.10: The finished Tweet button on both types of snippets

Next, let's set up the @IBActions that will be called when the buttons are pressed. Open up `TextSnippetCell` and add a function stub:

```
@IBAction func shareButtonPressed() {
    print("Tweet button pressed")
}
```

Then go over to `PhotoSnippetCell` and do the same. Finally, open up the `Assistant Editor` and connect the @IBAction from `TextSnippetCell` to the `Tweet` button in the text cell, and then do the same for the photo cells.

If you forget how to link @IBActions to UI elements, revisit *Chapter 4, Using Storyboards, Size Classes, and Auto Layout*, section on storyboards. (Hint: use the Connections Inspector). I could tell you here, but you'll learn more from having to work for it!

Once your Tweet buttons are linked to their respective @IBActions, if you run the app and click the buttons, you should see **Tweet button pressed** printed to the console. If that's all working, then it's time to post to Twitter!

Posting to Twitter

Now that we've got buttons set up to make tweets, it's time to get into the `Social.framework`. What we're going to do next is create an instance of and present a `SLComposeViewController`, which lets our user post a tweet. We're also going to pre-populate it with our snippet's data to make it easy for the user to post their snippets. Before we can do that though, we need to make some changes to our `shareButtonPressed()` functions in `TextSnippetCell` and `PhotoSnippetCell`.

Since we need to present a view controller (`SLComposeViewController`) from another view controller, we're going to need to run our `Social.framework` logic in our `ViewController` class. However, our button handling function is inside our `Cell` classes. How can we fix this? The short answer is by using a closure. In both the `TextSnippetCell` and `PhotoSnippetCell` classes, update your `shareButtonPressed()` function to look like this, while also adding a new `shareButton` closure as a property. We're going to set up the closure's code from our view controller, and then when we tap the button we're going to run that code. Pretty cool, huh?

```
var shareButton: (() -> Void)?

@IBAction func shareButtonPressed() {
    if let callback = shareButton {
        callback()
    }
}
```

Note how the `shareButton` property is an *optional closure*. This is why we use the `if let` syntax to unwrap the option, and then call the closure.

Now, all that we have left to do is to write the code that gets passed into the two closures. Back in `ViewController.swift`, first add `import Social` to the top of the file. Then head to the `tableView(_:, cellForRowAt:)` function, and let's take a look at where we set up our two cells. First, the text cell:

```
case .text:
    cell = tableView.dequeueReusableCell(withIdentifier:
"textSnippetCell", for: indexPath)
    (cell as! TextSnippetCell).label.text = (snippetData as!
TextData).textData
    (cell as! TextSnippetCell).date.text = dateString
```

```
        (cell as! TextSnippetCell).shareButton = {
            if SLComposeViewController.isAvailable(forServiceType:
    SLServiceTypeTwitter) {
                let text = (snippetData as! TextData).textData
                guard let twVC = SLComposeViewController(forServiceType:
    SLServiceTypeTwitter) else {
                    print("Couldn't create twitter compose controller")
                    return
                }
                if text.characters.count <= 140 {
                    twVC.setInitialText("\(text)")
                } else {
                    let tweetLengthIndex = text.index(text.startIndex,
    offsetBy: 140)
                    let tweetChars = text.substring(to: tweetLengthIndex)
                    twVC.setInitialText("\(tweetChars)")
                }
                self.present(twVC, animated: true, completion: nil)
            }
            else {
                let alert = UIAlertController(title: "You are not logged
    into twitter", message: "Please log into Twitter from the iOS Settings
    app.", preferredStyle: .alert)
                let dismissAction = UIAlertAction(title: "OK", style:
    .default, handler: nil)
                alert.addAction(dismissAction)
                self.present(alert, animated: true, completion: nil)
            }
        }
```

Here, you can see that we are setting the `.shareButton` closure to a chunk of code that will be executed when the `Tweet` button is pressed on a text cell.

First, we check to see if the Twitter service is available. If the user hasn't logged into Twitter from the iOS settings app, the user won't be able to post to Twitter, and they will be given the error message, which is presented in the `else` block towards the bottom.

If Twitter is available, we get the text out of our `TextData` object, and save it in a `text` constant for later. Then we create the view controller for creating a tweet, and store it in a `twVC` constant. We place this in a guard statement to ensure that we have a value, since it is an optional.

Finally, we have to check the length of our message; since Twitter can only support 140 characters or less, it's up to us to cut down the string if it's too long. Then, we can use the `setInitialText()` function on our `SLComposeViewController` to pre-populate the text field. Finally, we present the view controller. If all goes well, your app should look something like this when you post to Twitter:

Figure 8.11: Tapping the Tweet button lets us send the contents of our snippet to Twitter

To wrap things up, we'll create a similar closure to send to the `PhotoSnippetCell`. Since we don't have to check character length, this one is a bit easier to put together:

```
case .photo:
    cell = tableView.dequeueReusableCell(withIdentifier:
"photoSnippetCell", for: indexPath)
    (cell as! PhotoSnippetCell).photo.image = (snippetData as!
PhotoData).photoData
    (cell as! PhotoSnippetCell).date.text = dateString
    (cell as! PhotoSnippetCell).shareButton = {
        if SLComposeViewController.isAvailable(forServiceType:
            SLServiceTypeTwitter) {
            let photo = (snippetData as! PhotoData).photoData
            guard let twVC = SLComposeViewController(forServiceType:
                SLServiceTypeTwitter) else {
                print("Couldn't create twitter compose controller")
                return
            }
            twVC.setInitialText("Sent from Snippets™")
            twVC.add(photo)
            self.present(twVC, animated: true, completion: nil)
        }
        else {
            let alert = UIAlertController(title: "You are not logged
into twitter", message: "Please log into Twitter from the iOS Settings
app.", preferredStyle: .alert)
            let dismissAction = UIAlertAction(title: "OK", style:
.default, handler: nil)
```

```
            alert.addAction(dismissAction)
            self.present(alert, animated: true, completion: nil)
        }
    }
}
```

Again, first we are checking to see if Twitter is available, and if not, we give the user the same alert box. Then, we pull out the image data to the `photo` constant, and again create the `twVC` view controller. This time we manually set the text to a little tag line, and use a new function `add(image:)` to attach our photo to the tweet template. Finally, we present the view controller. If this all worked out, you should have a similar result:

Figure 8.12: Tapping the Tweet button on a photo snippet sets up a photo post for Twitter

And that's how you share text and images to social networks! See if you can figure out Facebook. Don't forget to `git commit` your work!

Summary

In this chapter, we learned about frameworks from many different angles. We talked about what they are, and how to add them to your projects. We looked at the biggest and most important iOS framework, `UIKit`, and learned about some of the most important system processes, like the view hierarchy. Then we looked at some more specific frameworks and added location data using `CoreLocation.framework`, and social media integration with the `Social.framework`. Now it's up to you to explore the documentation, and see what you can do with other frameworks in the iOS SDK!

If you haven't noticed yet, when we quit our app, none of our data gets saved, and we have to start over every time we launch the app. In the next chapter, we're going to dive into the world of `CoreData`, which will allow us to save and persist our data models across multiple sessions.

Working with Core Data

9

We've now spent three chapters working on building up the functionality for our note taking/journaling application, `Snippets`. However, while we've demonstrated a good amount of the core features such as content creation, 3D touch support, location tracking, and social sharing, we still don't have an application that a user can carry around with them and use.

We are lacking a key feature: *persistence*.

When a user closes our app or turns off their phone, they lose all of the snippets they've created. To me that sounds like a pretty terrible journaling application. In this chapter we're going to finally give our app's **model** the attention it deserves!

To accomplish our goal of persistent app data across multiple launches, we're going to be using the **Core Data** framework and its associated data containers. In this chapter, we're going to cover:

- What is Core Data?
- The data model components (entities, attributes, and relationships)
- Using the data model editor
- Adding Core Data support to an existing application
- Saving, fetching, and deleting data from our object graph

What is Core Data?

So what exactly is Core Data used for, and what is it capable of? To be technical, it is an object graph and persistence framework. To be less technical, it is a framework that makes it easy to save, change, track, and sort lots of data.

In this section, we're going to cover the model aspect of **Model-View-Controller (MVC)** again, and look at how Core Data ties into those ideas of separating data from views. Then, we're going to look at how Core Data represents data relationships, and finally, we'll learn how we can create our own specific descriptions of the data our app needs to manage.

Model revisited

In the very first chapter of this book, we took some time discussing the concept of MVC, and how we separate an application's data from its interface, and connect it through the controller. We've come a long way since then, and we've learned a ton about creating views and programming controllers.

However, as it stands now, our `ViewController` class is completely owning the model: it holds onto an array of data that it adds to and reads from. Let's go back and look at how the model is supposed to work in an MVC application (see *Figure 9.1*):

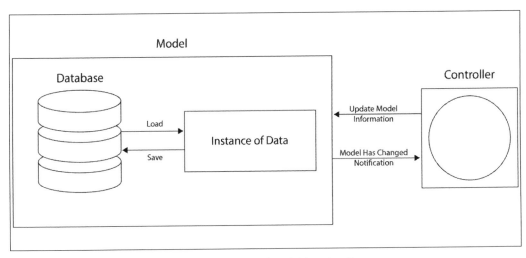

Figure 9.1: Diagram of model functionality

As you can see, we want to completely encapsulate our model. This will allow us to make changes to the model, without significant code changes in the controller, and down the line it will make it much easier to move the data. Right now, everything is stored locally on the device, but maybe in six months when we have 100,000 users we might want to start storing data in the cloud. No matter what your reasoning, proper model encapsulation will keep your app much easier to manage, and save you plenty of headaches in the future.

Throughout the rest of this chapter, we'll be exploring every aspect of *Figure 9.1*. I recommend that you continue to refer back to this diagram as you read through, and make mental notes about where the different parts of this chapter line up with it. It's very important to have a solid grasp of how your data is moving through your app!

So, looking at *Figure 9.1*, where does Core Data fit in with things? Actually, it takes care of the entire model box for us. On the backend, Core Data will interface with the saved data on the disk, and uses SQLite as its database to manage data. However, it also allows us to interface with this data at run time with instances of the data in a managed context (which we'll discuss in a bit), and deals with a lot of the *in-between parts* automatically.

Now, this isn't a book on database programming, so for our purposes we don't have to look any deeper than that, and Core Data is abstract enough that we really don't need to know any more! But if you're intrigued and want to know what's going on behind the scenes of Core Data, there is plenty of information about it online.

Entities, attributes, and relationships

Now, let's take a look at how Core Data works when it comes to defining our model. As I mentioned a bit earlier, Core Data manages an *object graph*. The object graph is the runtime version of a data model, which is a way of describing how different pieces of complex data are composed and relate to each other. This data model has three main parts: entities, attributes, and relationships.

Entities

The easiest way to think about an entity is as if it were an object. An entity has a name (like *person*) and is composed of the other two pieces, attributes and relationships. In our case, we'll create entities like `TextSnippet`, which will have attributes like *date*, *coordinate*, and *text*.

Attributes

While entities are the *objects*, attributes can be seen as the *properties*. An attribute is a piece of data with a certain data type. For example, our *person* entity might have a *name* attribute, which is of the string type, and an *age* attribute which is an integer. With Core Data, we can also set an attribute to be optional (the default) or required. If an attribute is required but isn't set, Core Data will throw an error. Attributes can also have default values.

Relationships

Finally, we have relationships which are pretty self-explanatory: they describe how two entities relate to one another. Going back to the *person* entity, let's imagine we also have a *house* entity. We can create a new relationship named *address* in the *person* entity, and connect it to the house. We can also create an inverse relationship by creating an *owner* relationship in the house and connecting it to the person.

Relationships can also be one of two types: *to-one*, and *to-many*. Our house/person example were both examples of *to-one* relationships, since each house had one owner, and each person had one address. However, multiple people can live in a house, so we can change the name of the *owner* relationship to be *resident*, and set it as a *to-many* relationship. Then the house can have as many residents as is needed.

It's also important to set rules for deletion with relationships. There are several things that can happen when an object gets deleted: it can *nullify* its relationship with related objects; it can *cascade* the deletion, deleting the connected object with it; or it can *deny* the deletion of the original object if the connected object exists.

With our person/house example, if a house gets deleted we shouldn't delete the people, since they might have other houses, but we should nullify their relationship to each other. How about a company/employee relationship? If the employee is deleted we should nullify the relationship with the company, but if the company itself is deleted, we should cascade that deletion down to the employee since they can no longer be employed if the company is gone.

Relationships are a very powerful tool, but are usually only useful when dealing with more complex data models. For our purposes they won't be used much, but it's good to understand how they work for future projects.

The data model editor

Now that we've learned about the three main components of the data model in Core Data, let's take a look at the editor! Let's create a little throwaway Xcode project to cut our teeth on Core Data before we set it up in our Snippets project. When starting this project, make sure to (finally) check off the box that says **Use Core Data** (*Figure 9.2*):

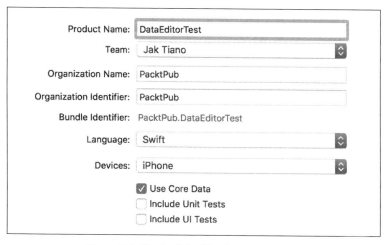

Figure 9.2: Check off the Use Core Data option

If you take a look at the project, you'll see some minor changes. In the `AppDelegate`, there's a *bunch* of new boilerplate code that sets up our managed context, but most interesting to us right now is the new `.xcdatamodeld` type file in our project navigator. This file is what describes our data model, and it uses a custom editor view to create entities, attributes, and relationships. Click on the file to open it and take a look:

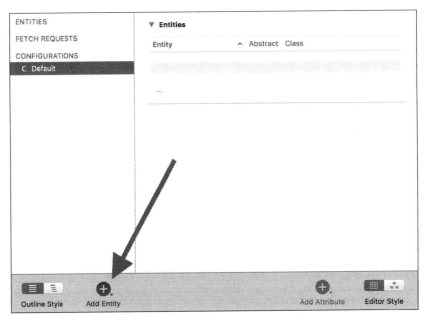

Figure 9.3: The Core Data data model editor

To start, there's not much going on. Let's add our first entity by clicking the **Add Entity** button on the bottom of the window, shown in *Figure 9.3*. We should now see a new entity named **Entity** under the **Entities** section on the left sidebar. In the middle of the editor window we have the ability to add new attributes, relationships, and *fetched properties* (don't worry about these for now).

For this example, let's use the **Company/Employee** model from the end of the last section to get us acquainted to the data model editor. First, change the name of our boring **Entity** to be **Company**. Then, in the attributes section, click the plus button to create a new attribute and call it `name`. Next to the attribute's name is a drop-down menu for the attribute's data type; select **String**. Now create another string attribute and call it `industry`:

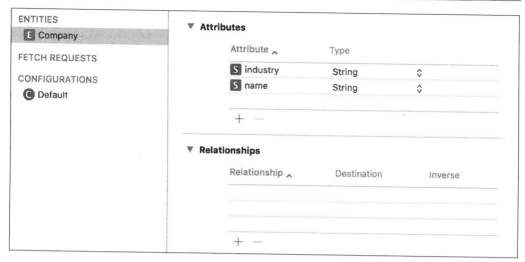

Figure 9.4: Our Company entity soso with its attributes set

Next, let's create another entity, this time named **Employee**. We'll add a `name` attribute of type `String`, and a `salary` attribute of type `Integer16`. If you select the `salary` attribute, and look in the attribute inspector (*option + command + 3*), you can see that we can set some data validation and default values. Let's enable a minimum of `40000` and a maximum of `200000`, with the default value of `40000`. This will ensure that our `salary` attribute always falls within one of these values, which can be useful in some scenarios.

Now that we have two entities, we can also create a relationship. Add a new relationship with the plus button, and name it `employer`. Next to its name, set the **Destination** of the relationship to our `Company` entity. For now, we'll leave the **Inverse** column blank:

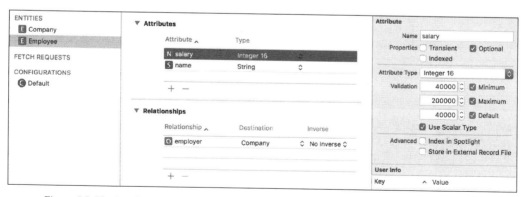

Figure 9.5: The Employee entity and its salary attribute selected with data validation edits made

Now that we have our `Employee` entity finished, let's head back to the `Company` entity and add a new relationship. Create the new relationship and name it `employee`, with the destination set to our `Employee` entity. This time, we will set the **Inverse** to the other relationship we made in the `Employee` entity; the `employer` relationship should be visible in the **Inverse** column dropdown.

The last relationship we made used the default values for its type and delete rule (*to-one* and *nullify*, respectively), so we didn't need to change them. However, our `employee` relationship needs to be of the type *to-many*, and the delete rule needs to be set to *cascade*.

To change these settings, click on the `employee` relationship in our `Company` entity, and then take a look at the attribute editor. You should see a set of dropdown options, below the `name` field. Set **Delete Rule** to *cascade*, and **Type** to *to-many*. Now the `Company` can relate to several employees, and when the `Company` is deleted, all of the employees are deleted with it.

Finally, let's take a look at the data model visualization feature. If you look in the lower right corner of the editor, there's a toggle called **Editor Style**. Toggle the style to the other mode, and you'll see a visual representation of your data model:

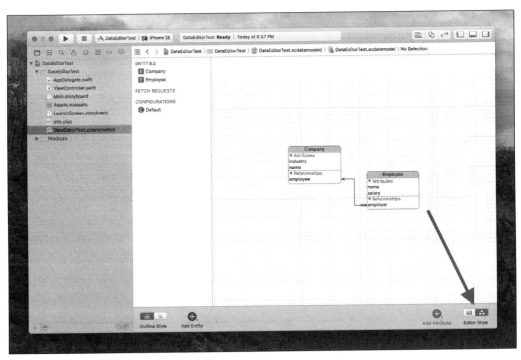

Figure 9.6: A visual representation of our data model

You can imagine how useful this can be later on when dealing with more complex data models! At this point, you know all of the basic tools for creating entities, attributes, and relationships, so play around a bit and see what kind of data you can model.

Preparing Snippets for Core Data

In the last section, we learned about how to start using Core Data in a project that already has the feature enabled from the beginning. However, our `Snippets` project was started *without* Core Data enabled so, before we can continue, we're going to have to prepare our project for use with Core Data. There are two things we need to do: set up the `managed context` and the rest of the Core Data stack in our `AppDelegate.swift` file, and then create the data model for Snippets using the editor we just covered. Before we get started, open your `Snippets` Xcode project (or use my final version from *Chapter 8, Exploring Common iOS Frameworks*), and import the `CoreData` framework.

Initializing the Core Data stack

So far, we've only looked at how to create a data model in Core Data. Now, we need to set up the code that will let us load, manipulate, and save our data. The objects that help us to do this are referred to as the `Core Data stack`. This is composed of three pieces: the managed object model, the persistent store container, and the managed object context.

> Most of the code in this section is taken from the boilerplate code added to a project when you enable Core Data using the checkbox at project creation time.
>
> This section might have some code that is a little tough to understand, but that's okay! The important part is that you understand what each part of the stack does, and why it's important.

Data model versus object graph

Before we can understand how this `stack` works together, we need to understand some other concepts. A few times throughout this chapter, I've mentioned something known as the `object graph`, and how Core Data is used to manage it. We've also spent a good amount of time learning about the *data model*, which Core Data is also responsible for. So before we move forward, let's look at how the two are related.

The *data model* is a description of a piece of data. The data model tells us that a *Person* must have a name and an age, and can have a *resident* relationship with a *House*. The data model is effectively a *blueprint*.

The *object graph* is a set of real data. It tells us that we have three actual people named *Emma*, *Tyler*, and *Natasha*, along with their ages and what *House* they each live in. The object graph is an *implementation* of a data set that follows the rules set by the data model. This is actually what is being loaded and saved by Core Data.

The NSManagedObjectModel

Armed with this information, let's now take a look at what is going on in the Core Data stack. The NSManagedObjectModel (usually abbreviated to **mom**) loads in a data model that we created in the data model editor. The mom is pretty much only used as a way for the NSPersistentStoreCoordinator to know what kind of data is being loaded. To create an instance of the NSManagedObjectModel, we need to load in the model from a file. While a bit counterintuitive, we are not actually going to load in the .xcdatamodeld file, but a file with the *same name* but a different extension: momd.

Navigate to your AppDelegate.swift file and add an import CoreData command to the top of the file. Then, scroll to the bottom of the class, and add the following code to create our NSManagedObjectModel:

```
// MARK: - Core Data stack
lazy var managedObjectModel: NSManagedObjectModel = {
    let modelURL = Bundle.main.url(forResource: "SnippetData",
withExtension: "momd")!
    return NSManagedObjectModel(contentsOf: modelURL)!

}()
```

 Here, we're declaring a lazy property with the *lazy* keyword. What this means is that the code inside the block will only initialize this property the first time some other object comes looking for it, *not* during initialization. This makes initialization much faster, and has the added benefit of making sure that time isn't spent initializing this property if no other object ends up needing it at runtime.

First, we get the location of our data model file from our application's resources using Bundle.main.url(forResource:), again using the filename from our .xcdatamodeld file, but with the momd extension instead. From there we can just instantiate the NSManagedObjectModel using that URL, and return it.

The NSPersistentStoreCoordinator

The next part of the Core Data stack is the NSPersistentStoreCoordinator. This object uses the managed object model to actually read and instantiate instances of objects from the *persistent store* based on the blueprints of the mom (the managed object model, not the mother). A simple way to think about the persistent store is that it is the saved data that exists on disk (it's not always that simple, but don't worry about that for now).

So, essentially, the NSPersistentStoreCoordinator uses the data model to know what the data should look like, and then coordinates creating new data and saving data to the disk. In practice, the managed context (which we will cover next) will do most of the heavy lifting with the persistent store coordinator, but we still need to set it up. Let's do that now:

```
llazy var persistentStoreCoordinator: NSPersistentStoreCoordinator = {
    let coordinator = NSPersistentStoreCoordinator(
managedObjectModel: self.managedObjectModel)
    let urls = FileManager.default.urls( for: .documentDirectory, in:
.userDomainMask)
    let url = urls.last!.appendingPathComponent("SingleViewCoreData.
sqlite")
    do {
        try coordinator.addPersistentStore(ofType: NSSQLiteStoreType,
configurationName: nil, at: url, options: nil)
    } catch {
        // Replace this to handle the error appropriately.
        let nserror = error as NSError
        print ("Unresolved error \(nserror), \(nserror.userInfo)")
        abort()
    }
    return coordinator
}()
```

First, we instantiate a new NSPersistentStoreCoordinator by passing in the managed object model. Again, this is so that the persistent store coordinator knows what the data will look like.

Next, we play around in the file system for a few lines of code in order to get the location of the database (the actual *persistent store*) that will be coordinated. Once we have that URL, we use a do/try/catch block to load the database from the URL. If it fails, we'll catch the error and need to handle it, but otherwise our NSPersistentStoreCoordinator is set up and ready to go!

The NSManagedObjectContext

Lastly, we have our NSManagedObjectContext, which is mainly what we'll be working with in our code. The purpose of the managed context is to provide an area to *play* with our data. It is here that we will edit data and create new instances of data; Apple describes the managed context as an *intelligent scratchpad*. When we are done creating, editing, and deleting data, the managed context can be used to tell the system to save our data, which flushes it through the persistent store and down onto the disk.

Let's set up our managed context now:

```
lazy var managedObjectContext: NSManagedObjectContext = {
    let coordinator = self.persistentStoreCoordinator
    var managedObjectContext = NSManagedObjectContext(
concurrencyType: .mainQueueConcurrencyType)
    managedObjectContext.persistentStoreCoordinator = coordinator
    return managedObjectContext
}()
```

First, we get a reference to our persistent store coordinator. Then we create a new instance of the NSManagedObjectContext class and pass in the concurrency type. Don't worry about this for now, but we're passing in .mainQueueConcurrencyType. Finally, after initializing the managedObjectContext, we assign its persistentStoreCoordinator to be our instance that we grabbed in the first line. This lets the managed object context know what database it is working with. Now we can return the fully set up context.

Final touches

We've now completely set up the Core Data stack in our AppDelegate. The managed object model describes our data, the persistent store coordinator interfaces with the database, and the managed object context lets us create, edit, and save data.

However, we can still do a little more in our AppDelegate to make using the stack a bit easier. Let's create a helper function at the bottom of our AppDelegate class that makes it really simple to save our data:

```
// MARK: - Core Data Saving support
func saveContext () {
    if managedObjectContext.hasChanges {
        do {
            try managedObjectContext.save()
        } catch {
            // Replace this to handle the error appropriately.
```

```
        let nserror = error as NSError
        print("Unresolved error \(nserror), \(nserror.userInfo)")
        abort()
    }
  }
}
```

The first thing we do in this `saveContext()` function is check to see if we've made any changes to our data. If not, then there is no point in saving! If changes have been made, then we try to save the data by calling the `save()` function in our managed object context. If the save is unsuccessful, we'll have to handle the error.

This helper function will make it easier down the line to save our data. Now, with one function call, we can make sure we are not saving data that doesn't need to be saved, in addition to handling errors.

Let's put our new `saveContext()` function to use. In your `AppDelegate` class, you should have several empty function stubs still in the class from when the project was created. Many of these are places where you can add code to run when the application enters and exits different states, like entering and exiting the background. There should also be a function called `applicationWillTerminate()`, which is called when an app is closed. This is a great time to make sure that the user's data is saved, so let's call our `saveContext()` function from here:

```
func applicationWillTerminate(_ application: UIApplication) {
    self.saveContext()
}
```

This will make it so that if any data accidentally goes unsaved, then our app will save it just before shutdown so that information is not lost.

Now we've got our stack set up, and some easy saving functionality ready to go!

Recreating the data model with Core Data

The only thing left to do before we can start saving data in our Snippets app is to recreate our data model for Core Data. Right now we have `SnippetData.swift`, which uses classes to model our data. In this section, we're going to make a new `.xcdatamodeld` file that will take the place of our `SnippetData.swift` file.

To begin, create a new file (*command + N*), and from the template chooser search for, and then choose `Data Model`. This will create a new `.xcdatamodeld` file in your project. Make sure to name it `SnippetData`, since this is what we told our `NSManagedObjectModel` our model file would be called.

Since we've already been over how to use the data model editor, I'm just going to give you some descriptions of the entities, and leave it up to you to create them and their attributes. However, one thing we didn't cover earlier was that you can have subentities, which act like subclasses. Since our existing `SnippetData.swift` data model uses subclassing to carry over redundant data, we're going to use subentities in our model. To create a subentity, select an entity from the entity sidebar and set the `parent` property from the attribute inspector. The entity will then `inherit` all of the parent entity's attributes and relationships.

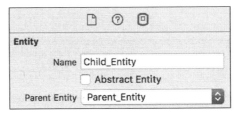

Figure 9.7: A close up of the attribute inspector showing the parent entity option

As you can see, you'll be able to select the **Parent_Entity** from a drop-down menu which contains all existing entities in your model. This means you'll have to create the parent entities first. Remember that you can also use the attribute inspector to set whether or not an attribute is optional or required.

First, let's create our `base` snippet type, which will be the parent of our other snippet data types. Here are the specifications for this entity:

Entity Name: Snippet		Parent: No Parent Entity
Attributes		
Key	**Type**	
date	Date	REQUIRED
latitude	Double	OPTIONAL
longitude	Double	OPTIONAL
type	String	REQUIRED

Next, we'll create and set up the text snippet entity:

Entity Name: Snippet		Parent: Snippet
Attributes		
Key	**Type**	
text	String	REQUIRED

Finally, we'll create our photo snippet entity:

Entity Name: Snippet		Parent: Snippet
Attributes		
Key	**Type**	
photo	Binary Data	REQUIRED

Make sure to double check all of your entities and attributes are set up correctly with the correct types, and the keys have *no spelling mistakes*. Once we start coding in the next section, any spelling mistakes here in the data model will give you errors when trying to retrieve data. If you set everything up the same way, your visual data model hierarchy should look like this:

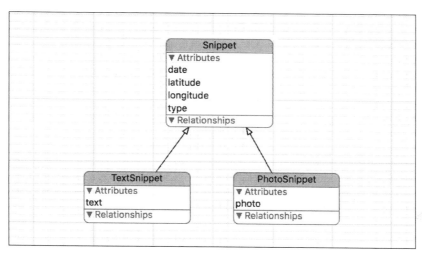

Figure 9.8: Our completed data model, represented in visual form

And with our data model completed, our Snippets project is completely ready to start using the persistence features of Core Data.

Persisting data

In order to implement persistence for our application's data, we need to do three things: save data, load data, and delete data. In this section, we're going to go through our ViewController class and remove all of the references to our old data model, and instead begin using our new Core Data compatible data model. As we go, we'll be introducing new ways of saving and loading our snippet data, and adding the ability to delete snippets.

Saving data

With our old data model, saving data consisted of two steps: create a new instance of a `SnippetData` subclass, and then add it to our `data` array. Now, with Core Data, the process is pretty similar but it takes a few more lines of code and uses some new concepts.

Before we can get started with our new save mechanisms, we're going to make two small changes. First, add an `import CoreData` command at the top of the `ViewController.swift` file, with the other `import` statements. Then, change the type of our `data` array so that instead of `[SnippetData]` type, it is `[NSManagedObject]` type.

```
var data = [NSManagedObject]()
```

`NSManagedObject` is the type of data that Core Data will load our `entities` into, as you will see shortly.

 Changing the type of our `data` array will result in giving your file several errors, since the complier is now expecting different data types everywhere. This is fine, since we're about to remove the rest of the references to `SnippetData`, and transition to using `NSManagedObject` for all of our needs.

With these changes made, let's move on to our first save function. Create a new function called `saveTextSnippet(text: String)`, and place it below the `createNewPhotoSnippet()` function.

Inside this function, we are doing three things: getting access to the Core Data stack, creating a new instance of an entity, and then configuring that entity. Let's start with getting access to the Core Data stack:

```
func saveTextSnippet(text: String) {

    let delegate = UIApplication.shared.delegate as! AppDelegate
    let managedContext = delegate.managedObjectContext
}
```

On the first line we are getting access to our application's delegate and then force casting it to our `AppDelegate` class, which is where we defined our Core Data stack in the last section. Now we can use `delegate` to get access to the `managedObjectContext` property in our `AppDelegate` class, which you'll remember is our main point of entry to Core Data functionality. It's a bit confusing to read it all, but basically what we did is create a shortcut to our `AppDelegate` with `delegate`, and to `NSManagedObjectContext` with `managedContext`. We'll be using both of these shortly.

Next, we are going to create a new data container. Earlier, we changed our data array from storing `SnippetData` objects, and instead made it hold `NSManagedObject` objects. So what is this `NSManagedObject` anyway? To put it simply, it is a shape shifting container that we can fill with any data that we want. To make sure that it works the way we want it to, we tell it what entity from our model that it is supposed to represent using what is called a `descriptor` object. Let's create the descriptor, and then the new data container:

```
func saveTextSnippet(text: String) {

    let delegate = UIApplication.shared.delegate as! AppDelegate
    let managedContext = delegate.managedObjectContext
        let desc = NSEntityDescription.entity(forEntityName:
            "TextSnippet", in: managedContext)

    let textSnippet = NSManagedObject(entity: desc!, insertInto:
        managedContext)
```

Here you can see that we first create the descriptor by passing in the name of the entity it represents, along with the `managedContext` that it will be a part of. Then, we create `textSnippet` which is an `NSManagedObject`. In the initializer, we pass in the `NSEntityDescription` object so that it knows what type of entity it represents, and then again we pass in the `managedContext` so it can be inserted into our `scratchpad`.

Now that we've created the new data object and added it to the `scratchpad`, we need to fill it with data and then save the changes to disk. In order to set all of the attributes that we defined in our `TextSnippet` entity in our data model, we'll need to use what is known as *key/value encoding*. This means that we will set properties of the object using the names of the properties instead of accessing them directly through code. To do this, we use the `setValue(_:  , forKey: )` function. Let's look at how that works as follows:

```
func saveTextSnippet(text: String) {

    let delegate = UIApplication.shared.delegate as! AppDelegate
    let managedContext = delegate.managedObjectContext
    let desc = NSEntityDescription.entity(forEntityName:
"TextSnippet", in: managedContext)

    let textSnippet = NSManagedObject(entity: desc!, insertInto:
managedContext)
    textSnippet.setValue(SnippetType.text.rawValue, forKey: "type")
    textSnippet.setValue(text, forKey: "text")
    textSnippet.setValue(NSDate(), forKey: "date")
    if let coord = self.currentCoordinate {
```

```
                    textSnippet.setValue(coord.latitude, forKey: "latitude")
                    textSnippet.setValue(coord.longitude, forKey: "longitude")
            }

        delegate.saveContext()
    }
```

First, we are setting the value for our `type` attribute. In our data model, we defined this as a string, and we are setting its value to the raw string behind the text value from the `SnippetType` enum (which is located in `SnippetData.swift`).

 Remember, you can access the backing data for an enum case by using `.rawValue`. We're using the enum data because it is safer than just writing Text, since we can just write `SnippetType.text.rawValue` anywhere in code to point to the same string, and spelling mistakes can't break anything.

Then, we are setting the value for our `text` attribute, and here we just set it to the string that is passed into the `saveTextSnippet()` function. After that, we set the value for our `date` attribute, which we set to the current date by instantiating a new `Date()` object, just like we did in the old data model.

If you think back to when we set up our data model, we made the latitude and longitude properties optional. That's because the user may not have allowed location services, or maybe the phone wasn't able to get a lock onto the user's location. In either case, the data model needed to support location data not being available. So, after we set the date we check to see if the `currentCoordinate` property has a value. If so, we set our latitude and longitude, but if not, that's okay too, we just don't set those values.

Finally, we call the `saveContext()` helper function that we wrote in our `AppDelegate` class.

Now that the save function is finished for our text snippet, let's hook it up. Find the `createNewTextSnippet()` function, and let's change the lines of code where we set the `saveText` closure.

```
    textEntryVC.saveText = { ( text: String ) in
        self.saveTextSnippet(text: text)
    }
```

Instead of creating a new `TextSnippetData` object, we are just calling the save function we just made, and passing in the text we want to save.

Great! Now let's tackle saving the photo snippet. For the most part, we're going to be doing a lot of the same things, with one major difference: we need to convert the image into a format suitable for saving. Let's create a new `savePhotoSnippet(photo: UIImage)` function:

```
func savePhotoSnippet(photo: UIImage) {

    let delegate = UIApplication.shared.delegate as! AppDelegate
    let managedContext = delegate.managedObjectContext
    let desc = NSEntityDescription.entity(forEntityName:
"PhotoSnippet", in: managedContext)
    let photoSnippet = NSManagedObject(entity: desc!, insertInto:
managedContext)
    let photoData = UIImagePNGRepresentation(photo)

    photoSnippet.setValue(SnippetType.photo.rawValue, forKey: "type")
    photoSnippet.setValue(photoData, forKey: "photo")
    photoSnippet.setValue(Date(), forKey: "date")
    if let coord = self.currentCoordinate {
        photoSnippet.setValue(coord.latitude, forKey: "latitude")
        photoSnippet.setValue(coord.longitude, forKey: "longitude")
    }

    delegate.saveContext()
}
```

Aside from the obvious change to the name of the entity we create (`photoSnippet` instead of `textSnippet`), there are only a few differences from the `saveTextSnippet()` function. First, we are telling the `NSEntityDescription` that the entity it is describing is the `PhotoSnippet` entity. Then, we are creating a new piece of data called `photoData`. This `photoData` is the raw data representation of our image, which we get by passing in our `UIImage` to the function `UIImagePNGRepresentation()`. Now that we have the raw .PNG data, we can use it to set the `photo` property of our `photoSnippet`.

To use the new save function, we're going to make some changes to the `imagePickerController()` function. The updated function should look like this:

```
func imagePickerController(_ picker: UIImagePickerController,
didFinishPickingMediaWithInfo info: [String : Any]) {
    guard let image = info[UIImagePickerControllerEditedImage] as?
UIImage else {
        print("Image could not be found")
        return
    }
    savePhotoSnippet(photo: image)
    dismiss(animated: true, completion: nil)
}
```

And with that, we've completely moved over to our new Core Data way of saving data! Unfortunately, we still have to load (or *fetch*) the data before it can be of any use to us. Let's do that now.

Fetching data

Right now, we have our `data` array which is expected to hold all of our snippet data. However, nowhere in our code do we populate our array with data! Let's fix this now.

Create a new function called `reloadSnippetData()`, and put it right below the `viewWillAppear()` function:

```
func reloadSnippetData () {

    let delegate = UIApplication.shared.delegate as! AppDelegate
    let managedContext = delegate.managedObjectContext
}
```

Before we start, we need to get our delegate and managed context so that we can ask the managed context to fetch our data. To do this, we need to use something called a `fetch request`. You can think of a fetch request as a way for us to describe what information we want from our database. In this case, we are going to set up our fetch request to ask for a certain type of entity ordered in a certain way:

```
func reloadSnippetData () {

    let delegate = UIApplication.shared.delegate as! AppDelegate
    let managedContext = delegate.managedObjectContext


    let request = NSFetchRequest<NSFetchRequestResult>(entityName:
```

```
"Snippet")
    let sortDescriptor = NSSortDescriptor(key: "date", ascending:
false)

    request.sortDescriptors = [ sortDescriptor ]
```

Here, we've created a new `NSFetchRequest`, and passed in the entity name that we want to retrieve. We pass in the `Snippet` entity name since that's the base entity of both our `TextSnippet` and `PhotoSnippet` entities; using the base entity name will return both.

After we create the fetch request, we also create a *sort descriptor*; a sort descriptor is attached to the fetch request and tells the database how we want the data sorted. When we create the `NSSortDescriptor`, we tell it that we want to sort the data based on the `date` attribute of the returned entities, and that the dataset should be descending (so, the ascending parameter is `false`). To attach the sort descriptor to our fetch request, we need to place it inside an array and then assign it to the fetch request's `sortDescriptors` property. We need to put it in an array since it's possible to attach multiple sort descriptors.

Finally, we need to execute the fetch request:

```
func reloadSnippetData () {

    let delegate = UIApplication.shared.delegate as! AppDelegate
    let managedContext = delegate.managedObjectContext

    let request = NSFetchRequest<NSFetchRequestResult>(entityName:
"Snippet")
    let sortDescriptor = NSSortDescriptor(key: "date", ascending:
false)
    request.sortDescriptors = [ sortDescriptor ]

    do {
        let fetchResults = try managedContext.fetch( request)
        self.data = fetchResults as! [NSManagedObject]
    } catch {
        let e = error as NSError
        print("Unresolved error \(e), \(e.userInfo)")
    }
}
```

To retrieve our data, we send the fetch request off to the managed context using the `fetch()` function, and put the results inside `fetchResults`. Since the fetch request can fail and throw an error, we place it inside a `do`/`try`/`catch` block, and handle any error that might occur. If there is no error, then we assign the results to our data array. So to recap, we got a reference to our managed context, set up a fetch request to grab `Snippet` entities ordered by date, and then fetched data from the managed context and stored it in the data array.

So now we've got a function that updates our data, but when should we use it? To keep things efficient, we should only fetch data when it changes. Right now, we are reloading our table view in the `viewWillAppear()` function. Let's reload our snippet data right before we reload the table view, so that its data is always fresh:

```
override func viewWillAppear(animated: Bool) {
    reloadSnippetData()
    tableView.reloadData()
}
```

Now, right before our view controller is about to come back on screen from a snippet creation view controller, we refresh our data, then refresh our table.

However, when our table reloads its data it still doesn't know how to handle the new Core Data objects in our data array! Let's update `tableView(cellForRowAt:)` so that it can read information out of the `NSManagedObjects`:

```
func tableView(_ tableView: UITableView, cellForRowAt indexPath:
IndexPath) -> UITableViewCell {

    let cell: UITableViewCell

        let snippetData = data[indexPath.row]
        let snippetDate = snippetData.value(forKey: "date") as! Date
        let snippetType = SnippetType(rawValue:
         snippetData.value(forKey: "type") as! String)!

    let formatter = DateFormatter()
    formatter.dateFormat = "MMM d, yyyy hh:mm a"
        let dateString = formatter.string(from: snippetDate)

    (...Additional code...)
}
```

At the top of the function, we're going to pull out all of the data that we need. First, we grab the relevant `NSManagedObject` out of the data array by grabbing the object at the index with the same row as our cell. So, if we're on row 3 of our table view, we pull out the `NSManagedObject` at index 3.

Now we have to extract data from our NSManagedObjects. When we were setting up the objects in our save functions, we used the setValue(_:, forKey:) function to insert data. Now, we can use the value(forKey:) function to extract data. First we pull out the date by getting the value for the key date, and force cast it to the Date type. After that we pull out the type string, and use that as the raw data to instantiate a SnippetType enum. Finally, we update our dateString to use the new snippetDate value we just made, instead of the old snippetData.date value we were using before:

```
func tableView(_ tableView: UITableView, cellForRowAt indexPath:
IndexPath) -> UITableViewCell {
    (...additional code...)

    switch snippetType
    {
    case .text:
        let snippetText = snippetData.value(forKey: "text") as! String
        cell = tableView.dequeueReusableCell( withIdentifier:
"textSnippetCell", for: indexPath) as! TextSnippetCell
        (cell as! TextSnippetCell).label.text = snippetText

    (...additional code...)
}
```

If we continue down the function, we get to the switch statement where we set up our Text and Photo snippet cells. At the beginning of our .text case, we are going to use the same value(forKey:) function to pull out the string for the text attribute, and assign it to a constant named snippetText. Now, we have to replace all instances of (snippetData as! TextData).textData with just snippetText. The first place we do that can be seen here, where we set the label text to snippetText, but there are a few more places where you should change this.

Once we've cleaned up our .text case, we should move on to the .photo case:

```
func tableView(tableView: UITableView, cellForRowAtIndexPath
indexPath: NSIndexPath) -> UITableViewCell {

    (...additional code...)

    case .photo:
        let snippetPhoto = UIImage(data: snippetData.value(forKey:
"photo") as! Data)
        cell = tableView.dequeueReusableCell(withIdentifier:
"photoSnippetCell", for: indexPath)
        (cell as! PhotoSnippetCell).photo.image = snippetPhoto
    (...additional code...)
}
```

When we saved our image, remember that we first had to convert it to `Data` before we could send it off to Core Data to be saved. Now that we've loaded it back in, we need to undo that process. Here, you can see that we are doing this by pulling out the raw data from the `photo` attribute, and passing it into a `UIImage` constructor that builds the image from `Data`.

Like in our `.text` case, we now have a much simpler `snippetPhoto` constant that we can use in place of the old `(snippetData as! PhotoData).photoData` that we were using before. Make sure to comb through the rest of the `.photo` case and replace all of these.

Once you've done that, our table view is now set up to load in all the data it needs from `NSManagedObjects`. So with saving and loading completely working through Core Data, everything should be working! To test it out, run the application on your device and make a few snippets. Then completely close the app, open it up again, and your snippets are still there!

Deleting data

While the prospect of retaining data across sessions is pretty awesome, we've now got a problem, we're stuck with every snippet we've ever made. Now that we can create and save new data, it only makes sense that we add the ability to delete saved data too.

Luckily for us, most of this functionality is built into the table view itself. If you've ever used an app that uses a table view (like Mail), you'll know that you can swipe on a cell to reveal a `Delete` button. Right now, our table view doesn't respond to a swipe, but we can change that by implementing a single function.

By implementing the `tableView(_:, commit:, forRowAt:)` function, our application knows that it can be edited, and in turn will enable the swipe to delete functionality. First, we'll start by creating an empty function stub in the `UITableViewDataSource` extension to see if the swipe is working.:

```
func tableView(_ tableView: UITableView, commit editingStyle:
UITableViewCellEditingStyle, forRowAt indexPath: IndexPath) {

}
```

After adding this function, run the app and then swipe from right to left on an existing `Snippet`. You should now see that you are able to delete the `Snippet` (*Figure 9.9*). However, tapping the delete button won't do anything... yet:

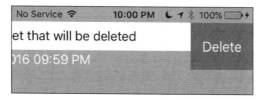

Figure 9.9: A snippet table view cell that has been swiped, exposing a Delete button

Now, let's look at what we have to do to actually delete the data. First, we need to delete the data from our managed context, and then we need to delete the actual table view cell that is presenting it. Let's fill out the function to do this now:

```
func tableView(_ tableView: UITableView, commit editingStyle:
UITableViewCellEditingStyle, forRowAt indexPath: IndexPath) {

    let delegate = UIApplication.shared.delegate as! AppDelegate
    let managedContext = delegate.managedObjectContext

    let currentObject = data[indexPath.row]
    managedContext.delete(currentObject)
    delegate.saveContext()
    reloadSnippetData()

    tableView.beginUpdates()
    tableView.deleteRows(at: [indexPath], with: .automatic)
    tableView.endUpdates()
}
```

At the top, we are again grabbing the delegate and `managedContext` for our Core Data stack. Then, we get the current object that we are dealing with, by asking for the object at the same index as our selected row (just like we did when setting up our cells). Once we have a reference to the current `NSManagedObject`, we pass it to our `managedContext` and tell it to delete the object. Once the object is deleted, we save the context to keep the change, and then finally reload our snippet data since it has changed.

Before we are finished, we also want to run a little animation to remove the cell from our table. To do this, we first call `tableView.beginUpdates()`. Then we tell the table view to delete the row at our current index path using the `.automatic` animation, before telling the table view to `endUpdates()`.

Now, when we actually press the **Delete** button that shows up when we slide, it will remove the associated object from our database, and then remove the cell from our table.

And now our journey with Core Data is complete! Our `Snippets` app has a brand new data model that can save, load, and delete data from a persistent store. Every time a user opens the app now, their data will still be there. We are one big step closer to finishing our first application! Before we leave, remember: `git commit`.

Summary

In this chapter, we learned a lot about Core Data. First we revisited the concept of the model within an MVC application, and learned about how entities, attributes, and relationships work in Core Data. We became acquainted with the Core Data model editor, and then used the editor to build up a real data model for our app. We also learned about the Core Data stack, which makes persistence work. Finally, we took all of this knowledge to implement saving, loading, and deleting permanent data in our app.

In the next chapter, we're going to take one more huge jump forward: learning how to use watchOS to create an Apple Watch companion app for your app. I could say more, but let's not spoil any of the fun.

10
Creating a watchOS Companion App

One of the most exciting development opportunities of the last few years became a reality when Apple officially announced they were making a smart watch companion to their iOS ecosystem: the Apple Watch. Since the watch released in April 2015, developers have been testing the limits of the wrist worn device, trying to overcome many of the interesting restrictions that result from its small size and limited computing ability.

The Apple Watch is very different from iOS devices. In this chapter, we're going to spend some time learning about what makes the Apple Watch different, and where its strengths lie. The focus will be on how to think *small*. To be more specific, we will be covering:

- How to design for the Apple Watch
- The components of a watchOS application
- How a watchOS app differs from an iOS app
- Building a full watchOS experience

Designing for the Apple Watch

While it may seem obvious from looks alone, it can be very easy to misunderstand the way that an Apple Watch differs from an iOS device like an iPhone. Many make the mistake of only focusing on how to shrink the user interface of their app into a smaller form factor, instead of really understanding how the Apple Watch is actually used.

Before we can move on to the more technical aspects of creating an Apple Watch companion app, it's important to look at these differences in use and expectations.

Using the watch

The most obvious difference between an Apple Watch and an iPhone, and I've already touched on this a few times, is the size. There is no way around it. The amount of screen real estate severely limits how much information can be presented, and how many inputs can be accepted.

A lot of developers also seem to underestimate how important it is that the watch is worn; it's not a device that comes out of a pocket when needed. There's a level of intimacy not present with an iPhone owing to the fact that the watch is in contact with your skin all day. It can also be tiring to hold a watch up to your face for more than 15 seconds!

Another big departure from the traditional iOS experience is the introduction of a new input method, which is the digital crown. This *scroll wheel* on the side of the watch allows users to scroll through lists without touching the screen, and clicking the crown acts as a *home* button that lets the user perform navigation commands depending on context.

Overall, using the watch can be distilled to three points: small, invisible, and intimate. It's a small device and there's no room for unneeded clutter. It's at its best when invisible; the user shouldn't have to constantly be remembering to interact with it. Finally, the watch is intimate and personal; it is highly customizable, and it touches and taps the user on the wrist.

Intended experience

With a better idea of what makes the Apple Watch different from an iOS device, let's now talk about how those differences change the experience that a watchOS app should provide.

Owing to the size of the screen, and the difficulty of holding up your wrist for extended periods of time, the optimal time for using a watchOS app is only a few seconds. Remember, at its core the Apple Watch is still a watch. Traditionally, people have only ever glanced at their wrists for a second or two to read the time, or check the date. Just because we *have* a touch screen, doesn't mean we should require its use to get access to the information we are looking for.

This ties nicely into the second point: an Apple Watch companion app is not meant to recreate the iOS experience on your wrist. It should really be used to put the most important data in your app, in a place that is more accessible than your pocket.

Some of the best apps on the watch are the simplest. For example, a budgeting app that only tells you how much you can spend on *food* that day. It doesn't make sense to give you the ability to look at transaction lists, or make budget edits on your wrist, but it's great to quickly check it if you should stop for a treat on the way home from work.

Similarly, some of the worst apps on the watch are the ones that try to do too much. Some apps try to squeeze the entire iOS experience onto the wrist, complete with multiple view controllers. Even Apple's Mail and Messages apps are a bit too bloated–scrolling through lists of messages is a pain. However, these apps are redeemed through their excellent use of notifications, since most users will probably never open the actual apps themselves but interface exclusively through their notifications.

Finally, it's worth noting that not every app needs a watchOS companion! The platform is still in its infancy, and it's clear that a lot of the apps on the watch are the result of very eager developers wanting to play with a new toy. But, as I've reiterated many times, the watch is small and intimate, and there's no room for unnecessary information. If your app doesn't have a real reason to live on a wrist, don't force it there.

To recap, a watchOS app should take no more than a few seconds to use, and should display only the most essential information from your app. If you can't do something that fits this description, it's okay to conclude that a watchOS companion is not needed for your app.

Apple's design principles

While everything up to this point has come from my extensive use of and development for Apple Watch, it's also a good idea to take a look at how Apple themselves expects us to design for the platform. Their design principles ultimately reflect what has already been discussed, so it also serves as a good wrap up. Apple's three design principles for Apple Watch are: Glanceable, Actionable, and Responsive. Watch apps should be glanceable, providing the most relevant information to the user as seamlessly as possible, weather from a complication, the dock, or the app itself. Applications are actionable when they think ahead for the user, presenting them with information they can act on just when they need it. Finally, apps should be responsive and quick to navigate through–unnecessary taps and wait times are eliminated.

Components of a watchOS app

Unlike iOS, where an app is mostly considered a single cohesive entity, watchOS applications have many different forms. There is the base *app*, which lives on the home screen, but there are also additional ways to interact with an *app* through *notifications* and a special watchOS interface known as *complications*, and finally by glancing at it in the *dock*. Each component of a watchOS app has its own strengths, and it's important to have a thorough understanding of how they all work together.

The watchOS app

The *app* on watchOS is the closest analog to what is traditionally seen as an app on iOS. It has a circular icon on the watch's home screen, and when you tap it you enter the full watchOS application. In a watchOS app, you can let the user tap buttons, scroll through content, and navigate through view controller hierarchies like in an iOS app. Later on, we'll talk about the features you have access to on the watch, but know that in the *app* you have access to everything:

Figure 10.1: The watchOS home screen, and the open Weather app

In watchOS 2.0 and onward, the watch applications will run directly on the device. In earlier versions, the iPhone would actually run the application and connect to the watch wirelessly. Running directly on the device gave the app better performance, but unfortunately apps were still quite slow. However, in watchOS 3.0 performance has been given top priority, and a user's favorite apps now always stay in memory making app launches instantaneous. Any app that has an active complication, or is kept in the dock is determined to be a *favorite*.

The main watch application is an important piece of your development efforts, but as you'll see shortly, it is not the most important part of the package. This is a pretty big departure from what we expect of iOS, but I think you'll see why this is true.

Dock snapshots

Different from the dock found on iOS, the watchOS dock is a live application view of your favorite apps just below the watch face. From the dock view, the app snapshot must be a single screen of information, because they cannot be scrolled from the dock. Buttons and interactions won't work either, because tapping on the app snapshot from the dock launches the full app. To make your application's dock snapshot as useful as possible, it should display only the most relevant information.:

Figure 10.2: The Weather application's dock snapshot, found below the watch face

When on the watch face screen, the user can press the long side button on the watch to bring up the dock. All of the user's docked applications are presented in a card-like format, swiping left and right to see their different apps.

Now, if you follow good watchOS design principles, a dock snapshot may be the primary use case for your application. Applications in the dock are very easy to get to, and the user can swipe through several apps very quickly. If you are displaying simple information (such as a gate number and boarding time for a flight), a dock snapshot will be more than enough for a user to quickly get the information they need.

Creating a good dock snapshot for your app presents an interesting challenge: you are required to cut down your whole watchOS application even further, presenting only the *most* essential information on a single screen. In practice, I find that I very rarely open an application from the home screen, and because of this I believe that earning a spot on a user's dock (only 10 apps can be docked) can make or break the usefulness of your watchOS application.

Notifications

While the dock is great for quickly finding *passive* information, notifications on Apple Watch are the primary method for dealing with *active* information. The common examples are e-mails and text messages. I rarely (or never) go into the messages or mail app on my Apple Watch to compose new messages. However, I interact with dozens of messages and e-mail notifications every day. Right from the notification, I can respond to a text with some pre-set answers, or use Siri dictation to respond with a simple answer. Usually, though, I just screen the texts and pull out my phone if they are urgent.

Notifications are a great way to present actionable information to your users. It's important to remember the intimacy of the watch here; if you're overloading your user's wrist with notifications that they don't care about, they *will* disable them altogether.

Complications

Finally, we have complications. The word is a term carried over from traditional watches, which would have sub-dials for stopwatches or little date markers that were referred to as *complications*. The term is used well, since complications on the Apple Watch are little icons or labels that you can optionally place on your watch face:

Figure 10.3: The Weather complication (in the upper left corner) displaying the current temperature

A complication can be seen as the ultimate summary of your application: you only get a very tiny rectangle to display information directly on the user's watch face. A great example is the complication for the built-in weather app, which displays the current temperature and nothing more. Tapping on the temperature launches the full weather application, making it very useful to not only get a quick gist of the weather, but to also bypass the home screen or dock to get more useful information.

One of the greatest new features in watchOS 2.0 is **Time Travel**, which allows you to turn the digital crown to look at the *future*. In addition to spinning the clock hands on the watch face, Time Travel will also update all of a user's complications to display the pre-computed *future* value, provided the developer supports the functionality. Using our weather example, spinning the watch a few hours into the future will change the temperature to read as the predicted temperature for that time:

Figure 10.4: The Weather complication showing the future temperature during Time Travel

As you can imagine, this is tremendously useful for people, and in my personal opinion is one of the greatest selling points of the watch. If you have an app that has any time sensitive information, supporting a Time Travel complication is the best way to make your app a must-have for Apple Watch owners.

Just as every iOS app doesn't need a watchOS app, not every watchOS app needs a complication. Sometimes the information in your app is not the right fit for such a time-oriented and compact summary, and a dock snapshot would serve you better. However, I believe that if you cannot come up with a useful dock snapshot, notification, or complication, there may be very little need for an app at all.

Architecture of a watchOS app

At this point, we've explored what an Apple Watch app is composed of, how it differs from iOS, and how it should function. Now it's time to take a look at how we actually write a watchOS app.

Before you get too worried, most of what we've learned so far will carry over to watchOS. We're still using Xcode, we're still using storyboards, and we're still using Swift. However, since battery life is a much bigger concern on watchOS, there are some pieces of the process that work a bit differently in order to keep the amount of actual processing time to a minimum. We're also working with considerably less performance than we are used to on iOS, so there is also going to be a bit more *magic* going on to ensure smooth operation—there isn't a lot of room for complex animations and the like.

Target bundles

First, let's talk about the different target bundles that are part of the Apple Watch target. Earlier in the book, we touched on what targets are, but as a quick recap: a target is a configuration for building a project, usually for a specific device. For a watchOS app, we have two target bundles that we need to put together; the Watch App bundle, and the Watch Extension bundle.

Watch App bundle

The Watch App bundle is a bit misleading; it contains all of the storyboards and assets needed to run your application. In the days of watchOS 1.0, this Watch App bundle is what would actually be installed on the watch itself, allowing quick loading of heavy assets like images. The Watch App bundle is where we will store the storyboard file containing our main app storyboard, as well as our storyboards for notifications. To store assets, we will use asset catalogs.

Watch Extension bundle

Unlike the Watch App bundle, the Watch Extension bundle is what *actually* runs your application's logic. This is where we are going to be writing all of the code that drives our watchOS application, as well as its glances, notifications, and complications.

The Watch Extension also existed in the watchOS 1.0 days, but it used to be loaded and run on the iOS device itself, streaming information between iOS and watchOS. After the upgrade to watchOS 2.0, the Watch Extension was then installed on the watch and run natively, giving apps an increase in performance. Now in watchOS 3.0, the most frequently used extensions are kept in memory, making application launches that much faster. Hopefully, at some point in the future, Apple will consolidate the two targets into a single target like with iOS apps now that they are both installed on the same device. While it doesn't really make a huge difference (we don't have to do anything special to access storyboards in the Watch App bundle), it would be a bit cleaner and less confusing to newcomers.

Interface controller

Over the course of the book, we've become very familiar with the View Controller, and its UIKit implementation UIViewController. We've built many custom view controllers to manage all of the different screens in our Snippets application, and have come to know them as the point of entry for building functionality in our test projects.

In *Chapter 8, Exploring Common iOS Frameworks*, we learned about UIKit and how it handles our application's view hierarchy. Unfortunately, watchOS does not operate in the same way. On the bright side, understanding how it *does* work is not important, so you don't have to learn a new system. What you do have to know is that the operating system itself is taking care of your views, and because of this we do not use UIViewController on watchOS. In its place, we have the WKInterfaceController (the **WK** prefix refers to **WatchKit**).

In order to keep things simple for developers, the `WKInterfaceController` class is designed very similarly to the UIViewController that we already know how to use, even though it works differently behind the scenes. Instead of `viewDidLoad()`, we now have `awake(withContext:)`, and instead of `willAppear()` and `didDisappear()`, we now have `willActivate()` and `didDeactivate()`, respectively. The name changes refer to the way the watchOS application life cycle works (which is outside the scope of this book), but you can think of them as functionally similar to the old UIViewController methods.

The Interface Controller is intended to be used in a pretty specific way. First, you should perform any set-up code in the `awake(withContext:)` function. Then, almost all subsequent functionality should be in response to button presses or other user interface element actions. Remember, the Apple Watch is not very powerful and shouldn't be doing complex computations.

Extension Delegate

While we haven't spent as much time with the App Delegate as we have with the View Controller, we are at least familiar with how it manages the life cycle of an iOS application. On our watchOS app, we have the Extension Delegate in the place of the App Delegate.

The Extension Delegate contains familiar methods like `applicationDidFinishLaunching()`, and similarly manages the life cycle of our watchOS application. The Extension Delegate is created automatically by the system, based on a key in the extension's `Info.plist` file. This is important to know if you choose to change the name of your `WKExtensionDelegate` subclass, and it is why I recommend that you use the pre-made extension delegate class that is given to you when you create a new watch kit extension.

The Extension Delegate also only works for the application. The Extension Delegate does not control any life cycle functionality for notifications or complications; those are all managed by the operating system itself.

Snippets for Apple Watch

Finally, it's time to begin development of our very own Apple Watch app! For our app, we are going to create a very simple feature: we will let users create a new text snippet using voice dictation. First we'll build the core application, and then we'll make a small complication to allow us to access the app right from the watch face.

Setting up our project

Before we get started, we have to set up our Snippets project to be ready for Apple Watch development. Open up your Snippets Xcode project again, or as always, you can grab my completed version from the *last* chapter (the *Chapter 9, Working with CoreData*, resources folder) if your project isn't quite up to speed yet.

To get our project ready for an Apple Watch app, we have to create the two new target bundles we discussed earlier. Go to **File | New | Target**, and then from the top bar select **watchOS**, and finally select the **WatchKit App** target type. Check out *Figure 10.5* to confirm you have the correct template:

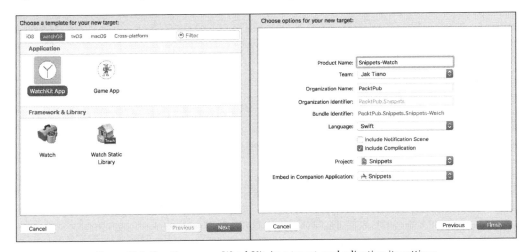

Figure 10.5: Creating a new WatchKit App target, and adjusting its settings

After you click **Next**, you'll be asked to finish setting up the new target. Name it Snippets-Watch, and then make sure you check off the **Include Complication** checkbox. We don't need the notification scene, since we won't be making a notification for our app. Click **Finish**. If you are asked to activate a scheme, do it.

Back in your project, you should see two new folders in your Project Navigator: Snippets-Watch and Snippets-Watch Extension. The first folder is for the Watch App bundle, which you'll remember is for your storyboards and assets. The second folder is for the Watch Extension bundle, which, again, is for all of your code.

Creating a watchOS storyboard

Building up a storyboard for an Apple Watch app uses the same tools that we used for iOS. We're still dragging objects out of our library onto our screens and then editing the objects' attributes; however, watchOS apps look considerably different than iOS apps and their UI elements use some new conventions. Let's learn about these differences as we walk through the process of building a screen for a watchOS app now.

First, navigate to the `Interface.storyboard` file inside the `Snippets-Watch` folder: you should see a storyboard labelled **Interface Controller.** Let's open up the object library and look around. You'll notice that there are fewer objects than there are in the iOS library. The Apple Watch UI is very minimal, which makes sense for a device so small.

We'll mostly be dealing with the familiar buttons, labels, and images, but the new **Group** object is one of the most important elements for watchOS storyboards. As its name implies, it allows us to group objects together in bunches. Unlike iOS storyboards where we can place UI elements anywhere on the screen, watchOS storyboards require us to place objects underneath the previous element. We can also change their horizontal (left, center, right) and vertical (top, middle, bottom) alignment, but that's it.

Groups are important because they allow us to treat multiple objects as one anchored element, and also let us set padding and change the layout from vertical to horizontal. If you were a bit of a wizard with **Auto Layout** you may find the watchOS method a bit limiting, but I find the watchOS method to be much simpler with practice.

For our interface, we're going to have a label along the top of the screen, with a big button beneath it that allows the user to create a new text snippet. Drag a label out onto the storyboard (notice how it gets placed automatically). Inside the label, type `New Text Snippet`.

Next, drag a button out below the label. From the Attribute Editor, change its content from Text to Group. This will allow us to place an image inside the button. To do that, just drag an image from the object library straight into the group. Now, from the Attribute Inspector, set the image's horizontal alignment to Center, so that it is centered inside the group. Finally, set both the height and width to Fixed with values of 130. You should now have a 130 x 130 square image centered inside your group, inside the button. Check *Figure 10.6* to see the Interface Controller as it is now:

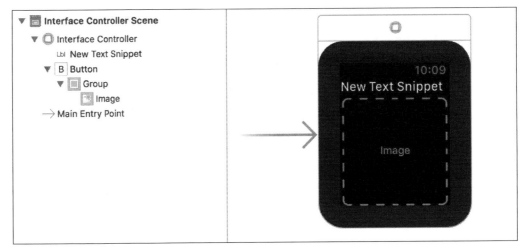

Figure 10.6: Our interface controller storyboard so far

To finish up this interface controller, let's give it a title. The title will be displayed in the upper left hand corner of the screen. We won't have many screens, so let's just give it the title Snippets so that the app name is always on the screen. Click on the **Interface Controller** icon (the yellow circle on top of the controller), and then from the Attribute Inspector, set the **Title** attribute to Snippets.

Next we'll create another interface controller for confirming the user's text input. Drag a new interface controller out from the object library, and place it next to our existing one. Then, add a label to the top of the screen and add a group underneath that. Place a another label inside the group, and then put three buttons underneath the group.

For the first label, set the text to say `Is this right?`. Next, select the group and set it to have custom insets, and then set all four insets to 6. Change the background of the group to be dark gray. Select the label inside the group and set the **Lines** attribute to `0`; this will make the label automatically adjust to the necessary number of lines depending on its contents. For the first button, set the text to `Yes, create it`. Set the second button to read `No, try again`. Finally, set the third button to say `Cancel`, and change the text color to red. Finally, set the title of the new interface controller to `Snippets`. When you're done, your interface controllers should look like they do in *Figure 10.7*.

Later, we'll fill the empty label with the text that gets recorded from dictation, and then use the buttons to confirm if they are correct:

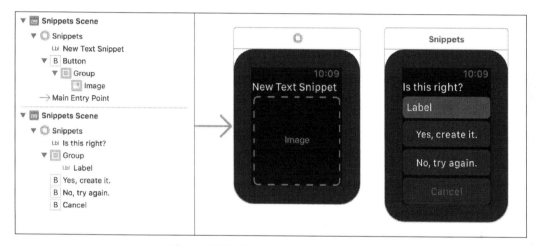

Figure 10.7 Both interface controllers set up

Before we're finished, we need to import and attach an image for our button. I've already included an image named `PlusButton.png` in the `Resources` folder for *Chapter 10, Creating a WatchOS Companion App*. To include it in or watchOS app, we need to create an image asset inside the `Assets.xcassets` file that is a part of the `Snippets-Watch` folder.

Open up that asset catalog, and then click the **+** button at the bottom of the file navigator in the left column of the asset catalog editor window. Choose **New Image Set**, name the asset `PlusIcon`, and then drag the `PlusButton.png` into the 2x slot for the image (*Figure 10.8*):

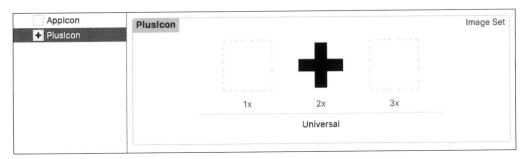

Figure 10.8: Setting up our button image

Now, with the `PlusIcon` asset still selected, open up the Attribute Inspector. Near the top of the Attribute Inspector, you should see a drop-down menu called **Render As**. Select `Template Image`. What this does is it lets the app know that our image shouldn't be interpreted as an image, but rather as a binary stencil where all the black pixels can be colored with a tint.

With the image asset set up, let's go back to the storyboard and select the image inside our button again. From the attribute inspector, set the image's **Image** attribute to use our new `PlusIcon` asset, and then right below that, set its **Tint Color** to a nice orange to match our Snippets color scheme. The image wont show in Interface Builder, but when you run the app it should be visible with the color you selected.

At this point, we've finished building our basic user interface! Select one of the simulators that includes an Apple Watch, then build and run the project to see our storyboard running in the simulator. Next, we're going to add functionality to the app by programming the interface controller.

Programming the interface controller

Our interface controller is going to be pretty simple. We need to create an action that gets called when we tap the new snippet button. Then we need to present the dictation controller and pass the result text into our confirmation controller. Depending on what the user chooses to do, we'll send the text back to our root controller. Let's start with programming the first controller.

Before we start, we're going to create an IBAction by control-dragging from the **New Snippet** button into the `InterfaceController.swift` file, and call the action `createNewTextSnippet()`. You may have to drag from the document outline to get the action from the button, because it might try creating an outlet for the image if you drag right from the storyboard. Then inside the default `InterfaceController.swift` file, delete the built-in `willActivate()` and `didDeactivate()` functions. At this point, your `InterfaceController` class should look like this:

```
import WatchKit
import Foundation

class InterfaceController: WKInterfaceController {

    override func awake(withContext context: Any?) {
        super.awake(withContext: context)

        // Configure interface objects here.
    }

    @IBAction func createNewTextSnippet() {

    }
}
```

Next, we're going to make it so that when we press the new snippet button it presents the text dictation input controller. We're going to place that in a function called `tryToGetText()`:

```
@IBAction func createNewTextSnippet () {
    tryToGetText()
}
```

To present the text input controller, we use a built in function called `presentTextInputController()`. The first parameter takes an array of strings that are used as predetermined test options, but we don't want that here so we pass in nil. The second parameter describes the type of input we want to allow. Since we don't want any emoji, we just use the `.plain` input mode. Finally, we pass in a completion handler, which we'll call `processResults`. Here's the final `tryToGetText()` function:

```
func tryToGetText() {
    presentTextInputController(withSuggestions: nil, allowedInputMode:
    .plain, completion: processResults)
}
```

Now we need to create the completion handler, processResults(). This function needs to be able to accept an optional array of Any ([Any]?), since that is what our text controller returns. In this function we're going to see if we can find a string in the first element of the results array, which means that our text entry was successful. If we find the string, we're going to present our confirmation interface controller:

```
func processResults(results: [Any]?) {
    guard let r = results?[0], let string = r as? String else {
        return
    }
    pushController(withName: "confirmation", context: nil)
}
```

There's still some work to be done in our root InterfaceController class, but first we're going to need to jump over and flesh out our confirmation interface controller. To start, let's create a new class for it. Right click on the Snippets-Watch Extension folder, then click **New File**. From the template selection dialog box, navigate to the **watchOS | Source** section, and choose WatchKit Class. On the next screen, set the name to ConfirmationInterfaceController, and make sure you set the subclass to WKInterfaceController (compare with *Figure 10.9*):

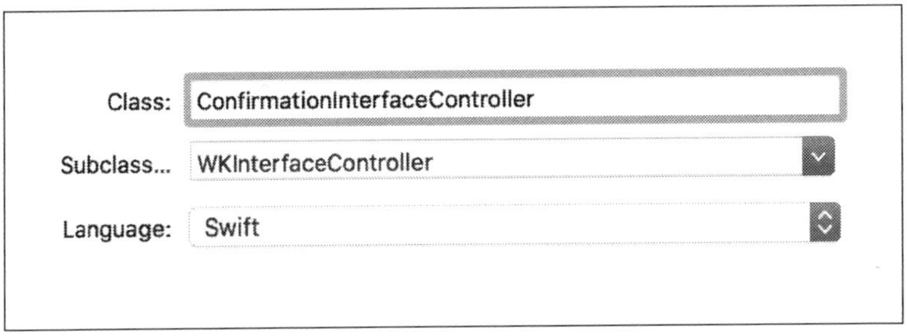

Class:	ConfirmationInterfaceController
Subclass...	WKInterfaceController
Language:	Swift

Figure 10.9: Creating a new subclass of WKInterfaceController

Finish up the creation of the new file, and then head over to the storyboard in our Watch App bundle, so we can connect this new class to the storyboard. Select the confirmation interface controller that we made in the storyboard, and from the Identity Inspector (*option + command + 3*) change the class to the ConfirmationInterfaceController that we just made. Then, from the Attributes Inspector (*option + command + 4*), set the **Identifier** to Confirmation. The storyboard is now connected to our code.

From the storyboard, pull up the Assistant Editor so we can make some connections. Create an outlet for the label inside the group, and call it `resultsLabel`. Then, create an `IBAction` for each of the three buttons, named `confirmText()`, `tryAgain()`, and `cancel()` respectively. Here's what the class should look like at this point:

```
class ConfirmationInterfaceController: WKInterfaceController {

    @IBOutlet var resultsLabel: WKInterfaceLabel!

    override func awakeWithContext(context: AnyObject?) {
        super.awakeWithContext(context)
    }

    @IBAction func confirmText() {

    }
    @IBAction func tryAgain() {

    }
    @IBAction func cancel() {

    }
}
```

Next, we need to transfer information from our root interface controller into this one. What we need to do is use the *context* parameter from `awake(withContext:)` to bundle up and transmit that data. First, let's create a new class named `ConfirmationContext` at the top of the `ConfirmationInterfaceController`. `swift` file that will be used to store all the data:

```
class ConfirmationContext {
    let textString : String
    let confirmAction: (String) -> Void
    let tryAgainAction: () -> Void

    init (textString: String, confirmAction: @escaping (String) ->
    Void, tryAgainAction: @escaping () -> Void) {
        self.textString = textString
        self.confirmAction = confirmAction
        self.tryAgainAction = tryAgainAction
    }
}
```

We've given it the ability to hold a string for the text data we are gathering, in addition to two closures that will be used in the button callbacks. We also add an `init` function to set up those values. Let's update our `awake(withContext:)` function to unpack this information from the context it receives:

```
var currentContext: ConfirmationContext?

override func awakeWithContext(context: AnyObject?) {
    super.awakeWithContext(context)

    if let c = context as? ConfirmationContext {
        currentContext = c
        resultsLabel.setText(c.textString)
    }
}
```

Above the function, we first create a new variable to store the current context so that we can access it later. Then, inside the `awake(withContext:)` function, we try to cast the incoming context to our `ConfirmationContext` class. If it's successful, we save that context to the `currentContext` variable, and set our label to the text that was inside.

Now that we have some closures from the context, let's use them to finish setting up our button callbacks:

```
@IBAction func confirmText() {
    popToRootController()
    if let context = currentContext {
        context.confirmAction(context.textString)
    }
}

@IBAction func tryAgain() {
    popToRootController()
    if let context = currentContext {
        context.tryAgainAction()
    }
}

@IBAction func cancel() {
    popToRootController()
}
```

In the `confirmText()` action, we first pop back to our root interface controller, and then execute the confirm action that was passed to the context, if it exists, and pass in the text string for that closure to process. We do something very similar in the `tryAgain()` action, but this time we run the try again action from our context, if it exists. Finally, in our `cancel()` action, we just pop back to the root controller, without running any additional code.

With those buttons finished, our confirmation interface controller is now complete. Now we just have to jump back to the original `InterfaceController.swift` file to set up the context that the `ConfirmationInterfaceController` is expecting:

Let's take a look at what the final `InterfaceController` class will look like:

```swift
class InterfaceController: WKInterfaceController {
class InterfaceController: WKInterfaceController {

    override func awake(withContext context: Any?) {
        super.awake(withContext: context)
    }

    @IBAction func createNewTextSnippet() {
        tryToGetText()
    }

    func tryToGetText() {
        presentTextInputController(withSuggestions: nil,
allowedInputMode: .plain, completion: processResults)
    }

    func processResults(results: [Any]?) {
        guard let r = results?[0], let string = r as? String else {
            return
        }
        let processText = { (text: String) in
            print ("processText: \(text)")
        }

        let confirmContext = ConfirmationContext(textString: string,
confirmAction: processText, tryAgainAction: tryToGetText)
        pushController(withName: "confirmation", context:
confirmContext)
    }
}
```

Inside the `processResults()` function, we create a new instance of the `ConfirmationContext` class, and then initialize it with the processed string, the `tryToGetText()` function for the `tryAgain` action, and a new closure called `processText()` for the `confirmAction`.

Right now, we are just going to print some debug text to the console when our text is processed; in the next section we'll be dealing with sending that back to iOS. We set the `processText` closure to take a single string parameter, and write it out to the console.

Now our watchOS app has a fully functioning interface! If you build and run this on a real Apple Watch, you'll be able to navigate through the entire app. However, the simulator doesn't support dictation, so you won't be able to use it there. As a workaround, let's add a text suggestion that you can click on in the simulator to bypass the need for dictation:

```
func tryToGetText() {
    presentTextInputController(withSuggestions: ["Test"],
allowedInputMode: .plain, completion: processResults)
}
```

In the `tryToGetText()` function, if we update the text input controller to have an array with a single string value you'll see that that `Test` string will show up on the text selection menu when you run the app now. This should allow you to test the app on the simulator if you don't own an Apple Watch.

Connecting to iOS with Watch Connectivity. framework

In order to have more robust communication between the Apple Watch and its connected iOS device, Apple introduced a new framework in watchOS 2.0 called Watch Connectivity. This framework allows us to send all kinds of information back and forth between devices, in many different ways.

For our purposes, we are going to need to send a message to our iOS app telling it that we have a new text snippet to create. This requires setting up a Watch Connectivity session on both the watchOS and iOS side of things, and then sending a message from watchOS and receiving it in iOS. We'll begin by setting up Watch Connectivity on the watch.

 Make sure to link the `WatchConnectivity.framework` file to your app from the main app's target.

Head over to the `InterfaceController.swift` file, and add an `import` `WatchConnectivity` statement to the top. Next, set our `InterfaceController` class to implement the `WCSessionDelegate` protocol:

```
class InterfaceController: WKInterfaceController, WCSessionDelegate {
```

Now that our class is set up with Watch Connectivity, we need to create a `WCSession` object, which is what manages the communications between the two devices. We're going to create a new `WCSession` property, and under that we add a function that the WCSessionManager protocol requires, but we don't need it so it just returns. Finally, we then set up our session when our interface controller starts up:

```
var session: WCSession?

func session(_ session: WCSession, activationDidCompleteWith
activationState: WCSessionActivationState, error: Error?) {
    return
}

override func awake(withContext context: Any?) {
    super.awake(withContext: context)
    session = WCSession.default()
    session?.delegate = self
    session?.activate()
}
```

First, we get the default session from the `WCSession` class and store it in our session property. Then we set the current class to be the session's delegate, and finally we activate the session.

With our session set up and active, we can now send messages to our iOS app. Inside the `processResults()` function, we need to change the closure that handles our final string. Now, we're going to bundle it up in a dictionary and send it off to our paired iOS device:

```
func processResults(results: [Any]?) {
    guard let r = results?[0], let string = r as? String else {
        return
    }

    let processText = { (text: String) in
        let info = ["textData":text]
        self.session?.sendMessage(info, replyHandler: nil,
errorHandler: nil)
    }
```

```
    let confirmContext = ConfirmationContext(textString: string,
confirmAction: processText, tryAgainAction: tryToGetText)
    pushController(withName: "confirmation", context: confirmContext)
}
```

Before we send the string to iOS, we need to put it into a dictionary. We create a new dictionary with a single key/value pair, with the key `textData` containing a value with our final text string. Then we can tell our session to send a message with our info.

 I'm not using a reply handler or an error handler here, so that I don't bore you with formalities, but I encourage you to try to think about how you might handle error cases, or how you might display syncing progress before the app replies with a success. In a final shipping application, you want to make sure your app is prepared to handle whatever might get thrown its way!

Now that watchOS is bundling up our string and sending it over to iOS, we need to get our iOS app ready to receive the data that is being sent to it.

Open up our `AppDelegate.swift` file, and add an import `WatchConnectivity` statement to the top. We need to also make our `AppDelegate` class implements the `WCSessionDelegate` protocol, just like our `InterfaceController`:

```
class AppDelegate: UIResponder, UIApplicationDelegate,
WCSessionDelegate {
```

At the top of the class, we're going to add another session property:

```
var session: WCSession?
```

Then we need to add some required functions:

```
func session(_ session: WCSession, activationDidCompleteWith
activationState: WCSessionActivationState, error: Error?) {
    return
}
func sessionDidBecomeInactive(_ session: WCSession) {
    return
}
func sessionDidDeactivate(_ session: WCSession) {
    return
}
```

Finally we can set up our session. In the application (`didFinishLaunching:`) function, we are going to that like so:

```
func application(_ application: UIApplication,
didFinishLaunchingWithOptions launchOptions:
[UIApplicationLaunchOptionsKey : Any]? = nil) -> Bool {

    if WCSession.isSupported() {
        session = WCSession.default()
        session?.delegate = self
        session?.activate()
    }
    return true
}
```

This time we check to see if `WCSession` is supported first, to make sure everything is ready to go with Watch Connectivity.

Now that WC is set up and our session is activated, we just have to wait for the message to come through! In order to receive the message, we need to implement a function from the `WCSessionDelegate` protocol, session (`didRecieveMessage`):

```
func session(_ session: WCSession, didReceiveMessage message: [String
: Any]) {
    if let textData = message["textData"] as? String, let vc = self.
window!.rootViewController! as? ViewController {
        DispatchQueue.main.async(execute: {
            vc.saveTextSnippet(text: textData)
            vc.reloadSnippetData()
            vc.tableView.reloadData()
        })
    }
}
```

First we try to pull out the text data from the dictionary, and we also try to get a reference to our root view controller. If both of those succeed, then we move on. Inside the function we call the `saveTextSnippet()` function and pass in the string from the watch, and then we reload the data and refresh our table.

You'll notice that there's a bit of new code wrapping the saving and reload code, which is `DispatchQueue.main.async(execute: {},` `{})`. What this does is make sure that code inside the block is being executed on the main thread. Since Watch Connectivity can be run in the background, this code block may be run on a background thread, and we can't adjust our views from a background thread.

Now that our iOS app can receive a message, extract the text and save it to our Core Data persistent store, our functionality is complete! *Figure 10.10* shows the final app running on an Apple Watch…

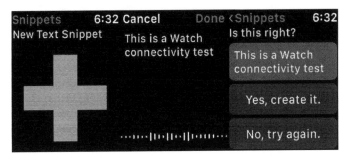

Figure 10.10: Using the app on our Apple Watch

And *Figure 10.11* shows the snippet we created showing up inside the iOS counterpart!

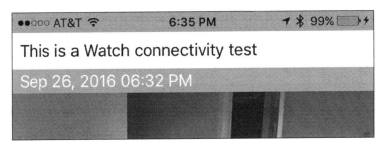

Figure 10.11: The resulting snippet created on our iOS device

Adding a complication

To complete our app, we're going to add a complication for our app. It's worth noting here that there isn't actually a great reason to add a complication to our app. Having a small button on the watch face to create a new text snippet is pretty useful, but it's not particularly timely or worth the space it takes up. Then again, that decision is up to the user! Just remember that this is not a great example of *when* to make a complication, but should be used as an example of *how* to make one.

First, let's go to the Xcode project settings, and select our `Snippets-Watch Extension` target, and select which complications are valid. We're only going to support **Circular Small**, **Modular Small**, and **Utilitarian Small**. Your checkboxes should look like this:

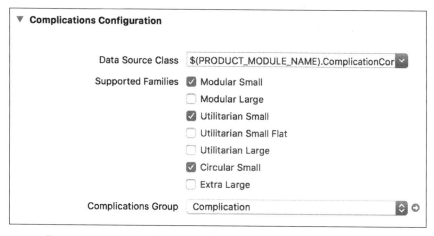

Figure 10.12: The complication configuration for our watch extension target

Next, we're going to configure the icon images that will be displayed in our complications. Inside the watch extension folder (`Snippets-Watch Extension`) there should be another asset catalog with a built in folder for complications, containing three empty image assets for Circular, Modular, and Utilitarian. Inside the resources folder for `Chapter 10`, I've included the correctly sized plus button images for all six slots, so drag those into the asset catalog now:

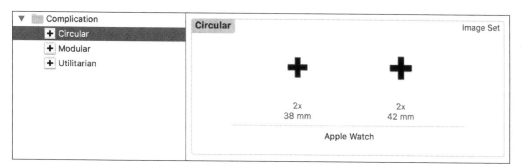

Figure 10.13: Our asset catalog filled with complication images

Like we did earlier, select all the image assets inside the asset catalog, and from the attribute inspector set the **Render As** attribute to **Template Image**.

Now that our app knows which complications it supports, and has the assets it needs, the rest of our work will be done in the ComplicationController.swift file. This file contains a class that implements the CLKComplicationDataSource protocol, which lets the Apple Watch request the data for the complication.

The first thing we'll do in here is set the Time Travel capabilities. Since our app doesn't have any time-sensitive data, we are not going to use Time Travel, and so we'll need to change the supported Time Travel directions by changing the first function like so:

```
func getSupportedTimeTravelDirectionsForComplication
(complication: CLKComplication, withHandler handler:
(CLKComplicationTimeTravelDirections) -> Void) {
    handler(nil)
}
```

Next, we need to return the correct data when the app asks for it. We'll be doing that in the getCurrentTimelineEntry(for complication:) function. Let's take a look at the code, and then break it down:

```
func getCurrentTimelineEntry(for complication: CLKComplication,
withHandler handler: @escaping (CLKComplicationTimelineEntry?) ->
Void) {

    var template: CLKComplicationTemplate

    switch complication.family
    {
    case .circularSmall:
        let t = CLKComplicationTemplateCircularSmallSimpleImage()
        let image = UIImage(named: "Circular")!
        t.imageProvider = CLKImageProvider(onePieceImage: image)
        template = t

    case .modularSmall:
        let t = CLKComplicationTemplateModularSmallSimpleImage()
        let image = UIImage(named: "Circular")!
        t.imageProvider = CLKImageProvider(onePieceImage: image)
        template = t

    case .utilitarianSmall:
        let t = CLKComplicationTemplateUtilitarianSmallSquare()
        let image = UIImage(named: "Circular")!
        t.imageProvider = CLKImageProvider(onePieceImage: image)
        template = t
```

```
    default:
        handler(nil)
        return
    }

    template.tintColor = UIColor.white
    handler( CLKComplicationTimelineEntry(date: Date(),
complicationTemplate: template) )
    }
```

So basically, what we are doing in this function is setting up a template for the complication and then returning that template at the end. So at the top we declare a `template` variable, which is of the type `CLKComplicationTemplate`. This is actually just a generic parent class, and we'll use specific subclasses to actually define the template.

To determine what template we should use, we run a switch statement on the `family` property of the complication that was passed into the function. If the family is `.circularSmall`, we set the template to the `SimpleImage` type for that family. If the family is `.modularSmall`, we set the template to the `SimpleImage` type for the modular family. And finally if the family is `.utilitarianSmall`, we set the template to `SmallSquare` for that family. In all cases, we grab the image from our asset catalog, put it inside a special `Image Provider` class that the watch uses, and then assign our template to the generic version. At the end we have a default case to catch any other family types (like `.utilitarianLarge` and `.modularLarge`, which we disabled).

Once we've set up each template, we set the `tintColor` to white. This makes sure our template images that are added are colored white instead of black. Otherwise, we wouldn't be able to see them on the black background!

Finally, we return a `CLKComplicationTimelineEntry` using the current date and our template by using the handler that was passed into the function. In order to check out the complications we made, switch the scheme (like we did with glances) to be the `Complication - Snippets-Watch` scheme, and run.

You should be able to just tap on the complication on the watch face to jump straight into the app. For power users, this might be a great shortcut to launch the app and record a quick memo. Check out *Figure 10.14* to see the complication across all the different templates we created:

Figure 10.14: Our final complication running on several different watch faces (Utilitarian, Modular, Circular)

You might also want to look at other watch faces and set them to use our new complication. To do that press (*command + shift + 2*) in the watch simulator to switch to force touch mode, and force touch on the watch face. Then use (*command + shift + 1*) to switch back to normal touch and swipe to select a new watch face. Try customizing some of the watch face complications to display our new Snippets complication.

Summary

And with that, we've built up a pretty solid Apple Watch companion app for our Snippets app! There's still a lot more to learn about watchOS, and the platform will only be expanding in the future, but in this chapter we've got a decent grasp of the basic design ideas behind watchOS, we learnt about the architecture of an app, and we learnt how to build an app complete with a glance and a complication! You should have enough experience at this point to use any part of this chapter that interested you as a diving board into Apple's documentation to learn even more about watchOS development. Go ahead and see what else you can do!

In the next chapter we're going to pull back from our Snippets app a bit and learn about some of the different sensors available in iOS. While they might not be particularly useful for this app, they're still an important part of a developer's toolkit (and a lot of fun to play with, too).

11

Advanced Input Using Sensors

When the iPhone was first announced, the multi-touch screen was the focal point of its high-tech appeal. However, it has always had a fantastic user interface due to the many other sensors that are built in, smoothing out every aspect of the user experience. The accelerometer knew when you tilted your device and rotated web pages automatically. A proximity sensor knew when your phone was up to your face so it would turn off the screen. An ambient light sensor would automatically adjust the backlight based on the room you were in.

Since those early days, each new iteration of the iPhone hardware has introduced more and more sensors that allow new generations of apps to provide even better experiences. Earlier in the book, we looked at very common input methods like multi-touch gestures, and positioning sensors like GPS with **Core Location**. In this chapter, we're going to take a look at some of the more advanced sensors, covering:

- Device information through UIDevice
- The basics of the Core Motion framework
- Using third-party charting frameworks to plot data
- Getting accelerometer data from the Apple Watch

In this chapter, we'll be taking a break from our Snippets project, so get ready to take a bit of a breather by learning some fun new ways to interact with an iOS device!

Due to the subject nature of this chapter, most of the code we'll be writing will not be possible to run in a simulator. If you don't have a device plugged in you can still follow along and learn, but you'll make the most of this chapter if you have the actual hardware.

Device status with UIDevice

Many of the simpler sensors available in iOS are exposed to us through the UIDevice class. Responsible for keeping track of the overall device state, this class has a bunch of little features that make it actually quite fun to poke around!

If you haven't already, create a new single view Xcode project; I called mine Sensors. Then, head over to your default view controller, and at the top of the class let's grab a reference to our current device to make it easier to get information later. Our class should start off looking like this:

```
class ViewController: UIViewController {

    let device = UIDevice.currentDevice()

    override func viewDidLoad() {
        super.viewDidLoad()
    }
}
```

Now let's see what we can do!

Accessing orientation state

One of the more important pieces of sensory information that you might need when developing your own apps is checking the current state of the device's orientation. In recent years, auto layout has made it less necessary to manually check for device orientation, but it's still a useful trick to know!

Let's start off by talking about how iOS represents orientation data. The device's orientation is defined using an enum called UIDeviceOrientation, of which all the cases are self-explanatory:

```
enum UIDeviceOrientation : Int {
    case unknown
    case portrait
    case portraitUpsideDown
    case landscapeLeft
```

```
case landscapeRight
case faceUp
case faceDown
}
```

To check the current orientation of the device, you can just access the `orientation` property like so:

```
device.orientation
```

However, usually it makes the most sense to not check what the orientation is, but to be notified when it *changes*. To detect orientation changes we have two options: be notified when the screen auto-rotates, or register directly to receive notifications when the orientation changes.

The first option works well when you need to know about orientation changes in the UI, since it is only called when the interface actually rotates. This is great because the orientation you get will match the orientation of the user interface, and can only ever be one of the *supported* orientations:

```
override func viewWillTransition(to size: CGSize, with coordinator:
UIViewControllerTransitionCoordinator) {
    switch device.orientation
    {
    case .landscapeLeft:
        print("Landscape Left")
    case .landscapeRight:
        print("Landscape Right")
    case .portrait:
        print("Portrait")
    case .portraitUpsideDown:
        print("Portrait Upside Down")
    default:
        print("Other orientation")
    }
}
```

To do this, we use the the `viewWillTransition(toSize:)` function, which lets us know when our screen is about to change sizes during a rotation event. Here, you can see that inside the function we're running a switch statement on `device.orientation`, which prints out the orientation based on the value.

The other option (being notified directly on device orientation change) is nice because it fires immediately, and doesn't care about what the *supported* orientations are. It also doesn't care what the user interface is doing, so it's perfect for when you really just need to know the orientation of the device.

To implement this, we need to register our view controller to receive the orientation change notifications. We'll do that right before our view is shown to the user:

```
override func viewWillAppear(_ animated: Bool) {
    let nc = NotificationCenter.default
    let oriSel = #selector(ViewController.onOrientationChange)
    let oriNot = NSNotification.Name.UIDeviceOrientationDidChange
    nc.addObserver(self, selector: oriSel, name: oriNot, object: nil)
}
```

Then we need to remove our class as an observer right after the view is taken away from the user:

```
override func viewWillDisappear(_ animated: Bool) {
    let nc = NotificationCenter.default
    let oriNot = NSNotification.Name.UIDeviceOrientationDidChange
    nc.removeObserver(self, name: oriNot, object: nil)
}
```

We're using a new class here called NSNotificationCenter. This is not the same notification center that is used to manage alerts that you get from apps on your iPhone. The NSNotificationCenter class processes *notifications*, which are essentially strings. It also manages lists of objects that are *listening* to each one of those notifications. When an object *posts* a notification to the notification center, it alerts all of the objects that are listening for that notification that it has been posted, and then all of those objects can react accordingly. So here, we are telling the notification center that our view controller wants to be alerted when the UIDeviceOrientationDidChangeNotification gets posted, and that when it does it should call the onOrientationChange function. So let's create that function now:

```
func onOrientationChange() {
    switch device.orientation
    {
    case .landscapeLeft:
        print("Landscape Left")
    case .landscapeRight:
        print("Landscape Right")
    case .portrait:
        print("Portrait")
    case .portraitUpsideDown:
```

```
        print("Portrait Upside Down")
    case .faceUp:
        print("Face Up")
    case .faceDown:
        print("Face Down")
    default:
        print("Other orientation")
    }
}
```

This function is very similar to the `viewWillTransition(toSize:)` function we created earlier, except that we can now detect the `.faceUp` and `.faceDown` orientations which do not trigger UI auto-rotation.

Try running this project on your device with one method enabled, and then the other. Spin your device around and see what results are spit out to the console!

Checking the proximity sensor

The proximity sensor is one of the little black circles near the earpiece on your iPhone. It detects when your face is close to the phone so that it can turn off the screen during calls. However, the same functionality is also available to developers to do with as they please.

Setting up proximity state changes is very similar to the way we used the notification center to check for orientation changes. Before we register for notifications, though, we need to tell the device to start monitoring the proximity sensor:

```
override func viewDidLoad() {
    super.viewDidLoad()

    device.isProximityMonitoringEnabled = true
}
```

Always remember to turn off the proximity sensor when you're done with it; there's no sense running the sensor if we don't need it!

Next we have to register for a new notification related to the proximity sensor. Let's update our `viewWillAppear()` and `viewWillDisapper()` functions to make our view controller listen for `UIDeviceProximityStateDidChangeNotification`, and call a function called `onProximityChange`:

```
override func viewWillAppear(_ animated: Bool) {
    let nc = NotificationCenter.default
    let oriSel = #selector(ViewController.onOrientationChange)
```

```
    let prxSel = #selector(ViewController.onProximityChange)

    let oriNot = NSNotification.Name.UIDeviceOrientationDidChange
    let prxNot = NSNotification.Name.UIDeviceProximityStateDidChange

    nc.addObserver(self, selector: oriSel, name: oriNot, object: nil)
    nc.addObserver(self, selector: prxSel, name: prxNot, object: nil)
}
```

Getting the hang of NSNotificationCenter? Next we have to create our callback function, onProximityChange():

```
func onProximityChange() {
    let proximity = device.proximityState ? "Near" : "Far"
    print(proximity)
}
```

Here, we're just checking to see what the new state is. If it's true (activated), we create a string that reads Near, and if it's false (not activated) we set it to Far. Then we print out the string.

> In that last function, we're using what is known as the ternary conditional operator. It is composed of three parts (the condition, the true return value, and the false return value) and is structured like this:
>
> ```
> (conditional statement) ? (if true return this) : (if
> false return this)
> ```
>
> The ternary conditional is usually useful in assignment cases like this one, where you want to assign one value if something is true, and something else if it is false.

If you build and run the app now, you should see that when you cover the proximity sensor with your finger, the screen will turn off and you'll get your Near/Far string printed out to the console. Unfortunately, the screen will always turn off with the proximity sensor, and there isn't anything you can do about it. (Also, some devices don't have a proximity sensor, like the iPod Touch, so keep that in mind!)

Getting battery status

One of the most fun pieces of data you can access is the user's battery level. In most cases there isn't anything particularly useful to do with this information, but with a little creativity anything is possible! For example, maybe you're making a game and you can add an achievement called *risk taker* if the user beats a difficult level when the battery is below 5% charge.

Anyway, accessing this information is very similar to the way we access the proximity state. However, this time there are *two* different notifications we can subscribe to: when the battery *level* changes, and when the battery *state* changes. The first one is just the percentage, but the second one is an enum, UIDeviceBatteryState, that looks like this:

```
enum UIDeviceBatteryState : Int {
    case unknown
    case unplugged
    case charging
    case full
}
```

In this example, we're going to subscribe to changes in the state, but you're welcome to check out the documentation and try to subscribe to changes in the battery level.

Since we've seen most of this code before, let's just lay it all out:

```
override func viewDidLoad() {
    super.viewDidLoad()

    device.proximityMonitoringEnabled = true
    device.batteryMonitoringEnabled = true
}

override func viewWillAppear(_ animated: Bool) {
    let nc = NotificationCenter.default
    let oriSel = #selector(ViewController.onOrientationChange)
    let prxSel = #selector(ViewController.onProximityChange)
    let batSel = #selector(ViewController.onBatteryStateChange)

    let oriNot = NSNotification.Name.UIDeviceOrientationDidChange
    let prxNot = NSNotification.Name.UIDeviceProximityStateDidChange
    let batNot = NSNotification.Name.UIDeviceBatteryStateDidChange

    nc.addObserver(self, selector: oriSel, name: oriNot, object: nil)
    nc.addObserver(self, selector: prxSel, name: prxNot, object: nil)
```

```
        nc.addObserver(self, selector: batSel, name: batNot, object: nil)
}

override func viewWillDisappear(_ animated: Bool) {
    let nc = NotificationCenter.default
    let oriNot = NSNotification.Name.UIDeviceOrientationDidChange
    let prxNot = NSNotification.Name.UIDeviceProximityStateDidChange
    let batNot = NSNotification.Name.UIDeviceBatteryStateDidChange

    nc.removeObserver(self, name: oriNot, object: nil)
    nc.removeObserver(self, name: prxNot, object: nil)
    nc.removeObserver(self, name: batNot, object: nil)
}

override func viewWillDisappear(animated: Bool) {
    let nc = NSNotificationCenter.defaultCenter()
    let oriNot = UIDeviceOrientationDidChangeNotification
    let proNot = UIDeviceProximityStateDidChangeNotification
    let batNot = UIDeviceBatteryStateDidChangeNotification
    nc.removeObserver(self, name: oriNot, object: nil)
    nc.removeObserver(self, name: proNot, object: nil)
    nc.removeObserver(self, name: batNot, object: nil)
}
```

Again, first we set battery monitoring to Enabled. Then we register our battery state change notification in viewWillAppear, and unregister in viewWillDisappear. Finally, we need to create our callback function, onBatteryStateChange:

```
func onBatteryStateChange() {
    switch device.batteryState
    {
    case .unplugged:
        print("Battery Unplugged")
    case .charging:
        print("Battery Charging")
    case .full:
        print("Battery Full")
    default:
        print("Battery State Unknown")
    }
}
```

Here, we check the device's battery state, and print out some results depending on its current state. We could also use `device.batteryLevel` to get the exact charge of the battery.

Introduction to Core Motion

Many applications, games in particular, love to use the accelerometer sensor in the iPhone to let the user precisely tilt their device as an interaction mechanism. In the last section we used `UIDevice` to get notifications about general orientation changes of the device, but there is a way to get much more precise data: the **Core Motion** framework. In this section, we'll be taking a look at some of the sensory data available through the `CMMotionManager` class.

Before we get started, let's reset our `ViewController` class to get rid of our `UIDevice` experiments, and start with our Core Motion experiments (you can create a new project if you don't want to get rid of the old code):

```
import UIKit
import CoreMotion

class ViewController: UIViewController {

    let motionManager = CMMotionManager()

    override func viewDidLoad() {
        super.viewDidLoad()
    }
}
```

Remember to link the `CoreMotion` framework before you import at the top of the view controller. We've also initialized a `CMMotionManager` object at the top of the class so that we have access to it throughout the next few examples.

Accelerometer

Let's first begin by setting up and pulling data from the accelerometer. If you've never heard of an accelerometer before, or don't know what it does, it's quite simple: it measures linear acceleration from both gravity and movement. This means we can not only get orientation information from the accelerometer, but also process how its movement changes over time:

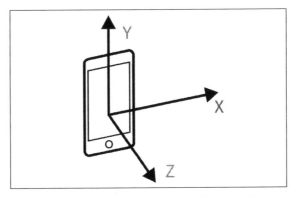

Figure 11.1: Linear motion along the x, y, and z axes of the device

The kind of math and algorithms that would be necessary to really analyze this raw data would be far outside the scope and subject matter of this book, so we're just going to focus on how to get the raw data.

In order to get the data from the accelerometer, we're going to need to do three things: create a function that handles data updates; create a new operation queue to run the data processing; and configure the motion manager and begin updates.

First, we'll create a new function called `onAccelerometerUpdate()`, which will be notified every time the accelerometer updates. Since this function will be sent to the `CMMotionManager` to be used as a handler, it needs to conform to the `CMAccelerometerHandler` signature, which is defined as:

```
(CMAccelerometerData?, Error?) -> Void
func onAcelerometerUpdate(data: CMAccelerometerData?, error: Error?) {
    if error == nil, let d = data {
        print("x \(d.acceleration.x)")
        print("y \(d.acceleration.y)")
        print("z \(d.acceleration.z)")
    } else {
        print("Error: \(error?.localizedDescription)")
    }
}
```

We check to see that there is no error, and then we unwrap the CMAccelerometerData optional value. Inside the if statement, we are printing out the x, y, and z component of the accelerometer data (all three values range from -1.0 to 1.0). If we detect an error, we print it out in the else statement.

Next, we need to create a new OperationQueue for our updates to run on. The easiest way to think about an operation queue is that it is a separate area to execute commands. By default, our code runs on the main operation queue. Since the accelerometer data may update many times per second, we create a different queue for it to run on so that it doesn't slow down the main queue.

At the top of the class, we'll create a new operation queue like this:

```
let motionQueue = OperationQueue()
```

Finally, we need to configure our CMMotionManager for accelerometer updates, and then tell it to begin running those updates:

```
override func viewDidLoad() {
    super.viewDidLoad()

    if motionManager.isAccelerometerAvailable {
        motionManager.accelerometerUpdateInterval = 0.25
        motionManager.startAccelerometerUpdates(to: motionQueue,
withHandler: onAccelerometerUpdate)
    }
}
```

In the viewDidLoad() function, we first need to check if the accelerometer is available by checking the isAccelerometerAvailable property of our motionManager. If it returns true, then we continue with the setup by setting the frequency that the updates are run. In this example I'm setting the update interval to 0.25 (in seconds), which gives us four updates per second. If we were doing real processing on the accelerometer, this would be far too slow, but it's fine just for looking at the values coming out.

Finally, we begin polling the sensor by telling it to start updating the accelerometer and passing in our motionQueue, and the name of our handler function. Let's take a look at all of this together before running the project on our device:

```
let motionManager = CMMotionManager()
let motionQueue = OperationQueue()

override func viewDidLoad() {
    super.viewDidLoad()
    if motionManager.isAccelerometerAvailable {
```

```
        motionManager.accelerometerUpdateInterval = 0.25
        motionManager.startAccelerometerUpdates(to: motionQueue,
    withHandler: onAccelerometerUpdate)
        }
    }

    func onAccelerometerUpdate(data: CMAccelerometerData?, error: Error?)
    {
        if error == nil, let d = data {
            print("x \(d.acceleration.x)")
            print("y \(d.acceleration.y)")
            print("z \(d.acceleration.z)")
        } else {
            print("Error: \(error?.localizedDescription)")
        }
    }
```

Again, our motion manager is set up, then sent a new operation queue and a reference to a handler function that can process the accelerometer data. If you build and run this project on your device, you should see the x, y, and z values being printed out to the console.

Gyroscope

The accelerometer is similar to the gyroscope. While the accelerometer detects translation along the x, y, and z axes, the gyroscope detects rotation around those axes:

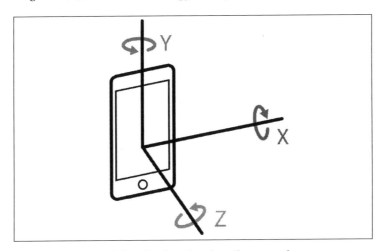

Figure 11.2: Rotational motion along the x, y, and z axes

Using the gyroscope is very similar to using the accelerometer; we still need to set up our motionManager with an operation queue and a handler to process the data. Let's take a look at what the code looks like:

```swift
class ViewController: UIViewController {

    let motionManager = CMMotionManager()
    let motionQueue = OperationQueue()

    override func viewDidLoad() {
        super.viewDidLoad()

        if motionManager.isAccelerometerAvailable {
            motionManager.accelerometerUpdateInterval = 0.25
            motionManager.startAccelerometerUpdates(to: motionQueue,
withHandler: onAccelerometerUpdate)
        }

        if motionManager.isGyroAvailable {
            motionManager.gyroUpdateInterval = 0.25
            motionManager.startGyroUpdates(to: motionQueue,
            withHandler: onGyroUpdate)
        }
    }

    func onAccelerometerUpdate(data: CMAccelerometerData?, error:
NSError?) {
        if error == nil, let d = data {
            print("x \(d.acceleration.x)")
            print("y \(d.acceleration.y)")
            print("z \(d.acceleration.z)")
        } else {
            print("Error: \(error?.description)")
        }
    }

    func onGyroUpdate(data: CMGyroData?, error: Error?) {
        if error == nil, let d = data {
            print("x \(d.rotationRate.x)")
            print("y \(d.rotationRate.y)")
            print("z \(d.rotationRate.z)")
        } else {
            print("Error: \(error?.localizedDescription)")
        }
    }
}
```

To read information from the gyroscope, we needed to add two chunks of code. In the `viewDidLoad()` function, we create a similar check to see if a gyroscope is available on the current device, then set up an update interval, and then start the update process.

Here, we're using the same `OperationQueue` as last time; we've already moved the processing of the main queue that was the primary concern, so there's no reason to create another one.

Finally, we create a new data handler function, this time called `onGyroUpdate()`. Similar to the accelerometer data handler, this function's signature follows the `CMGyroHandler` definition, which is as follows:

```
typealias CMGyroHandler = (CMGyroData?, Error?) -> Void
```

Inside our data handler, we are checking for errors and then printing out the relevant information to the console. Here we are printing out the x, y, and z components of the `rotationRate` property inside the `CMGyroData` object that gets passed into the function. These are all represented as radians per second along their respective axis.

Before you build and run, comment out the line with `startAccelerometerUpdates` so that the accelerometer data isn't also being printed out to the console. Then run the project, and have a look at the raw gyroscope data being reported. With this gyroscope information, you could create a pretty accurate steering wheel for a driving game! Try to think about the other things you could do with the raw rotation information.

CMDeviceMotion

Now, these last two sections are really great to get some low level data from your iPhone's sensors, but the `CMMotionManager` provides a great way to get calibrated data with bias removed automatically by Core Motion: `CMDeviceMotion`. This class contains a handful of sensory data that has already been processed by algorithms in Core Motion.

Since we're already familiar with the way we configure `CMMotionManager` to begin polling sensors, I'll just leave the code here for you to look at; you should already know how it works:

```
class ViewController: UIViewController {

    let motionManager = CMMotionManager()
    let motionQueue = OperationQueue()

    override func viewDidLoad() {
```

```
            super.viewDidLoad()

        if motionManager.isDeviceMotionAvailable {
            motionManager.deviceMotionUpdateInterval = 0.25
            motionManager.startDeviceMotionUpdates(to: motionQueue,
    withHandler: onMotionUpdate)
        }
    }

    func onMotionUpdate(data: CMDeviceMotion?, error:Error?) {
        if error == nil, let d = data {
            print("Acceleration X: \(d.userAcceleration.x)")
            print("Acceleration Y: \(d.userAcceleration.y)")
            print("Acceleration Z: \(d.userAcceleration.z)")

            print("Gravity X: \(d.gravity.x)")
            print("Gravity Y: \(d.gravity.y)")
            print("Gravity Z: \(d.gravity.z)")

            print("Rotation X: \(d.rotationRate.x)")
            print("Rotation Y: \(d.rotationRate.y)")
            print("Rotation Z: \(d.rotationRate.z)")

            print("Magnetic Field X: \(d.magneticField.field.x)")
            print("Rotation X: \(d.rotationRate.x)")
            print("Rotation Y: \(d.rotationRate.y)")
            print("Rotation Z: \(d.rotationRate.z)")

            print("Magnetic Field X: \(d.magneticField.field.x)")
            print("Magnetic Field Y: \(d.magneticField.field.y)")
            print("Magnetic Field Z: \(d.magneticField.field.z)")
        } else {
            print("Error: \(error?.localizedDescription)")
        }
    }
}
```

This time, in the `onMotionUpdate()` function, we're printing out a lot more data. That's because the `CMDeviceMotion` class captures a full snapshot of all of the device's motion (hence the name). This makes `CMDeviceMotion` really useful for when you need to get a lot of *clean* motion data from your device, which is great if you don't plan on writing any of your own data processing algorithms. Let's look at each piece of data that `CMDeviceMotion` provides.

User acceleration

Since the accelerometer data is being processed by Core Motion, it is able to separate the forces that are being detected. User acceleration is the component of the accelerometer data that represents what the user is doing to the device.

Gravity

As a continuation of user acceleration, gravity is the component of the accelerometer forces that (obviously) represent gravity. When the phone is upright in portrait mode, you'll see close to a -1 value on the y axis, meaning straight down.

Rotation rate

The rotation rate property is similar to the rotation rate property of the CMGyroData class we used earlier, however this data has had its bias removed by Core Motion.

Magnetic field

The magnetic field property gives you the total magnetic field vector that surrounds the device, excluding the device's bias.

Charting motion data

We've been learning how to access a lot of cool information from the sensors in our iOS devices, but we haven't really been putting that information to use. Since the data processing involved in using that data is beyond the scope of this book, let's do something a bit more visual: charting it.

Displaying information through charts is a really useful feature you can add to an app that collects or generates any kind of data. Charts are simple, visual ways to communicate complex information, and can really create new meaning for a user. In this section, we'll be learning about a third-party open source charting library called iOS Charts, and then we'll apply it to some new sensor data that we'll pull from Core Motion.

Charts

Included in the resources folder of this chapter, is an open source charting library called `iOS Charts`. The library was ported by Daniel Gindi from an Android charting framework by Philipp Jahoda, and you can find the original GitHub repository here: `https://github.com/danielgindi/Charts`. I've included a copy of the version I used with the resource files just in case it changes by the time you read this, and things work differently.

Importing the framework

Since we're using a third-party framework, importing it will be a bit different than when we import Apple provided frameworks. The first thing we need to do is drag the `Charts.xcodeproj` file *into* our existing Xcode project. This file can be found in the resources folder of this chapter under `Resources/Charts/Charts.xcodeproj`:

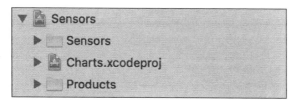

Figure 11.3: Another Xcode project nested in our Xcode project

Now, click in our original Xcode project (**Sensors**) and then scroll down to the bottom of the general settings page. You should see a section called **Embedded Binaries**, which is above the **Linked Frameworks and Libraries** section we've been using to add Apple frameworks to our project. If you click the + button, you should see some `Charts` frameworks to import from inside the `Charts.xcodeproj` file; choose the iOS one:

Figure 11.4: We've added an embedded binary from the Charts.xcodeproj

Now that we've added the binary to our project, we actually need to *build* the project once so that the binary gets loaded. You can press *command + B* to just build the project without running.

With the framework loaded, we are now free to import the `Charts` framework inside our code just like the Apple frameworks we've been using up to this point. Open up our `ViewController.swift` file, and at the top add:

```
import UIKit
import CoreMotion
import Charts
```

Now we're ready to start charting!

Setting up the storyboard

To display a graph on screen, we're going to create a custom view using one of the classes that exists inside the new `Charts` framework we just imported: `LineChartView`. To begin, open up the `Main.storyboard` file, and add a new `UIView` to the view controller, and then pin all four sides to the edges (set edge pin constraints with a value of `0`).

Next, select the view in the storyboard and open up the `Identity Inspector`. In the past, we've set storyboard objects to be custom subclasses of UI classes, but this is the first time we're going to set a storyboard object to be a class from inside a framework. To do this, first set the class to `LineChartView`. Next, we need to set the module (right underneath the custom class) to `Charts`. If you don't tell the `Identity Inspector` which module (framework) the class is from, it will look in the default module and throw an error at run time:

Figure 11.5: Our configured Identity Inspector with custom class and module

Finally, we must create an outlet for `LineChartView`. Open the `Assistant Editor` and control drag from the view in your storyboard to the `ViewController` class, and create an `IBOutlet` for it named `lineChartView`. If everything worked out, you should now have a line of code like this at the top of the class:

```
@IBOutlet weak var lineChartView: LineChartView!
```

Our line chart view is now set up in Interface Builder, and ready to be programmed!

Filling the chart with data

Before we move on to some new types of sensor data in Core Motion, let's test our new line chart using `DeviceMotion` data we're already capturing from the `onMotionUpdate()` function. This will also give us a chance to understand how the line chart needs to have its data formatted.

The iOS `Charts` framework requires us to set up data in a very specific way. First, we have a `Data Entry` object, which represents a single point of information, and consists of the data value, and the x-index. Then, when we have a bunch of these entries we put them together and give them a label and it becomes a `Data Set`. Finally, we take the data set and a list of labels for each x value to create a `Chart Data` object. This full chart data gets sent to the chart view, which then renders the data.

To start, let's create a new property at the top of the class, underneath the label outlet we just made. It will be a new data set, which we will add to as we get new data points:

```
@IBOutlet weak var lineChartView: LineChartView!
var dataSet = LineChartDataSet(yVals: [], label: "Values")
```

Next, we'll add a new function stub called `addChartPoint()`, which takes in a double value, and a string name. Then, in our `onMotionUpdate()` function from earlier, we'll clear out all of the print statements and instead just add a chart point using the x value from the gravity information:

```
func onMotionUpdate(data: CMDeviceMotion?, error:Error?) {
    if error == nil, let d = data {
        addChartPoint(data: d.gravity.x)
```

Finally, we'll fill out the addChartPoint() function. First, we add a new data entry to the data set by using the index of the current number of entries as the x value, and using the data we pass in as the y value. We then add that data point to your data set. Next, we create a new LineChartData object, attach our updated data set to it, and then set that to the data property of our lineChartView. Now our line chart has updated data.

```
func addChartPoint(data: Double) {

    let newDataPoint = ChartDataEntry(x: Double(dataSet.entryCount),
y: data)
    dataSet.addEntry(newDataPoint)

    let chartData = LineChartData()
    chartData.addDataSet(dataSet)
```

```
        lineChartView.data = chartData

        DispatchQueue.main.async(execute: {
            self.lineChartView.notifyDataSetChanged()
            self.lineChartView.setNeedsDisplay()
        })
    }
```

The last thing we need to do is tell the line chart that it needs to redraw itself. Normally, we would just need to call the two lines:

```
    lineChartView.notifyDataSetChanged()
    lineChartView.setNeedsDisplay()
```

However, the setNeedsDisplay() function is part of UIKit, and all user interface function calls need to happen on the main thread. Now, multi-threading is a bit beyond the scope of what we're covering in this book, but we're calling addChartPoint() from the onMotionUpdate() function which is being run on the motionQueue, which exists on a *separate thread*. So, like earlier in the book, we use DispatchQueue.main.async() to execute those two lines on the main thread.

If this is all over your head, that's fine! The main takeaway is that setNeedsDisplay() needs to be inside that code block for it to work properly and redraw the chart. Let's take a look at the final updated code for our new view controller:

```
    import UIKit
    import CoreMotion
    import Charts

    class ViewController: UIViewController {

        let motionManager = CMMotionManager()
        let motionQueue = OperationQueue()


        @IBOutlet weak var lineChartView: LineChartView!
        var dataSet = LineChartDataSet(values: [], label: "Values")

        override func viewDidLoad() {
            super.viewDidLoad()
```

```
        if motionManager.isDeviceMotionAvailable {
            motionManager.deviceMotionUpdateInterval = 0.25
            motionManager.startDeviceMotionUpdates(to: motionQueue,
withHandler: onMotionUpdate)
        }
    }

    func onMotionUpdate(data: CMDeviceMotion?, error:Error?) {
        if error == nil, let d = data {
            addChartPoint(data: d.gravity.x)
        } else {
            print("Error: \(error?.localizedDescription)")
        }
    }

    func addChartPoint(data: Double) {

        let newDataPoint = ChartDataEntry(x: Double(dataSet.
entryCount), y: data)
        dataSet.addEntry(newDataPoint)

        let chartData = LineChartData()
        chartData.addDataSet(dataSet)
        lineChartView.data = chartData

        DispatchQueue.main.async(execute: {
            self.lineChartView.notifyDataSetChanged()
            self.lineChartView.setNeedsDisplay()
        })
    }
}
```

At this point you should be able to build and run the project, and see a live updating chart that shows the values of gravity forces on the *x* axis. Still not something that's too useful, but we'll start charting some more useful information next!

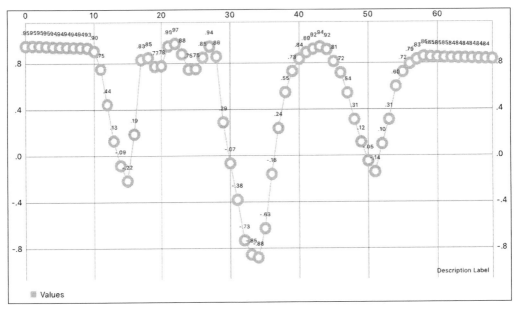

Figure 11.6: Our finished line chart outputting the live values of gravity from our device's accelerometer

Pedometer

Now that we've got a system set up to chart data, let's start looking at more interesting information. While iOS has always given developers access to the low-level sensor data, over the years Apple has started to process more and more motion data, especially since dedicated motion co-processors (the M7/M8/M9/M10 chips) were added to the iPhone starting with the 5s. One of the new pieces of data that came along with the new motion co-processors was the pedometer data. Let's dive into the pedometer and chart the number of steps the user has taken each day over the last week.

Before we get started, let's strip out all of the old `DeviceMotion` tracking that we had, but leave in all of the `Chart` functions. Our starting view controller should look like this:

```
import UIKit
import CoreMotion
import Charts

class ViewController: UIViewController {
```

```
@IBOutlet weak var lineChartView: LineChartView!
var dataSet = LineChartDataSet(values: [], label: "Values")

override func viewDidLoad() {
    super.viewDidLoad()

}

func addChartPoint(data: Double) {

    let newDataPoint = ChartDataEntry(x: Double(dataSet.
entryCount), y: data)
    dataSet.addEntry(newDataPoint)

    let chartData = LineChartData()
    chartData.addDataSet(dataSet)
    lineChartView.data = chartData

    DispatchQueue.main.async(execute: {
        self.lineChartView.notifyDataSetChanged()
        self.lineChartView.setNeedsDisplay()
    })
}
}
```

Before we get started, we're going to need to add a privacy description to the project's Info.plist – you know the drill. In Info.plist, create a new key named Privacy - Motion Usage Description, and for the value, put Needs to access pedometer data.". Now our app will be allowed to ask the user for permission to use pedometer data.

To access this pedometer data, we need to use a Core Motion class called CMPedometer. At the top of our ViewController class, let's instantiate a new CMPedometer object that we can use to access this information:

```
let pedometer = CMPedometer()
```

Next, in the viewDidLoad() function, we need to check to see if the current device has step counting capabilities available. To do this, we use a *class method* of the CMPedometer class called isStepCountingAvailable(). A class method is a method that we call on the class itself; we don't need an instance of an object. Here's what that looks like:

```
if CMPedometer.isStepCountingAvailable() {
    loadHistoricPedometerData()
}
```

If step counting *is* available, we're going to call a function named
`loadHistoricPedometerData`, which we're going to create right now!

```
func loadHistoricPedometerData() {

    let now = Date()
    let secPerDay = TimeInterval(60 * 60 * 24)
    let secPerWeek = secPerDay * 7
    let lastWeek = Date(timeInterval: -secPerWeek, since: now)
    let lastWeekTime = lastWeek.timeIntervalSince1970

    for i in 1...7 {
        let startTime = lastWeekTime + ( secPerDay * Double(i - 1) )
        let endTime = lastWeekTime + ( secPerDay * Double(i) )
        let startDate = Date(timeIntervalSince1970: startTime )
        let endDate = Date(timeIntervalSince1970: endTime )
        pedometer.queryPedometerData(from: startDate, to: endDate,
withHandler: processPedometerData)
    }
}
```

This function plays around with `Date` and `TimeInterval` to query the pedometer
for data for each day in the last week. First we grab the current date, and then create
some simple variables to hold the number of seconds in a day, and number of
seconds in a week. After that, we get the `Date` representation of exactly a week ago
by passing in the negative amount of seconds in a week with the `since parameter`
set to `now`. Finally, we get the `TimeInterval` representation of last week from the
`lastWeek` `Date`.

After we have all these starting values, we do some fancy work inside a `for` loop.
Each iteration passes through the loop, and our goal is to get the starting date and
ending date of a specific day, starting from a week ago. So if it is Sunday night, first
we get the date starting from *last* Sunday night and ending on last Monday night. By
repeating this seven times, we get the last seven days.

At the end of each iteration through the `for` loop, we call a function from the
pedometer called `queryPedometerData()`, where we then pass in the start date and
end date for that day, along with a handler function called `processPedometerData`,
which looks like the other motion data handlers we've created earlier in the chapter.
Calling this query function will give us all of the pedometer data that lies in between
the date ranges:

```
func processPedometerData(data: CMPedometerData?, error: Error?) {
    if error == nil, let d = data {
        addChartPoint(data: d.numberOfSteps.doubleValue)
```

```
    } else {
        print("Error: \(error?.localizedDescription)")
    }
}
```

The `processPedometerData()` function is pretty straightforward. We check to see if there was an error, and if not we try to unwrap the data that gets passed in. If we successfully unwrap the data, we just add a chart point using the `numberOfSteps` property of the `CMPedometerData` that gets passed into the function. Remember, this `CMPedometerData` only contains data that was created between the start and end dates we gave the pedometer. The end result of all this is that we create a data point for each of the last seven days containing the number of steps walked that day.

In addition to just `numberOfSteps`, the pedometer data also keeps track of the distance the user had walked/ran (using the `distance` property), their cadence, which is the number of steps per second (using the `currentCadence` property), and the user's pace, which is measured as the number of seconds per meter (using the `currentPace` property).

If you try to build and run the project on your device, the app will ask for permission to access your pedometer data; allow it. What you should see is something like this:

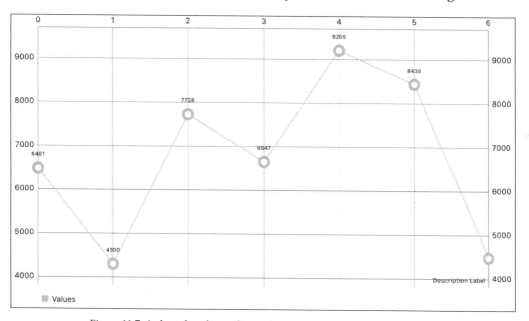

Figure 11.7: A chart that shows the user's step count over the last seven days

Now, even if you're running this on a device, there's a possibility that it doesn't track pedometer data and your chart will be empty. Even if it does track steps there's still a possibility that there won't be a step count, especially if you're trying this on a development only device that sits on a desk all day! My chart is actually showing my own step count, since I'm using my day-to-day phone that has all of my movement data.

Altitude

One of the coolest sensors that exists in the newest iPhones (the 6, 6s and 7) is the barometer. The barometer measures air pressure, which allows us to measure the relative changes in altitude of a device. Before we get started, let's again clear out the functionality we just added with the pedometer.

At the top of our class now, let's get a reference to the CMAltimeter class, which is what interfaces with the barometer to get altitude data. We're also going to need another OperationQueue to process data like with the accelerometer earlier, so create one of those too:

```
let altimeter = CMAltimeter()
let altimeterQueue = OperationQueue()
```

Then, in the viewDidLoad() function, we need to check to see if the current device supports the altimeter, so we use another class method like so:

```
if CMAltimeter.isRelativeAltitudeAvailable() {
    altimeter.startRelativeAltitudeUpdates(to: altimeterQueue,
withHandler: processAltimeterData)
}
```

If the device supports the altimeter functionality, then we start running updates on the altimeterQueue just like we were doing earlier with the accelerometer and gyroscope. Here we pass in processAltimeterData as the data handler, which should look familiar:

```
func processAltimeterData(data: CMAltitudeData?, error: Error?) {
    if error == nil, let d = data {
        addChartPoint(data: d.relativeAltitude.doubleValue)
    } else {
        print("Error: \(error?.localizedDescription)")
    }
}
```

Here, we create a new chart point that uses the `relativeAltitude` property of our `CMAltitudeData,` and give it the name `relative altitude`. Now, every time our app gets a new altitude reading, it will plot the point on our line chart.

Here's how the final code should look for reading the altimeter data:

```
class ViewController: UIViewController {

    let altimeter = CMAltimeter()
    let altimeterQueue = OperationQueue()

    @IBOutlet weak var lineChartView: LineChartView!
    var dataSet = LineChartDataSet(values: [], label: "Values")

    override func viewDidLoad() {
        super.viewDidLoad()

        if CMAltimeter.isRelativeAltitudeAvailable() {
            altimeter.startRelativeAltitudeUpdates(to: altimeterQueue,
withHandler: processAltimeterData)
        }
    }

    func processAltimeterData(data: CMAltitudeData?, error: Error?) {
        if error == nil, let d = data {
            addChartPoint(data: d.relativeAltitude.doubleValue)
        } else {
            print("Error: \(error?.localizedDescription)")
        }
    }

    func addChartPoint(data: Double) {

        << This code has not changed since we wrote it >>
    }
}
```

If you don't have a device that has the proper hardware to test on, this is what the app would look like as the phone is moved up and down:

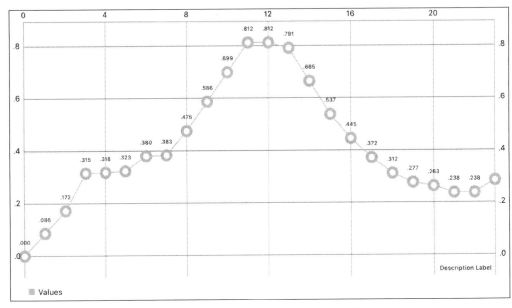

Figure 11.8: The relative altitude data charted as I move my iPhone up and down

At this point we've played with almost all of the sensors available to us on iOS. As I'm sure you can tell, most sensors are interfaced in similar ways, so I encourage you to dig around the documentation and see what other sensors you can play with!

Sensors on Apple Watch

Now, while we've exhausted most of our sensory options on iOS, there's still plenty of room to explore on watchOS! In this section, we'll combine what we've learned about sensors in this chapter with the watchOS development we learned in the last chapter. The end goal is to get information from the Apple Watch's accelerometer, and then bring it back to iOS and display it on a chart. Let's do it!

Once again, before we start let's clear out our `ViewController` class to get rid of the altimeter processing that we were playing with in the last section. Your `ViewController.swift` file should look like this as we begin our Apple Watch experiment:

```
import UIKit
import CoreMotion
import Charts
```

```
class ViewController: UIViewController {

    @IBOutlet weak var lineChartView: LineChartView!
    var dataSet = LineChartDataSet(values: [], label: "Values")

    override func viewDidLoad() {
        super.viewDidLoad()
    }

    func addChartPoint(data: Double) {

        let newDataPoint = ChartDataEntry(x: Double(dataSet.
entryCount), y: data)
        dataSet.addEntry(newDataPoint)

        let chartData = LineChartData()
        chartData.addDataSet(dataSet)
        lineChartView.data = chartData

        DispatchQueue.main.async(execute: {
            self.lineChartView.notifyDataSetChanged()
            self.lineChartView.setNeedsDisplay()
        })
    }
}
```

Setting up an extension

Before we can start programming, we need to create the watchOS extension targets. (I won't go into full detail here, so if you need some more detail, feel free to refer to *Chapter 10, Creating a WatchOS Companion App*). Create a new app target (**File** | **New** | **Target**), select WatchKit App, from the watchOS tab, name it Sensors-Watch, and activate the scheme when prompted.

At this point, run the app in a joint simulator like iPhone 6s + Apple Watch - 38mm just to make sure that the extension is set up and running properly. If the simulator launches, we're all set to go!

Getting sensor data on Apple Watch

With watchOS 2, Apple opened up a bunch of iOS APIs to the watchOS development platform (and even more in watchOS 3!). On watchOS we also have access to Core Motion API, which means that getting accelerometer data is going to be pretty much exactly the same as getting it on iOS! Open up the `InterfaceController.swift` file inside the `Sensors-Watch Extension` folder, and let's set up accelerometer polling:

```swift
import WatchKit
import Foundation
import CoreMotion

class InterfaceController: WKInterfaceController {

    let motionManager = CMMotionManager()
    let motionQueue = OperationQueue()

    override func awake(withContext context: Any?) {
        super.awake(withContext: context)

        if motionManager.isAccelerometerActive {
            motionManager.accelerometerUpdateInterval = 0.5
            motionManager.startAccelerometerUpdates(to: motionQueue,
withHandler: onAccelerometerUpdate)
        }
    }

    func onAccelerometerUpdate(data: CMAccelerometerData?, error:
Error?) {
        if error == nil, let d = data {
            print("acceleration x \(d.acceleration.x)")
        } else {
            print("Error: \(error?.localizedDescription)")
        }
    }

    override func willActivate() {
        super.willActivate()
    }
    override func didDeactivate() {
        super.didDeactivate()
    }
}
```

At this point, this code should look very familiar to you. Remember to import the Core Motion framework. At the top of the class we create a `CMMotionManager` object, and a new `OperationQueue` to process the data on. Then, inside the `awake(withContext:)` function, we check to see if the accelerometer is available, and if so we set the update interval and begin updating the accelerometer.

I've called attention to the update interval, since I'm setting it to `0.5`. Since we're running on the Apple Watch, we are running it a bit slower so we don't overload it. If you truly need a higher sampling rate you can set it to be faster, but since we're just experimenting I've set it to two updates per second.

Finally, we create the `onAccelerometerUpdate()` function which processes the data that gets sent from the accelerometer. For now, we're just printing it out to the console.

And that's it! Pretty much exactly the same as we do on iOS, which is what makes the Core Motion API so great. Now let's bundle up that data and send it back to iOS.

Sending and displaying data on iOS

In order to get the data back to iOS, we're going to use the Watch Connectivity framework that we explored in the last chapter. We'll start by sending it out from the watchOS app, and then go back to the iOS `AppDelegate` to receive the data we send:

```
import WatchKit
import Foundation
import CoreMotion
import WatchConnectivity

class InterfaceController: WKInterfaceController, WCSessionDelegate {

    let motionManager = CMMotionManager()
    let motionQueue = NSOperationQueue()
    var session: WCSession?


    public func session(_ session: WCSession,
    activationDidCompleteWith activationState: WCSessionActivationState,
    error: Error?) {
        return
    }

    let motionManager = CMMotionManager()
    let motionQueue = OperationQueue()
```

```
        override func awake(withContext context: Any?) {
            super.awake(withContext: context)
            session = WCSession.default()
            session?.delegate = self
            session?.activate()

            if motionManager.isAccelerometerAvailable {
                motionManager.accelerometerUpdateInterval = 0.5
                motionManager.startAccelerometerUpdates(to: motionQueue,
        withHandler: onAccelerometerUpdate)
            }
        }

        func onAccelerometerUpdate(data: CMAccelerometerData?, error:
        Error?) {
            if error == nil, let d = data {
                sendDataToiOS(data: d.acceleration.x)
            } else {
                print("Error: \(error?.localizedDescription)")
            }
        }

        func sendDataToiOS(data: Double) {
            let info: [String: Any] = ["data" : data]
            session?.sendMessage(info, replyHandler: nil, errorHandler:
        nil)
        }

        override func willActivate() {
            super.willActivate()
        }
        override func didDeactivate() {
            super.didDeactivate()
        }
    }
```

First, we need to link the `WatchConnectivity` framework, and then import it at
the top of the file. Then, we set our `InterfaceController` class to implement
the `WCSessionDelegate` protocol. Next, we create a variable property to hold a
reference to the watch connectivity session, and implement a required function of
the `WCSessionDelegate` protocol. After that, we create and set up the session in the
`awake(withContext:)` function.

With our session set up, we can jump down to the bottom of the class and create a new function called sendDataToiOS(), which takes a Double as a parameters. Inside the function, we create a new dictionary that holds the data and the string, and then we use the sendMessage() function of the session to send that dictionary off to iOS:

```
import UIKit
import WatchConnectivity

@UIApplicationMain
class AppDelegate: UIResponder, UIApplicationDelegate,
WCSessionDelegate  {

    var session: WCSession?

    func session(_ session: WCSession, activationDidCompleteWith
activationState: WCSessionActivationState, error: Error?) {
        return
    }
    func sessionDidDeactivate(_ session: WCSession) {
        return
    }
    func sessionDidBecomeInactive(_ session: WCSession) {
        return
    }

    var window: UIWindow?

    func application(_ application: UIApplication,
didFinishLaunchingWithOptions launchOptions:
[UIApplicationLaunchOptionsKey: Any]?) -> Bool {
        session = WCSession.default()
        session?.delegate = self
        session?.activate()

        return true
    }

    func session(_ session: WCSession, didReceiveMessage message:
[String : Any]) {
        if let data = message["data"] as? Double {
            let vc = window?.rootViewController as! ViewController
            vc.addChartPoint(data: data)
        }
    }
}
```

Like in the last file, we have to implement some empty functions that are required by the `WCSessionDelegate` protocol.

Once we've finished implementing all of the highlighted required methods, we can implement the session(`didReceiveMessage:`) function which is what receives the dictionary we sent from watchOS. In there, we try to unwrap the data the elements from the dictionary as the correct types. If it succeeds, we get a reference to our root view controller and then call the `addChartPoint()` function to add the data from our Apple Watch's accelerometer to the chart.

At this point, everything should be set up! We pulled the accelerometer data on the watch, then packaged it up and sent it off to iOS where the `AppDelegate` received and unwrapped the data, before sending it off to our chart. Here's me flailing my wrist:

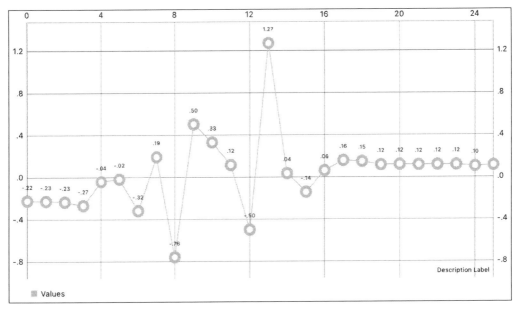

Figure 11.9: The accelerometer data being pulled from the Apple Watch on my wrist

Hopefully, this demonstrated how simple it should be to get all the other sensory data off the Apple Watch and into an iOS app.

Summary

We just learnt a ton about sensors, in addition to a handful of other good stuff! We learnt about `UIDevice`, and the basic device state sensory information it contains. Then we discovered Core Motion, and learnt how to create new operation queues to process sensory data. After that we learnt how to link a third-party library, and charted data from the iPhone's pedometer and altimeter. Finally, we took all of our sensory knowledge to watchOS by pulling accelerometer data from an Apple Watch into a chart on our iPhone.

In the next chapter, we'll be looking at our last major element of iOS programming in this book: notifications. We're on the home stretch, and we're just about ready to start diving into the tools Xcode provides to test, debug, optimize, and wrap up our project. Let's keep going!

12
Sending Notifications

When building an application, most of the interactions will take place while users are actually inside the app. Users are interacting with user interface elements, and your app can respond to their input in real time.

However, sometimes your app may receive information from a server, or be alerted that some scheduled action is happening while the user isn't inside the app. A lot of times, your app can just process these things the next time the app launches, like when your Facebook feed refreshes when you enter. However, other times the information coming in is time-sensitive, or of higher importance, and you need to let the user know what's going on, even if the app is closed

In these situations, you can send the user a notification. Notifications are presented to the user in many forms, and can provide a handful of ways for the user to respond to the information being presented. In this chapter, we're going to cover:

- Local versus remote notifications
- Scheduling local notifications
- Creating categories and actions for notifications
- Using badges and sounds
- Writing code to handle incoming notifications

Introduction to user notifications

Chances are that if you've used an iOS device, you're very familiar with the user notification system. We'll review the components of notifications so that we're refreshed prior to coding, but before we do that it's worth taking a second to talk about *notifications* in iOS.

If you remember in the last chapter, when we were getting orientation changes, we used a class called `NotificationCenter` to register for notifications. These *system* notifications are completely different from *user* notifications, which are visual elements that alert a user about things going on inside an app. Those system notifications were strictly code, notifying us, as a programmer, about things going on in other parts of our application's code.

You'll see later on when we start coding that we are dealing with the `UUNNotificationContentandUNNotificationTrigger` objects for user alerts, as opposed to the `Notification` objects we used to be notified of coding events. It can be a little confusing to new programmers, so just keep it in mind that there are different meanings for the word *notification*.

Components of a user notification

A user notification can take many forms, depending on what makes sense for your app and what the user allows in their notification preferences. One of the most common forms is the banner, where the notification is presented at the top of the screen:

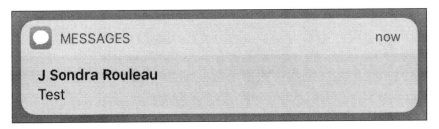

Figure 12.1: A banner notification

Some apps also use what are known as *badges*, the little red circles that appear in the corner of an app icon with a number letting the user know how many notifications are waiting for them. For apps that hold a number of actionable objects (like a mail or to-do app), a badge can add a lot of value:

Figure 12.2: A badge being shown in the corner of the built in messages app

Notifications that are received when the user's phone is locked can also be presented on the lock screen of the device. Lock screen notifications can also include a **slide to reply** action. These notifications allow the user to slide the notification to jump to a state of the application where they can act on the notification:

Figure 12.3: A notification on the lock screen with a slide action

Users can also swipe down from the top of their screen to access the notification center, which keeps a chronological list of all notifications that have not been read, and also lets them slide to act:

Figure 12.4: A notification in the notification center

As we move through the chapter, we'll learn how all of these capabilities are designed and implemented through the code in your application.

Local versus remote notifications

When working with notifications, there are two different types that we can use: local and remote notifications. Both look identical to the user, taking the forms we just discussed. The difference lies in how the notifications are created: local notifications are created and scheduled on the device, while remote notifications are delivered to the device from a server through a network connection.

Remote notifications are a bit complex; handling them as a notification is pretty much the same as a local notification, but actually setting up a server to create the notification and communicate with the **Apple Push Notification (APN)** service is beyond the scope of what we're covering in this book. Instead, we'll focus on local notifications.

By the end of the chapter you'll have the *front end* skills to handle notifications, so that later on in your career you could easily learn the additional skills required to fully use remote notifications.

Adding notification support to Snippets

It's time to jump back into our Snippets project! In this section, we'll be adding a daily notification that reminds the user to capture snippets from their day. To do this we need to register our app with the system to receive notifications, and then we need to schedule it.

As always, feel free to open your existing Snippets project, or use the completed project from *Chapter 10, Creating WatchOS Companion App*, since we didn't use it in *Chapter 11, Advanced Input Using Sensors*.

Getting permission to send notifications

In order for your app to use notifications, you need to register the app with the system. Much like earlier in the book, when getting permission to use location and other services, this will prompt an alert for the user to accept or decline.

To set up our app with proper permissions, we need to request authorization from the system. This makes the most sense to do in the AppDelegate's application(did FinishLaunchingWithOptions:) function, so let's go there and update our code:

```
func application(_ application: UIApplication,
didFinishLaunchingWithOptions launchOptions:
[UIApplicationLaunchOptionsKey : Any]? = nil) -> Bool {

    if WCSession.isSupported() {
        session = WCSession.default()
        session?.delegate = self
        session?.activate()
    }

    let center = UNUserNotificationCenter.current()
    center.requestAuthorization(options: [.alert, .badge, .sound]) {
granted, error in
        if !granted {
            print("Notifications are not allowed")
        }
    }

    return true
}
```

First, we grabbed a reference to the `UNUserNotificationCenter`, which is what manages the device's user notifications. Then, we request authorization for our app to schedule notifications with the options **alert**, **badge**, and **sound**. This means our application will be allowed to present alert/banner notifications, app icon badges, and notification sounds.

If you build and run the app now, you should get a prompt that asks if `Snippets` can send the user notifications (make sure to press **Allow**):

Figure 12.5: Our app asking for permission to send the user notifications

Our app is now configured to schedulenotifications.

Scheduling a local notification

To schedule a notification, we are going to need to configure a new `UNNotificationRequest` object. The notification request itself is composed of two main pieces: `Content` and a `Trigger`. Let's write a new function in our `AppDelegate`to create and configure everything we need to schedule a notification:

```
func scheduleReminderNotification() {

    let center = UNUserNotificationCenter.current()
    center.getPendingNotificationRequests() { pendingRequests in

        guard !pendingRequests.contains(where: { r in r.identifier ==
"Snippets.Reminder"}) else {
            print("Notification already exists")
            return
        }

        let content = UNMutableNotificationContent()
        content.title = "Reminder"
        content.body = "Have you snipped anything lately?"
```

```
        content.sound = UNNotificationSound.default()

        var fireDate = DateComponents()
        fireDate.hour = 12
        let trigger = UNCalendarNotificationTrigger(dateMatching:
fireDate, repeats: true)

        let request = UNNotificationRequest(identifier: "Snippets.
Reminder", content: content, trigger: trigger)

        center.add(request, withCompletionHandler: nil)
    }
}
```

First we get a reference to the current UNUserNotificationCenter, which we will use to schedule the notification later. Then we check to see if there are already any scheduled notifications in our app by calling the getPendingNotificationRequests() function. If there are notifications, we check to see if it contains a notification whose identifier matches Snippets.Reminder. If there is no reminder notification, then it's time for us to make one.

We start off by creating a new instance of UNMutableNotificationContent. Then we give the content an alert title, body text, and a sound to play.

After that, we create a trigger, which dictates when the notification will be presented to the user. There are several different kinds of notification triggers, such as a time interval, a calendar date, or even a location. In this case, we're going to use a calendar trigger, asking the notification to be sent every time it is 12 o'clock. To do that is simple: we create a DateComponents() object, and set the hour property to 12. Then, we create a UNCalendarNotificationTrigger object, pass in the fireDate, and tell it to repeat. Now the notification is set to trigger every day at 12.

Finally, we create a notification request using an identifier (Snippets.Reminder), along with the notification content and the trigger. Then we add the notification request to our UNUserNotificationCenter, which registers the notification with the system.

To wrap up our scheduling, we just call our scheduling function in our application(didFinishLaunchingWithOptions:) function after we check the authorization status:

```swift
func application(_ application: UIApplication,
didFinishLaunchingWithOptions launchOptions:
[UIApplicationLaunchOptionsKey : Any]? = nil) -> Bool {

    if WCSession.isSupported() {
        session = WCSession.default()
        session?.delegate = self
        session?.activate()
    }

    let center = UNUserNotificationCenter.current()
    center.requestAuthorization(options: [.alert, .badge, .sound]) {
granted, error in
        if granted {
            self.scheduleReminderNotification()
        }
    }

    return true
}
```

Figure 12.6: The remindernotification on the lock screen

Advanced notifications

So right now, we've got our notification registered to be delivered every day at noon. But that's only scratching the surface with what we can do with notifications. In this section we'll add actions, badges, and custom sounds.

Categories and actions

When you receive a notification in iOS, sometimes you can 3D touch on the notification or pull it down to reveal quick response actions. We can add our own notification actions by creating `UNNotificationAction` objects, adding them to a `UNNotificationCategory`, and then assigning a category to a notification's content.

To begin, let's create a new function that will take care of setting up all of the categories and actions. We'll modify our `application(didFinishLaunchingWithOptions:)` function like so:

```
let center = UNUserNotificationCenter.current()
center.requestAuthorization(options: [.alert, .badge, .sound]) {
granted, error in
    if granted {
        center.setNotificationCategories( self.
getNotificationCategories() )
        self.scheduleReminderNotification()
    }
}
```

Now let's get to work setting up those categories. We'll create the `getNotificationCategories()` function (which returns a Set of categories), and then implement our first action:

```
func getNotificationCategories () -> Set<UNNotificationCategory> {

    let textAction = UNNotificationAction(identifier: "Snippets.
Action.NewText ", title: "New Text Snippet", options:
[.authenticationRequired, .foreground])
}
```

Here, we're creating a new action called `textAction`, which will ultimately allow us to create a new text snippet right from the notification banner. We give it an identifier of `Snippets.Action.NewText`, and a title of `NewTextSnippet`. In the options array, we give it the `.authenticationRequired` option to make sure the user's phone is unlocked to be allowed to use the action. We also add the `.foreground` option to let the app know to launch the app when the action is pressed.

Next, we need to create another action for creating a photo snippet. The parameters are all pretty much the same, except that we replace the word `Text` with `Photo` throughout:

```
func getNotificationCategories () -> Set<UNNotificationCategory> {

    let textAction = UNNotificationAction(identifier: "Snippets.
Action.NewText ", title: "New Text Snippet", options:
[.authenticationRequired, .foreground])
}
```

Finally, we need to create a category to hold these actions. We first create an instance of UNNotificationCategory, and set the identifier to Snippets.Category. Reminder. We'll be using this identifier later to assign categories to our notifications. Then, we just pass in the actions as an array. We aren't using any intent identifiers (which are related to Siri), or any options so we leave those arrays blank:

```
func getNotificationCategories () -> Set<UNNotificationCategory> {

    let textAction = UNNotificationAction(identifier: "Snippets.
Action.NewText ", title: "New Text Snippet", options:
[.authenticationRequired, .foreground])

    let photoAction = UNNotificationAction(identifier: "Snippets.
Action.NewPhoto", title: "New Photo Snippet", options:
[.authenticationRequired, .foreground])

    let reminderCategory = UNNotificationCategory(identifier:
"Snippets.Category.Reminder", actions: [textAction, photoAction],
intentIdentifiers: [], options: [])

    return Set<UNNotificationCategory>( [reminderCategory] )
}
```

Once the category is fully set up, we create a set of UNNotificationCategory objects, and then return it.

With our new Snippets.Category.Reminder category set up, we just need to assign this category to our daily reminder notification's content:

```
let content = UNMutableNotificationContent()
content.title = "Reminder"
content.body = "Have you snipped anything lately?"
content.sound = UNNotificationSound.default()
content.categoryIdentifier = "Snippets.Category.Reminder"
```

Now, the next time you get your daily reminder, you can pull down or 3D touch to see two buttons to create a text or photo snippet!

If you don't feel like waiting until noon to see if it worked, see if you can figure out how to add a new `BarButtonItem` to your storyboard (next to the `New` button), and have it call an `IBAction` in `ViewController.swift` that creates a new test notification with the category set to `Snippets.Category.Reminder`. (This is how I took the photos below).

Here is what this should look like in a banner notification:

Figure 12.7: The reminder notification with actions being displayed from a banner

These are the actions in the notification center:

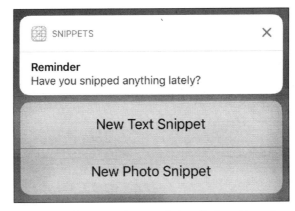

Figure 12.8: The reminder notification with actions being displayed from the notification center

Finally, this is what our actions look like on the lock screen:

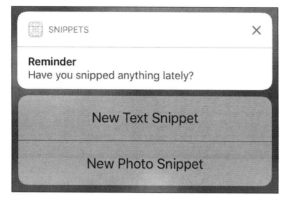

Figure 12.9: The reminder notification with actions being displayed from the lock screen

Awesome! The only problem now is that these buttons don't do anything yet. In order to respond to the action, we need to create an extension of the `AppDelegate` class that implements the `UNUserNotificationCenterDelegate` protocol, and then write a function that receives action responses.

To start, let's create the extension at the bottom of the `AppDelegate.swift` file, and add the empty handler function:

```
extension AppDelegate: UNUserNotificationCenterDelegate {

    func userNotificationCenter(_ center: UNUserNotificationCenter,
    didReceive response: UNNotificationResponse, withCompletionHandler
    completionHandler: @escaping () -> Void) {

        }
    }
}
```

This function passes in a handful of parameters, but we're mostly concerned with the `response` here. We're going to look at the action identifier of the response to see what we should do:

```
func userNotificationCenter(_ center: UNUserNotificationCenter,
didReceive response: UNNotificationResponse, withCompletionHandler
completionHandler: @escaping () -> Void) {

    switch response.actionIdentifier {
        case "Snippets.Action.NewText":
            let vc = self.window!.rootViewController as!
ViewController
```

```
        vc.createNewTextSnippet()

    case "Snippets.Action.NewPhoto":
        let vc = self.window!.rootViewController as!
ViewController
        vc.createNewPhotoSnippet()

    default:
        break
    }

    completionHandler()
}
```

Finally, we need to call the `completionHandler()` closure that is passed in, otherwise the app will crash. Then to finish everything off, we set the delegate of the `UNUserNotificationCenter` back up in the `application(didFinishLaunchingWithOptions:)` function.

```
let center = UNUserNotificationCenter.current()
center.delegate = self
center.requestAuthorization(options: [.alert, .badge, .sound]) {
granted, error in
    if granted {
    center.setNotificationCategories( self.getNotificationCategories())
        self.scheduleReminderNotification()
    }
}
```

Try pressing the buttons on the notifications now, and you'll launch the app into the correct snippet creation view controller!

Before we move on, lets acknowledge that this code is very similar to the code we wrote much earlier in the book that handled the 3D touch shortcuts. As a little challenge, see if you can go back to that earlier code, and separate it a bit better into smaller functions, so that we can reuse that code here in our notification handlers.

We also dealt with an edge case with the shortcuts: if the user was already creating a snippet when the shortcut was used, the app asked the user if they wanted to throw away the other snippet, or continue editing it. See if you can also get that functionality working with the notification handlers!

Badges

In most apps where detail is paid attention to, badges on the app icon correspond to the number of items awaiting the user's action inside the app. Our application is pretty simple and doesn't have particularly urgent notifications, so we normally wouldn't implement icon badges for our current feature set. However, for the sake of learning, let's do it anyway!

Here's the good news about icon badges: they're ridiculously easy to implement. We only need to add one line of code to our notification set up:

```
func scheduleReminderNotification() {
    let center = UNUserNotificationCenter.current()
    center.getPendingNotificationRequests() { pendingRequests in

        guard !pendingRequests.contains(where: { r in r.identifier ==
"Snippets.Reminder"}) else {
            print("Notification already exists")
            return
        }

        let content = UNMutableNotificationContent()
        content.title = "Reminder"
        content.body = "Have you snipped anything lately?"
        content.sound = UNNotificationSound.default()
        content.categoryIdentifier = "Snippets.Category.Reminder"
        content.badge = 1

        var fireDate = DateComponents()
        fireDate.hour = 12
        let trigger = UNCalendarNotificationTrigger(dateMatching:
fireDate, repeats: true)

        let request = UNNotificationRequest(identifier: "Snippets.
Reminder", content: content, trigger: trigger)

        center.add(request, withCompletionHandler: nil)
    }
}
```

Now, when our notification comes in, it will set the badge number to 1. In order to clear the number when the user comes back into the application, we'll implement the `applicationDidBecomeActive()` function, and set the badge number to zero when the application is opened:

```
func applicationDidBecomeActive(_ application: UIApplication) {
    application.applicationIconBadgeNumber = 0
}
```

Try this out and see how the badge number changes!

Figure 12.10: Our snippets app with a notification badge displayed

Now, the bad news about badge numbers: we are *hardcoding* the number to set the badge number. This obviously won't work if there are more kinds of notifications that can show up!

In the event that you're using remote notifications that are pushed from a server, you'll have to keep track of those numbers yourself on the server, and send them in with the notification. If using local notifications, you'll have to do some fancy tracking to keep updating the numbers of all pending notifications. Every situation is different, and it's up to you to figure out the best solution for managing the badge number associated with notifications for your app.

Custom sounds

Adding sound to a notification can really add some weight to the alert. Using a custom sound is also a great way to give your app some character. Like badges, adding sound is a pretty simple task.

First, drag in the `CustomSound.caf` file from the chapter 12 resources folder into your Xcode project. When importing, make sure you copy the files and include them in your app target. The settings should look like this:

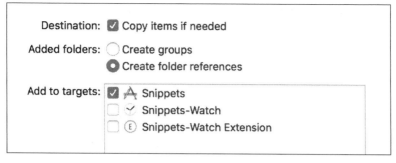

Figure 12.11: The import settings for our CustomSound.caf file

Once the sound is imported into the project, we use the
UNNotificationSound(named:) initializer, instead of UNNotificationSound.
default() like before:

```
func scheduleReminderNotification() {
    let center = UNUserNotificationCenter.current()
    center.removeAllPendingNotificationRequests()
    center.getPendingNotificationRequests() { pendingRequests in

        guard !pendingRequests.contains(where: { r in r.identifier ==
"Snippets.Reminder"}) else {
            print("Notification already exists")
            return
        }

        let content = UNMutableNotificationContent()
        content.title = "Reminder"
        content.body = "Have you snipped anything lately?"
        content.sound = UNNotificationSound(named: "CustomSound")
        content.categoryIdentifier = "Snippets.Category.Reminder"
        content.badge = 1

        var fireDate = DateComponents()
        fireDate.hour = 17
        fireDate.minute = 13
        fireDate.second = 40
        let trigger = UNCalendarNotificationTrigger(dateMatching:
fireDate, repeats: true)

        let request = UNNotificationRequest(identifier: "Snippets.
Reminder", content: content, trigger: trigger)

        center.add(request, withCompletionHandler: nil)
    }
}
```

Now, build and run the project, and you should get a custom sound when the notification arrives! (Make sure to turn your sound on).

If you prefer to use the default sound, you can use the following code instead:

```
reminderNotification.soundName = UILocalNotificationDefaultSoundName
```

> If your custom sound isn't playing, you might have to uninstall the app, reboot your phone, clean the Xcode project (*command + shift + K*), and reinstall the app. Sometimes things get a little finicky! ! Also worth noting is that as of the writing of this book, iOS 10.0 is the current version of iOS, and this issue should be fixed in iOS 10.1.

Receiving notifications while in the app

We've got a pretty solid set of notification functionality going right now, but there's still one big piece missing: what happens if a notification is received while the user is currently inside the app?

iOS responds to notifications differently when the app is in the foreground vs the background. So far, all of our code has been telling the notification what to display on the banner, what sounds to play, what to change the badge number to. However, we don't need to do any of this when inside the app, since we can much more effectively tell the user something important just happened!

As I mentioned with the badges, there's no real reason to interrupt the user to remind them to make a snippet when they're already in the app, but we'll look at how to do this for educational purposes.

What we are going to do is present the user with an alert to let them know what is going on with the notification. We'll be using the UIAlertController to display the notification information, and let the user act.

To receive notifications while the application is in the foreground, we need to implement a different handler in our UNUserNotificationCenterDelegate class extension. Let's head to the extension and add this new function:

```
func userNotificationCenter(_ center: UNUserNotificationCenter,
willPresent notification: UNNotification, withCompletionHandler
completionHandler: @escaping (UNNotificationPresentationOptions) ->
Void) {
    let content = notification.request.content
    if content.categoryIdentifier == "Snippets.Category.Reminder"{
    }
}
```

First, we're creating an if statement to see what category the notification belongs to. Right now we only have the `Snippets.Category.Reminder` category, but later on we might have more; it's best to plan ahead to prevent bugs in the future:

Next we are going to create an alert to present to the user:

```
func userNotificationCenter(_ center: UNUserNotificationCenter,
willPresent notification: UNNotification, withCompletionHandler
completionHandler: @escaping (UNNotificationPresentationOptions) ->
Void) {
    let content = notification.request.content
    if content.categoryIdentifier == "Snippets.Category.Reminder"{
        let vc = self.window!.rootViewController as! ViewController

        let alert = UIAlertController(title: content.title, message:
content.body, preferredStyle: .alert)

        let newTextSnippetAction = UIAlertAction(title: "New Text
Snippet", style: .default) { (action: UIAlertAction) in
            vc.createNewTextSnippet()
        }
        let newPhotoSnippetAction = UIAlertAction(title: "New Photo
Snippet", style: .default) { (action: UIAlertAction) in
            vc.createNewPhotoSnippet()
        }
        let cancelAction  = UIAlertAction(title: "Cancel", style:
.cancel, handler: nil)

        alert.addAction(newTextSnippetAction)
        alert.addAction(newPhotoSnippetAction)
        alert.addAction(cancelAction)
        vc.present(alert, animated: true, completion: nil)
    }
}
vc.present(alert, animated: true, completion: nil)
    }
}
    }
}
```

First we grab a reference to the root view controller. Then we instantiate the alert itself, using the notification content's title and body for the alert's title and message, respectively. After that, we create the three actions we want to allow the user to do: create a new text snippet, create a new photo snippet, or cancel. To wrap things up, we add our actions and present the alert controller to the user:

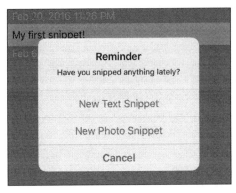

Figure 12.12: The alert letting us know we received a notification while inside the app

And with that, we've implemented a pretty basic way to let the user know of a notification that was received.

Summary

In this chapter, we learned about the user notification system in iOS. We looked at handful of ways that notifications are presented to users, and then added notification support to our Snippets app. Along the way, we learned a bit more about the `Date` and `DateComponents` classes, and scheduled a daily reminder for the user to check in with the app. We also looked at how to add badge numbers to our notifications, and how to play custom sounds with them as well. Finally, we built a simple alert to relay information to the user when a notification is received while the app is in the foreground.

From here, you should have a solid base with the notification system to venture out and try your hand at implementing remote notifications. You'll need to look into the APN service, and learn how to handle the server side of things, but once the notifications make it to the iOS device, you should have a decent handle of how to implement them into your app!

With this chapter, we've finished the development of our app. In the last four chapters, we'll be jumping back into the tools that Xcode gives us to wrap things up. In the next chapter, we'll be taking a look at unit testing in Xcode, which allow us to make sure that each part of our app is functioning as expected.

13
Writing Unit Tests

We've finished building our app! We've implemented a handful of features, and everything works as expected. And we had no real setbacks along the way! However, this is not the norm: you usually don't have a guide helping you through your project.

When working on a software project, your code base can sometimes get a bit unruly. When a project gets big enough, you might start touching old code to add new functionality, when suddenly, your whole app is broken! Something you had been fumbling with must have been important, because now you've got a mess on your hands.

In this chapter, we'll be covering the concept of unit tests, and code testing in general. The goal of writing tests for your code is to make sure that all of your code is performing its intended function, and to let you know as soon as that stops being the case. Specifically, we'll learn about:

- What are unit tests?
- Testing tools provided by Xcode
- Using the XCTest framework
- Setting up and writing tests in an Xcode project
- Testing interface elements with UI Tests

Introduction to unit tests

Depending on how and when you began learning about software development, the concept of unit testing may or may not be a part of your vocabulary. Often used in bigger projects with larger teams, unit testing can be seen as a waste of time for smaller developers who don't have the time or resources to spend on writing tests.

Regardless of your past experiences with unit tests, they're a great tool and an important part of Xcode's toolset, and it will be up to you to decide when to use them. Before we get into how they work in Xcode, let's first talk a bit about unit tests in general.

What is a unit?

So, the idea of *testing* seems pretty clear, but what exactly is a unit? It's up for a bit of interpretation, but generally you should think of a unit as the smallest piece of code that performs a discernible function. For example, if I have a function that processes some data and outputs some result, that could be a unit that we could test. In other cases, an entire class may be a unit, if it only serves one purpose.

Once we break down our program into its discernable units, what exactly are we testing? There are many opinions on the subject of what percentage of units you should test: 20%? 50%? 100%? Ultimately, it's up to you. Sometimes there are clear *problem areas* in your source code, with high complexity and a lot of room for things to go wrong. If you've only got a handful of developers on your team, creating some good tests for those problem areas can save a lot of headaches down the line. On the other hand, if you're a company like Uber and your app is the lifeblood of a billion dollar company, maybe you should focus on some more thorough testing!

Why use unit testing in the first place?

The purpose of unit testing is to double check that your code is doing what you meant it to do in the first place. For example, let's say we have a function that takes in two integers and returns their sum. We could write a unit test where we pass in 2 and 2, and make sure that it returns 4. If, later on, we implement the new Addition Engine Turbo 2017™®, we may find that our unit test starts failing because it returns 5.

Assuming that we are running our tests quite frequently, we will be alerted to the fact that parts of our code base are no longer acting as intended. We'll also know that the problem is with our addition function.

These two reasons are some of the most compelling arguments to implement unit testing: early detection, and isolated issues. Every programmer can see the value in finding issues early and easily, but these aren't the only reasons to use unit tests. By writing tests you must critically think about the components of your source code, which forces you to think about the design of your code. This additional pass can also help you identify problems in your architecture.

In the end, taking the time to write out unit tests will force you to write code that is cleaner and less prone to fail, and if it does fail you'll know exactly when and where.

Unit tests in action

Let's get started with writing our first unit tests in Xcode. First, we'll start off in a clean project while we learn the basics, and then later on we'll integrate unit testing into our `Snippets` project.

In this section, we'll start by learning how to set up a project with unit testing capabilities. Then we'll take a look at how to write a unit test using the `XCTest` framework. Finally, we'll take a look at how to run our tests and measure their results.

Setting up the project

Time to set up a new project, you know the drill. But not so fast! This time we're going to be exploring the last two settings that we haven't yet used in the project creation process: the **Include Unit Tests** and **Include UI Tests** options (seen in *Figure 13.1*):

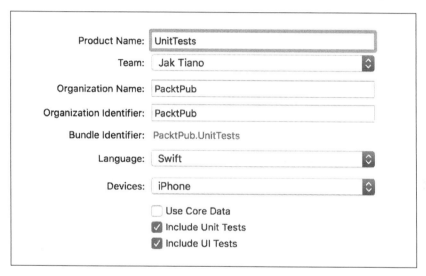

Figure 13.1: We've enabled the two testing checkboxes during project setup

Checking off these two boxes will make sure that the new project you're about to create will have all of the necessary set up taken care of to begin writing unit tests right out of the gate. We're also including UI tests, but we won't be touching those until later in the chapter. We're just including them now to speed things up later.

Once you finish setting up the project, take a look around and notice the differences. Most notably, we have two new targets in our app: the `UnitTestsTests` target and the `UnitTestsUITests` target, each with their own folder in the project hierarchy. If we look inside the `UnitTestsTests` folder, we have a single `UnitTestsTests.swift` file, which is where we'll be writing our tests later on.

To finish our project setup, let's create a basic model class with a few example functions that we can write tests for. Create a new file called `TestModel.swift`, and define it like so:

```swift
import Foundation

class TestModel {

    func example1() -> Int {
        return 1
    }

    func example2() -> Int {
        return 2
    }

    func example3() -> Int {
        return 2
    }


}
```

Also, take care when creating this new file that you are including it with the application target, and not the unit testing target. If you had a file open from the testing targets (like the `UnitTestsTests.swift` file) when you created the new file, it will try to default the new file's target to the testing target. To give you a visual, make sure your target checkbox is similar to the one shown in *Figure 13.2* when you create the file:

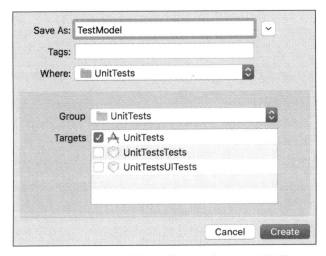

Figure 13.2: Creating the new TestModel.swift file with the correct UnitTests target selected

If you're not sure if you selected the correct target, you can open the file inspector (*option + command+ 1*) to see the same set up of checkboxes for what targets the file belongs to.

Once the new file is created, filled out, and belonging to the correct target, our new project should be fully set up with unit test capabilities and some simple code to run tests on. Let's get to testing!

Writing tests with XCTest

Before we start writing tests, we should take a look at the testing navigator, which will be our base of operations when it comes to unit testing. It's the fifth tab on our navigation sidebar, so you can jump to it with the keyboard shortcut *command + 5*. It should look similar to *Figure 13.3* right now:

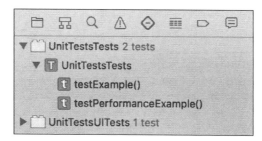

Figure 13.3: Our test navigator at the start of our project

Here, you can see our two testing targets represented by little white blocks. We have the **UnitTestsTests** target and the **UnitTestsUITests** target that were created when we started the project. Underneath these two targets are all of the classes within the target, and underneath each class are all of the testing methods. The testing class template comes with two example tests, named `testExample()` and `testPerformanceExample()`. It also has two `setUp()` and `tearDown()` functions, which allow you to do any set up for the tests that will be run in that class, but they aren't tests and don't show up in the test navigator.

However, a class named **UnitTestsTests** isn't very descriptive, so let's jump back to the project navigator, delete the `UnitTestsTests.swift` file, and then come back to the test navigator. If you look at the bottom of the test navigator, you should see a search field, and to the left a little plus button. This lets us add new testing targets and testing classes to our project. If you click it and select new **Unit Test Class**, you can create a new testing class to replace the one we just deleted.

However, we can also just create one from scratch. Create a new file (*command + N*), choose a Swift file, then select the **UnitTestsTests** group, and add it to the **UnitTestsTests** target:

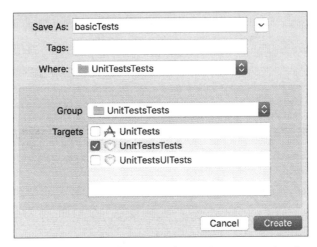

Figure 13.4: The correct file settings for creating a new testing class

Inside our new testing class, we're going to want to import the XCTest framework, and fill in our file with a class declaration that inherits from XCTestCase:

```
import XCTest
@testable import UnitTests

class BasicTests : XCTestCase {


}
```

We need to import the XCTest framework, which is what allows our code to interface with Xcode's testing capabilities. This is where the XCTestCase class comes from, which our class needs to inherit from to enable testing. You'll see that it's ready for testing since there will be a little diamond in the editor margin next to the class name. We also have something new at the top of our file: a @testable import statement. This allows us to have access to all parts of the imported module; even internal/private pieces. This is convenient, because it lets us keep the correct access on our code, while still being able to test it.

Remember that our project name is `UnitTests`. By default, our project is defining a new Swift module with the same name as our project, so when we import `UnitTests`, we are importing our project's code module, not a unit testing framework… it's a bit confusing, I know. To make things a bit clearer, if our project name was `CoolProject`, then our Swift module would also be called that, and we'd use `@testable import CoolProject`.

In order for `@testable` to work, you need to ensure your main app target enables testability. To check, click on the Xcode project in the project navigator, make sure the `UnitTests` target is selected in the sidebar, then select the **Build Settings** tab, and search for **Enable Testability**. You should see something similar to *Figure 13.5*. Make sure that your app target has testability enabled on **Debug**, and *not* for **Release**. Your project may already be set properly:

Figure 13.5: Enabling testability in the build settings for our main app target

So with our base class, we've imported the necessary testing features with `import XCTest`, then we imported our application's code module with `@testable import UnitTests`. Finally, we set up our class to be testable by making sure it inherits from the `XCTestCase` class.

Time to write our first test. A unit test is written like any other function, but with two rules: the function name *must* start with `test`, and it *should* use an `XCTAssert` function if you actually want it to do anything. To try this out, let's write a test for our first example function in our `TestModel()` class:

```
func testExample1() {
    let model = TestModel()
    XCTAssertEqual(model.example1(), 1)
}
```

First, we create an instance of our model. Then we use an XCTAssert function, in this case XCTAssertEqual(), which takes two inputs. If the result is true, then the test continues. If a test method makes it to the end without hitting an XCTAssert function that fails, then the test is considered passed. So, in this case, our test will pass if our Example1() function returns 1. If everything worked out properly, your code should look like *Figure 13.6*. The diamonds next to the class and test methods indicate that Xcode has detected a test that will be run:

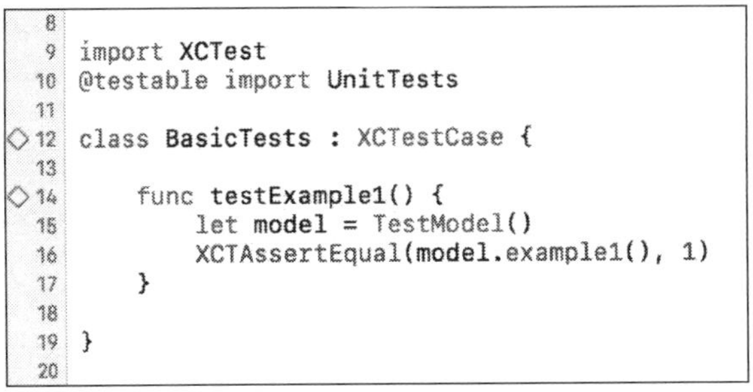

```
 8
 9  import XCTest
10  @testable import UnitTests
11
12  class BasicTests : XCTestCase {
13
14      func testExample1() {
15          let model = TestModel()
16          XCTAssertEqual(model.example1(), 1)
17      }
18
19  }
20
```

Figure 13.6: A simple test for a simple function, with the testing diamonds shown in the margin

Next, let's create a test for our other two example functions in our model:

```
class BasicTests : XCTestCase {

    var model: TestModel!

    override func setUp() {
        model = TestModel()
    }

}

    func testExample1() {
        XCTAssertEqual(model.example1(), 1)
    }

    func testExample2() {
        XCTAssertEqual(model.example2(), 2)
    }

    func testExample3() {
        XCTAssertEqual(model.example3(), 3)
    }

}
```

We now have three individual tests that will run, testing all components of our model. We check to make sure that `example1()` returns 1, that `example2()` returns 2, and `example3()` returns 3. Now, we could have also written a test like this:

```
func testExamples() {
    XCTAssertEqual(model.example1(), 1)
    XCTAssertEqual(model.example2(), 2)
    XCTAssertEqual(model.example3(), 3)
}
```

This would check all three examples, and fail if any one of the examples failed. Since our functions are so simple this might be okay, but this is a great time to remember the idea of units. If one of our example functions fails, will it be easy to find out exactly which function failed? In this case not really, so we'll keep them separate.

We also use the `setUp()` function to initialize our `TestModel`, since the `setUp()` function gets called before each test. This ensures we have a fresh version of our model for each test. In this case it doesn't matter, but it's a good habit to develop.

Running tests

Now that we have a completed testing class with unit tests for our model code, let's get to running the tests! There are several ways to run tests, both from the testing navigator, and from the test class code editor itself. You can also use *command + U* to run all of your tests at once. But first, let's try from the test navigator.

From the test navigator, you can select any target, class, or test method individually and click the play button that appears on the far right side of the navigator to run that test (or all the tests in that class, or all the tests in that target). Let's run the tests in our `BasicTests` class by clicking the play button, shown in *Figure 13.7*:

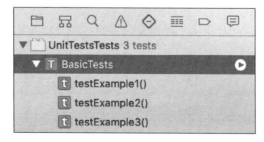

Figure 13.7: The BasicTests testing class highlighted in the test navigator

Running the test will launch the simulator (or launch on your device, if it's plugged into Xcode), and begin running the app, before finally executing the tests. Once they've completed, you should see:

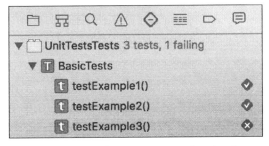

Figure 13.8: The test navigator after running tests, showing that one test failed

Oops! One of our tests failed. It looks like our `example3` test isn't working as expected. Let's first check to see that the test we wrote is correct. We're checking to see that `example3()` is returning a value of 3, so our test is in fact working properly, so there must be an issue with our `example3()` code. Let's jump into our `TestModel` class to see what the issue is:

```
func example3() -> Int {
    return 2
}
```

There's the issue! The `example3()` function is returning 2 instead of 3. We must have copy and pasted, or mistyped somewhere. Luckily we caught the error early. Let's fix that up:

```
func example3() -> Int {
    return 3
}
```

Now, let's head back to our testing class. If we go down to the `textExample3()` function and hover over the failed testing diamond, it will turn into a *run test* button (see *Figure 13.9*). Since we think we fixed the issue, lets click that button to rerun that test:

```
 8
 9  import XCTest
10  @testable import UnitTests
11
12  class BasicTests : XCTestCase {
13
14      var model: TestModel!
15
16      override func setUp() {
17          model = TestModel()
18      }
19
20      func testExample1() {
21          XCTAssertEqual(model.example1(), 1)
22      }
23
24      func testExample2() {
25          XCTAssertEqual(model.example2(), 2)
26      }
27
28      func testExample3() {
29          XCTAssertEqual(model.example3(), 3)
30      }
31
32  }
33
```

Figure 13.9: The red x's become run test buttons in the margin of the editor for our test class

In our current project, our tests are really light, so there's no reason to not just run them all again. But in bigger projects, tests may be a bit heavier, so running only one at a time can be quite the time saver. So, once you run the failed test again, you should find that everything worked!

```
 8
 9  import XCTest
10  @testable import UnitTests
11
12  class BasicTests : XCTestCase {
13
14      var model: TestModel!
15
16      override func setUp() {
17          model = TestModel()
18      }
19
20      func testExample1() {
21          XCTAssertEqual(model.example1(), 1)
22      }
23
24      func testExample2() {
25          XCTAssertEqual(model.example2(), 2)
26      }
27
28      func testExample3() {
29          XCTAssertEqual(model.example3(), 3)
30      }
31
32  }
33
```

Figure 13.10: Our test class with all tests passing!

Great! We've now run all of our tests, fixed the errors, and have a clean slate of passed tests. Writing new tests as we add functionality to the app, and running tests frequently can help to make sure any possible bugs are caught early and often.

Implementing tests for Snippets

Now that we've cut our teeth on unit testing in Xcode, let's apply our new skills back in our `Snippets` application. In this section, we'll learn how to set up unit tests in an existing project that didn't start with testing targets, and then write some tests for our application to ensure everything is working as expected.

Setting up the Snippets project

Setting up our project with unit tests is relatively simple. Since we're starting out without anything, we're going to need to create a new unit testing target, and then make sure all of our build settings are set properly:

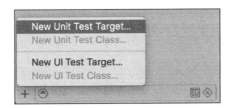

Figure 13.11: Creating a new unit test target from the test navigator

To begin, open up the test navigator, and then, from the plus button at the bottom (*Figure 13.11*), choose new **Unit Test Target...**. From there, we'll give the new target a name of `SnippetsTests`, and set the project to be `Snippets` and the target to be tested as `Snippets` (see *Figure 13.12*):

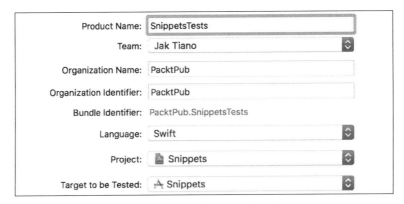

Figure 13.12: Setting up the new unit testing target

Next, we need to make sure that our project's module is testable. Like in the last section, head to the main app target's build settings, search for **Enable Testability**, and make sure it is turned on for **Debug**:

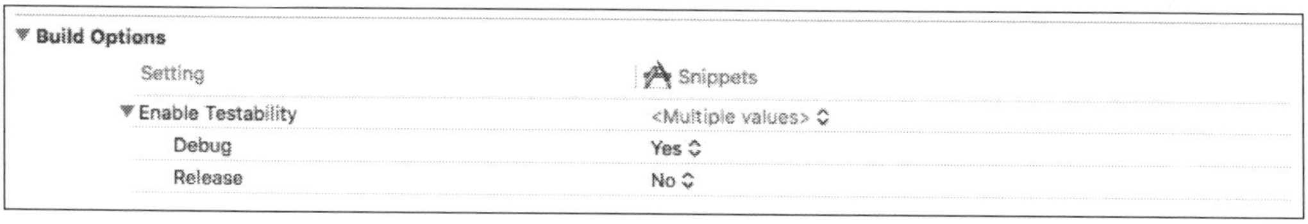

▼ **Build Options**		
Setting	🅰 Snippets	
▼ Enable Testability	<Multiple values> ◇	
Debug	Yes ◇	
Release	No ◇	

Figure 13.13: Making sure our Snippets project is testable

Preparing our testing class

Now that our project is set up with a testing target, let's make sure our testing class has everything it needs to run tests. Before we can do that, however, we need to know what kind of tests we are going to write.

One of the most important parts of our app is that it is saving data correctly. We are going to write a test that checks to make sure that there is no data loss from when our view controller saves a text snippet to when it loads that data back in later. To do this, we are going to need access to our view controller, and we're also going to need to make sure that our core data model is ready to interface with our tests.

To start, open the new SnippetsTests folder, and then select the `SnippetsTests.swift` file and let's get our imports set up, along with the `setUp()` function stub:

```
import XCTest
import CoreData
@testable import Snippets

class SnippetsTests: XCTestCase {

    var vc: ViewController!
    var moc: NSManagedObjectContext!

    override func setUp() {
        super.setUp()
    }
}
```

At the top, we're making sure we have `XCTest`, in addition to `CoreData`, which we'll be using quite often, and finally our `Snippets` module. Then, inside the class, we are creating references to our `ViewController` and our `ManagedObjectContext`.

Next, we have to actually set up the references in the `setUp()` function. We're also going to have to clear out our `CoreData` information before each test so that we can be sure everything is working correctly:

```
class SnippetsTests: XCTestCase {

    var vc: ViewController!
    var moc: NSManagedObjectContext!

    override func setUp() {
        super.setUp()

        let sb = UIStoryboard(name: "Main", bundle:
        Bundle.main)
        vc = sb.instantiateInitialViewController() as! ViewController

        let delegate = UIApplication.shared.delegate as!
        AppDelegate
        moc = delegate.managedObjectContext

        clearOutCoreData()
    }

    func clearOutCoreData() {
        // to do next
    }
}
```

Here, we're getting a reference to our storyboard, then instantiating our root view controller and setting it to our `vc` reference. After that, we get our `AppDelegate` and then pull out a reference to our managed object context from the core data stack, and save that into our `moc` variable for later. Finally, we call our `clearOutCoreData()` function, which we'll fill out now:

```
func clearOutCoreData() {
    var data: [NSManagedObject]!

    let fetchRequest = NSFetchRequest<NSFetchRequestResult>(entityNa
me: "Snippet")
    do {
        let fetchResults = try moc.fetch(fetchRequest)
        data = fetchResults as! [NSManagedObject]
    } catch {
        let e = error as Error
        print("Unresolved error \(e.localizedDescription)")
    }

    for d in data {
```

```
        moc.delete(d)
    }
}
```

For this function, we are essentially creating a fetch request that will grab all of our snippet data, store it in an array, and then loop through the data and delete each entry from our object context.

Now, before each test, our `setUp()` function will create a fresh instance of our view controller, grab a reference to the managed object context, and then clear out the core data database. Now let's put it to use!

Writing a data validation unit test

In our test, we're going to call the `saveTextSnippet()` function of our `ViewController` to write out a new text snippet, and then read that data back in and make sure it is correct.

We'll start by creating a new function called `testSaveTextSnippet()`. At the top of the function, we'll define the string we're passing in, and then call the function on our view controller;

```
func testSaveTextSnippet() {

    let testString = "test"
    vc.saveTextSnippet(text: testString)
}
```

That's the easy part! Now we need to load in the `NSManagedObject` that was created, and check the data that was saved. To start, we'll pull out all of the snippet data from our core data model. Since we just cleared it out, it should be empty except for the new data we just created:

```
func testSaveTextSnippet() {

    let testString = "test"
    vc.saveTextSnippet(text: testString)

    // get data from core data
    var data: [NSManagedObject]!
    let fetchRequest = NSFetchRequest<NSFetchRequestResult>(entityNa
me: "Snippet")
    do {
        let fetchResults = try moc.fetch(fetchRequest)
        data = fetchResults as! [NSManagedObject]
    } catch {
        let e = error as Error
```

```
        print("Unresolved error \(e.localizedDescription)")
        XCTFail()
    }

}
```

First, we define an array of NSManagedObjects, and create an NSFetchRequest that asks for all Snippet entities. We try to run the fetch request, and if it succeeds we store it in the data array. However, if it fails, we are calling a function called XCTFail(). As you can probably guess, this causes the test to fail immediately. If we can't read back the data we just saved, then something has definitely gone wrong so it makes sense to automatically fail the test.

After we have the information loaded into the data array, it's time to validate the data that is inside our Snippet:

```swift
func testSaveTextSnippet() {

    let testString = "test"
    vc.saveTextSnippet(text: testString)

    // get data from core data
    var data: [NSManagedObject]!
    let fetchRequest = NSFetchRequest<NSFetchRequestResult>(entityNa
me: "Snippet")
    do {
        let fetchResults = try moc.fetch(fetchRequest)
        data = fetchResults as! [NSManagedObject]
    } catch {
        let e = error as Error
        print("Unresolved error \(e.localizedDescription)")
        XCTFail()
    }

    // validate data
    let snippet = data[0]
    if let rawType = snippet.value(forKey: "type") as? String, let
string = snippet.value(forKey: "text") as? String {
        XCTAssertEqual(SnippetType(rawValue: rawType), SnippetType.
text)
        XCTAssertEqual(string, testString)
    } else {
        XCTFail()
    }
}
```

We first pull out the first element in the data array: this is our snippet. Then we try to access values inside the `NSManagedObject` using `value(forKey:)` and cast them to the expected type. If any of these operations fail it will fall through to the else statement, and we'll call the `XCTFail()` function again to fail the test.

However, if we're able to read all the data properly, then we run it through some `XCTAssertEqual()` functions. First, we check to see that the type is correct (we expect the type to be `.text`), and then we check to see if the text is correct by using the `testString` that we passed in initially.

If you run the test, you should (hopefully) see that everything is working as expected!

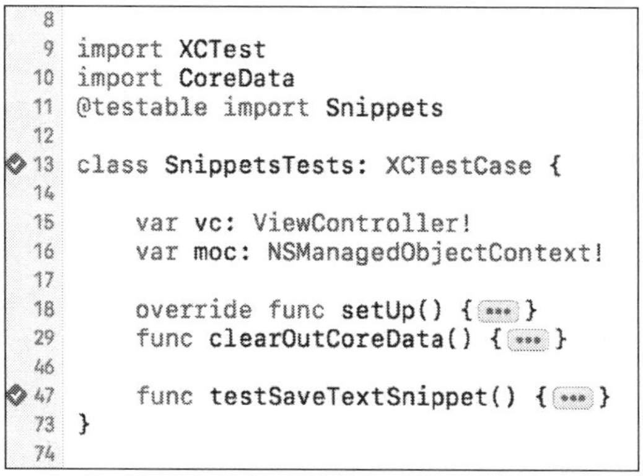

```
 8
 9  import XCTest
10  import CoreData
11  @testable import Snippets
12
13  class SnippetsTests: XCTestCase {
14
15      var vc: ViewController!
16      var moc: NSManagedObjectContext!
17
18      override func setUp() { ••• }
29      func clearOutCoreData() { ••• }
46
47      func testSaveTextSnippet() { ••• }
73  }
74
```

Figure 13.14: Our unit test is passing!

Checking code coverage

Earlier in the chapter when we were discussing the concepts behind unit testing, we touched on the idea of how much of your code you should test. This is called *code coverage*. In Xcode 7, we can actually gather data to see exactly what the code coverage of our tests are. This can be very useful to you when writing tests, for obvious reasons. As I mentioned the last time we talked about this, your target for code coverage is up to you.

To enable your project to collect code coverage data, we need to update the settings for our testing scheme. To open the scheme editor, use the keyboard shortcut *command* + < (which is actually *command* + *shift* + ,), or navigate from the menu bar to **Product** | **Scheme** | **Edit Scheme**:

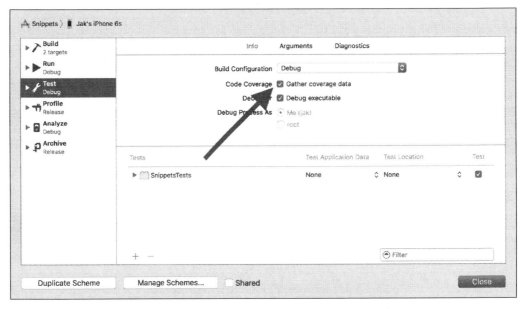

Figure 13.15: Enabling coverage data collection in our test scheme

Once we open the scheme editor, select the **Test** scheme from the sidebar, and then underneath the **Build Configuration** dropdown, check the box for **Gather coverage data** (*Figure 13.15*). This makes it so that when we run our tests, Xcode looks to see what code is being run during tests, and reports that information back to us.

The best way to understand this is to see it in action. With code coverage data now being gathered, lets run our tests again (*command* + *U*). Once the tests have been completed, open the `Results Navigator` (*command* + *8*), and then select the most recent test operation (*Figure 13.16*):

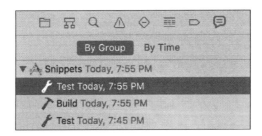

Figure 13.16: Selecting the results from the most recent test

Once the test is selected, you should see the editor window fill with information about the tests that were run. However, there is also a tab along the top of the editor window, and in the middle there should be a **Coverage** tab. Click on it, and you should see detailed information about what parts of your code are covered by your last execution of tests (*Figure 13.17*):

Figure 13.17: Selecting the results from the most recent test

Testing UI in Xcode 8

Writing unit tests helps to make sure your application's model and controller code are working properly, but as apps get more and more complex views, it's becoming increasingly important to test the interface of our apps as well. In Xcode 7, Apple introduced a new UI testing feature that allows us to do just that.

How does UI testing work?

When building an app, we have a certain way that our logic is expected to function. Earlier, we expected that by passing an input string to our save function we would get a data representation of a new snippet on disk, so we wrote a test to ensure this was happening. This same idea can be applied to the actual user interface, instead of the logic behind it.

For example, in our app, we want to make sure that when the New button is tapped, the user is presented with an action sheet for them to choose an option from. We could write a unit test to check the button code, but that won't check to make sure that the button event is firing properly in the first place, and that we're getting the proper UI response. UI testing aims to fix these shortcomings by essentially letting us code a fake user who taps on the screen, and letting us check to see what happens.

Adding the UI testing target

Before we can start writing UI tests, we need to create a separate UI test target, which must be separate from the unit test target we made earlier. This can be accomplished from the same plus button at the bottom of the test navigator (*Figure 13.18*):

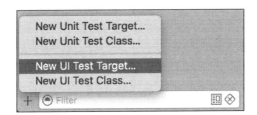

Figure 13.18: Creating a new UI test target from the test navigator

Make sure the new target settings are correct; check with *Figure 13.19* before creating it:

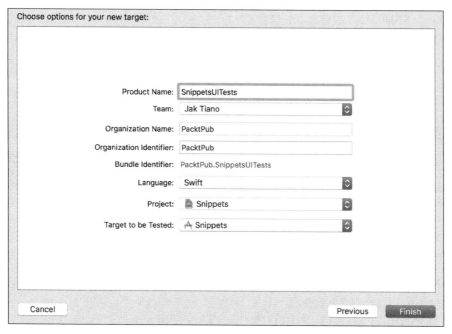

Figure 13.19: The correct settings for the new UI test target

We now have our UI test target added to the project, and we've been given a testing class to write our tests in, named `SnippetsUITests.swift`. It starts off a bit bloated, so let's cut that down to something a bit more manageable before moving on:

```swift
import XCTest

class SnippetsUITests: XCTestCase {

    override func setUp() {
        super.setUp()
        continueAfterFailure = false
        XCUIApplication().launch()
    }

}
```

Using the UI recorder

Now that we've got a testing class set up, we begin the daunting task of programming our *fake user* to play with our app, or do we? As a part of Xcode's robust testing suite, Apple has included a feature called the UI recorder that is built right into our UI testing class.

As the name implies, it is quite literally a record button that allows us to *show* Xcode what we want it to do by doing it ourselves! It then watches, and translates our actions into code that allows our test to repeat our actions later. To get a better idea of how this all works, it's best to see it in action: let's make a test!

Earlier, we said that we would want to check to make sure that when we tap the new button, our action sheet is presented. That's what we'll test now. Create a new function for this test:

```
func testSnippetSelectionOnNewPress() {

}
```

Now comes the fun part; click inside the brackets of the function, and then look along the bottom bar of the editor window. You should see a little record button (the red circle) next to the blue breakpoint icon. If you click the record button, your app will be launched, and then Xcode will start tracking your input and translating it to code on the fly!

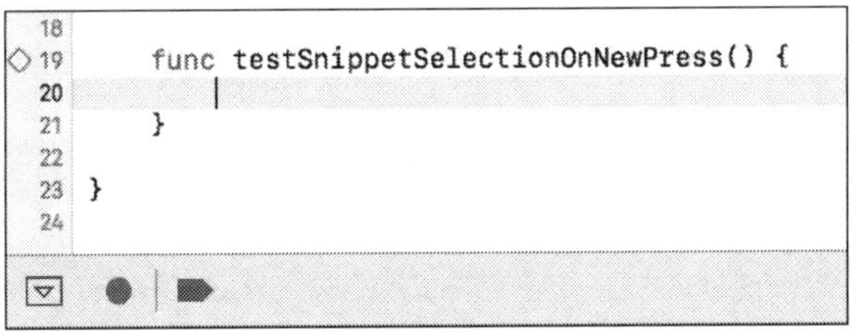

Figure 13.20: The UI recorder button on the bottom bar

Try clicking around on your application screen to see what happens in Xcode. Watch as it creates code based on what you're doing. Once you've had your fill, click the record button again to stop recording. Now delete all of the junk code you created, run the recorder again, and this time, just click New and stop the recording. You should be left with something like this:

```
func testSnippetSelectionOnNewPress() {
    XCUIApplication().toolbars.buttons["New"].tap()

}
```

This is the code that Xcode generated for us when we clicked that button. As you can see, it's very readable, and after a bit of practice you could easily write these tests by hand! But for now, the UI recorder is an invaluable tool to get our tests up and running as quickly as possible.

So, now that we have tapped our button, we need to check to make sure that the action sheet was presented to the user. However, this presents an issue: UI changes don't happen instantaneously. We need a way to wait a little bit to see what happens. To do this, we'll create an `expectation` then wait for a set amount of time to see if expectations are met:

```
func testSnippetSelectionOnNewPress() {

    // reference to application
    let app = XCUIApplication()

    // create and set expectation
    let selectionAlert = app.staticTexts["Select a snippet type"]
    let exists = NSPredicate(format: "exists == true")
    expectation(for: exists, evaluatedWith: selectionAlert, handler:
nil)

    // tap button and wait for expectation
    app.toolbars.buttons["New"].tap()
    waitForExpectations(timeout: 1, handler: nil)
}
```

First, we are getting a reference to the application. Next, we create an `XCUIElementQuery` for something with the text `Select a snippet type` (which is the title of our action sheet), and then we create an `NSPredicate` for checking if the exists property is `true`. Then, we set an expectation for the `selectionAlert` to have `exists == true`. To finish our test, we tap the new button, and then give the test one second to see if the expectation becomes `true`:

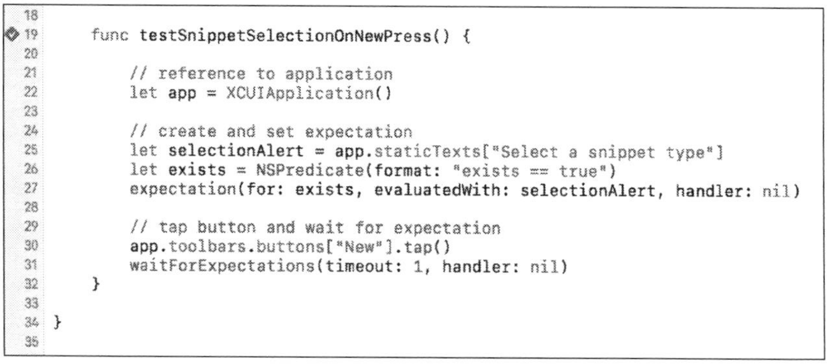

```
18
19   func testSnippetSelectionOnNewPress() {
20
21       // reference to application
22       let app = XCUIApplication()
23
24       // create and set expectation
25       let selectionAlert = app.staticTexts["Select a snippet type"]
26       let exists = NSPredicate(format: "exists == true")
27       expectation(for: exists, evaluatedWith: selectionAlert, handler: nil)
28
29       // tap button and wait for expectation
30       app.toolbars.buttons["New"].tap()
31       waitForExpectations(timeout: 1, handler: nil)
32   }
33
34 }
35
```

Figure 13.21: Our final passing UI test

If you run UI tests, you'll see that the app is launched in the simulator, and the actions you performed are mimicked (buttons will be virtually tapped, etc.). There's still a lot for you to go out and learn about UI testing, but this short primer should give you enough of a footing to understand the basics and get your feet wet.

Summary

In this chapter, we learnt about the subtle art of testing your code with more code. It's a very useful skill, and can save plenty of headaches throughout the development process. We looked at what unit tests are and why they're important, and then spent some time learning how to use them in Xcode. Once we were comfortable, we added unit tests to our Snippets project, and wrote a somewhat more complicated test that worked with Core Data. From there, we talked about code coverage and learnt how to use Xcode to visualize how thorough our tests are on our codebase. Finally, we dipped our toes into the water of UI testing in Xcode 7, and tested a button in our Snippets app.

In the next chapter, we continue the theme of cleaning up our project, and making the code safer and less prone to failure. We'll be covering the many debugging tools available in Xcode 8 that help you make sure that your apps are running smoothly and error free. Combined with the testing features we covered in this chapter, understanding the debugging tools will make sure your code is rock solid.

14
Debugging an iOS Application

In the previous chapter, we learned about how to use unit tests to prevent problems in your code from occurring in the first place. While preventative measures are great, what happens when you can't prevent an issue? Your unit test fails, your new feature isn't working as intended, the app is crashing for an unknown reason, any way you slice it, you've got a bug!

With unit tests and debugging under your belt, by the end of this chapter you'll be well on your way to building clean, efficient, bug-free applications that prevents both user and developer frustration.

In this chapter, we're going to cover:

- Debugging with `print()`, breakpoints, and the call stack
- Using advanced debug tools like the Address Sanitizer
- Fixing visual issues with the View Debugger

Basic debugging practices

When programming an app, you will no doubt encounter many little snags along the way. After some time, you might not even notice some of the smaller issues you run into because of how quickly you can resolve them. In this section, we'll look at some of the most basic ways to look at what is going on inside your app so that you can navigate around the issues you may encounter.

print()

Sometimes, the simplest answer is the best answer. Using a print statement to write a string out to the console can be a quick and effective way to get a status report from inside your app. The print() function is defined in the Swift standard library of functions, and lets you write strings to the console with some minor formatting options:

```
print("hello world!")
```

The print function, while usually used to print a single string, can also accept several string parameters to print, along with a separator and a terminator string:

```
print("apple","orange","banana", separator:"##")
output ->"apple##orange##banana?

print("apple","orange","banana", terminator:"!")
output ->"apple orange banana!"

print("apple","orange","banana", separator:"##", terminator:"!")
output ->"apple##orange##banana!"
```

The print() function can be a useful way to send out messages to the console when execution reaches a certain point of your code, or to check to see how many times something is looping through a certain part of code.

However, even though it is a basic tool, mastering the art of when to use a print statement can take a bit of time. For most beginners, what they really mean to do is use breakpoints.

Breakpoints and the debug area

Breakpoints are the bread and butter of any good debugging tool kit. At its core, a breakpoint system allows you to place a marker on a line of code, then run the code until it hits that line before it pauses. Once the code is paused, you're able to step through the code line by line to see how the code executes, and look at how the variables change. This is all done in the *debug area*:

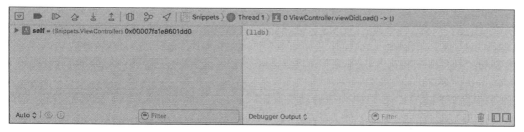

Figure 14.1: The debug navigator

The debug area is composed of three main parts (*Figure 14.1*), the variables view on the left (in **blue**), the console view on the right (in **green**), and the debug toolbar on top (in **red**).

Variables view

In the variables view, we can see the values inside all of the variables that are in the scope of our break point. So, if we place a break point inside a function and the debugger pauses there, we can see all of the variables inside that function here. In *Figure 14.2*, you can see the value of a variable x is 0, which was just an Int. that I threw into a test function.

You can also see the self variable, which represents the current class instance (in this case, a ViewController). Since this is a complex object and not a basic data type, there is a dropdown arrow next to it that allows us to inspect its properties:

Figure 14.2: The variables view

Along the bottom of the variables view there are a few more options. From the left, we first have a dropdown to change the mode; by default it is set to **Auto**, but it can also be changed to only show local (which is similar to **Auto**, but more strict), and a third option that gives you much more detailed information that we really won't be needing to use.

Next to the dropdown is an eye icon that lets you quick look a variable that is selected in the variable list. This can be useful for certain data types like images; using quick look on a UIImage will show you that image. The little information icon next to the eye prints out a description of the selected variable to the console.

Finally, on the far right of the variable view is a filter that allows you to search through the variables in the view. In this screenshot it's not particularly useful, but when code gets more complicated and we have more variables it can be quite useful.

Console

Next to the variables view is the console. We've been using the console throughout the book, but it's worth giving it a bit of extra attention now. Most of the console area is dedicated to outputting text from inside your application, usually from print() statements, or from inside the iOS SDK. When your app crashes, you'll also see some output in the console:

Figure 14.3: The debug console

In *Figure 14.3*, you can see a line that says Printing description of x: 0. This is actually the result of me pressing the information button while the x variable was selected in the variables view that we just looked at. The 1 on the last line was the result of me placing a print(1) statement in my program.

Along the bottom of the console, you can see a dropdown that switches between `debugger` mode, and `target` mode. Debugger mode only shows output from the debugger, which would be output like the `Printing description...` text that was written by interacting with the debugger. Target mode only shows output that came from our application target; in other words, this is the output straight from your code. `All Output` will show you both types of console output.

On the bottom right there is a trash can that clears the console, in addition to two little icons that are not actually a part of the console, but which toggle the variables view and console from being shown.

Debug toolbar

The debug toolbar is your home base for debugging. It is from the debug toolbar that you can enable and disable breakpoints, and step through code. The debug toolbar will only show up while your application is running. Looking at *Figure 14.4*, you can see a row of icons going from left to right; let's step through each one:

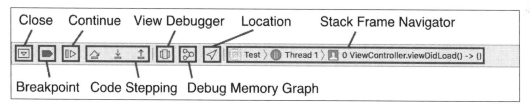

Figure 14.4: The debug toolbar

First, we have a downward arrow: this just closes (and opens) the debug area below the toolbar. You can also use *command* +*shift*+ *Y* to accomplish the same thing.

Next, we have the breakpoint icon. This enables and disables breakpoints. If it is filled in, and blue, that means breakpoints are enabled, and your code will stop and wait at breakpoints that you have specified. Click it and it will become an outline, meaning that the debugger ignores the breakpoints in your code. Just after the breakpoint icon is the continue button. Once your program is stopped at a breakpoint, you can click this button to continue the execution.

The next three buttons let you navigate through your code when paused at a breakpoint. When your app is running but not paused at a breakpoint, the buttons will be greyed out and disabled. The first angled arrow is the step over button, which lets you go to the next line of code by stepping *over* any function calls. Similarly, the down arrow after that is the step in button, which lets you go into a function on the current line if one exists. The third button (up arrow) is a step out button, which allows you to go up one level of code. So, if you step into a function and press the step out button, you'll pop back out to the scope of the original function.

After the codestepping buttons is the View Debugger button, which we'll be covering in detail, later on in the chapter. Next is the debug memory graph button, which is a very useful advanced debugging tool, but a little too advanced for us to talk about right now. The location icon next to the memory graph button allows you to simulate a location for an app running in the simulator. Finally, the last piece of the toolbar lets you choose the **stack** frame navigator for a paused application. We'll be talking about the call stack in the next section.

Now that we've looked at every component of the debug toolbar, lets put it to use by stepping through the process of using a breakpoint. Open up the Snippets project, and navigate to the ViewController.swift file. We're going to place a breakpoint inside the viewDidLoad() function, since that runs right at the beginning of execution. To place the breakpoint, just click in the left margin of the editor window with the line numbers. (If you're using your own project file and not the one from the resources folder, you might be on different line numbers):

```
23      // MARK: - UIKit
24      override func viewDidLoad() {
25          super.viewDidLoad()
26          imagePicker.delegate = self
27          locationManager.delegate = self
28          locationManager.desiredAccuracy = kCLLocationAccuracyBest
29          locationManager.distanceFilter = 50.0
30
31          tableView.estimatedRowHeight = 100
32          tableView.rowHeight = UITableViewAutomaticDimension
33
34          askForLocationPermissions()
35      }
```

Figure 14.5: The viewDidLoad() function with a breakpoint placed on line 31

Once you place the breakpoint, build and run the project. The code should stop at the breakpoint, and the debug toolbar should now allow you to use the code stepping buttons:

```
23      // MARK: - UIKit
24      override func viewDidLoad() {
25          super.viewDidLoad()
26          imagePicker.delegate = self
27          locationManager.delegate = self
28          locationManager.desiredAccuracy = kCLLocationAccuracyBest
29          locationManager.distanceFilter = 50.0
30
31          tableView.estimatedRowHeight = 100         Thread 1: breakpoint 1.1
32          tableView.rowHeight = UITableViewAutomaticDimension
33
34          askForLocationPermissions()
35      }
```

Figure 14.6: The program execution is paused on line 31

If you press the `step over` button a few times (the angled one), you should be able to step through each line of code, one at a time. Once you get to line **34** (in my project, maybe different on yours) which has the `askForLocationPermissions()` function call, click the `step in` button. You should see that the code jumps into that function, and your execution is now at the beginning of the `askForLocationPermissions()` function:

```
140     func askForLocationPermissions () {
141         if CLLocationManager.authorizationStatus() == .notDetermined {
142             locationManager.requestWhenInUseAuthorization()   Thread 1: step in
143         }
144     }
145 }
```

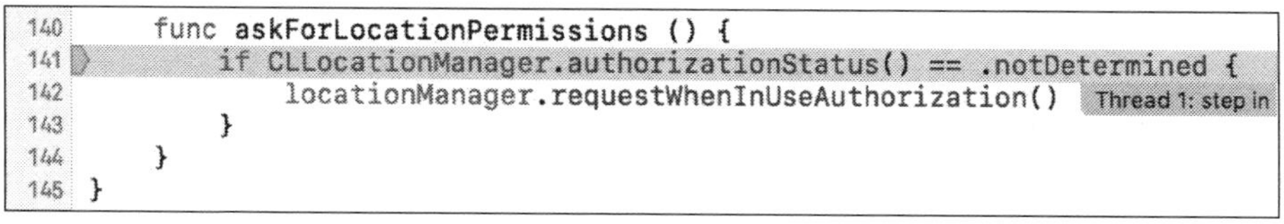

Figure 14.7: The execution has stepped into the askForLocationPermissions() function

Now, if you click the step out button, you'll see that the execution will eject you out of the `askForLocationPermissions()` function, and back out to the `viewDidLoad()` function. Finally, click the continue button next to the breakpoint icon to continue running the program as normal.

Sometimes you get unexpected behavior when your app is running, and you suspect that values are not being assigned correctly. In this case, it would be very useful to know how your variable is changing. Before we move on from breakpoints, let's see how we can use breakpoints to inspect how a variable can change at runtime. Let's create a temporary function to test this functionality with, and call it inside the `viewDidLoad()` function:

```
override func viewDidLoad() {
    super.viewDidLoad()
    imagePicker.delegate = self
    locationManager.delegate = self
    locationManager.desiredAccuracy = kCLLocationAccuracyBest
    locationManager.distanceFilter = 50.0

    tableView.estimatedRowHeight = 100
    tableView.rowHeight = UITableViewAutomaticDimension

    askForLocationPermissions()
    variableViewTest()
}
func variableViewTest() {
    var x = 0
    x = 1
    x = 2
}
```

Next, let's place a breakpoint on the first line of the `variableViewTest()` function, and run the project. You should see the program execution break on that first line. However, take note of the variables view shown as follows:

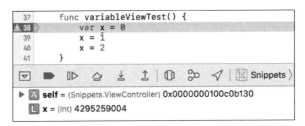

Figure 14.8: The first line of our variableViewTest(), with x still unassigned

On this first line, our variable view is showing x having a value of `4295259004`, which means that it hasn't been initialized yet. It's important to know that if the debugger is paused on a line, it means that that line hasn't been executed yet. Let's click the `step over` button to see another example:

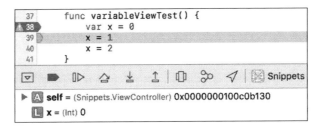

Figure 14.9: The second line of our variableViewTest(), with x set to the value of the last line

Now, with the program on the second line (x = 1), we can see in the variables view that x is set to 0 right now. Again, that's because we executed the last line, but have not yet executed the current line. Now let's step over two more lines until we're at the end:

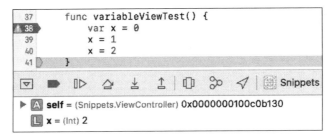

Figure 14.10: The end of the variableViewTest() function, where x has its final value

In *Figure 14.10*, you can now see that at the end of the function, all of the lines have been executed and that x is equal to 2.

When debugging your own applications, you can use this technique to place breakpoints and inspect a variable (or the property of an object) by stepping through code and seeing how things change.

The call stack

One of the last core pieces of a good debugging suite is the **call stack**. The call stack lets you see what functions have been called (in order) to get to the point in the program's execution that you are in now:

Figure 14.11: Call stack (on the left) while we are stepping through the variableViewTest() function

Found in the **Debug Navigator** (*command + 6*), the call stack shows you the current execution point of your code on every thread of your application. Since we aren't dealing with multithreading concepts in this book we'll just stick to **Thread 1**, which is the main thread and where your application code is being executed.

With the first line of the `variableViewTest()` function still set up with a breakpoint, let's run the program again, but this time look at what is going on with the call stack:

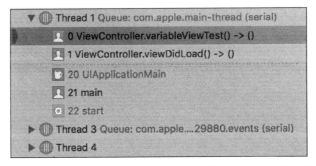

Figure 14.12: The call stack while the program execution is paused at a breakpoint inside variableViewTest()

At the top of the call stack, we see that we are inside a dropdown labeled **Thread 1**. As I said, this is our main thread, and this is where all of our application and UI code is run (unless we choose to do otherwise). From there, we have a list of *stack frames*, each numbered by how far away they are from the current stack frame.

Notice how there is a dotted line after stack frame 1, and then it jumps to 19. By default, Xcode collapses a bunch of frames that aren't important, because they don't have debug information and are mostly inside other libraries like `UIKit`. Click the little blue sandwich button at the bottom of the debug navigator to see the full stack:

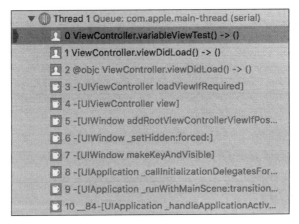

Figure 14.13: The full call stack, showing the full list of stack frames

This information is good to see to understand how your app is running, starting by calling the `main` function, and then drilling down through function calls until you hit your current function, but usually we can leave this turned off.

But wait, what is a stack frame in the first place? Essentially, every time you call a function, you dig down into the *stack* and create a new frame of reference for program execution. Imagine you had a piece of paper with text on it. Calling a function is like cutting that piece of paper between two lines of text, pulling them apart, and putting another full piece of paper between the two pieces. Then you do that again on the new piece of paper, etc. Each time we do this we create a new stack frame, creating a big nested list describing how our program got to the current line of execution.

Now, this is great for learning, but it can also be very useful when debugging a program crash. Sometimes a function is being called from several places in your code, but only one or some of those function calls are creating a crash. Instead of trying to mentally figure out all of the reasons a line of code might crash in a function, we can look at the call stack to see exactly how we got to this line of code and give us a better idea of what's going on.

To test this out, let's get rid of the breakpoint (right click on the breakpoint and select delete), and manually add a program ending error to our `variableViewTest()` function:

```
func variableViewTest() {
    var x = 0
    x = 1
    fatalError()
    x = 2
}
```

Using the `fatalError()` function can be very useful to make sure your program doesn't get to *very bad places* in your code while testing, but here we're just using it to induce a program failure. When your program crashes, you'll see that the call stack shows up telling you exactly where the program crashed.

It also gives you information about the crash in the console, and captures the state of variables in the variables view:

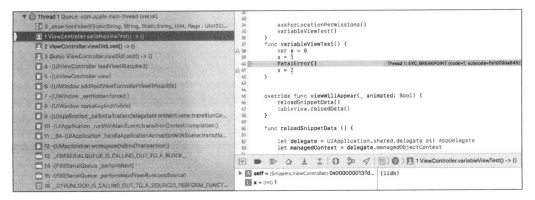

Figure 14.14: The state of debug information after a program crash

With this crash information, we can look at the call stack to see how we got to this point of the program. If we click on higher stack frames, we can actually jump to those frames and see the state of the local variables there as well.

Advanced debugging tools

With these basic practices under your belt, you're in a good position to deal with most of the issues that will come your way on a normal day. But sometimes, you have to deal with bugs that are anything but normal. In this section, we'll cover two advanced features in Xcode 8 that allow you to find some hidden bugs.

Don't think of these as the only advanced techniques you need to know, but as the beginning of a long education in how to deal with unruly code.

Address Sanitizer

The **Address Sanitizer** was one of the best new debugging features added to Xcode 7. If you're new to programming, you might not have had enough coding experiences to truly feel the pain that the Address Sanitizer solves.

With Swift, the language is designed to be safer with memory management, and in most cases you don't have to think about memory allocations at all. However, in C and Obj-C code, memory (mis)management can cause all kinds of trouble.

For example, in C, it is perfectly valid to allocate a new array with a size of four elements, and then try to access the fifth element. Not only is it valid, but that code will actually *run*. When used, it will *overflow* the size of the array and grab whatever data might be sitting just outside of that array in memory. It can also change those bits, meaning that if a value isn't reading properly, there may be a memory issue *anywhere* in your program that is accessing something it shouldn't be.

As you can imagine, this is a nightmare. Luckily, though, the Address Sanitizer solves these kinds of problems. Even though you might be using only Swift right now, you may start using others' code (or writing your own code) written in C or Obj-C, so this may very well save you many headaches down the line.

To test the Address Sanitizer, let's quickly make a new test project. However, this time, set the language to *Objective-C*. Scary, I know! Once you open up the project, things might look a little different, but let's open up the file called ViewController.m and rewrite the viewDidLoad() method like so:

```
- (void)viewDidLoad {
    [super viewDidLoad];

    int* myArray = malloc( sizeof(int) * 2 );
    myArray[0] = 0;
    myArray[1] = 1;
    myArray[2] = 2;

    NSLog(@"%i", myArray[3]);
}
```

This may look a little strange if you've never used C or Obj-C before, but you should still be able to understand that we are creating an array of ints (with a size of 2 ints). We then set values for index 0, 1, and 2. That last index is invalid, since we only have two ints, and thus only index 0 and 1 are valid. After that, we use NSLog (which is similar to print() in Swift) to write out the value at index 3 of the array.

Here's the really scary part: build and run the project, and it works! Let's look at the console to see what's going on:

```
17  - (void)viewDidLoad {
18      [super viewDidLoad];
19
20      int* myArray = malloc( sizeof(int) * 2 );
21      myArray[0] = 0;
22      myArray[1] = 1;
23      myArray[2] = 2;
24
25      NSLog(@"%i", myArray[3]);
26  }
```

▽ ● ‖ △ ↓ ↑ ⬭ ✂ ⬳ ▦ Address Sanitizer

```
2016-10-24 14:04:52.762414 Address Sanitizer[6823:2030802] 0
```

Figure 14.15: Our app is printing out some memory garbage for the value at index 3 of our array

The app runs fine without any crashes, and our log statement even printed out a number to the console. In this case it's reading out 0, which is extra dangerous because that can seem like a perfectly valid value. You can see how this can cause unpredictable behavior!

Let's get the Address Sanitizer up and running to see how it handles these issues. To do that, you'll need to edit our debug scheme (*command + shift + ,*). Go to the diagnostics tab of the scheme editor (*Figure 14.16*) and check the **Address Sanitizer** box:

Figure 14.16: Enabling Address Sanitizer for our debug scheme

Now that the Address Sanitizer is running, build and run the project one more time, and:

```
17  - (void)viewDidLoad {
18      [super viewDidLoad];
19
20      int* myArray = malloc( sizeof(int) * 2 );
21      myArray[0] = 0;
22      myArray[1] = 1;
23      myArray[2] = 2;                                   Thread 1: Heap buffer overflow detected
24
25      NSLog(@"%i", myArray[3]);
26  }
```

▽	■	▷ △ ↓ ↑ ▯ ✂ ◁	▦ Address Sanitizer ⟩ ⬤ Thread 1 ⟩ ▮ 5 -[ViewController viewDidLoad]

```
2016-10-24 14:11:27.553654 Address Sanitizer[6826:2032059]   Heap left redzone:       fa
2016-10-24 14:11:27.553678 Address Sanitizer[6826:2032059]   Heap right redzone:      fb
2016-10-24 14:11:27.553718 Address Sanitizer[6826:2032059]   Freed heap region:       fd
2016-10-24 14:11:27.553752 Address Sanitizer[6826:2032059]   Stack left redzone:      f1
2016-10-24 14:11:27.553764 Address Sanitizer[6826:2032059]   Stack mid redzone:       f2
2016-10-24 14:11:27.553775 Address Sanitizer[6826:2032059]   Stack right redzone:     f3
2016-10-24 14:11:27.553786 Address Sanitizer[6826:2032059]   Stack partial redzone:   f4
2016-10-24 14:11:27.553796 Address Sanitizer[6826:2032059]   Stack after return:      f5
2016-10-24 14:11:27.553807 Address Sanitizer[6826:2032059]   Stack use after scope:   f8
2016-10-24 14:11:27.553848 Address Sanitizer[6826:2032059]   Global redzone:          f9
2016-10-24 14:11:27.553872 Address Sanitizer[6826:2032059]   Global init order:       f6
2016-10-24 14:11:27.553884 Address Sanitizer[6826:2032059]   Poisoned by user:        f7
2016-10-24 14:11:27.553895 Address Sanitizer[6826:2032059]   Container overflow:      fc
2016-10-24 14:11:27.553906 Address Sanitizer[6826:2032059]   Array cookie:            ac
2016-10-24 14:11:27.554084 Address Sanitizer[6826:2032059]   Intra object redzone:    bb
2016-10-24 14:11:27.554096 Address Sanitizer[6826:2032059]   ASan internal:           fe
2016-10-24 14:11:27.554107 Address Sanitizer[6826:2032059]   Left alloca redzone:     ca
2016-10-24 14:11:27.554131 Address Sanitizer[6826:2032059]   Right alloca redzone:    cb
2016-10-24 14:11:27.554142 Address Sanitizer[6826:2032059]
==6826==ABORTING
```

Figure 14.17: The Address Sanitizer catches our memory bugs

That's more like it! When our program is running, the Address Sanitizer is running on top of the application to check how the memory is being managed, and is able to spot issues like this one. As you can see on the side, not only does it tell you where it found an issue, but it also says what the issue is. In this case, it's letting us know that there was a heap buffer overflow, which means we went outside of the boundaries of the array we defined.

When catching an error like this, the Address Sanitizer also captures a full snapshot of our program, so we can inspect variables in the variables view, and look through the call stack too.

If we delete the line of code causing the issue, you'll see that it catches our invalid access in the NSLog function too.

As an advanced feature, the Address Sanitizer offers some more functionality for more advanced users. For example, from the call stack, we can look at the blocks of memory directly (*Figure 14.18*) when the Address Sanitizer finds an error, but this is a bit beyond the scope of this book:

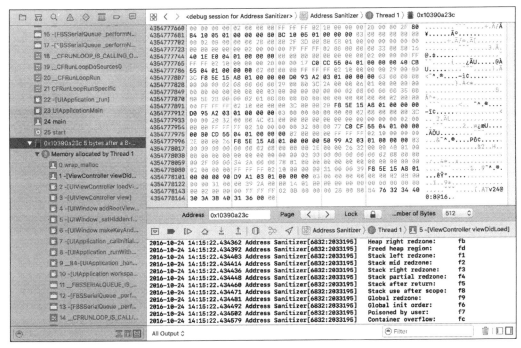

Figure 14.18: Viewing the heap memory allocation from the debug navigator with the Address Sanitizer

Performance gauges

While we'll be covering performance profiling in more detail in the next chapter on optimization, the simple performance gauges found in the debug sidebar can also be used to keep an eye on app vitals for debug reasons (hence their location in the debug sidebar):

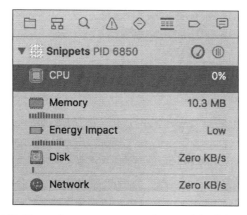

Figure 14.19: The performance gauges at the top of the debug navigator

These performance gauges include the CPU, memory, disk, and network gauges, in addition to the energy gauge that only appears when testing on a physical device.

CPU and memory gauge

The CPU and memory gauges let you see the hardware resources your app is using. High CPU or memory usage is not necessarily a bad thing if your app is doing intensive work, but if you're seeing high readings or spikes in these gauges when you don't think there should be any, it may be indicative of a bug somewhere in your code:

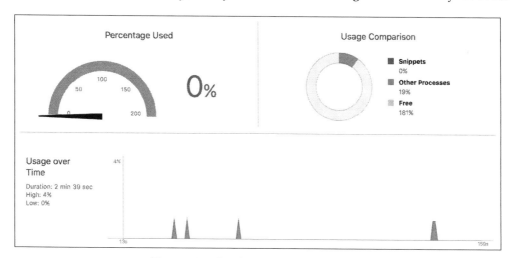

Figure 14.20: The editor view of the CPU gauge

This is a simple view of what our **Snippets** app looks like at rest. We're not doing anything, so this is justifiably using zero percent of the CPU. However, what happens if I create a function that runs a `for` loop that increments an integer to 1,000,000 every frame?

Figure 14.21: The CPU gauge with an intense loop running every frame

That's a bit more intense! Not really a *good* use of that processing power, but it's definitely more laborious.

The memory gauge is pretty similar to the CPU gauge, but obviously measures your memory usage instead of CPU:

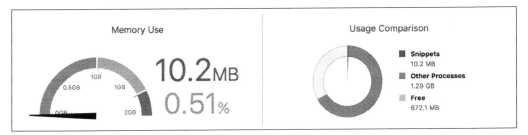

Figure 14.22: The memory gauge while running Snippets in the simulator

Remember to check in on these gauges occasionally to see if there are any spikes so that you can catch resource issues early.

Disk and network gauge

While the CPU and memory gauges are helpful to gauge the amount of resources your app is using, the disk and network gauges are helpful to check in on *data activity*, which is a term I just made up to describe data flowing in and out of your app:

Figure 14.23: The disk read/write gauge

The disk gauge shows you the rate of the data being written to your local storage, and the data being read from local storage. Here you can see that we had 32.6 MB read from the disk, which was mostly in the boot up process of the application, and then reading our CoreData information. There's also 1MB of write activity, which happened when I created and saved a few snippet while running the application.

Underneath these gauges, we can see a histogram of when the data was read and written:

Figure 14.24: The network read/write gauge

The network gauge shows the same information, except for data sent and received over a network connection. Since our app doesn't use a network connection at all, we're seeing zeroes across the board.

These two gauges are a good place to check to see if your app is needlessly reading, writing, sending, or receiving data. These operations are usually somewhat costly, so it's a good idea to make sure they are under control.

Energy gauge

Unlike the other four gauges, the energy impact gauge is only usable when you are testing on an actual device. When running your app on a device, Xcode automatically tracks the energy impact of the different components of an app, and then gives you an overall energy impact rating:

Figure 14.25: The energy impact gauge while on the home screen of Snippets

When developing an app, you should make sure that there is no **Energy Impact** while the user isn't actively interacting with it. If they are actively interacting, the **Energy Impact** should still be low, unless the user knowingly started an intensive process.

These guidelines can help you find unexpected bugs in your code. If your app is sitting idle and you see any energy impact, it can be a warning that some part of your codebase isn't working as intended.

Visual debugging

As app development has become more and more visual with the use of storyboards, we, as developers, have an increasing number of places that things can go wrong outside of our actual code. In the last chapter we looked at how UI tests allow us to test user interaction scenarios, but we can also *debug* our interfaces when things go wrong. To do that, we're going to use Xcode's **View Debugger**.

When we were looking at the debug toolbar earlier in the chapter, we looked at the `View Debugger` button, but didn't use it. (It's the one that looks like three rectangles.) Let's build and run our project, and then click it to launch the View Debugger:

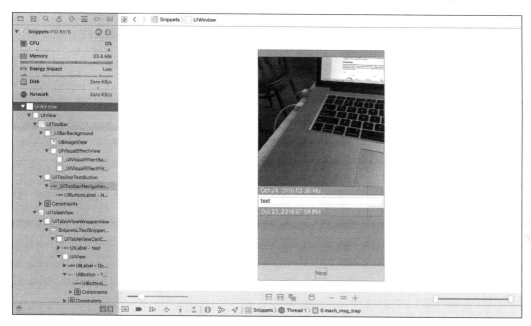

Figure 14.26: The View Debugger paused on a frame of our Snippets app

So what just happened? Xcode paused our app, and then loaded the entire view hierarchy into the editor. Along the left side of the screen (in the debug navigator) we can see all of the UI elements in their hierarchy, much like the document outline in a storyboard. However, these are all the real objects that are created at runtime and are captured straight from the device. In addition to the hierarchy, we have a visualizer in the main editor window on the right.

Along the bottom of the editor we have some buttons that allow us to get a better idea of what is going on in our views. The first button will let you see clipped content, and the third button (two intersecting boxes with lines inside) is actually a dropdown that lets you switch to a wireframe mode:

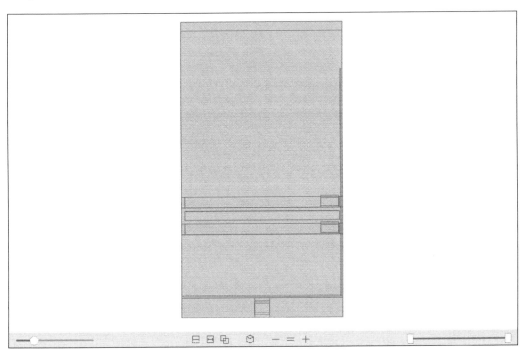

Figure 14.27: The View Debugger in wireframe mode

The wireframe mode can be helpful to quickly see if your bounding boxes have gotten mixed up from Auto Layout at runtime, while also giving you a better idea of how your UI is actually structured. In addition to this, one of the most useful features of the View Debugger is its 3D mode:

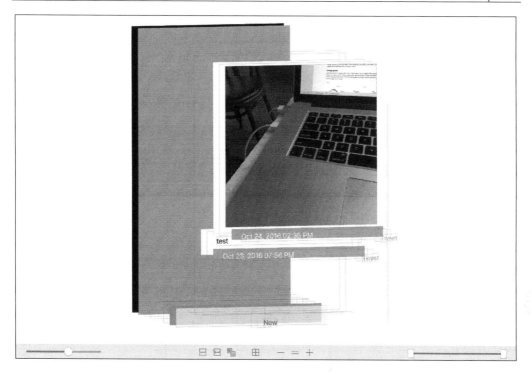

Figure 14.28: The View Debugger in 3D view mode

The 3D mode can be activated by clicking the cube button at the center of the bottom of the editor, or by simply dragging on the white space in the editor. When in 3D view mode, the layers of your application's hierarchy become much easier to understand. If you have layering issues with your app's UI, this can be a lifesaver (coupled with the clipping views toggle).

The slider on the bottom left of the window allows you to spread the layers closer and farther away from each other, while the range slider on the bottom right lets you clip which parts of the hierarchy you want to see.

You can also click on elements in the hierarchy to highlight them in the editor window, and vice versa. If you double-click on an element, you will hide all of the elements higher on the hierarchy, and only show that element and its children. This can be useful for isolating parts of the UI to investigate small pieces:

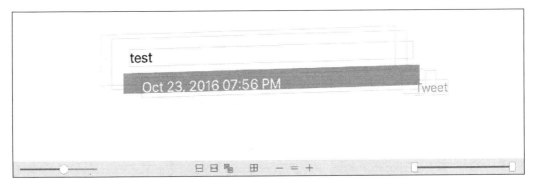

Figure 14.29 An isolated element in the View Debugger

With these tools, you can quickly investigate and spot issues in your view hierarchies by inspecting a real snapshot of your running app's UI.

Summary

In this chapter, we looked at many ways to debug applications that are misbehaving, in addition to learning some ways to check on the overall *health* of the app. First, we looked at some basic debugging practices such as printing, using breakpoints, and understanding the call stack. Then we looked at some advanced debugging tools like Address Sanitization, which helped us solve hard to find bugs in C and Objective-C code. We also learned about the performance gauges in the debug navigator, which help us stay alert to any major issues that don't necessarily cause a crash. Finally, we looked at the View Debugger, which helps us visualize any bugs that we may have in our view hierarchies.

In the next chapter, we'll be looking at some of the tools that Xcode provides for optimizing our app's performance and file size. After we look at optimization, we're going to put some final touches on our app and declare it a finished v1.0 app!

15
Optimizing Your App

So here we are with an app that is feature complete (for this first release), tested, and debugged. What's left to do? A lazier developer would call it done and just ship the app, but there's still some performance we can squeeze out of our app, and detail work to be done.

To do this, we're going to look at the features in Xcode that help us optimize our app's performance. There are also tools to help us optimize the amount of space the app takes up on the user's device. In this chapter, we're going to cover:

- The Instruments performance analysis toolset
- **Asset slicing** using asset catalogs in Xcode
- **Bitcode** compiling
- On-demand resources

Introduction to Instruments

When writing and debugging code, you can often get caught up in the frustrations of questions like *why isn't this working* and *how can I make this feature more obvious to the user?* However, once you've got everything functioning in the way you like, it's time to ask some questions that have less visible and less immediate impact. *How can we make our app run faster? Is this function as simple as it needs to be? Are we wasting any processor time?*

These are questions of *optimization*: once our product is functionally complete, we need to go back and make sure we did everything right. Because these questions don't have easily visible answers, we're going to have to use some tools to get the job done. In the case of optimization, that tool is **Instruments**.

Instruments is an analysis and profiling tool that gives a detailed look at what is going on under the hood of your app. (You may remember that we took a very quick look at it all way back in *Chapter 1, Starting Your iOS Journey*). Instruments is a collection of profiling tools, each of which are a different *instrument* of analysis, hence the name. There are tons of these little tools inside the Instruments app, but for now we're going to explore three of the most commonly used instruments for profiling the performance of your apps: the **Time Profiler** instrument, the **Allocations** instrument, and the **Leaks** instrument.

Time Profiler instrument

Arguably one of the most straightforward and intuitive tools, the Time Profiler does just what it says it will: it looks to see how long your app takes to *run*. However, it does so at a high granularity by checking to see how much time your app spends executing all of the functions inside your code. This allows you to quickly see which parts of your code are using up the most time, and helps you have a good idea of where the best place to start optimizing may be.

Let's get to it. Open up `Snippets` (as always, there's a fresh copy of the Xcode project in the resources folder of the last chapter if you need it), and then build our app for *profiling*. To do this, we'll use *command + I* (instead of *command + R*), or **Product | Profile** from the menu bar. This will build the app, and then launch **Instruments**. You should see a screen like this, asking you to choose a profiling template:

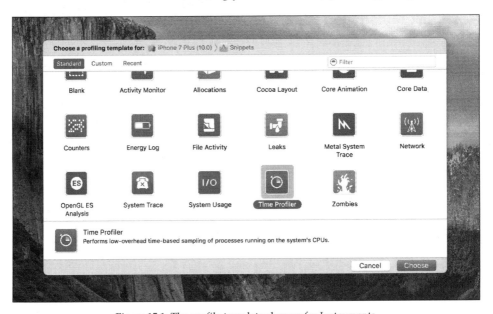

Figure 15.1: The profile template chooser for Instruments

Like I said, there are a lot of these! They're listed in alphabetical order, so scroll down a bit, select the **Time Profiler**, and click **Choose**. This will open a new Instruments document that is ready to use the Time Profiler.

Anatomy of an Instruments document

Before we learn about the Time Profiler specifically, lets take a little time to get a feel for what is going on inside this Instruments document:

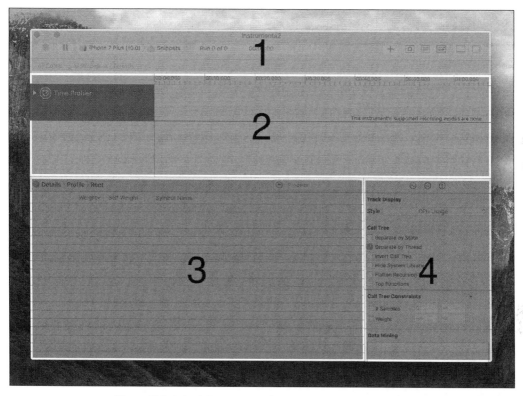

Figure 15.2: A fresh Instruments document, ready to profile time

At the top (box **1** in *Figure 15.2*), we have the toolbar. Starting from the left, we have the record and pause buttons. Clicking the record button will actually *begin* profiling your app by launching it and recording the activity. Likewise, pause will pause the profiling. Then we have some information on the device and process being monitored. On the right, the plus button allows you to add additional instruments to your document (though we will just stick to one at a time).

In box number **2**, we have the actual instrument data that is processed from the device. We just have the Time Profiler active, so that's all we see for now. Once it starts running, we'll have metrics running across the view horizontally.

In box **3**, we have the **Detail** window. This window will look different for each specific instrument that is used. In this case, it is going to show us something similar to the call stack that we used when debugging, but it will be telling us how much time was spent in each part of the stack.

Finally, in box **4**, we have the **Detail Inspector**. You can jump around between the tabs along the top using *command + 1*, *command + 2*, and *command + 3*. There are some useful tools in these inspectors, but the second tab (**Display Settings**, *command + 2*) is really the only one we care about right now, because it allows us to configure some settings for our detail window. Before we move on from the display settings, check off the boxes for **Invert Call Tree** (this shows us the bottom of the stack first, instead of the top), and **Hide System Libraries** (we don't care about time spent in system library code; we can't fix any of that!).

Using the Time Profiler

Now that we've got our bearings on the Instruments document window, let's get to profiling! Press the record button on the toolbar to launch the app, and begin profiling. Make sure that your device is plugged in and unlocked first.

It is always recommended to test directly on your device. Since the simulator is just that, a *simulator*, there's not really much of a point to testing performance with it. Always test directly on a device to get a better idea of how things are working.

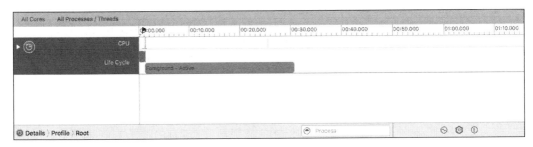

Figure 15.3: The Time Profiler after fiddling with Snippets for about 30 seconds

In the instrument data view along the very top, we can see the CPU usage over time, including spikes at different points in time. Below that, we can see the life cycle of the app, where it is mostly running active in the foreground. If we look at the detail window below, we can see a list of all the functions in our app as a **Call Tree**, showing us which functions used the most percentage of our app's time.

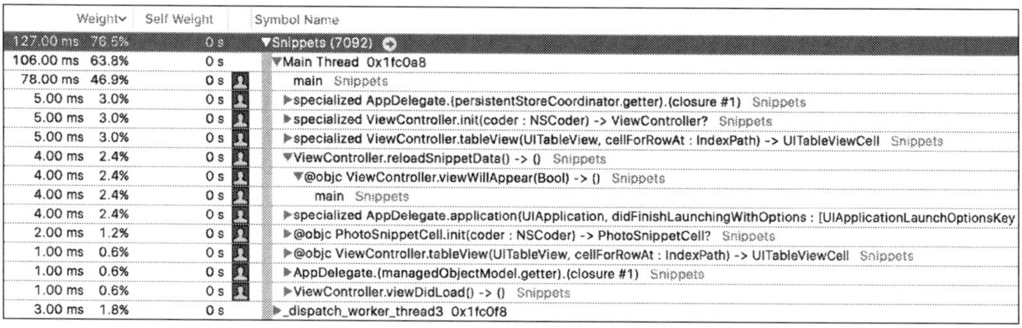

Weight˅		Self Weight	Symbol Name
127.00 ms	76.5%	0 s	▼Snippets (7092) ➕
106.00 ms	63.8%	0 s	▼Main Thread 0x1fc0a8
78.00 ms	46.9%	0 s	main Snippets
5.00 ms	3.0%	0 s	▶specialized AppDelegate.(persistentStoreCoordinator.getter).(closure #1) Snippets
5.00 ms	3.0%	0 s	▶specialized ViewController.init(coder : NSCoder) -> ViewController? Snippets
5.00 ms	3.0%	0 s	▶specialized ViewController.tableView(UITableView, cellForRowAt : IndexPath) -> UITableViewCell Snippets
4.00 ms	2.4%	0 s	▼ViewController.reloadSnippetData() -> () Snippets
4.00 ms	2.4%	0 s	▼@objc ViewController.viewWillAppear(Bool) -> () Snippets
4.00 ms	2.4%	0 s	main Snippets
4.00 ms	2.4%	0 s	▶specialized AppDelegate.application(UIApplication, didFinishLaunchingWithOptions : [UIApplicationLaunchOptionsKey
2.00 ms	1.2%	0 s	▶@objc PhotoSnippetCell.init(coder : NSCoder) -> PhotoSnippetCell? Snippets
1.00 ms	0.6%	0 s	▶@objc ViewController.tableView(UITableView, cellForRowAt : IndexPath) -> UITableViewCell Snippets
1.00 ms	0.6%	0 s	▶AppDelegate.(managedObjectModel.getter).(closure #1) Snippets
1.00 ms	0.6%	0 s	▶ViewController.viewDidLoad() -> () Snippets
3.00 ms	1.8%	0 s	▶_dispatch_worker_thread3 0x1fc0f8

Figure 15.4: The detail view of the Time Profiler, showing the amount of time that was spent in each function

In my case, the most used function was the getter for `persistentStoreCoordinator` in the `AppDelegate` class, so I clicked on the little arrow that shows up on the far right of a row when you hover over it to see more details. From there, I could see all the function calls that happen inside that function:

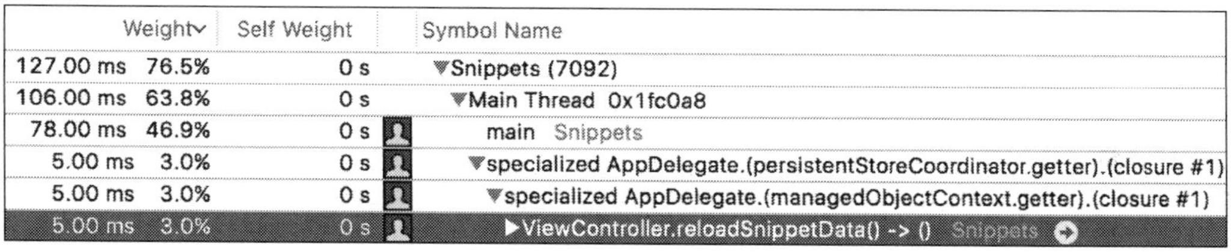

Weight˅		Self Weight	Symbol Name
127.00 ms	76.5%	0 s	▼Snippets (7092)
106.00 ms	63.8%	0 s	▼Main Thread 0x1fc0a8
78.00 ms	46.9%	0 s	main Snippets
5.00 ms	3.0%	0 s	▼specialized AppDelegate.(persistentStoreCoordinator.getter).(closure #1)
5.00 ms	3.0%	0 s	▼specialized AppDelegate.(managedObjectContext.getter).(closure #1)
5.00 ms	3.0%	0 s	▶ViewController.reloadSnippetData() -> () Snippets ➕

Figure 15.5: More information about a high-use function call

Once there, I could see that the most time consuming part of this function was *another* function call to my `reloadSnippetData()` function. By right clicking on that function call, I selected the option **Reveal in Xcode**. This opened my Xcode document to show me the `reloadSnippetData()` function, allowing me to look through it for performance issues myself.

```
44    func reloadSnippetData () {
45
46        let delegate = UIApplication.shared.delegate as! AppDelegate
47        let managedContext = delegate.managedObjectContext
48
49        let request = NSFetchRequest<NSFetchRequestResult>(entityName: "Snippet")
50        let sortDescriptor = NSSortDescriptor(key: "date", ascending: false)
51        request.sortDescriptors = [ sortDescriptor ]
52
53        do {
54            let fetchResults = try managedContext.fetch( request)
55            self.data = fetchResults as! [NSManagedObject]
56        } catch {
57            let e = error as NSError
58            print("Unresolved error \(e), \(e.userInfo)")
59        }
60    }
```

Figure 15.6: Inspecting my reloadSnippetData() function after seeing its performance in Instruments

After looking through the function, it seems that there isn't much we can do to optimize it; the big time sink appears to be the fetch request we send to our **Core Data** database. Luckily, even though this was taking up a big percentage of our app's run time, it wasn't really causing any major performance issues, or causing any noticeable lag.

Let's take a quick look at another way to connect the Time Profiler to your code. Heading back to the Call Tree from *Figure 15.5*, when I double click on the `reloadSnippetData()` line, I'm presented with a look of what's going on in Xcode directly inside Instruments:

```
39    override func viewWillAppear(_ animated: Bool) {
40        reloadSnippetData()                                              5x
41        tableView.reloadData()
42    }
43
44    func reloadSnippetData () {
45
46        let delegate = UIApplication.shared.delegate as! AppDelegate
47        let managedContext = delegate.managedObjectContext
48
49        let request = NSFetchRequest<NSFetchRequestResult>(entityName: "Snippet")
50        let sortDescriptor = NSSortDescriptor(key: "date", ascending: false)
51        request.sortDescriptors = [ sortDescriptor ]
52
53        do {
54            let fetchResults = try managedContext.fetch( request)
55            self.data = fetchResults as! [NSManagedObject]
56        } catch {
57            let e = error as NSError
58            print("Unresolved error \(e), \(e.userInfo)")
59        }
60    }
```

Figure 15.7: Double clicking on a row in the Call Tree gives us a look at the code from inside Instruments

This is a great way to preview the code without leaving Instruments. However, we can't edit any code from Instruments, and will ultimately have to go back to Xcode if we want to make any changes.

Normally, you should be able to tell pretty quickly if there is a major issue with your code by skimming the most time-consuming functions. They're measured in milliseconds (1000 ms in 1 second), so if you see a lot of time being spent in a function that you don't think should be taking that long, you should investigate it.

Allocations instrument

From a programmer's standpoint, memory usage is one of the most important things to keep in mind when trying to optimize your app. When in iterative development mode, you might not be thinking too much about what is happening with your device's memory, because you're not even sure if the feature you're working on is going to make it into the final build!

However, eventually you will need to go through your code and make sure that you aren't creating a huge memory mess by creating new objects all the time when it isn't necessary. The allocations tool is a great way to get a quick idea of what your memory allocations look like in your code, and it can help you spot messy patches.

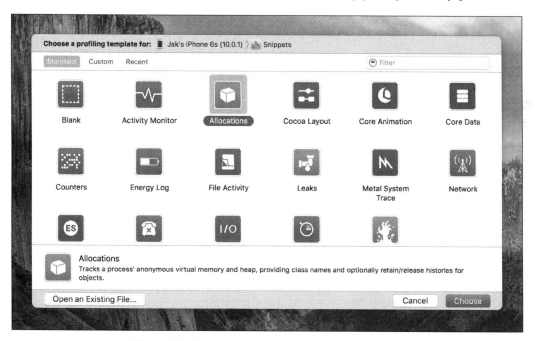

Figure 15.8: Creating a new allocations profiling document

To try this out, let's build our app for profiling again (*command* + *I*). Make sure you closed the old Instruments document first. This time, we're going to select the **Allocations** profiler, and click **Choose**. Once we have our Instruments document open, press the record button to begin profiling it. Once running, create and save a new text snippet, and then do the same for a photo snippet before stopping the profiling session. You should have an instrument view that looks similar to this:

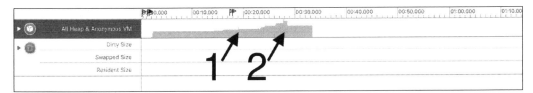

Figure 15.9: Example of an Allocations profiling session

You can see two spikes from memory allocations where we present the text snippet view controller (arrow **1** in *Figure 15.9*) and where we present the photo snippet view controller (arrow **2** in *Figure 15.9*). Here, you can see that memory goes up when the controller is presented, and then goes back down once it is dismissed. This is the first sign that things are working pretty well. Next, let's take a deeper look at the detail view:

Graph	Category	Persistent B...˅	# Persistent	# Transient	Total Bytes	# Total	Transient/Total Bytes
☑	All Heap & Anonymous V...	21.78 MiB	39,163	215,548	251.54 MiB	254,711	
☐	All Heap Allocations	9.28 MiB	39,073	215,029	198.38 MiB	254,102	
☐	All Anonymous VM ⊙	12.50 MiB	90	519	53.16 MiB	609	
☐	VM: Image IO	4.38 MiB	6	29	6.97 MiB	35	
☐	VM: CoreData Object IDs	4.02 MiB	1	0	4.02 MiB	1	
☐	CFData (store)	2.69 MiB	96	3,739	3.70 MiB	3,835	
☐	VM: Foundation	1.78 MiB	2	6	4.52 MiB	8	
☐	VM: Swift metadata	528.00 KiB	33	0	528.00 KiB	33	
☐	UIMorphingLabel	528.00 KiB	11	0	528.00 KiB	11	
☐	VM: SQLite page cache	512.00 KiB	8	7	960.00 KiB	15	
☐	Malloc 8.00 KiB	480.00 KiB	60	31	728.00 KiB	91	
☐	Malloc 4.00 KiB	384.00 KiB	96	261	1.39 MiB	357	
☐	VM: CoreAnimation	368.00 KiB	21	42	4.98 MiB	63	

Details 〉 ⊞ Statistics 〉 Allocation Summary — Instrument Detail

Figure 15.10: The detail view during an allocations Instruments session

In the detail view we can see all of the memory that was allocated during the session. The category is the object type, which is then followed by all types of memory information. The most important number to us (for now) is the **Persistent Bytes** column, which lets us know how much memory is actually staying used for each category. To continue keeping things simple for beginners, the **All Heap Allocations** category is the best place to focus, since that is mostly where the objects you create will go.

So this information is great, but what are we supposed to do with it? It would be more useful to have some data at different points in the program to compare along the way. Using a tool called **Generation Analysis**, we can do just that! First, from the **Display Settings Inspector** (*command + 2*), set the allocation type to **All Heap Allocations**, then hit the record button to begin a new round of profiling.

Above the **Allocation Type** section of the **Display Settings Inspector** is another section called **Generation Analysis** with a single button called **Mark Generation**. With the app running under the Allocation instrument, here's what we're going to do:

1. Click the **Mark Generation** button in Instruments.
2. Tap the **New** button in the running Snippets app; select `Text`.
3. Write `Hi` and the press **Done**.
4. Repeat steps *1* through *3* five times.

Now let's talk about what we just did, and take a look at the data we got back from this process:

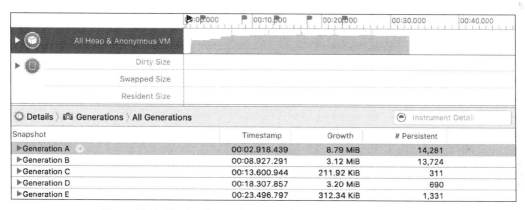

Figure 15.11: The detail view during an allocations instruments session

Every time we clicked the **Mark Generation** button, we were making a little flag that held all of the memory allocations from that generation. Then we executed a task before marking a new generation. By doing this several times, we get a good idea of whether our memory usage is staying the same through the tasks, or increasing over time.

In the **Detail Inspector** (as seen in *Figure 15.11*), we can see an overview of each generation, including the amount of memory growth between generations. We can also scrub through the instrument view to get a number representing the allocated memory at any point on the timeline. From looking at all of these numbers, I can see that the overall memory fluctuates between 17.8 MB and 18.3 MB across all of my generations, so I think it's safe to say that there are no major issues with our memory allocations.

Leaks instrument

While the Allocations instrument tracks all memory allocations, the Leaks instrument is specifically tailored to finding memory leaks in your code. Like the Address Sanitizer that we looked at in the last chapter, the Leaks instrument is mostly useful when profiling older Obj-C and C code, since memory management can be a bit trickier. We'll take a brief look at it anyway though, since you'll inevitably touch some old code at some point!

 A *memory leak* is when you create space in your device's memory, but lose the address for that memory without clearing it first. This means that there is still data in the memory, but you have no way to access it anymore.

Again, close your old Instruments document, then build your project for profiling with *command + I*. This time select **Leaks** from the profiling template picker:

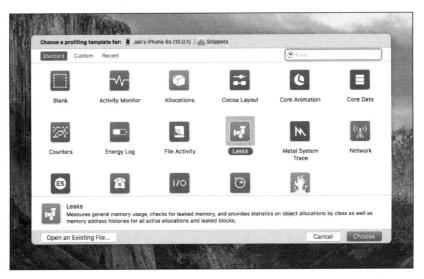

Figure 15.12: Choosing the Leaks instrument from the profiling template picker

Once the document is created, you'll notice that this template also gives you an Allocations instrument! In the future, you could just use this single template to check for both allocation issues and memory leaks.

Click record to begin profiling the app, and then create some snippets like we did earlier. Then, let's click on the **Leaks** instrument, and check out our **Details** view.

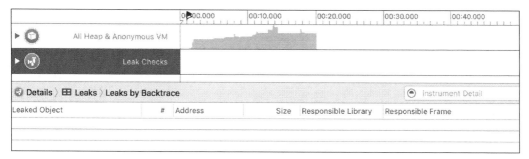

Figure 15.13: Viewing Leaks in the Instruments and detail views

Luckily, we don't have any leaks in our current application. However, fixing anymemory issues that would arise here is a bit beyond the scope of this book, and not all too interesting. The important takeaway is that you get acquainted with setting up this tool, and knowing that it exists to help you find these memory issues when they arise.

App Thinning

While code performance is an obvious area to focus our optimization efforts, it's not the only one. When building our application for distribution (as we'll be doing very soon!), it becomes important to start thinking about the file size that the app will take up on the device. In this case, we're not talking about optimizing the speed at which the app runs, but optimizing how the actual assets that make up the app are packaged.

To keep apps lean, Apple has introduced a new strategy called **App Thinning** that makes sure your app download contains only the assets and information that it needs. App Thinning has three main components: asset slicing, bitcode compilation, and on-demand resources.

Slicing

When Apple introduced Universal builds for applications, there was only one version of the iPhone and one version of the iPad. This meant that when downloading a universal app, you were getting two versions of the app, which isn't too bad. However, since then, things have changed considerably. We now have three different versions of the iPhone with different screen resolutions (iPhone SE, 7s and 7s Plus), two sizes of iPad, and two sizes of iPad Pro. Not to mention two versions of the Apple Watch, and the Apple TV to top it off! If we let people download real universal builds for applications now, they'd be huge bloated messes that had a lot of information that devices didn't need.

The concept of slicing removes the unnecessary files, and makes sure that only the resources that each specific device needs is downloaded. Here's how it works:

- You categorize resources using asset catalogs in Xcode
- The full app gets uploaded to iTunes Connect
- Apple's servers take care of splitting up resources based on devices
- A user downloads the app from the app store, only receiving the resources needed for their device

As you can see, most of the heavy lifting is taken care of on Apple's end, which makes our lives much easier. However, we do have to do a bit of work up front by placing all of our resources into asset catalogs and flagging them properly. Let's open up Snippets and see how this works by adding some app icon resources to an asset catalog.

Start by opening the Assets.xcassets file inside your main Snippets folder (not the watch extension ones). Inside should be two assets, **AppIcon** and **Brand Assets**. Click on the **AppIcon** image set, and you should see the following:

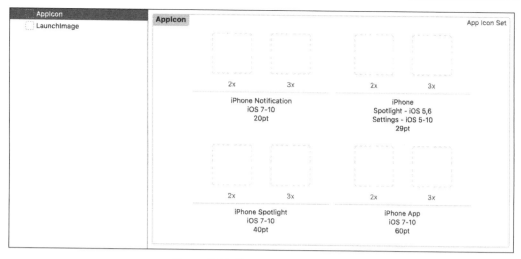

Figure 15.14: The empty app icon asset

You'll notice that there are a ton of slots for many different image sizes (and detail levels). This is the beginning of our slicing journey: setting up the app icon for all of the different resolutions of phones! In the resources folder of this chapter, I've included a folder of icons at different resolutions and detail levels. For example, in the first slot you should put `icon_29@2x.png`, since it's looking for the 2x size of the 29pt icon. Drag each image into the asset catalog, and you'll have something that looks more like this:

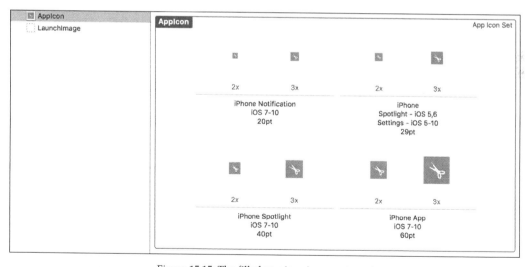

Figure 15.15: The filled app icon image set asset

It should be fairly obvious that each image in this set is registered with a specific device type and screen size. This means that an iPhone 7 won't be downloading the iPhone 7 Plus images. In fact, it will only be downloading the 2x versions of the iPhone images. So even though we've got 8 icons in the asset catalog, the iPhone 6s will only end up with 4.

While we're at it, let's go ahead and add all the Apple Watch icon images to the `Assets.xcassets` file inside the `Snippets-watch` folder, using the icons I have provided in the `icons-watch` folder in the `Chapter 15` resources folder:

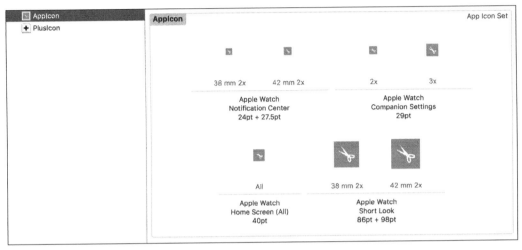

Figure 15.16: The filled apple watch icon image set asset

Now, this is great for app icons, but what about other images? Or even assets that aren't images? Well, asset catalogs let us create our own sliced assets. Let's try it out. Go back to the main application catalog, then at the bottom of the asset catalog's set list on the left, there is a plus button to create a new asset. Click it, then select **New Image Set**. Rename the image set to `Example`:

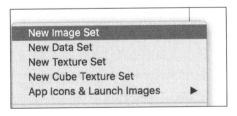

Figure 15.17: Creating a new image set asset

Once created, the image set will be configured for a universal app. However, we can add more information to give more specific data for different devices. If you open the **Attribute Inspector** while the image set is selected, you'll see more options for the asset (*Figure 15.18*):

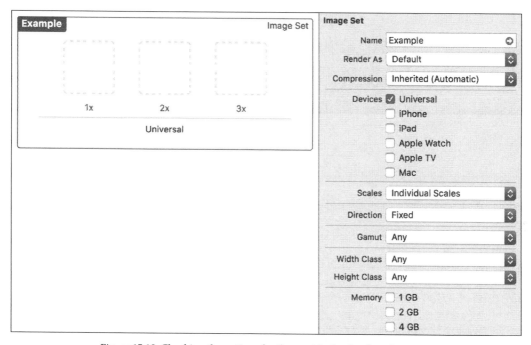

Figure 15.18: Checking the options for the asset in the Attribute Inspector

In the Attribute Inspector, you'll see that we can set a number of flags that we can support. We can choose from a set of devices, some permutations of size classes, the amount of memory a device has, and the type of graphics performance available on the device.

Let's say we're building an app for iPhone, iPad, and Apple TV, and this image asset doesn't care about anything else. We can uncheck `Universal` then check off all three platforms, and see the asset change accordingly:

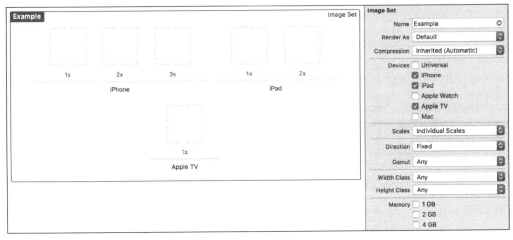

Figure 15.19: A more specific configuration for our new image asset

At this point, we can drag in our images, and know that we'll have tailored images for each platform without worrying about bloating our app's file size. To access the correct image from code, we only need to reference the base name (in this case, `Example`), and the asset catalog will make sure the correct version is used at run time.

In addition to custom images, we can also use asset catalogs to slice *any* type of file. Let's say we have a custom configuration file that we load in at run time to set up our graphics pipeline. But we have a different file depending on the graphics available, and the amount of RAM the device has.

Create a new asset, but this time choose **New Data Set**, and name the asset `GraphicsConfig`. Select the asset, and then check off the **4GB** option, along with the **Metal 2v2** and **Metal 3v2** options in the **Attribute Inspector** (*Figure 15.20*):

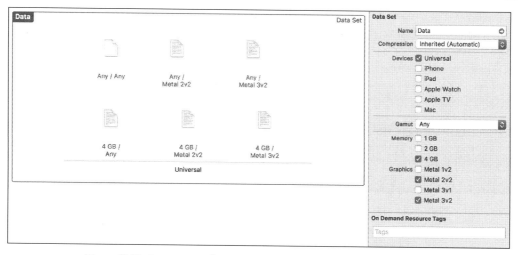

Figure 15.20: A custom configuration asset for different graphics capabilities

With these options enabled, we now have a grid of six possible configurations to load, depending on the device. I've also included a set of .txt files in the resources folder of this chapter (called graphics configs) that you can drag into the data set. Right now these are just tiny example files, but in a bigger production app, you might have a ton of files like this that can now be customized per device without sacrificing app file size.

Bitcode

When you compile your app, your code gets translated into machine code that runs on your device's processor. Usually, once complied for a specific processor architecture, that executable can only be run on that processor. However, with Bitcode, Apple compiles your app to an intermediate state, which Apple can then re-compile at their end for specific devices.

What this means for you is that if Apple changes their processors in future devices, Apple can recompile your app for the new processors, and your app will *just work*. You don't have to recompile and reupload your app to work with the new processors. It also allows them to optimize builds for each individual device. Bitcode isn't so much a feature for you to use as much as it is a new way for your code to be deployed easily to many different devices.

Figure 15.21: Enabling bitcode from the Xcode project's build settings

By default, Bitcode is enabled on an iOS project. If you're working on a different type of project or just want to double check, you can go to the build settings of the Xcode project and search for `bitcode`. Just make sure that the **Enable Bitcode** flag is set to **Yes**.

On-demand Resources

Sometimes when building an app, there is no way around requiring a large amount of asset resources. For example, if you are building an advanced 3D game, you may have many levels worth of 3D meshes and textures, in addition to audio. Instead of downloading several hundred or thousands of megabytes of data at the initial download time, you can store some of those assets in the cloud and pull them down as needed. These assets are called **On-demand Resources (ODR)**.

When creating an app that has some assets that are only used occasionally, like an app tutorial, or levels in a game, offloading those assets to the cloud until you need them can save a ton of space in your app's file size. To use ODR, we are going to tag assets in our asset catalog, and then pull down resources associated with that tag. We first need to create and set up our tags, then we'll load the resources, and finally we'll purge them.

Creating tags

Let's take the graphics `config` files that we created earlier and set them as resources to be downloaded on demand. First, we need to create a tag for this resource group so that we can use it to download the resource later. Go to the Xcode project settings, and open the **Resource Tags** tab, which should be two to the right of the default **General** tab. Click the **+** button along the top to create a new tag, and call it `Graphics` (*Figure 15.22*):

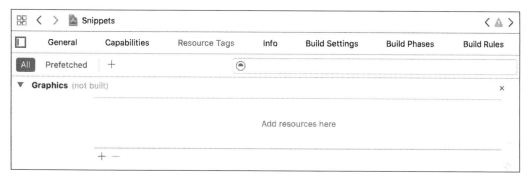

Figure 15.22: We created an empty Graphics tag for on demand resources

From inside the tag, we can use the plus button at the bottom to add files to the tag, which then become part of that ODR bundle. However, if we want to get more specific, we can go inside our asset catalogs to tag specific assets.

Open up the `Assets.xcassets` catalog, and select the `GraphicsConfig` asset. From the **Attribute Inspector**, you should see a section called **On-demand Resource Tags**. If you type in the name of the tag we just made, it should autocomplete and you should have a tag that looks just like *Figure 15.23*:

Figure 15.23: A resource in an asset catalog using an ODR tag

If we go back to the resource tags in the Xcode project editor, we should now see that we've added a new resource to the `Graphics` tag:

Figure 15.24: The Graphics tag now contains an asset from our asset catalog

At this point, we're now ready to load the resource from code.

Loading resources

To load the resources, we need to fetch the resources from the app store. We do this using an `NSBundleResourceRequest` object. Let's open our `ViewController.swift` file and make some changes to load in our ODR.

```swift
var resourceRequest: NSBundleResourceRequest!

override func viewDidLoad() {
    super.viewDidLoad()
    imagePicker.delegate = self
    locationManager.delegate = self
    locationManager.desiredAccuracy = kCLLocationAccuracyBest
    locationManager.distanceFilter = 50.0

    tableView.estimatedRowHeight = 100
    tableView.rowHeight = UITableViewAutomaticDimension

    askForLocationPermissions()

    fetchODR()
}

func fetchODR() {
    let tags = Set(arrayLiteral: "Graphics")
    resourceRequest = NSBundleResourceRequest(tags: tags)
```

```
resourceRequest.beginAccessingResources { ( error: Error? ) in

  if error != nil {
    print("graphics resources were not loaded")
    return
  }
  print("resources can now be accessed as usual")
  }
}
```

Here, we've created a new function called `fetchODR()`. It first creates a new set of tags, in this case just the `Graphics` tag that we've made. Then we initialize an `NSBundleResrouceRequest` object using the tags. Finally, we request to download the resources, and create a completion handler that prints out whether or not the download was successful.

Once our download succeeds, the resources will be a part of our application bundle, and can be accessed just as if they had been part of our app the whole time.

Purging resources

To get rid of ODRs that we no longer need, we just need to tell the `NSBundleResourceRequest` that we are no longer using it. This is why we need to keep a reference to the bundle resource request.

```
resourceRequest.endAccessingResources()
```

Calling the `endAccessingResources()` function from anywhere in your code will tell the bundle resource request that we no longer need the associated assets, and that it can remove them from the system when necessary.

If you're interested in learning more about ODR, then you should check out Apple's documentation. There's enough information to spend a whole chapter just discussing the many ways to interact with ODR, like getting download progress information, setting download priority, and managing multiple tags. However, here we learnt just enough to get up and running.

Summary

In this chapter, we learnt about how to use the Instruments set of tools to profile our code in multiple ways. We used the Time Profiler to see which parts of our code took the most amount of time to run, and then we used the Allocations and Leaks instruments to see which parts of our app were using the most memory. Then, we looked at other ways to optimize our app's file size and assets, instead of its code. To cut down our app's file size, we reviewed Apple's guidelines for App Thinning, including slicing, Bitcode, and ODRs.

In the next chapter, we take our final application and learn how to deploy it to TestFlight for beta testing, and finish our journey by pushing the final version of `Snippets` to the App Store!

Distributing an iOS App
16

We've done it all. We learned the tools, designed and built an application, and now it is tested, debugged, and optimized. The only thing that is left to do is put it somewhere that people can download it! To distribute our app, we'll be using Apple's distribution platform called **iTunes Connect**. There's not much else to say, so let's get straight to it. In this chapter we will cover:

- Creating a new app page in iTunes Connect
- Archiving your app and uploading to iTunes Connect
- Using iTunes Connect to distribute TestFlight builds
- Submitting final builds to the App Store for download

Preparing iTunes Connect

While we've been able to spend the majority of this book in the Xcode suite of development tools, it's time to jump into something new. iTunes Connect is a web portal that allows you, the developer, to set up all of the app information that is necessary to have a store page on the App Store.

For this part of the process, iTunes Connect is going to be our new home base. We'll head back to Xcode to do our final export of our application, but otherwise we'll be in iTC. Here's the downside: you must be a paid developer to access iTunes Connect and distribute applications. If you don't have a paid developer license, you should either buy it now, or just read through this chapter and wait to follow it when you have your own app ready to distribute.

Registering a bundle identifier

When we first began developing our application, we had to give our app a `Bundle ID`. This ID was in reverse domain syntax, and gave our app a unique identifying string. When setting up your app for distribution, you need to register that specific ID with your developer account. To do this, we actually have to visit the Developer Member Center first, which is where we signed up for our developer account all the way back in the first chapter. Here's the link: `http://developer.apple.com/membercenter/`:

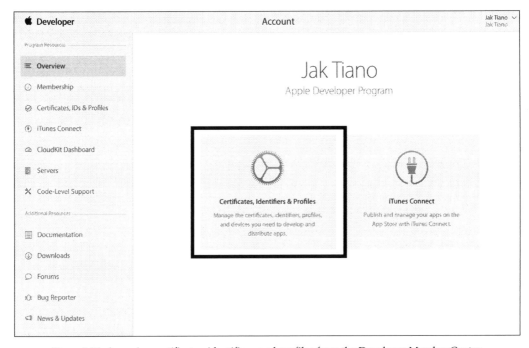

Figure 16.1: Accessing certificates, identifiers, and profiles from the Developer Member Center.

Once you sign in, you should see a screen like in *Figure 16.1*; this is the **Member Center** dashboard. From here, you want to click on the highlighted link in *Figure 16.1*, which will bring you to the **Certificates, Identifiers & Profiles** area. This is where you will be registering your `Bundle ID`:

Figure 16.2: How to create a new bundle identifier from the member center.

On the next screen, you'll want to click on the **App IDs** link underneath the **Identifiers** section of the navigator on the left of the page (pointed out by arrow number 1 in *Figure 16.2*). You can see that my account has a ton of **App IDs**, but yours will be empty if you've never done this before. To create a new ID, click the plus button in the upper right of the window, as shown from arrow **2** in *Figure 16.2*.

This will start guiding you along the App ID creation process. In the **App ID Description** box, you can give this any label you want, it's only for your own personal organizational purposes. Leave the **App ID Prefix** at its default setting (you should only have one anyway). The important part is the **App ID Suffix** category. Here, you have to make sure to use the same `Bundle ID` that is in your Xcode project. (This is very **important**. You can find this information near the top of the **General** tab of your Xcode project's settings.):

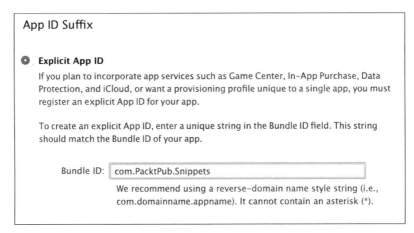

Figure 16.3: Setting the correct App ID Suffix for the new ID

Again, we need to do this so that we have a unique ID tied to our account for our app. Below the suffix is an area where you can check off what services you want to enable for this `App ID`. We aren't using any of these services in our app, so we can leave them as they are. Hit **Continue** at the bottom of the page, and you'll be presented with an overview of the new `App ID`:

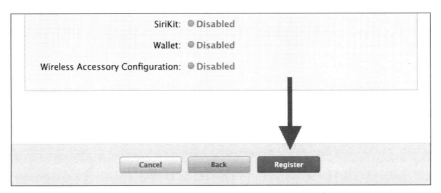

Figure 16.4: Register the new ID from the bottom of the review page

To finish creating the new ID, scroll to the bottom of the page and click the **Register** button.

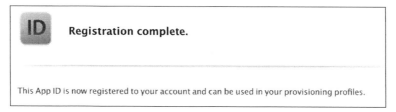

Registration complete.

This App ID is now registered to your account and can be used in your provisioning profiles.

Figure 16.5: We've successfully set up our new App ID

That's all there is to it! Time to head over to iTunes Connect.

Creating a new app record in iTunes Connect

Now that we have an App ID, we can create a new app record. Before we can upload our app to the app store servers, we need to set up a landing pad on iTunes Connect that has an app name and a `Bundle ID` associated with it. That's what our app record is. Later on, this is where we'll put our app icon, screenshots, and description that will be shown on the App Store:

Figure 16.6: Logging into the iTunes Connect dashboard

To begin, head over to `http://itunesconnect.apple.com` and log in with your developer credentials. Once inside, we're going to navigate to the **My Apps** section; the others aren't important to us right now (but they will be once you start selling your own apps!).

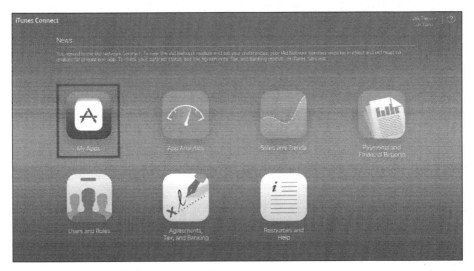

Figure 16.7: Click on the My Apps icon to view and create app records

The next screen will be empty for you, but in *Figure 16.8* you can see what your apps dashboard will look like once you've built enough of your own apps! To create your first app record, click the plus button in the upper left corner, and then select **New App**:

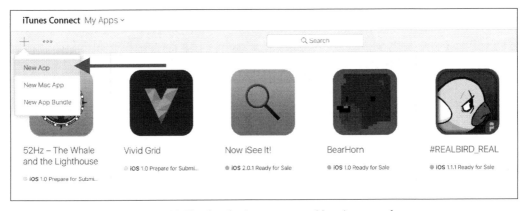

Figure 16.8: Use the plus icon to create a New App record.

From there, you'll be shown a popup box that lets you fill in the details of your app.
Check the **iOS** box, give it a name, and select the default language:

Figure 16.9: Setting up a new app record in iTunes Connect.

Here's the first tricky part: the name needs to be completely unique from every other
app on the app store. So even though our app's name is `Snippets`, that name had
already been taken, so I needed to add a little subtitle. Once you've given the app
a name, we need to select the `Bundle ID` that this app uses. From the dropdown,
select the App ID we just made in the last section; this is why we needed to register
the App ID first! Finally, we need an `SKU` ID. This string is a unique product
code identifying your app, and isn't shown anywhere in the app store. I used
`JTPP2016001`, because it's `JT` (my initials) followed by `PP` (for Packt Publishing)
then `2016` (for the current year) and then a `001` for good measure.

Once you've filled out all of the details, you can click **Create** at the bottom of the box.
We have now completed the initial set up of the app record for `Snippets`. There's
still a lot more to do in here later, but let's head back to Xcode one last time, package
up our build, and upload it to our app record!

Uploading to iTunes Connect

With the app record set up, we're ready to make the final build of our app and upload it to iTunes Connect. Due to the possibility of this section being very tricky, I recommend you use my final version of the Snippets project which is located in the Chapter 16 resources folder, to minimize the possibility of bugs:

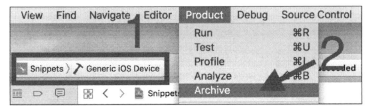

Figure 16.10: Setting our code signing properties for our build

With the Snippets project open, on the Xcode toolbar change the destination device to **Generic iOS Device** (as seen in *Figure 16.10*). This makes it so that when we build, it is for a generic device, instead of for a specific device or simulator.

Next, we need to *archive* our app. This is a different type of build that can be uploaded to the app store. To do this, go to **Product | Archive** on the menu bar (the second arrow in *Figure 16.10*):

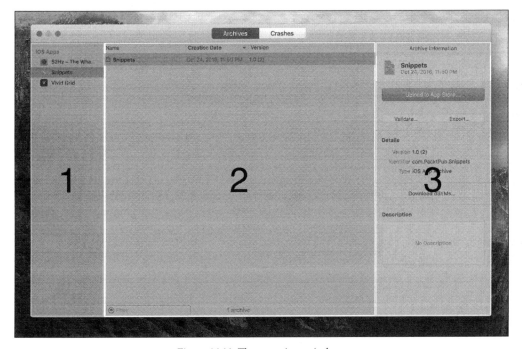

Figure 16.11: The organizer window

Once the archive is complete, Xcode will open the Organizer window, showing you the completed archive. The Organizer window is composed of three sections: the app browser on the left (labeled area 1 in *Figure 16.11*); the archive browser in the middle (labeled area **2** in *Figure 16.11*); the archive information inspector on the right (labeled area **3** in *Figure 16.11*). On the left we want to make sure we have selected the Snippets app, and then in the center we've selected the most recent (and only) archive that has been made:

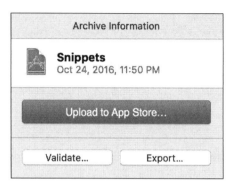

Figure 16.12: The archive inspector options

On the right, in the inspector, we have a couple of options. We can **Upload to App Store...**, **Validate...**, or **Export...** the archive. While we could just immediately try to upload, it's always a good idea to validate the archive first:

Figure 16.13: Select your development team to validate the archive

Once you click **Validate…**, you'll be asked to choose your team. Normally, you'll just pick your developer name from the drop-down list. Once you click **Choose**, the archive will be processed for a little bit, and then present you with a summary screen, detailing how the archive's components and settings (*Figure 16.14*):

Figure 16.14: The archive validation summary screen

Click on **Validate**, and the process will begin. This may take a few minutes, but once it's done, you should be shown a confirmation screen like in *Figure 16.15*:

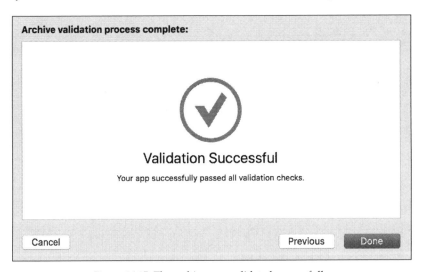

Figure 16.15: The archive was validated successfully

Once your archive validation is complete, you're ready to upload to the app store. Click on **Upload to App Store...** in the archive information inspector, and you'll be greeted by a very similar process to the validation. Select the team, and confirm the summary screen, and your app will begin the process of uploading to the App Store:

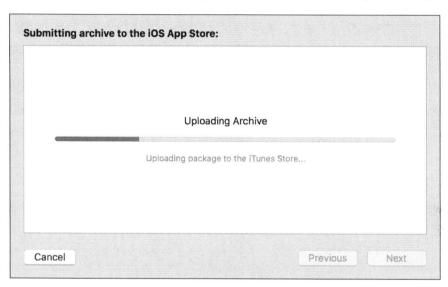

Figure 16.16: The archive uploading to the App Store

Once it's done, you'll be greeted by a success screen similar to the validation one. Now, even though the validation may have succeeded, your upload might not. There are a lot of errors that may occur here, and there is really no way for me to help you troubleshoot them all from here. If you're getting an issue, my first recommendation is to try this section again with my version of the project if you were using your own. This is because I got my project 100% through this process. If my project isn't working, then Apple may have changed some of the upload requirements, and you might have to search the web a bit to find a solution. (If you were using a different Bundle ID in your project, make sure to update my projects Bundle ID to match.)

 It might take a few minutes for your archive to finish processing on iTunes Connect after uploading it in the last step. You'll get an email when it's done.

Releasing the app

The app is uploaded and ready to go on iTunes Connect. Next, we'll put the final touches on the app record by uploading screenshots and icons, and filling out the necessary descriptions. Finally, we'll push out builds on TestFlight, and submit for review to the App Store.

Finalizing store assets

So we've got an app, but how do we let customers learn about it before they download it? From iTunes Connect, we can upload a video, screenshots, description text, and icons to help potential customers get an idea of what the app is about. I've included a folder inside this chapter's resources called `iTunes Connect Resources` that you can use to fill out the information in this section:

Figure 16.17: Our build is now available in iTunes Connect

First, let's go back to the app record in iTunes Connect. Once your archive has finished uploading and is processed, it will show up in the sidebar of the app record with the version number and status (*Figure 16.17*). Click on it to go to the information for that build. It is there that we will set the screenshots, icons, and descriptions for that version. At first, it should look something like *Figure 16.18*:

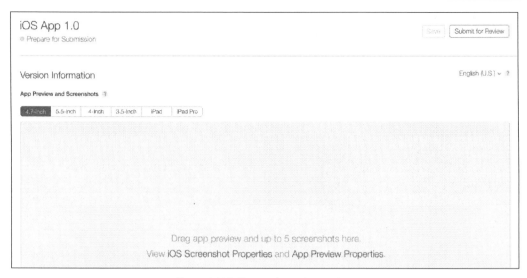

Figure 16.18: Our app's version settings

Now, since our app supports iPhone, we need to include screenshots for all four versions of iPhone. Inside the `iTunes Connect Resources` folder I gave you, there is a single screenshot for each device size. You can drag those screenshots right into the gray box to upload them. Below the screenshots, we have a box for the app description. In the `iTC Resource` folder is a text file containing an app description that I wrote, if you don't want to write your own. Copy and paste the description into iTunes Connect. You'll also need to fill in some keywords and a support URL for a real app submission:

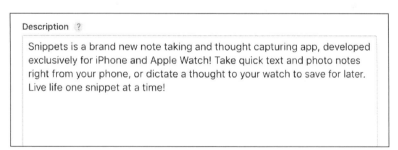

Figure 16.19: Filling out the app description

Below the description is the area where we can set up the Apple Watch information for our app. We can include an icon for the watch app, in addition to screenshots. Again, I have an icon file and an Apple Watch screenshot available in the `iTC` `Resources` folder. Just drag them into the browser window:

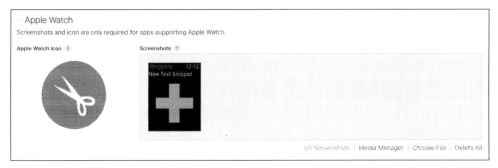

Figure 16.20: Filling out the apple watch app information

After the Apple Watch settings, we have to choose the actual build associated with this version. Click the **Select a build** text to bring up a box to select the build, shown in *Figure 16.21*. Select the build, and click done:

Figure 16.21: Selecting the 1.0 build we uploaded in out archive

Below the build selection, we have to upload the app icon that will be displayed on the store page. You can drag in the same `icon_1024.png` file from the `iTC` `Resources` folder for the icon. Make sure you also fill out the **Copyright** section.

Finally, all the way at the bottom of the page, we have the ability to select how the app gets released. Since the app needs to go through approval, we can have the app automatically go on sale when it is approved or we can manually release the app ourselves after it's approved. We can also set a date for the app to automatically release, assuming it has been approved by then. We're just going to leave this at **Automatic release this version**:

Figure 16.22: Selecting the option for how the version gets released once approved

Click the **Save** button in the upper right corner of the window to save all our changes. At this point, we're finished setting up the app version settings, but before we can move on to distribution we need to set some info on pricing and availability. On the sidebar above the version tab, click on the **Pricing and Availability** tab (*Figure 16.23*):

Figure 16.23: Moving the Pricing and Availability tab

Once in the pricing tab, we need to set a pricing tier, and the territories where the app will be available. By default, the app is available in all territories (countries), so we'll leave that as is:

Figure 16.24: Choosing the free pricing tier for Snippets

To set the initial pricing tier, click on the dropdown that says **Choose** and pick a price that makes sense for your app. In this case, I'm choosing the free tier.

 To release paid applications, you'll need to sign some contracts in the **Contracts** section of iTunes Connect. Due to the legal nature of this, I'll let you do this on your own, if you choose to use a paid tier.

One last thing before we move on: we need to set a category for our app. Head back to the **App Information** tab, scroll down a bit, and change the **Category** to something that makes sense. I chose **Lifestyle** in this case:

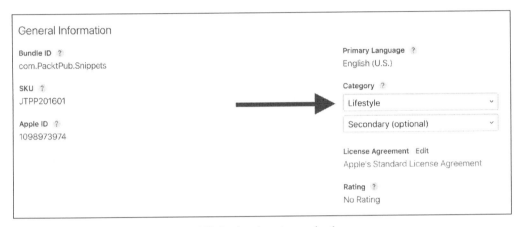

Figure 16.25: Setting the category for the app

Now our app is ready for distribution.

Distributing on TestFlight

The first method of distribution that we will look at is TestFlight. This is a platform that is used for beta-testing applications with a limited number of users. Once your app is finished, it is usually a good idea to distribute it to a small number of people first to check for bugs. No matter how thoroughly you check your own app for bugs, there will always be things you miss, and the best way to find them is to put your app in the hands of other people.

To distribute your app through TestFlight, click on the **TestFlight** tab along the top of the window (*Figure 16.26*):

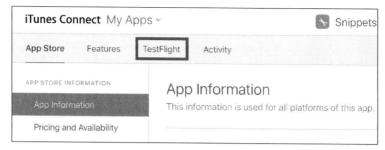

Figure 16.26: Moving to the TestFlight tab

Once in the **TestFlight** tab, you'll see some fields asking for a feedback email, and some marketing/privacy URLs. Fill those in with some placeholders for now, but when running a real app beta, you'll want to make sure you have a good system for dealing with beta users.

Along the sidebar in the TestFlight section, you should see tabs for **Internal Testing** and **External Testing**. Let's set up an internal test, since it's a bit quicker than an external test:

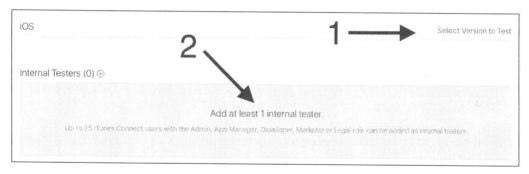

Figure 16.27: Setting up an internal test

To set up an internal test, you need to select a build and add testers. To select a build, click the **Select Version to Test** button (arrow **1** in *Figure 16.27*), and then choose our 1.0 build from the resulting dialog box. Next, add an internal tester to the build. Internal testers must be people that are part of your app development team on iTunes Connect, so right now that means only you. If you click on the text that says **Add at least 1 internal tester** (arrow **2** in *Figure 16.27*), you'll be given a list of eligible members. Select yourself. Now, if you look in the upper right corner, you can click the **Start Testing** button (*Figure 16.28*). This will send an email to you (and any other testers that might be added in the future) alerting them that a new TestFlight build is available to you/them.

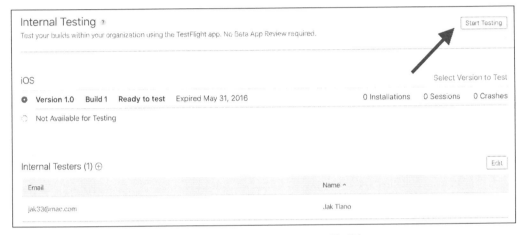

Figure 16.28: Start testing an internal build

External testing works in almost the exact same way, except that when you add a build you need to answer a few more questions and submit the app to a beta review, which is similar to the app store review process (except usually faster). With external testing, you're allowed to add anyone to the test with just their email, they don't need to be an iTunes Connect team member. You are also allowed up to 2,000 external testers, making it a great platform to get some widespread feedback without releasing to the full app store.

Submitting to the App Store

Actually submitting the app for review is pretty easy at this point. Back in the App Store section (not TestFlight), if you click on your version in the sidebar, there will be a button in the upper right corner that says **Submit for Review**. If you click this button, you'll be notified of any issues with your information. You may have to fill out some reviewer information, or clean up some fields you may have missed. However, if everything is in order, that's it. It's off to be reviewed, and in about a week your app will be live on the App Store, as long as it passes review.

Summary

In this chapter we brought our iOS development journey to a close. We learned about how to register an App ID to our developer account, and then used that to create an app record on iTunes Connect. Then, we uploaded the archive to iTunes Connect, we filled out the app's store page information. We wrapped everything up by learning how to distribute our app on TestFlight, and ultimately submitted our app to be reviewed for the App Store.

Thanks for coming along on this journey with me! I hope you learned a ton, and had a great time learning about the many facets of iOS development. If you ever have any questions, feel free to tweet at me (@jakintosh).

You are now an iOS developer!

Index

Symbols

3D touch app shortcuts
creating 217
handling, in app delegate 220-225
Info.plist, setting up 218-220

A

Address Sanitizer 396-399
allocations instrument 415-418
app
App Store, submitting to 449
releasing 442
store assets, finalizing 442-446
TestFlight, distributing on 446-448
Apple Watch
designing for 279
experience 280, 281
sensors 334
using 280
Apple Watch, snippets
about 288
complication, adding 304-306
interface controller, programming 292-298
iOS connecting to, WatchConnectivity.
    framework used 298-302
project, setting up 288
watchOS storyboard, creating 289-292
application loader 10
application management, UIKit
    fundamentals
about 230
UIDevice class 231

app thinning
about 419
Bitcode 425, 426
On Demand Resources (ODR) 426
slicing 420-425
arrays 80, 81
auto layout
about 115
constraints 117-122
issues, resolving 123
view hierarchy 116, 117

B

badges 355, 356
breakpoints
about 386, 387
console 388, 389
debug toolbar 389-392
variables view 387, 388
builds
and run 53, 54
creating 53
device, running on 54, 55

C

call stack 393-395
classes
creating 89-92
class extensions 98, 99
closures 95, 96
CMDeviceMotion
about 320, 321
gravity 322

magnetic field 322
rotation rate 322
user acceleration 322

code
gesture data, reading 213
gestures, adding from 211
gestures, creating through 211, 212
image scale, changing 214, 215

collection types
about 80
arrays 80, 81
dictionaries 81, 82

Command Line Tools 26

comments 88

complications, watchOS app
about 284, 285
adding 302-306

conditional statement
guard statement 83
if statement 82
switch statement 83, 84

constants 76

constraints 117-122

controller
creating 57-62

Core Data
about 254
attributes 255, 256
data model editor 257-261
data model, recreating 265-267
entities 255, 256
model 254, 255
relationships 255-257
snippets, preparing for 261
stack, initializing 261

Core Data stack, initializing
about 261
data model, versus object graph 261, 262
final touches 264, 265
NSManagedObjectContext 264
NSManagedObjectModel 262
NSPersistentStoreCoordinator 263

Core Location 307

CoreLocation.framework
CoreLocation permissions,
setting up 236-240

location data, adding to Snippets 243-245
users location, getting 240-242
using 236

Core Motion
about 315
accelerometer, using 316, 317
CMDeviceMotion 320
gyroscope, using 318-320

CPU and memory gauge 401, 402

D

data
deleting 276-278
fetching 272-276
persisting 267
saving 268-272

data model
versus object graph 261, 262

data model editor 257-261

data types 76

data validation unit test
writing 375-377

debugging, practices
about 385
and breakpoints 386, 387
print() function 386

debugging, tools
about 396
Address Sanitizer 396-399
CPU and memory gauge 401, 402
disk and network gauge 402, 403
energy gauge 404
performance gauges 400

debug navigator 34

debug toolbar 389-392

developer
about 2
deployment 3
development 3
pre-production 2
project setup 3

developer account
adding 28, 29

development plan
creating 157-159

device status, checking with UIDevice
  about 308
  battery status, obtaining 313, 314
  orientation state, accessing 308-311
  proximity sensor, checking 311, 312
dictionaries 81, 82
disk and network gauge 402, 403
displays, UIKit fundamentals 235
distributed version control system 132
documents, UIKit fundamentals 235

E

editor
  about 36
  assistant editor 40, 41
  standard editor 36-39
  version editor 42
energy gauge 404
entities 256
enumerations (enum) 94
error handling 100, 101
explicit type 77

F

feature list
  assembling 154, 155
files
  creating 47
  existing files, importing 51
  groups and folders 52
  managing 47
  new resources, creating 48-50
  resource types 47
for in loop 84
frameworks
  about 227, 228
  linking, in project 228-230
functions 86

G

gestures
  adding, from code 211
  adding, from storyboard 207

gestures, human interface guidelines
  about 204
  standard gestures 204, 205
  usage guidelines 205, 206
  working 206, 207
Git
  about 131
  adding, to local repository 137-141
  GitHub hosted repository, using 141-145
  local repository, creating 136
  setting up, in Xcode 135
GitHub hosted repository
  using 141-145
guard statement 83

H

Human Interface Guidelines (HIG) 204

I

IBActions 59
IBOutlets 59
if statement 82
implicitly unwrapped 79
implicit type 77
Info.plist
  setting up 218-220
instruments
  about 409, 410
  allocation instrument 415-418
  leaks instrument 418, 419
  time profiler instrument 410, 411
**integrated development
      environment (IDE) 25**
iOS Charts
  about 323
  filling, with data 325-328
  framework, importing 323
  reference link 323
  storyboard, setting up 324
iTunes Connect
  about 431
  bundle identifier, registering 432-435
  new app record, creating 435-437
  preparing 431
  uploading to 438

iTunes Connect, uploading to
  about 438-441
  archiving 439-441

L

leaks instrument 418, 419
local notification
  versus, remote notifications 345
local repository
  creating 136
loops
  about 84
  for-in loop 84
  repeat-while loop 86
  while loop 85

M

Mac App Store (MAS) 26
minimum viable product (MVP) 154
model
  creating 57-62
Model-View-Controller (MVC)
  about 11, 12, 254
  Controller 15, 16
  Model 12, 13
  on iOS 19-21
  on web 16-19
  View 14
motion data
  altitude 332-334
  charting 322
  iOS Charts 323
  pedometer 328-332

N

New Snippet
  about 159
  button 160-163
  SnippetData model 160
notifications
  sending, permission getting for 346
  support, adding to Snippets 346
notifications, advanced
  badges 355, 356
  categories and actions 350-352

notifications, receiving while
  in app 358-360
  sounds 356-358
notifications, watchOS app 284
NSManagedObjectContext 264
NSManagedObjectModel 262
NSPersistentStoreCoordinator 263

O

On Demand Resources (ODR)
  about 426
  resources, loading 428, 429
  resources, purging 429
  tags, creating 427, 428
optionals 78, 79

P

pages 73, 74
performance gauges
  about 400, 401
  CPU and memory gauge 401, 402
  disk and network gauge 402, 403
  energy gauge 404
Photo Snippet, implementing
  about 179
  data entry 180-183
  SnippetData model, updating 179
playgrounds
  about 66
  previews, using 69-72
  setting up 66-69
pre-production
  about 154
  development plan, creating 157-159
  feature list, assembling 154, 155
  visual design 155, 156
print() function 386
printing 88
printing, UIKit fundamentals 236
project, settings
  about 42
  Capabilities tab 45, 46
  General tab 44
  Info tab 46, 47
  Project targets 43
protocols 97

R

registered developer
about 21
free developer account, registering 22
paid developer account, registering 22, 23
relationships 256, 257
repeat-while loop 86
resources 73
results view 70
rich comments 74, 75

S

segues 111, 112
Select Snippet type
about 163
alert controller, creating 165-167
SnippetData model, updating 164
sensors, Apple Watch
data, displaying in iOS 337-340
data, sending in iOS 337-340
extension, setting up 335
obtaining 334-337
size classes
about 123
in action 129
selecting 125
slicing 420-424
Snippet dates
about 196
data, saving to model 197, 198
SnippetData model, updating 196, 197
view and controller, updating 198-201
Snippets
about 153
notification support, adding 346
prototype cells, creating 186-190
scrolling through 185
table view, populating 191-196
Social.framework
Twitter, posting to 249-252
using 246
views, setting up 246-248
sounds 356-358
standard gestures 204, 205

storyboard
about 103
gestures, adding from 207
getting started 104, 105
image, flipping 209, 210
screen flow 106-111
segues 111-115
setting up 207-209
view controllers 106-111
structs
creating 92, 93
Swift basics 75
Swift Features
about 95
class extensions 98, 99
closures 95-97
error handling 99-101
protocols 97, 98
switch statement 83, 84

T

team, working on
about 4
designers 4
investors 6
other developers 5
project managers 5
TestFlight 4
Text snippet 154
Text Snippet, implementing
about 167
SnippetData model, updating 168
Text entry View Controller 169-176
time profiler instrument
about 410, 411
document, anatomy 411, 412
using 412-415
type inference 77

U

UIButton 57
UIDevice
used, for checking device status 308
UIKit fundamentals
about 230
application management 230

views 231
UILabel 57
UI testing
  in Xcode 7 379
  target, adding 380, 381
  UI recorder, using 382-384
  working 380
unit tests
  about 361
  in action 363
  project, setting up 363-365
  running 369-372
  unit 362
  uses 362
  writing, XCTest used 365-368
unit tests, implementing for Snippets
  about 372
  code coverage, checking 377-379
  data validation unit test, writing 375-377
  Snippets project, setting up 372, 373
  testing class, preparing 373-375
unwind segue 113
unwrapping 78
user notifications
  about 343, 344
  components 344, 345
  local, versus remote notifications 345
utilities sidebar 35

V

variables 77
version control
  about 132
  branches, creating 149-151
  branches, merging 149-151
  pull, push, and commit 145-147
  using, in Xcode 145
  version editor 147, 148
view
  creating 57-62
views, UIKit fundamentals
  about 231
  coordinate systems 234
  drawing 232
  hierarchies 233, 234
visual debugging 404-408

W

Watch App bundle 286
WatchConnectivity.framework
  used, for connecting to iOS 298-301
Watch Extension bundle 286
watchOS app
  about 282
  architecture 285
  complications 284, 285
  components 282
  notifications 284
watchOS app, architecture
  extension delegate 287
  interface controller 286, 287
  target bundles 286
  Watch App bundle 286
  Watch Extension bundle 286
while loop 85
work
  testing, in simulator 62, 63
workspace
  setting up 55, 56

X

Xcode
  about 6
  developer account, adding 28, 29
  installing 26-28
  navigating 32, 33
  new project, creating 30-32
Xcode 7 toolset
  about 6
  Application Loader 10
  instruments 9
  iOS and watchOS simulator 8, 9
  Xcode 6, 7
Xcode developer portal
  URL 27
Xcode, navigating
  debug area 35
  editor 33
  navigator sidebar 34
  utilities sidebar 35
XCTest
  used, for writing tests 365-369

Made in the USA
Middletown, DE
05 November 2017